POWER PROJECTIONS

P9-DUG-730

ARCTIC OCEAN

Finland

Est.
Lat.
th.

Soviet Union

The United States Government has not recognized the incorporation of Estonia, Latvia, and Lithuania into the Soviet Union.

Romania

Bulgaria

ce

Turkey

Cyprus

Lebanon

Israel

Egypt

Saudi Arabia

Syria

Iraq

Jordan

Kuwait

Bahrain

Qatar

U.A.E.

Oman

Yemen

YAR

PDR

Aden

Sudan

Ethiopia

R.

Uganda

Kenya

aire

Rwanda

Burundi

Tanzania

Zambia

Malawi

Somalia

Djibouti

Zimbabwe

tswana

Mozambique

Madagascar

Mauritius

th
ca

Swaziland

Lesotho

Comoros

Seychelles

Maldives

Iran

Afghanistan

Pakistan

Nepal

Bhutan

India

Bangladesh

Burma

Sri Lanka

Mongolia

China

Laos

Thailand

Cambodia
Kampuchea

Vietnam

N. Korea

S. Korea

Japan

Hong Kong (U.K.)
Macau (Port)

(Occupied by Soviet Union since 1945, claimed by Japan.)

PACIFIC OCEAN

Malaysia

Singapore

Brunei

Philippines

South China Sea
(25–30 Ships, Average)

Soviet Airfield and Naval Base
Cam Ranh Bay

Indonesia

Papua
New Guinea

Nauru

Solomon
Islands

Kiribati

Tuvalu

Western
Samoa

Vanuatu

Fiji

Tonga

Indian Ocean
(15–20 Ships, Average)

INDIAN OCEAN

Australia

New
Zealand

SSB/SSBN Operating Areas . . . .

Soviet Naval Access . . . .

Airfield Access . . . .

Mutual Defense Treaties . . . .

SOURCES:
The World Fact Book, CIA, US Gov't Printing Office, 1987.
1986, Yearbook on International Communist Affairs, Richard F. Staar, Ed., Hoover Inst. Press.
1987, Soviet Military Power, US Department of Defense, US Gov't Printing Office.
Data on Communist Parties is often sparse and judgment, especially of Socialist-Military dictatorships, is tentative. No US Government publication seems to cover the task adequately. (Ed.)

Boundary representations are not necessarily authoritative

MESMERIZED BY THE BEAR

The Soviet Strategy of Deception

MESMERIZED BY THE BEAR

The Soviet Strategy of Deception

Edited by
Raymond S. Sleeper

Dodd, Mead & Company
New York

In Memoriam

Allen T. Klots
1921–1987

Enthusiastic supporter, articulate advisor,
meticulous editor, and friend.

Copyright © 1987 by Raymond S. Sleeper

All rights reserved

No part of this book may be reproduced in any form
without permission in writing from the publisher.
Published by Dodd, Mead & Company, Inc.
71 Fifth Avenue, New York, New York 10003
Manufactured in the United States of America
Designed by Marilyn E. Beckford

First Edition

1 2 3 4 5 6 7 8 9 10

Library of Congress Cataloging-in-Publication Data

Mesmerized by the bear.

Includes index, and map of Soviet Global Power Projections
1. Soviet Union—Military policy. 2. Soviet Union—
Foreign relations—1945-   . 3. Deception.
I. Sleeper, Raymond S.
UA770.M48 1987   355′.0335′47   87-13336

ISBN 0-396-09026-5

CONTENTS

MESMERIZED BY THE BEAR

The Soviet Strategy of Deception

Introduction
Congressman Jack Kemp

Over the past seventy years, the United States has sought to live peacefully and cooperatively with the Soviet Union. Shortly after the Bolshevik Revolution, the United States provided the new USSR with massive economic and agricultural aid. Our industries worked to modernize and in many cases to create a Soviet industrial base. Later, during World War II, the Allied powers, true to their peaceful motives, demobilized their military forces. In less than a year, U.S. military strength fell from over 6,000,000 to under 200,000.

The Soviets' response has been to mock American goodwill. They have provided arms and support to America's enemies around the world, overthrown legally constituted governments in Eastern Europe, and reneged on their promise to hold free elections at home. Their armies remained in Eastern Europe after World War II, and they continued to expand their military capability even though the Western powers had virtually disarmed.

For the Soviets evidently the war was not over. As a result, the United States was stimulated to create an economic program that became the basis for the European recovery, the Marshall Plan, and to form a Western defensive alliance, NATO, in response to Soviet aggression.

From the beginning of the nuclear age, the United States has sought to reduce the risk of nuclear war. Even in the midst of the Soviet takeover of Eastern Europe, the United States extended to the Soviets the very first olive branch in the field of disarmament: the Baruch Plan, which offered international control over atomic energy and weaponry, though we had a nuclear monopoly at the time. The Soviets flatly rejected the American offer and launched a cynical propaganda campaign for "disarmament." Their objectives were to sabotage U.S. defense programs in order to facilitate their own armaments programs and leapfrog ahead of the United States.

For years, the perception of U.S. policymakers was that the Soviets wanted to achieve only strategic parity. But by the late 1970s, it was clear that the Soviet objective was to achieve dominant, first-strike superiority.

In the 1970s the United States pursued a detente policy, trying yet again to achieve normal relations with the Soviet Union. Agreements for technical and economic assistance were signed, and once again aid flowed from the West into Soviet-bloc countries. The Soviet response, as before, was to capitalize on the opportunity to expand their military machine, subvert the governments of numerous Third World nations, sponsor revolutions, and subject millions of innocent people to Communist oppression.

The policy of the United States has been a continuing and repeating sequence of hopes, followed by disappointment and disillusionment, and then, by a return to those original hopes.

Clearly, something is wrong. All signs point to the strong possibility that there are serious errors in our perceptions of the Soviet Union and our expectations of what can be accomplished with them. But perhaps most in error is our failure to ask what is wrong, to look into the process and determine why the cycle we are caught in seems to be no more than that—a cycle in which our hopes, desires, and expectations are continually being frustrated.

This book is a collection of essays by a variety of experts, all of whom have been addressing from different perspectives that same question, "What is wrong?" In the process they have all arrived at remarkably similar conclusions. The first and most important of these concerns the very nature of the Soviet Union. The collected authors conclude that coherent policy toward the Soviet Union cannot be formulated without a realistic understanding of the "nature of the beast." Contrary to so much of the wishful thinking of our political leaders and diplomats, the authors all recognize that the Soviet Union is an aggressive and expansionist power whose unremitting goal is to destroy all competing societies and coalesce the remains into one worldwide socialist "community" run by Moscow. This goal has been clearly expressed by all the Soviet leaders since the inception of the USSR. Moreover, the goal is ingrained into the Soviet system in such a way that short of a major upheaval, any expectations of fundamental change in this Soviet objective are unrealistic.

The basis of the West's misperceptions of the Soviet Union, the authors argue, is not due just to traditional Western optimism, although that is an important factor. Additionally, they point to the massive application of Soviet deception. This deception is designed to bring about precisely those misperceptions that have been the basis of false expectations and Western foreign policy failures. The authors show how the Soviets employ deception as a strategic weapon, not just in war but in peacetime too, in accordance with the dictum laid down over two thousand years ago by the ancient Chinese military philosopher Sun Tzu, who wrote, "To subdue the enemy without fighting is the acme of skill."

Deception has always walked arm in arm with conspiracy, aggression, and violence, whether in the realm of domestic or foreign affairs. Communist parties require deception as an essential element of their revolutionary takeovers and their concept of "government." Both require the conspiracy of a privileged and well-organized few to dominate the masses and eliminate all political opposition. As deception proved invaluable in subduing all "class enemies" internally, it is only natural that it should be employed as a weapon against all external "class enemies"—which is how the United States and other democratic nations are characterized.

Our own democratic form of government makes us particularly vulnerable to deception. Democracy requires freedom and openness. People must be able to think, to write, and to speak freely. Unfortunately, it is exactly this kind of climate that is most susceptible to manipulation and poisoning by deception and disinformation—especially if citizens are not vigilant and active in their pursuit of the truth.

This book on Soviet strategic deception is especially timely. Following the disappointments of detente and arms control, with its accompanying string of Soviet violations, we are once again hearing calls for more detente and more arms control treaties. We hear the familiar arguments about how the Soviet Union is changing for the better, how "we can do business" with Mr. Gorbachev, who is allegedly a new and nicer kind of Soviet leader. We are being urged to work even harder and to seize this "unique and historic opportunity" to reach new arms control accords, to put aside the problems of the past, and to make real peace with the USSR. Those who look upon all this with skepticism are being branded as strident anti-Soviets—implying that being anti-Soviet is a prejudice instead of a cautious lesson from history.

But times have changed since the "detente" years of the 1970s, changed in a direction that makes consideration of the issues raised in this book so crucial. It is easy to dismiss foreign threats when the hostile forces are economically weak, industrially backward, and militarily inferior, as the Soviet Union was from 1917 until recently. By the mid-1970s, however, the Soviet Union had established clear military superiority in most areas in which comparisons are conducted. Also, following the infusion of U.S. technology and financial assistance of the 1970s, it has become misleading to speak disparagingly about the Soviet economy, especially given its demonstrated capacity to incorporate technological advances into the design of its military equipment, often much faster than we do in the United States. Such disparaging comments are based all too often on Western values and objectives, which do not correspond to those of the Soviets. From its own perspective, the Soviet Union is a major power now in all important respects. Under the circumstances, if our perceptions and expectations prove to be in error, that could rapidly grow to be a very serious, perhaps even a catastrophic error. It was precisely such a grave intellectual error, a failure to perceive reality properly—in that case, the true nature and purpose of Nazism—that proved to be the decisive catalyst for World War II. In the nuclear age, we cannot afford such errors.

This is why the essays in this book are worth the most serious consideration. They cover a wide range of topics, from something as basic as the Soviet use of language to the nuclear arms race; from arms control and treaties to the military utilization of space; from religion and economics to the so-called wars of national liberation with which the United States is now confronted in Latin America.

The common theme that rings strong and clear through all the essays is the focus of the introductory essay by Michael Voslensky, that the Soviet Union is "An Empire Based On Lies." Dr. Voslensky and Mr. Bukovsky, both former citizens of the USSR, characterize this as the fundamental essence of the Soviet Union.

One of the continuing problems the world faces is the threat of nuclear war. Here deception is shown to play an important role in Soviet strategy, which encompasses arms control, military doctrine, and preparations for war. But hand in hand with each part of Soviet strategy is the technique of hiding it from the West. When these analyses are laid side by side with studies of the utility of treaties with the Soviets and the Soviet concept of peace, the failures of nuclear arms control become understandable, however unpleasant their implications.

Ambassador Nitze's paper goes to the heart of the problem of perceptions and anticipations. How can there be a meeting of the minds, an agreement to live and work in peace and harmony, when by the word *peace* the Soviets mean the condition that is reached after all competing societies have been destroyed?

Similarly, the expression "peaceful coexistence" leads us to more misconceptions and semantic non sequiturs, because the Soviets mean not "live and let live," which is the Western interpretation, but rather the waging of lethal covert war using all forces and means to destroy the West, as Sun Tzu advised, without the need for those direct military engagements that have become so dangerous in the nuclear age.

Perhaps the most disquieting theme that also runs through the individual essays is the failure of the West to see what is happening. The Soviet practice of deception would be less important if it were not successful—if we were not actually being deceived. The opinion of many professionals in the intelligence community is, indeed, that Soviet deception is not all that successful. But this analysis is belied by a variety of case studies presented in this book. As is pointed out, the Soviets spend over $3 billion each year just to misinform the world about their intentions and activities.

How, the reader will ask, can informed decisions be made about such important issues as aid to the movement in Nicaragua? And what is it about the President's Strategic Defense Initiative that really bothers the Soviets? Who is there to explain these issues to the public or to the Congress when it is time to decide on whether to fund these programs? How does the interested citizen who is unable to devote the hours analyzing these issues, as authors of the essays in this book have done, achieve an objective understanding when faced with the product of a massive and sophisticated Soviet propaganda apparatus? Unfortunately, there are no labels reading, "Caution: Believing these data can be dangerous to your country's health."

The final fundamental message in this book is that the real target of the Soviet deception is the public—citizens of nations around the world, and especially here in the United States. Certainly, the Soviets work to deceive political leaders and government administrators. Yes, their targets have also included the media and academia. But ultimately they recognize that political power in America comes from the people and is most reflected in Congress. In a sense, deception is a massive advertising campaign in which the product is deliberately misrepresented so that the consumers are trapped and robbed of their property and protection without knowing what has happened until it is too late. This is the Soviet strategy: to keep the people misinformed until it is too late for them to react to the truth.

That is why this book was written. It is for the public, and for the protection of those values we cherish.

About the Authors

Congressman Jack Kemp

Congressman Jack Kemp is currently serving his eighth term in the U.S. House of Representatives, where he holds a key leadership position as chairman of the House Republican Conference. He was elected to Congress in 1970 following thirteen years of leadership as a quarterback in the American and National Football Leagues.

Congressman Kemp, whose western New York district encompasses much of suburban Buffalo, was a quarterback for the Buffalo Bills from 1962 to 1969. He helped lead the team to League championships in 1964 and 1965 and was twice selected All-League Quarterback, once with the San Diego Chargers in 1960 and later with the Buffalo Bills in 1965. He was president of the AFL Players Association for five years and helped negotiate one of the most comprehensive pension contracts in professional football history. Kemp was selected as the Most Valuable Player in the League in 1965, and in 1983 he received the National Football Foundation and Hall of Fame's Gold Medal for excellence in leadership both on the football field and in the nation's legislative arena.

During his years in Congress, Representative Kemp's top priority has been the reform of our nation's fiscal, monetary, and economic policies in order to restore full employment without inflation.

In 1981 Congressman Kemp's tax reform legislation—the Kemp-Roth Bill, providing for a 30 percent reduction in marginal tax rates for all and "indexing" of the tax code—was in large part adopted by Congress and the Administration. In 1984 he introduced a far-reaching tax reform bill that would lower the top personal rate to 25 percent, simplify the tax code by closing inefficient loopholes, and broaden the nation's tax base while protecting families and the working poor.

Congressman Kemp has been a leader in promoting reform of the Federal Reserve's monetary policy. In the spring of 1984 he introduced monetary reform legislation designed to reduce uncertainty and speculation in financial markets by requiring the Federal Reserve to publish monetary policy decisions on the day they are adopted. A companion bill was also introduced to establish long-term price stability as the overall objective of Federal Reserve monetary policy, providing a "price rule" for stabilizing the value of the dollar. This was designed to help bring down interest rates without causing inflation.

Mr. Kemp, together with Democratic Congressman Robert Garcia of the South Bronx and Congressional Black Caucus leader Bill Gray of Philadelphia, has been a pioneer for the concept of free enterprise zones. They have formed a unique bipartisan coalition in Congress to revitalize the inner cities of America by providing special tax and regulatory incentives to encourage entrepreneurship and job creation in the private sector of the urban economy.

As the ranking Republican on the Foreign Operations subcommittee of the House Appropriations Committee, Representative Kemp is a key leader in redesigning and reforming U.S. security and economic assistance programs to strengthen Free World alliances and to develop U.S. foreign policy credibility. In 1984 Congressman Kemp served as a senior counselor to the President's National Bipartisan Commission on Central America, which was chaired by former Secretary of State Henry A. Kissinger, and he was a U.S. observer to the 1984 presidential elections in El Salvador.

Representative Kemp is also a member of the House Budget Committee and the Task Force on National Defense. In 1983 he was a member of a U.S. congressional delegation visiting Moscow and Leningrad. He was an active congressional delegate to the SALT talks in Geneva from 1979 to 1981, to the Jerusalem Conference on International Terrorism in 1979, and to the 1984 Washington Conference on Terrorism sponsored by the Jonathan Institute.

Congressman Kemp and his wife, Joanne, are dedicated to the cause of human rights, with particular emphasis on the plight of Soviet Jews. They also helped to establish CREED, the Christian Rescue Effort for the Emancipation of Dissidents, an organization devoted to improving the conditions of Christians behind the Iron Curtain.

Congressman Kemp is the author of *An American Renaissance: A Strategy for the 1980s; The American Idea: Ending the Limits to*

Growth; and he is coeditor, with Professor Robert Mundell of Columbia University, of *A Monetary Agenda for World Growth.*

Born and educated in Los Angeles, Mr. Kemp received his B.A. from Occidental College in 1957.

Jack and Joanne are the parents of four children: Jeffrey, Jennifer, Judith, and James. Their hometown is Hamburg, New York, and they have a residence in Bethesda, Maryland.

Dr. Michael S. Voslensky

Dr. Michael S. Voslensky was born in Berdjansk, USSR, on June 12, 1920. Educated at Moscow University, The Moscow State Pedagogical Institute, The Moscow State Institute of International Relations, and The German Academy of State and Law at Potsdam, he is one of the true experts on the Soviet system.

He held positions while in the USSR as lecturer and as a translator at the Nuremberg Trials; he served in the Council of Ministers of the USSR, in the World Peace Council in Prague, the Presidium of the Academy of Sciences of the USSR, as professor at Lumumba University, and as vice president of the Historian's Commission. He left the USSR in 1972.

He held positions as visiting professor in universities in Vienna, Münster, and Hamburg and at the Max-Planck-Institute in Starnberg.

In 1977 he was deprived of Soviet citizenship and is now an Austrian citizen.

He has written five books and 450 articles. He is famous for his book, *Nomenklatura, The Soviet Ruling Class,* which has appeared in fourteen countries.

Dr. Voslensky is a member of the American Association for the Advancement of Slavic Studies and the Committee of International Solidarity with the Afghan Resistance.

He is presently the director of the Institute of Contemporary Soviet Research, Munich, Federal Republic of Germany.

David S. Sullivan

David S. Sullivan works for the U.S. Senate as principal national security adviser to several Republican senators in leadership positions.

After a lengthy career at the Central Intelligence Agency, where he analyzed Soviet strategy and nuclear force modernization, Mr. Sullivan resigned in 1978 to join the staff of Senator Lloyd Bentsen, Democrat of Texas. In 1981 he accepted an appointment in the Reagan Administration as a senior official of the Arms Control and Disarmament Agency but later returned to his present position on Capitol Hill to help implement the President's defense policies in Congress. He is presently Legislative Assistant for Military Affairs and Arms Control for several senators.

Mr. Sullivan was educated at Harvard University (B.A. cum laude, 1965) and at Columbia University, where he received a master's degree in International Affairs.

He is a major in the U.S. Marine Corps Reserve and saw active service in the Vietnam War in Marine Combat Intelligence.

His previously published works number more than twenty articles and books on national security and include *The Bitter Fruit of SALT: A Record of Soviet Duplicity* and *The Fatal Flaws of SALT II*.

Mr. Sam Cohen

Mr. Sam Cohen is retired after a forty-year career in nuclear weapons issues. While with the U.S. Army, he was assigned to the Manhattan Project at Los Alamos in 1944, working on the atomic bomb development. In 1947 he joined the RAND Corporation, beginning his career as a nuclear weapons analyst. Over most of Mr. Cohen's career, he has worked on and conducted studies dealing with nuclear weapons. In the course of this work, he developed the technical military concept of the "neutron bomb" in 1958. He has consulted over the years with the Los Alamos and Livermore nuclear weapons laboratories, the U.S. Air Force, and the Office of the Secretary of Defense. He has authored (and coauthored) numerous articles and books dealing with nuclear weapons issues. Five recent books are: *Tactical Nuclear Weapons: An Examination of the Issues* (New York: Crane, Russak and Company, 1978); *Echec à la Guerre* (Paris: Editions Copernic, 1979); *The Truth About the Neutron Bomb* (New York: William Morrow and Company, 1983); *We Can Prevent World War III* (Ottawa, Ill.: Jameson Books, 1985); *Reflections on Nuclear Testing* (Stanford, Cal.: Hoover Institution Press, 1986).

Dr. William R. Van Cleave

Dr. William R. Van Cleave is professor of International Relations and director of the Defense and Strategic Studies Program at the University of Southern California and Senior Research Fellow for National Security at the Hoover Institution, Stanford University. He is also a member of the Executive Committee of the Board of Directors of the Committee on the Present Danger, and he is codirector of the annual summer International Seminar on National Security at Christian Albrechts University, Kiel, West Germany. He is the author of numerous publications on national defense, international security affairs, strategy, and arms control.

From 1969 to 1971, Dr. Van Cleave was a member of the first U.S. SALT delegation and a special assistant in the Office of the Secretary of Defense. In 1976 he was a member of the presidential "B-Team," which was charged with reviewing national intelligence on Soviet strategic programs and objectives and preparing a competitive national intelligence estimate. During the presidential campaign of 1979–1980, Dr. Van Cleave was senior defense adviser and defense policy coordinator for Ronald Reagan; after the election he was director of the Department of Defense transition team.

Dr. William R. Kintner

Dr. William R. Kintner is listed in the Marquis *Who's Who in the World* as an educator, which aptly summarizes a varied career. A 1940 West Point graduate, he fought in World War II at Normandy and into Germany, and he commanded an infantry battalion on Pork Chop Hill in the Korean War. He received a Ph.D. from Georgetown University in 1949 and subsequently served in many government agencies dealing with U.S. national security, including the CIA, the NSC, and the White House. In 1961 he retired from the army and became a professor of political science at the University of Pennsylvania.

He helped organize and became the deputy director of the Foreign Policy Research Institute in 1961, then became the director and the president of the Institute. In 1976 Dr. Kintner was appointed ambassador to Thailand. He became professor emeritus at the University of Pennsylvania in 1985. He is the author of numerous books, including *The Front is Everywhere*, 1950; *Protracted Con-*

flict, 1959; and *A Forward Strategy for America,* 1961. His latest book, *Soviet Global Strategy,* was published in 1986. During 1973–75 he was the U.S. ambassador to Thailand. In 1985 he was appointed a member of the United States Peace Institute.

David Martin

David Martin worked for the U.S. Senate for over nineteen years. He was staff assistant and speechwriter for Senator Thomas J. Dodd of Connecticut. He was an adviser for foreign policy, national defense, and internal security. He was senior analyst for the Senate Subcommittee on Internal Security for over six years. In this capacity he helped organize and conduct hearings on terrorism, drugs, control of explosives, and internal security.

He has written numerous articles on internal security, is the author of two books on Yugoslavia in World War II, and is the editor of a series of three books about Hungary under Soviet rule. He has recently published a booklet, *Screening Federal Employees: A Neglected Security Priority,* and is associate editor of *Law and National Security Intelligence Report* of the American Bar Association.

John Rees

John Rees is a senior editor of *Conservative Digest.* For the past eighteen years he has published the authoritative biweekly *Information Digest,* well known for its reports on organizations that populate the extreme shores of political thought and on terrorist groups throughout the world. In addition to making frequent television and radio appearances, Mr. Rees is the author of many articles, published both in America and in Europe, on terrorism, espionage, technology transfer, counterintelligence, and U.S. foreign policy. He was attacked by the U.S. left for alerting the Reagan Administration to Soviet penetration of the U.S. nuclear freeze campaign. His best-known book in this area is *The War Called Peace,* which details Soviet active measures designed to influence the European and American peace movements.

Mr. Rees is national editor of the Mid-Atlantic Research Associates' publication, *Early Warning.*

Ambassador Paul H. Nitze

On December 5, 1984, Paul H. Nitze was asked to serve as a special adviser to the President and the Secretary of State on arms control matters. Ambassador Nitze had been head of the U.S. delegation to the intermediate-range nuclear forces negotiations with the Soviet Union, which convened on November 30, 1981, in Geneva, Switzerland.

During the preceding seven years, Mr. Nitze was a consultant on defense policy and international relations to various government departments and private industry firms. He was also chairman of the Advisory Council of the Johns Hopkins School of Advanced International Studies; a director on the boards of Aspen Skiing Corporation, Twentieth Century-Fox Film Corporation, Schroders, Inc., American Security and Trust Company, the Ethics and Public Policy Center, and the Atlantic Council of the United States; trustee emeritus of the Aspen Institute for Humanistic Studies and the George C. Marshall Research Foundation; and chairman of policy studies for the Committee on the Present Danger.

In the spring of 1969 Mr. Nitze was appointed representative of the Secretary of Defense to the U.S. delegation to the Strategic Arms Limitations Talks with the Soviet Union, a position he held until June 1974, at which time he resigned.

Mr. Nitze served as Deputy Secretary of Defense, Secretary of the Navy, Assistant Secretary of Defense for International Security Affairs, a member of the Board of Economic Warfare, and vice chairman of the U.S. Strategic Bombing Survey. He held senior positions in the U.S. State Department, including as the director of the State Department's policy planning staff.

Mr. Nitze left the federal government in 1953 to become president of the Foreign Service Educational Foundation in Washington, D.C., a position he held until January 1961.

Graduated cum laude in 1928 from Harvard University, Mr. Nitze subsequently joined the New York investment banking firm of Dillon Reed and Company. In 1941 he left his position as vice president of that firm to become financial director of the Office of the Coordinator of Inter-American Affairs.

Born in Amherst, Massachusetts, on January 16, 1907, Mr. Nitze is married to the former Phyllis Pratt and has four children: Heidi, Peter, William, and Anina. Mr. Nitze maintains his legal residence in Washington, D.C., and has a residence in Bel Alton, Maryland.

Raymond S. Sleeper

Raymond S. Sleeper was born in Laconia, New Hampshire, in 1914, attended the University of New Hampshire, graduated from West Point in 1940, and received a master's degree from Harvard in 1949. He was an instructor at the Air War College and director of Project Control.

His military service ranged from a pilot of B-17s in World War II to chief of war plans for the commander in chief, Pacific Area Command, to commander of the Foreign Technology Division, Wright Patterson Air Force Base near Dayton, Ohio.

In his postmilitary life he has served with the American Security Council and as professor of cybernetics at the University of Tennessee Space Institute in Tullahoma, Tennessee.

He is presently the director of the National Security Division of the Leadership Foundation, and the director of the Coalition for Freedom Through Truth.

Colonel Sleeper has published numerous articles and is the author of *Project Control* (unpublished) at the Air University, Maxwell Air Force Base, Ala., and *A Lexicon of Marxist-Leninist Semantics*.

Dr. Joseph D. Douglass, Jr.

Dr. Joseph Douglass is a Washington-based defense analyst. Over the past twenty-five years, he has performed or managed a wide variety of national security studies. His fields of expertise include nuclear strategy and technology, modern chemical and biological warfare, Soviet strategy and decision-making, intelligence and deception, command and control for nuclear war, and arms control. His most recent work has been in the involvement of foreign nations in international drug and narcotics trafficking, arms control, applications of modern technology to chemical and biological warfare, strategic nuclear war termination, and advanced radar technology for intelligence applications.

Dr. Douglass has worked with the U.S. government, where he was deputy director, Tactical Technology Office, Advanced Research Projects Agency, and with Washington area defense contractors System Planning Corporation, JAYCOR, and IRT. He has also been associated with SANDIA Corporation and the Institute for

Defense Analyses, where he worked as a member of the Weapon Systems Evaluation Group. He has served on numerous defense science board studies and is currently a consultant to the Arms Control and Disarmament Agency. He also serves on the editorial board of *Strategic Review* and on advisory boards of the Institute for Foreign Policy Analysis, American Security Council, and Reason Foundation.

Dr. Douglass has lectured extensively in the United States and in Europe. He has authored or coauthored numerous articles and books, including *Soviet Strategy for Nuclear War* (Hoover Institute), *Soviet Strategy for War in Europe* (Pergamon), *America the Vulnerable: The Threat of Chemical and Biological Warfare* (Lexington), *Why the Soviet Union Violates Arms Control Treaties* (Pergamon-Brassey's), and *Communist Decision-Making: An Inside View* (Pergamon-Brassey's).

Dr. Douglass studied at Cornell University, where he received a B.S., M.S., and Ph.D. in electrical engineering.

Charles B. Dickens

Charles B. Dickens has had twenty-seven years of intelligence experience, twenty-six of which were with the Central Intelligence Agency. Twenty years of his service were abroad at nine posts in eight different countries. Mr. Dickens worked primarily in operational management positions. His last position was that of chief of the Foreign Liaison Branch in the Directorate of Operations, where he had an Agency oversight responsibility on the propriety of the operational cooperation, training, and the technical assistance provided to foreign intelligence services. His guidance to the CIA stations around the world provided for a CIA role in implementing human rights policies that would not wreak havoc with our foreign liaison relationships.

His service abroad included briefings of foreign presidents and cabinet ministers. In awarding a State Department decoration to Mr. Dickens, his role in stopping a military action was described as crucial to the success of U.S. policy in the country concerned.

Mr. Dickens is the author of several articles, among them *Human Rights and Foreign Policy Under the Carter Administration—The Distortion of an Ideal,* studies for the National Security Council, and papers on intelligence legislation. He has lectured to the CIA staff, to audiences across the United States, and has appeared on U.S. and Canadian TV.

Mr. Dickens graduated from North Dakota State University and was a member of Phi Kappa Phi. He attended a wide range of schools and seminars affiliated with his service.

Mr. Dickens has native fluency in Spanish, having lived and served in Latin America for thirty years. He was born in Buenos Aires, Argentina, the son of American parents, and is a member of the Sons of the American Revolution.

His father, Fred W. Dickens, born in Eureka Springs, Arkansas, is renowned in Argentina as the Olympic coach who gave to Argentina in the Twenties and Thirties a period of sporting excellence still known as the Golden Era of Argentine athletics. His mother, Grace Gesell Dickens, born in La Crosse, Wisconsin, was the inspiration for her children's interest in foreign affairs.

James E. Oberg

James E. Oberg is a professional space engineer in Houston, Texas, working on the Space Shuttle project. He is generally considered one of the West's leading experts on the Soviet space program. His book, *Pioneering Space,* issued by McGraw-Hill, is very well known. He has researched the KAL 007 atrocity carefully and has published on the tragedy at length.

He is the author of *Red Star in Orbit, Mission to Mars, New Earths,* and *UFO's and Outer Space Mysteries,* as well as many magazine articles for such publications as *Omni, Science Digest,* and *Analog.*

Herbert Romerstein

Herbert Romerstein is a senior policy officer on soviet disinformation and active measures for the U.S. Information Agency. He had previously served as a professional staff member for the U.S. Congress for eighteen years. The views he expresses are his own and do not necessarily reflect those of the U.S. government.

Dr. William Fletcher

William C. Fletcher, A.B., B.D., Ph.D., is professor and director of Soviet and East European studies at the University of Kansas. He was President of the Centre de Recherches et d'Etude des Institutions Religieuses in Geneva, Switzerland, from 1965 to 1970. Before that he was a research associate at the Research Institute on Communist Strategy and Propaganda in the School of International Relations at the University of Southern California.

Dr. Fletcher is internationally recognized as one of the world's leading authorities on religion in the USSR. He has published widely on topics in this field, including ten books. These include *The Russian Orthodox Church Underground 1917-1970* (London, Oxford University Press), 1973, and *The Moderns: Moulders of Contemporary Theology* (Grand Rapids, Michigan, Zondervan), 1962.

Dr. Fletcher received his A.B. cum laude from UCLA, his B.D. from California Baptist Theological Seminary, and his Ph.D. at the University of Southern California.

Dr. Steven Rosefielde

Dr. Steven Rosefielde is a professor of economics at the University of North Carolina, Chapel Hill, and adjunct research professor of national security affairs at the U.S. Navy Postgraduate School. He served as a coordinator of the US–USSR Joint Cooperative Research Program on Science and Technology. A graduate of Harvard University, he is the author of more than fifty books and articles on Soviet economics and the economics of socialism.

Vladimir Bukovsky

Vladimir Bukovsky spent twelve years in Soviet prisons because he spoke out against the inequities and injustices in Soviet life, in schools, in the community, and in the life of the ordinary Soviet citizen.

He was first arrested while in high school in the early 1960s. He was expelled later from the university and was attacked by the KGB for publicly reading unpublished poets. Later he was sentenced to the prison hospital at Leningrad.

He studied Western books, learned English, learned the Soviet prison system, and even manipulated it, as his striking autobiography *To Build a Castle* describes—sometimes in harrowing detail.

He came to the United States in 1976. He is currently studying neuroscience at Stanford University.

Mr. Smith

Mr. Smith came to Washington to help formulate U.S. foreign policy. He quickly realized something was wrong. He has described what he considers to be wrong with U.S. policy toward the Soviet Union and what can be done about it. He wishes to remain anonymous in order to be more effective in his work.

General Bernard A. Schriever, USAF (Ret.)

General Bernard A. Schriever, USAF (Ret.), headed all Air Force ballistic missile and space development programs from 1954 to 1966. Following retirement, he was elected board chairman of Schriever & McKee, Inc., of Washington, D.C.

The last seventeen years of General Schriever's military career were spent in positions of high responsibility in military research and development, including commander of the Air Force Systems Command (1959-66). General Schriever gained fame as the director of the Air Force ballistic missile program, which developed and deployed the Thor, Atlas, Titan, and Minuteman missile systems. He also directed the development of a number of space programs.

General Schriever was born in Bremen, Germany, on September 14, 1910. He immigrated to the United States in 1917 and was graduated from Texas A&M in 1931 with a bachelor of science degree. He started his military career that same year when he accepted a reserve appointment in the field artillery. He earned his wings as a second lieutenant in the Army Air Corps in June 1933; in 1937 he reverted to inactive status to become a pilot for Northwest Airlines. Reentering the service as a second lieutenant in the Regular Army Air Corps in October 1938, he remained on active duty until August 31, 1966. In 1942 he obtained a master of science degree in aeronautical engineering from Stanford University. He has been awarded the Army Distinguished Service Medal, the USAF Distinguished Service Medal with one Oak Leaf Cluster, the Legion of Merit, the Air Medal, and the Purple Heart.

He is a director of American Medical International, Control Data Corporation, Eastern Airlines, Emerson Electric, and Wackenhut Corporations.

General Schriever has received honorary doctor of science degrees from Creighton University, Rider College, Rollins College, and Adelphi College. He has been awarded a doctor of aeronautical science degree from the University of Michigan and doctor of engineering degrees from Brooklyn Polytechnic Institute, Pennsylvania Military College, and Morton College. Loyola University, in Los Angeles, has conferred an honorary doctor of laws degree on General Schriever. He is a fellow of the American Institute of Aeronautics and Astronautics.

In 1980 General Schriever was enshrined in the Aviation Hall of Fame.

Contributors

Many individuals helped produce *Mesmerized by the Bear: The Soviet Strategy of Deception*. The following people and organizations contributed direct support for the research, preparation, and publication of the study:

Edward Durell
George R. Wackenhut
Wackenhut Corporation
Dr. S. Jerome Tamkin
Tamkin Foundation
Wallace R. Persons
A.C. Wedemeyer
L.R. Hafstad
Royce Diener
James Q. Brett
Dr. David Meroney
Harold E. Watson
Robert E. Wilson

Tom F. O'Neil
Granville A. Morse
Philip Lukin
Jim R. Lyons
Stanley M. Rumbough, Jr.
Senator George Murphy
Joseph I. O'Neill, Jr.
Sam M. Fleming
Gene J. DeMatteo
Marianne Mele Hall
Oliver Presbrey
Martha Rountree

THE EMPIRE OF LIES

Dr. Michael S. Voslensky

Alexander Solzhenitsyn coined a formula that he addressed to all those living in the Soviet Union: *Zhit' ne po lzhy*—"to live without lie." Why did this appeal have to be launched by the great Russian writer to his countrymen? Why has this principle become so eminently important in today's Russia?

A System Born in Lies

The Soviet system pretends to be "real socialism" built up according to the teaching of Karl Marx. Is this true?

Marx's main theses are:

That the proletariat is a class generated by capitalist development. It is the most progressive class of the society because its class interests objectively coincide with the interests of mankind. Struggling for these interests, the proletariat will overthrow capitalism in a proletarian revolution. In this way the last form of class exploitation will be deleted. A real democracy—a "dictatorship of the proletariat"—then will be installed.

That "dictatorship of the proletariat" will be the last form of the State. The State is an apparatus of the ruling class for oppressing the other classes of the society. As soon as there is no class oppression, the State will wither away. Thus a Communist society will be born: a classless society without state, army, police, or bureaucracy. Everybody will work according to his capacity and receive according to his needs.

This unsophisticated utopia contains an important element: it proclaims the proletariat as the force bound to overthrow the existing order and to establish the dictatorship of the proletariat, a premise allegedly necessary for general happiness. Marx wrote that philosophers should not only explain but above all *change* the world.[1] The proletarian innovation in a rather traditional utopia was a political lever for changing the world. Marx was very proud of his idea of the dictatorship of the proletariat. He considered it to be his main contribution to the philosophy of history.[2]

There were at least two lies in this contribution.

The first one was that, when speaking about the proletariat, Marx did not mean the real working class. His complete disinterest in this class was clearly demonstrated. Living in industrial England and writing about the proletariat and its exploitation by the capitalists, Marx did not pay even a short visit to a factory to see this exploitation and to meet members of the "most progressive" class. The real workers were alien to the intellectual and elitist Marx. Speaking about the proletariat, he meant the revolutionary intelligentsia pretending to be an avant-garde of the proletariat.

Why did they choose as "their" class just the proletariat? Because of a certain similarity between the situation of the working class and that of the intelligentsia, both earning their living by selling their single commodity, labor, to the employer. But similarity does not mean identity. The interest of the revolutionary intelligentsia in the working class was generated not by a sentimental solidarity but by a practical consideration: the small leftist groups were unable to seize power; they tried to persuade the workers to overthrow the existing order. Then the revolutionary intellectuals of the Marx-Engels type could come to power—in the name of the proletariat. Thus a dictatorship of the proletariat would actually be a dictatorship of these intellectuals—not in any sense of the proletariat.

The second lie was the assertion that such a dictatorship would be the most perfect democracy, leading to a classless society and to the disappearance of the State. A dictatorship is and can be only the opposite of a democracy. Even a "dictatorship of a majority over a minority," as Marx and then Lenin put it, would remain a clearly undemocratic rule. But the so-called dictatorship of the proletariat, i.e., of a group of left-wing intellectuals, had nothing to do with majority rule. And it was not clear why these intellectuals, should they indeed grasp power, would renounce it and allow the State to "wither away." One had to expect that they, on the contrary, would use the State in order to change the world according to their views or, more accurately, according to their interests. This was quite apparent in Marx's time. His critics (for instance, Bakunin) stressed that the application of Marx's teachings would inevitably mean the end of any democracy. Thus, as we see, one could have detected in the ideas of Marx the germ of a development that led to the creation of a new ruling class. It is difficult to say whether Marx understood the ambiguities of his teachings, but it is beyond doubt that Lenin did.

In his most important work, *What Is To Be Done?* Lenin proclaimed the Marxist theory a dogma. In the same book he developed a plan, clearly opposed to this dogma.

Historical materialism considers any revolution, including the proletarian one, the result of the steady growth of the productive forces in the society. Under the pressure of these forces it results in an explosion of the "production relations," the social framework of the society. A new framework arises, giving space for the further growth of the productive forces. This explosion is a revolution. Thus, according to the Marxist theory, only a development in material production leads to a revolution. This means, as Marx and Engels stressed, that a socialist revolution is possible only in a highly developed capitalist society.

Lenin, on the contrary, saw a proletarian revolution just as an overthrow of a "bourgeois" government by the Communists in an armed insurrection. For this reason he advocated setting up an "organization of professional revolutionaries" as the main lever to bring about a proletarian revolution. Lenin did not pay much attention to the stage of development of the productive forces. Engels stated that the proletarian revolution would take place at first in England, the United States, France, and a bit later in Germany, all in accordance with the level of their economic development; Lenin, on the contrary, planned the first proletarian revolution in underdeveloped, still-feudal, czarist Russia. The difference between Marxist theory and Lenin's planning was obvious, and the talented politician Lenin was fully aware of it. Lenin was in fact a revisionist of Marxism, going much further than Edward Bernstein or Karl Kautsky. Thus Lenin's proclaiming Marxism a dogma and his arguments against the "revisionists" were lies.

Even more of a lie was Lenin's affirmation that an overthrow of the Russian government by the Bolshevik organization of professional revolutionaries would bring with it the realization of the Marxist utopia. In fact Lenin never really planned to attain this idealistic aim; he wished just to establish the Bolsheviks' full control over Russia and to expand this control worldwide. Lenin's real aim was to create, as he used to say, a "World Republic of the Soviet."

This was a plan of world domination of the Soviet State, not of a classless society without either State or domination.[3]

Thus the second thick layer of lies marked the creation of the Soviet Union in December 1922.

The third layer came with Stalin's rise to power. With Lenin's support, he was elected General Secretary of the Party's Central Committee in April 1922. Like Lenin, who presented himself as the most orthodox Marxist, Stalin presented himself as the most fervent Leninist. But under the slogan of struggle against deviationists from Lenin's "general line," Stalin persecuted Lenin's closest comrades in arms, followers, the old Bolsheviks. Stalin's dictatorship was not a dictatorship of the proletariat. Trotsky called it the "dictatorship over the proletariat." But it wasn't a dictatorship of Lenin's revolutionary intellectuals, either: they were purged under different pretexts as Trotskyists, Bukharinists, Zimovievists, or as participants of several oppositions. The Great Terror of the years 1936–38, with its show trials, mass executions, the deportation of millions of people to the terrible NKVD camps, was the final stage of these persecutions. A dictatorship of the new ruling class, the *nomenklatura*, was established as the logical result of this development, started by Marx, continued by Lenin, and achieved by Stalin.

Let us scratch off the thick layer of propagandistic lies and see the main features of the social and political structure called "real socialism." Those interested in more details can find them in *Nomenklatura.*[4]

The society consists of five classes. Among the elite are:

1. *The ruling class:* the political bureaucracy, called by the insiders nomenklatura and by the outer world, the Party. This class has a monopoly of power in all spheres of the country's life: politics, economy, law, culture, and ideology. It is very privileged and constitutes a kind of a new aristocracy.

2. *The intelligentsia:* a class of specialists having no political power but some privileges and a higher standard of living than the bulk of the population.

In the direct producers are:

3. *The working class:* underprivileged, exploited, and underpaid, a class of workers of the early capitalistic epoch hailed by the official propaganda as "the leading class of the socialist society."

4. *The kolchoz peasantry:* underprivileged, exploited, and badly paid, a class of feudally dependent peasants, even officially considered as a

second-rate class. The employees, the working class, and the peasantry
are developing together toward a united class of "toilers", i.e., of
producers.

5. *The forced labor class:* the state slaves, very like those of the ancient
   world: people in prisons, camps, and administrative exile, deprived
   of practically every right, treated like cattle, existing at the mercy of
   the KGB.

The most important class of this society is certainly the nomenklatura.
Its hard core is the Party apparatus, from the district (*rayon*) Party
committees to the Party Central Committee with, at its head, the
two "directive organs"—the Politburo and the Secretariat of the
Central Committee—both presided over by the General Secretary.
In this hard core of the nomenklatura is concentrated the political
decision-making as well as the appointment of all nomenklaturists—
in the Party apparatus itself and outside it, in the key positions in the
State, economy, science, and art, everywhere. An important part of
the nomenklatura is the "stabilizers" of the "real socialist" society: the
political police, the military, and the propaganda managers. The role
of the rank-and-file members and candidates of the Party (there are 18
million now) is as a link between the nomenklatura and the population.
The compensation for this particular devotion is the better prospect
for a member of the Party to make a career and, in a case of particular
zeal, to become a member of the nomenklatura.

The dictatorship of the nomenklatura is no longer a one-man
dictatorship. It is an oligarchy ruled by dictatorial methods. This
fully corresponds to the character of "socialist property," the collective property of the nomenklatura. It is managed by the Soviet
State, which is the administrative apparatus of the nomenklatura. If
we apply Marxist terminology, the nomenklatura is the exploiting
class of the society: nomenklatura takes over the "surplus-value"
produced by the workers, the peasants, and the State slaves. It
distributes this wealth according to its egoistic class interests. So a
huge part is spent on the privileges of the nomenklatura, on the
stabilizers, on the production of military strength (the military-
industrial complex), and on the policy of expansion (diplomacy,
propaganda abroad, subversion, espionage, financing of Communist
parties and different pro-Soviet movements, and so on).

Lenin quite correctly stated that every monopoly, with its absence of competition, necessarily leads to parasitism. The nomenklatura, this class with full monopoly of power, becomes ever more

parasitic. This class gives society less than it takes from it. This process of the parasitic degeneration of the ruling class is reflected in the poor performance of the Soviet economy, the stagnation of Soviet cultural life, and the widespread wish of intellectuals to emigrate from the USSR, held back only by restrictive measures.

Such is, in short terms, the system that arose—legitimately or not—from Marx's teaching and that calls itself—correctly or wrongly—the "real socialism."

Born in lies, this system can live only in lies. Otherwise, its nomenklatura rulers would have to accept that in Russia a social structure has been built up that is just the opposite of the Marxist utopia. Instead of a classless society without State, army, police, or bureaucracy, without class exploitation, privilege, or parasitism, a new class society has come into being, with an exceedingly powerful State, a huge army and police, and with a political bureaucracy as a ruling, exploiting, privileged, and parasitic class.

The nomenklatura cannot afford to tell this truth and must tell lies. Soviet propaganda continues to repeat the thesis proclaimed by Stalin in November 1936: Soviet society consists of two classes—the workers and the kolchoz peasants, as well as a stratum of intelligentsia.

To what class do Stalin's heirs in the Kremlin belong, and their huge Party apparatus, the KGB, and so on? Are they workers, or peasants, or intellectuals? They are not. They all belong to the nomenklatura. Mankind has known classes that tried to conceal their negative features, but the nomenklatura is the first class in history attempting to conceal its very existence.

The Soviet sociological literature mentions vaguely that there is in the intelligentsia a "section" (or even militarily, "detachment") that is specialized in "governing" (or "controlling") the others. The "governors" (or "controllers") are just a section of a "stratum," while the "governed" "controlled" are the rest of the Soviet population. No member of this important section is named. It reminds one of a science fiction novel by the famous Soviet writers the brothers Stroogatski, in which they ironically pictured a society ruled by an anonymous oligarchy of the "unknown Fathers."

The unknown Fathers in the Soviet Union and in the other States of the Soviet bloc have a name: nomenklatura. But one would search in vain for this name in Soviet encyclopedias or handbooks. Only in the manual for Party schools can one detect this term and its definition: "The nomenklatura is the group of the most important positions; the candidates for these positions are examined, recommended, and confirmed by the Party committees (district, city, region, etc.). The nomenklatura members can be relieved of their positions only with the consent of the respective Party committee. Persons elevated to the nomenklatura are those in key positions."[5] The group possessing the totality of the key positions in the country is evidently the most important group in the society. But not only do the names and the members of this group not appear in the Soviet handbooks; neither does the term *nomenklatura*. The ruling class of the USSR is concealed; it is secret.

The class of the State slaves is secret as well: the number of detained and exiled, in camps and prisons, the living and working conditions there, the mortality rates—all these are top secret.

A system jealously concealing even its own structure, pretending to be the opposite of what it really is, must practice overall secrecy and deception. The tradition of the conspiratorial organization of professional revolutionaries largely contributed to this spirit of secrecy and of steady lying after the organization came to power in October 1917. But it is no explanation; it merely sharpened and made particularly ridiculous this secrecy and deception as one of the main features of the system. The feature as such is due neither to the tradition nor to the individual amorality of the leading apparatchiks; it is an objective necessity for the system. That is why it is typical of every country of "real socialism," independently of its history and of the individuals at the top. The attempt to present the dictatorship of a parasitic and selfish oligarchy as a realized utopia cannot live without utmost secrecy and constant deception.

People in the non-Soviet world can hardly imagine the amount of everyday lies and deception a citizen of a "real socialist" country is confronted with. He is told that he is much better off than people in the West; that he is free and that they are not, that his living standard is higher and is rising. He knows that just the opposite is true, but he must repeat these lies. He is told to "quietly look into the future," although he is afraid of this future with its uncertainty; but he must repeat the lies. He is told that all citizens in socialism are equal, although he knows that there are the privileged, the underprivileged, and the totally unprivileged. He must pretend to elect the governing bodies, while he knows that the elections are just a dull formality: there is always one candidate and no choice. He is told that the socialist economy is flourishing, although he knows that is is in an extremely bad state. He must line up every day in order to obtain the most primitive consumer goods and elementary products. He is told that "socialist legality" guarantees his rights, although he knows that he fully depends on the arbitrary decisions of the Party apparatus and its secret police. He is told that the Soviet Union pursues a policy of peace, although he knows that the Soviets are waging a war in Afghanistan, that they have annexed or subjugated several countries, and that a huge war machine has been built up in the USSR and continues to grow.

The citizen must repeat all these lies. He must show himself enthusiastic over every official pronouncement of the General Secretary, although they usually deserve at best to be shamefully passed unnoticed. He must try to make people believe that he shares the official thesis of the infallibility of the Party.

In short, the citizen is forced not only to listen to but to repeat lies. If he does not, he will be punished. The official lie is obligatory. Those who tell the truth about the structure and functioning of "real socialism" are put on trial for slandering the Soviet State and social system and sentenced to several years of detention. Soviet law deters the citizen from telling the foreigners even nonclassified information that has not been officially published. Westerners visiting the Soviet Union are agreeably surprised that Soviet citizens are always speaking to them about peace. These travelers do not realize that this is practically the single topic on which a Soviet national is allowed to speak with foreigners—of course, he repeats the theses of official propaganda. I have never heard Soviet citizens talk among themselves about peace or disarmament; should one start talking of it, he would be considered a fool.

The nomenklaturists are fully aware of the popular skepticism toward official lies. Such expressions as "he is lying like a radio broadcasting" or "tell the truth, you are not in a Party meeting" are well known in all strata of the population. But it would be wrong to think that the Soviet authorities feel very uneasy about it. The times when they really tried to persuade the people are over; they are trying now to persuade people that it's better to parrot the official lies, because any other approach would achieve nothing but would damage these people. This appeal to realism, backed by repression, seems to be reasonable. It is followed by the majority of the population, as in any totalitarian society. But the official slogans and phrases have become largely accepted meaningless clichés and nothing more. It is a kind of mask that people take off at home or with their friends and that they eagerly would take off in a political or military crisis. The nomenklatura must live with it, and the people must live with the nomenklatura.

Only the fact that the Soviet authorities do not worry whether their subjects believe their propaganda or not can explain the cynicism with which these subjects are told obvious lies. Soviet soldiers sent to Afghanistan are told that they will have to fight there against Americans, Chinese, and Pakistanis; only in Afghanistan do the officers tell the newcomers that the enemy will be the Afghans. This change provokes neither surprise nor indignation: the soldiers quietly realize that they have been lied to once more.

Constant lying becomes a normal attitude of the rulers and of the ruled in the Soviet Union. They lie even when there is no real incentive to do so. So Andropov's disinformation service stubbornly launched a "special rumor" (a KGB term for mouth-to-ear disinformation) that Andropov had no wife—until at his funeral his crying widow appeared on the Red Square at the head of the mourning family.

It is just this mentality that brought the Soviet leadership to the extensive use of disinformation as a means of foreign policy. Normally, States use misinformation of the enemy in wartime in order to support their military operations. The Soviet Union is the first State to use large-scale disinformation activities at all times. KGB General Agavants, an Armenian, the longtime Soviet espionage chief (*rezident*) in France, shaped and was the chief of the Soviet disinformation service. Such services were created in all other Warsaw Pact countries. Ladislav Bittman, former deputy chief of this service in Czechoslovakia, published two revealing books about his experiences after his defection to the West in 1968.[6] By the end of the 1960s Andropov, then chairman of the KGB, reorganized the disinformation service and made it even more efficient. In recent years we were witnesses of worldwide Soviet disinformation operations. So they tried to present the shooting down of the Korean airliner over Kamchatka as a "defensive measure" against an alleged U.S. intelligence operation; to describe the attempt to kill the Pope as an action of the right-wing Turkish terrorists with the CIA behind them; even to ascribe to the CIA the assassination of Indira Gandhi. The kidnapping by the KGB of the Soviet defector in England, Oleg Bitov, was also used by Moscow for dissemination of disinformation.

The Soviet disinformation's quality usually does not correspond to the level of the KGB effort in disseminating it. Produced by bureaucrats having normally a rather poor knowledge of the West and Western mentality, these lies show only too clearly their objectives. As a matter of fact, a careful analysis of Soviet lies is an interesting source for detecting Moscow's intentions. Nevertheless, Soviet disinformation is not counterproductive. It is always aimed at circles in the West that are for different reasons interested in accepting the invented "news" at its face value. It is easy to find such circles in a pluralistic society. That is why even frankly stupid Soviet lies usually find an audience in the West. But this is another phenomenon—that of Western self-deception—and it is a special topic.

The dissemination of lies has always a reverse side: the concealing of the truth. As we have stated in the first part of this chapter, official lies and secrecy go hand in hand in the USSR.

Of course, every State has degrees of secrecy. In the Soviet Union these degrees start with For Service Use Only and rise through Secret and Strictly Secret to the highest Kremlin level of secrecy. This may sound exaggerated, but in the USSR this is still in the framework of the normal.

The official paranoia begins beyond these degrees of secrecy. The Soviet citizen knows that any nonclassified information that has not been recently made public could be considered secret, and he can be punished for disclosing it. It is this mentality that brought the Soviet authorities to proclaim the bulk of the USSR territory an "area closed to foreigners"; only some big cities and a couple of regions prepared for international tourism are open. The same mood of secrecy is shown by the ridiculous Soviet unwillingness to reveal the names and numbers of their missiles, tanks, military ships, and planes. In the U.S.-Soviet arms control talks, the Soviets reveal no information about their weapons at all. All the information comes from the U.S. intelligence!

Even the General Secretary of the Party Central Committee uses in his public pronouncements the NATO denominations—for instance, "SS-20" missiles (instead of their Soviet name, "Pioner"). Everything linked with the foreigners, or the international connections, is considered as forbidden to the average Soviet citizens. I remember how the deputy executive secretary of the Soviet Peace Committee, Leonid Kapitonovich Makarchenkov (identified by John Barron as a KGB officer),[7] demanded that the judge in a civil trial exclude the public; the solicitor was a former committee staff member and had worked abroad at the World Peace Council two years before.

Overall secrecy is stupid only at first glance. Certainly in many cases it is exaggerated, but the purpose is evident. Since the nomenklatura must present Soviet society as the opposite of what it really is, it is necessary not only to disseminate lies but also to conceal the truth.

All this is understandable. But is it possible? Will not people see the reality behind the lies and secrecy? It is agreeable to be optimistic, but it is better to be realistic. Of course, in the long run people discern lies from truth. But it would be wrong to underestimate Marx's and Lenin's thoughts about truth and about the possibility of creating an artificial consciousness in the heads of people. Marx shaped the formula that an idea winning the minds of the masses becomes a material force. He did not say that this idea must be correct; it can also be a wrong idea. Lenin drew a logical conclusion that a conscience must be brought into the masses. We know how successful Hitler and Goebbels were in achieving this task. So were, to a lesser extent, the Bolsheviks, as well.

Lies and deceptions are political weapons and tactics of the Soviets. This is clear practically to everybody, in the West as in the East. But it is necessary to realize that they are not just tactics that could be easily changed. Neither the new General Secretary nor the Soviet leadership as a whole can renounce these lies. Deceptions and lies are, under the dictatorship of the nomenklatura, not only systematic, they are systemic. Deceptions and lies in all politically relevant matters are an organic consequence of "real socialism's" very nature.

It is for all these reasons that Alexander Solzhenitsyn coined the formula for all those living in the Soviet Union, "To live without lie," to tell the truth.

The West should have no illusions: the lies will continue as long as the system of "real socialism" exists.

President Reagan called the Soviet Union an "Evil Empire." This provoked much indignation and protest. After fifty years of life there, with all the ups and downs, innumerable events, encounters, feelings, and thoughts, I do not know whether the USSR is an evil empire. Is it an empire that can be trusted? Is it a good one?

Notes

1. Karl Marx and Friedrich Engels, *Theses on Feuerbach*, Collected Works. (Moscow, Progress Publishers, 1975), vol. 5.
2. Karl Marx and Friedrich Engels, *Selected Works*. (1975), vol. 2, p. 410.

3. Lenin, *Collected Works*. (Moscow, Progress Publishers, 1963–70), vol. 5.

4. Michael S. Voslensky, *Nomenklatura, The Soviet Ruling Class. An Insider Report*. (N.Y.: Doubleday & Co., 1984).

5. *Partijnoje Stroitel'stvo. Ucebnoje Posobije*. (Moscow, 1981), p. 300.

6. Ladislav Bittman, *The Deception Game*. (Syracuse, N.Y.: Syracuse Univ. Research Corp., 1972). Also *Zum Tode Verurteilt*. (München: Roitman Verlag, 1984).

7. J. Barron, *KGB: The Secret Work of Soviet Secret Agents*. (N.Y.: Reader's Digest Press, 1973), p. 534.

SOVIET
DECEPTION IN
ARMS CONTROL

David S. Sullivan

President Ronald Reagan stated bluntly on April 2, 1985, that "The Soviet Union virtually outnumbers us in any type of weapon you want to name." President Reagan has publicly conceded that the Soviet Union has achieved overwhelming strategic superiority over the United States at least seven times since 1982.

These declarations of a starkly true fact have extremely serious consequences for world peace, but this fact of U.S. strategic nuclear inferiority is not well known around the Free World or even in the United States.

The full implications of the reality of Soviet strategic superiority have yet to be fully understood in U.S. politics, defense planning, budgeting, and diplomacy.

How have the Soviets achieved this strategic superiority so decisively and so successfully without provoking an American response?

In a nutshell, the arms control process has been responsible for Soviet strategic superiority. A strong element of Soviet deception and duplicity has been involved.

Arms Control
Has Led to
Soviet Superiority

President Reagan himself realized this fact as early as May 9, 1982, when he stated:

> So far, the Soviet Union has used arms control negotiations primarily as an instrument to restrict U.S. defense programs, and in conjunction with their own arms buildup, as a means to enhance Soviet power and prestige.

An awareness of this truth is now beginning to permeate U.S. defense and intelligence establishments. For example, the Defense Department stated recently that:

> The Soviet Union regards arms control negotiations as arenas of political conflict in which important military advantages can be gained or lost. The Soviet leadership does not think in terms of mutuality or perceive arms control negotiations as a means of reducing arms. They attempt at every turn to achieve strategic advantage.

Another recent Defense Department statement was even more critical of the arms control process:

> Current Soviet policy on arms agreements is dominated by their attempts to derive unilateral advantage from arms negotiations and agreements, by accepting only arrangements that permit continued Soviet increases in military strength while using the negotiation process to inhibit Western increases in military strength.

Even the U.S. intelligence community, which so often has underestimated Soviet strategic strength and misperceived Soviet intentions, has finally reached the same conclusion. The most recent Central Intelligence Agency National Intelligence Estimate on Soviet strategic forces was declassified in June 1985 by the White House and released to the U.S. Senate. NIE-11-3-8-85 states:

> Soviet leaders view arms control policy as an important factor in advancing their strategy of achieving strategic advantage. Moscow has long believed that arms control must first and foremost protect the capabilities of Soviet military forces relative to their opponents.

Defense Secretary Caspar Weinberger was even more succinct when he stated in December 1984 that "We now face precisely the situation that SALT I and SALT II were supposed to prevent."

President Reagan's National Security Adviser, Robert McFarlane, was quoted in January 1986 as saying:

> The U.S. strategic buildup has not worked, and has done nothing to close the window of vulnerability. In fact, American

land-based missiles have become even more vulnerable to Soviet first strike attack over the past few years.

President Reagan has made four historic reports to Congress on Soviet arms control treaty violations. The first was on January 23, 1984; the second was on October 10, 1984; the third was on February 1, 1985; and the fourth was on December 22, 1985.

Each of these four presidential reports to Congress on Soviet arms control treaty violations was in response to an amendment that U.S. Senator Jim McClure (R–Idaho) sponsored and that was either unanimously or overwhelmingly passed by the U.S. Senate.

These four presidential reports support the reasonable conclusion that arms control treaties with the Soviets have undermined American security, not safeguarded it. Arms control treaties have enormously strengthened the Soviet Union while weakening the United States. Yet because this conclusive fact seems so startling to so many observers, we must also conclude that the Soviets have used the arms control process and arms control treaties as a bold instrument of massive deception to promote their own thrust to military supremacy over the United States. In fact, however, there has long been overwhelming evidence that the Soviets use diplomacy and international law as important tools in their arms control deception program.

The Four Presidential Reports on Soviet Violations

The fact that these reports were rendered at all is historic and unprecedented. For the first time in our history, a U.S. President has openly accused the Soviet Union of violating Strategic Arms Limitation Treaty (SALT) commitments. These four reports, made by formal messages to Congress, are irrevocable and, though still incomplete, must be applauded. Even the liberal pro–arms control Arms Control Association has concluded that Soviet "violations of arms control agreements cannot be overlooked or excused." But the implications of these violations for American national security and for world peace are extremely serious. These implications have not yet been addressed within the U.S. government, however, despite urgent and repeated requests to President Reagan beginning on March 1, 1984.

In addition to addressing the military implications of the Soviet SALT violations and deceptions, we need to summarize these presidentially confirmed Soviet arms control treaty violations. Moreover, when these violations were first released, they were downplayed both by the White House and by the media, so they are not, in fact, well known at all. It is important to note further that these findings were unanimously agreed upon by the national security departments and agencies of our government. There were neither dissenting footnotes nor disagreeing qualifications by any part of the Executive Branch to these presidential reports to Congress. There are now 106 Soviet arms control treaty violations agreed and confirmed by the Executive Branch and reported by the President to Congress.

These 106 violations are summarized, for the first time aggregated in one place publicly, as follows, according to the different treaties violated.

Presidentially Confirmed
Expanding Pattern of Soviet SALT II
Break-Out Violations
—Total of Twenty-two

A. **SS-25 mobile ICBM—prohibited second new type ICBM.**
   1. Development
   2. Flight testing (irreversible)
   3. Deployment since 1985—over eighty, plus launchers, a "direct violation"
   4. Rapid-refire capability—doubles force
   5. RV-to-throw-weight ratio (and doubling of throw weight over old SS-13 ICBM)—probable covert SS-25 two or three MIRV capability
   6. Encryption of telemetry, a "direct violation"
B. **SNDVs**
   7. Strategic Nuclear Delivery Vehicle limit of 2,504. Soviets are at least sixteen to over six hundred SNDVs over the number they had when SALT II was signed in 1979, thus illustrating the fundamental inequality of SALT II.
C. **SS-N-23 SLBM**
   8. Heavy throw weight prohibited
   9. Development

    10. Flight testing (irreversible)
    11. Deployment on Delta IV and III Class submarines
    12. Encryption of telemetry

D. **Backfire intercontinental bomber**
    13. Arctic basing; increasing intercontinental operating capability
    14. Probable refueling probe; increasing intercontinental operating capability
    15. Production of more than thirty Backfires per year for five years, making more than ten extra Backfire bombers

E. **CCD**
    16. Expanding pattern of camouflage, concealment, and deception (*maskirovka*), deliberately impeding verification

F. **Encryption**
    17. Almost total encryption of ICBM, SLBM, and SLCM telemetry

G. **Launcher-Missile Relationship**
    18. Concealment of relationship between SS-16, SS-24, and SS-25 missiles and their mobile ICBM launchers
    19. Confirmed deployment of fifty to two hundred banned SS-16 mobile ICBM launchers at Plesetsk test range, now being replaced by a similar number of banned SS-25 mobile launchers

H. **Falsification of SALT II Data Exchange**
    20. Operationally deployed SS-16 launchers not declared
    21. AS-3 Kangaroo long-range air-launched cruise missile range falsely declared to be less than six hundred kilometers and not counted

I. **Excess MIRV fractionation**
    22. SS-18 super-heavy ICBM: NIE reportedly says SS-18 deployed with fourteen warheads each, adding 1,212 warheads

These Soviet SALT II violations have enormous strategic significance, both militarily and politically. Altogether they amount to Soviet strategic offensive superiority. First, they result in over six hundred more Soviet SNDVs than are allowed by SALT II. Second, they augment the already overwhelming Soviet first-strike capability actually codified with U.S. agreement in the terms of the SALT II Treaty itself. Even more important, U.S. unilateral compliance with the unratified SALT II Treaty, which the Soviets are confirmed to be violating at will, actually demonstrates Soviet strategic offensive superiority to the world. If the numbers themselves did not demonstrate Soviet superiority, then overt U.S. agreement to unequal levels of forces in complying, contrary to its own laws and Constitution, with an unratified SALT II Treaty clearly demonstrates U.S. submission to Soviet superiority. And the Soviets are estimated to be preparing to deploy over seven hundred more mobile ICBM launchers by 1987 in addition to their already overwhelming 6-to-1 superiority in ICBM warhead capabilities. The Soviets are already thus ten to fifteen years ahead of the United States in strategic offensive capabilities.

Presidentially Confirmed
Expanding Pattern of Soviet SALT I
ABM Treaty Break-Out Violations
—Nine Violations

1. The siting, orientation, and capabilities of the Soviet Krasnoyarsk ABM battle management radar "directly violates" three provisions of the SALT I ABM Treaty.

2. Over one hundred ABM-mode tests of Soviet SAM-5, SAM-10, and SAM-12 surface-to-air missiles and radars are "highly probable" violations of the SALT I ABM Treaty. Two high Soviet officials have even admitted that their SAMs have been tested and deployed with a prohibited ABM capability.

3. The Soviets "may be developing" and deploying a territorial, nationwide ABM defense, which violates the SALT I ban on developing even a "base" for a "nationwide defense." President Reagan has stated that "this is a serious cause for concern." The Secretary of Defense has testified that the "Soviets have some nationwide ABM capability" already.

4. The mobility of the ABM-3 system is a violation of the SALT I ABM Treaty.

5. Soviet rapid relocation without prior notification of an ABM radar, creating the Kamchatka ABM test range, and mobility of the ABM-3 radar, were "violations" of the ABM Treaty.

6. Continuing development of mobile "Flat Twin" ABM radars, from 1975 to the present, is a violation of the prohibition on developing and testing mobile ABMs. The Soviets are now mass producing the ABM-3 system for rapid nationwide deployment.

7. Soviet ABM rapid reload capability for ABM launchers is a "serious cause for concern." The State and Defense Departments state that the Soviets "may" have a prohibited reloadable ABM system.

8. Soviet deliberate camouflage, concealment, and deception activity impedes verification.

9. Confirmed Soviet falsification of the deactivation of ABM test range launchers is a violation of the ABM Treaty dismantling procedures.

These Soviet violations of the SALT I ABM Treaty have enormous significance, both military and political. The Soviets are planning to deploy over four thousand mobile ABM interceptors by 1987, for a nationwide ABM defense. They can already defend almost 20 percent of their strategic forces, and soon they will be able to defend 50 to 66 percent. The Soviets are over ten years ahead of the United States in strategic defenses.

Presidentially Confirmed
Expanding Pattern of Soviet SALT I
Interim Agreement
—Five Break-Out Violations

1. Soviet deployment of the *heavy* SS-19 ICBM and the medium SS-17 ICBM to replace the light SS-11 ICBM was a circumvention defeating the object and purpose of the SALT I Interim Agreement. Article II of the Interim Agreement prohibited heavy ICBMs from replacing light ICBMs. This violation alone increased the Soviet first-strike threat by a factor of five.
2. Soviet deployment of modern SLBM submarines exceeding the limit of 740 SLBM launchers without dismantling other ICBM or SLBM launchers, which the Soviets actually admitted was a violation.
3. Soviet camouflage, concealment, and deception deliberately impeded verification.
4. Circumvention of SALT I by deploying SS-N-21 and SS-NX-24 long-range cruise missiles on converted Y Class SLBM submarines, which "is a threat to U.S. and Allied security similar to that of the original SSBN."
5. "The U.S. judges that Soviet use of former SS-7 ICBM facilities in support of the deployment and operation of the SS-25 mobile ICBM is a violation of the SALT I Interim Agreement."

Presidentially Confirmed
Expanding Pattern of Soviet Violations
of Nuclear Test Bans
—Over Seventy Violations

1. Over twenty atmospheric nuclear weapons tests, August through September 1961, in violation of the 1959 Mutual Test Ban Moratorium.

2. Over thirty conclusively confirmed cases of Soviet venting of nuclear radioactive debris beyond their borders from underground nuclear weapons tests, in violation of the 1963 Limited or Atmospheric Test Ban Treaty.

3. Over twenty cases of Soviet underground nuclear weapons tests over the 150-kiloton threshold in "probable violation" of the 1974 Threshold Test Ban Treaty.

The many Soviet nuclear test ban violations have allowed the Soviets to develop and test much more lethal warheads for their new ICBMs, SLBMs, and cruise missiles. Thus these Soviet violations have enormous strategic significance.

Presidential Confirmation of Soviet Violations of the Kennedy-Khrushchev Agreement on Cuba of 1962

The Soviets breached a unilateral commitment by sending offensive weapons—intercontinental nuclear-delivery-capable bombers, nuclear-delivery-capable fighter bombers, and various kinds of nuclear missile submarines—back to Cuba, beginning in 1969.

On September 14, 1983, President Reagan for a second time confirmed that the Soviet Union had violated the Kennedy-Khrushchev agreement that ended the Cuban missile crisis: "That agreement has been abrogated many times by the Soviet Union and Cuba in the bringing of what can only be described as offensive weapons, not defensive, there." This presidential statement has been backed up by the CIA director, the chairman of the Joint Chiefs of Staff, and the under secretary of defense for policy. Even the State Department concedes that the Soviets have violated the "spirit" of the agreement.

Presidentially Confirmed Expanding Pattern of Soviet Violations of Biological and Chemical Weapons Bans

1. "The Soviets have maintained an offensive biological warfare program and capability in direct violation of the 1972 Biological and Toxin Weapon Convention." The United States has no defenses against this capability. The Sverdlovsk Anthrax explosion of April 1979, killing several thousand Soviets, is direct evidence of this capability.

2. "Soviet involvement in the production, transfer, and use of chemical and toxic substances for hostile purposes in Southeast Asia and Afghanistan are direct violations of the 1925 Geneva Protocol." Tens of thousands of innocent men, women and children suffered horrible deaths from these Soviet atrocities, which are also violations of the Genocide Convention.

3. The Soviets violated the Conventional Weapons Convention by using booby-trap mines and incendiary devices against civilians in Afghanistan.

4. The U.S. Government has determined that the Soviet Union is violating the 1975 Helsinki Final Act by its inadequate notifications of its Warsaw Pact military exercises.

5. The Soviets violated the Montreux Convention of 1936 by transiting the Turkish Straits repeatedly with aircraft carriers. (The Turkish Government, a signatory of the Montreux Convention, repeatedly protested these violations to the Soviets, to no avail.)

6. The Soviets breached the 1982 Brezhnev SS-20 moratorium, their unilateral commitment to end SS-20 deployment, by completing SS-20 launcher positions and continuing to deploy new SS-20s.

In sum, twenty-two of the presidentially confirmed Soviet violations relate to the SALT II Treaty, nine relate to the SALT I ABM Treaty, and five relate to the SALT I Interim Agreement. Many relate to the nuclear weapons ban agreements. Nothing whatsoever has been done by the Reagan Administration to counteract these Soviet arms control violations. Until the Reagan Administration, all previous administrations had claimed that if the Soviets were ever caught violating even one arms control treaty, the United States would have to reassess the entire spectrum of our relations with them. Complete U.S. inaction in the face of these presidentially confirmed Soviet violations demonstrates that this was a false premise. In fact, U.S. inaction can be interpreted as appeasement of the Soviets. Instead of reassessing our relations with the Soviet Union, the Reagan Administration actually resumed arms control negotiations with the Soviets aimed at achieving a new arms control treaty and has even agreed to hold a summit meeting with the Soviets in its quest for a new arms control treaty.

A reasonable explanation of these confirmed Soviet violations is that they are measures to test U.S. intelligence capabilities and U.S. political will. Further, the violations and the expanding pattern of Soviet camouflage, concealment, and deception activities may be a preparation or a cover for more extensive violations taking place already or planned for the future. The United States still has no long-range or even short-range strategy to deter or to counteract Soviet violations. But most important, Soviet violations are aimed at increasing strategic superiority.

America is now witnessing the Soviet SALT break-out deployment of hundreds of illegal new-type ICBMs, carrying illegal new MIRVed warheads covertly, being camouflaged illegally, and defended by thousands of launchers for several illegal mobile camouflaged ABM systems, using an illegal nationwide system of large ABM battle management radars.

Additional Reagan Administration Charges of Soviet Treaty Violations

1. Soviet violation of the 1945 Yalta Agreement, by denying free elections in Poland.
2. Soviet violation of the 1945 Potsdam Agreement, by occupying Eastern Europe.
3. Soviet violation of the United Nations Charter, through threatened aggression against Poland, in 1980–81.
4. Soviet violation of the Paris Peace Accords on ending the Indochina War, by continuing to build up the North Vietnamese military.
5. Soviet violation of various international agreements governing civil aviation, by the brutal KAL 007 shoot-down murder incident of 1983.
6. Soviet violation of the 1972 Incidents at Sea Agreement during the attempts to recover the KAL 007 black box. In fact, there is strong evidence that the Soviets shot down KAL 007 in the first place in order to cover up some of their SALT II violations (such as a test of their illegal SS-25 second new-type ICBM, with full encryption of electronic telemetry signals) planned for that very night of August 31, 1983.

The Defense Department has stated that the United States should vigorously pursue compliance issues with the Soviet Union and demand that the Soviets take corrective action when we detect violations. If this fails, the United States should be prepared to take those measures necessary to maintain our national security in the face of Soviet violations.

But the Soviets are directly challenging the essence of the United States democratic political system by their forty-six confirmed, conclusively agreed-upon arms control violations. They are boldly gambling that American democratic leaders cannot muster the leadership or collect the bipartisan political consensus necessary to demonstrate the political will to compensate for the Soviet SALT violations. The Soviets believe, with some justification derived from their direct experience with American appeasement, that American political leaders are paralyzed and demoralized and unable to galvanize public support to challenge the Soviets and counteract their threats to our collective allied security.

The Soviets are demonstrating self-confidence and have reason to. The Soviets know full well that they have an overwhelming 4-to-1 numerical advantage in ICBM warheads (counting the Defense Intelligence Agency's best estimate of fourteen warheads on each of 326 superheavy SS-18 ICBMs, giving the Soviets 8,500 ICBM warheads to only 2,100 for the U.S.). Their accuracy and megatonnage advantages give them over a 6-to-1 or even an 8-to-1 advantage in first-strike counterforce capabilities. The Soviets also have simultaneously over a 14-to-1 advantage in intermediate-range nuclear force warheads against NATO. The Soviets are apparently deploying a nationwide ABM defense, probably capable soon of defending not only Moscow but also ICBM fields and all the USSR. Thus the Soviets are able to threaten the United States with a strategic offensive first strike, and soon they may even be largely immune from a limited U.S. retaliation.

Eighteen Additional Soviet SALT Circumventions or Violations

Assistant Secretary of Defense Richard Perle has testified to the Senate that the existing violations reports from the President are "illustrative only," and that "twenty to twenty-five" more Soviet violations remain to be publicly confirmed by the President to the Congress. The following eighteen additional Soviet SALT violations have been widely discussed in the press.

1. Developing and testing the Soviet SS-18 ICBM rapid-reload and refire capability as a circumvention of all the SALT II ceilings, doubling the Soviet SS-18 force.

2. Soviet failure to dismantle 18 SS-9 Fractional Orbital Bombardment ICBMs banned by the SALT II Treaty, which also circumvented the SALT I ICBM ceiling.

3. Soviet deployment of SS-11 ICBMs at SS-4 MRBM soft launch pads for covert soft launch in circumvention of all SALT I and SALT II ceilings.

4. Soviet maintenance of several thousand stockpiled ICBMs, SLBMs, and strategic cruise missiles as potentially operational, thus circumventing all SALT II ceilings.

5. Soviet development and deployment of the SS-24 rail mobile ICBM, which will be above SALT II launcher ceilings, and which reportedly may have heavier throw weight than the Soviet heavy SS-19 and which therefore is a prohibited new very heavy ICBM.

6. Probable Soviet exceeding of the SALT II ceiling of 820 MIRVed ICBMs, by reportedly deploying covertly MIRVed mobile SS-25 ICBMs, and by preparations to deploy MIRVed SS-24 mobile ICBMs.

7. Soviet failure to deactivate old ICBMs on time, in violation of the SALT I ICBM ceilings and 1974 dismantling procedures, and continuous falsification of official deactivation reports between 1975 and 1981.

8. Ongoing Soviet deployment of the mobile SS-16, mobile SS-24, and mobile SS-25 ICBMs, which circumvents and defeats the object and purpose of SALT I, because it is inconsistent with the U.S. SALT I Unilateral Statement against mobile ICBM deployment.

9. Violation of the late Soviet President Brezhnev's 1972 SALT I pledge not to build mobile ICBMs.

10. Violation of the late Soviet President Brezhnev's 1972 SALT I pledge to dismantle the entire G Class of strategic missile submarines.

11. Soviet violation of the SALT II ceilings of 1200 MIRV ICBM and MIRV SLBMs, and the 1320 ceiling on MIRV launchers and intercontinental bombers with long-range ALCMs, through deployment of excess MIRVed ICBM and MIRVed SLBMs and over fifty Bear H bombers and over three hundred intercontinental Backfire bombers capable of carrying long-range ALCMS.

12. Soviet circumvention of the SALT I ABM Treaty, by giving the Moscow ABM-3 complex the capability to defend over three hundred adjacent MIRVed ICBM silos.

13. Soviet violation of the 1971 agreement to reduce the risk of outbreak of nuclear war by jamming U.S. early-warning detection systems, failing to notify the United States of this jamming, and failing to notify the United States of the early April 1984 salvo launch of multiple SS-20s toward the United States.

14. Soviet achievement of "unilateral advantages" through their circum-ventions, violations, and negotiating deceptions related to SALT I and II. These Soviet unilateral advantages violate the 1972 agreement on basic principles of U.S.-Soviet relations, which is specified in the preamble to the SALT II Treaty as a fundamental element of SALT II.

15. Soviet violation of the June 1973 agreement on the prevention of nuclear war, through their hostile actions and hostile threats in the October 1973 Middle East War. (The Federal Republic of Germany has made this charge against the Soviets.)

16. Soviet direct interference with U.S. national technical means of SALT verification in a reported 1980 incident in which a Soviet intelligence satellite rendered a U.S. satellite useless during a key Soviet missile test. The incident is a clear violation of SALT I and II provisions. Moreover, the Soviets have reportedly blinded U.S. satellites with lasers and are jamming U.S. electronic collection satellites and other systems.

17. SALT II permits no increase in the throw weight of the superheavy SS-18 ICBM and no new type of very heavy ICBM to replace it. The Soviets appear to be doing both: developing a third new type of ICBM that is even heavier than the SS-18.

18. Any follow-on to the heavy SS-24 will have to be within 5 percent of its throw weight and other characteristics or else it is a prohibited new-type ICBM. The SS-24 follow-on under development is a fourth new-type ICBM, when SALT II allows only one new-type ICBM, and the SS-24 follow-on also appears to have even more throw weight than the heavy SS-24, which is already probably heavier than the SS-19.

The Soviets have thus gained overwhelming strategic superiority over the United States through their SALT violations, and thus they will be very reluctant to correct their violations. Indeed, deliberate Soviet efforts to counter U.S. "spies in the skies" strongly indicate a Soviet intention to continue to circumvent and violate treaties.

Soviet Intent to Deceive

As noted at the outset, according to a Department of Defense statement of March 28, 1984:

> The Soviet Union regards arms control negotiations as arenas of political conflict in which important military advantages can be gained or lost. The Soviet leadership does not think in terms of

mutuality or perceive arms control negotiations as a means of reducing arms. They attempt at every turn to achieve strategic advantage.

One Soviet military theorist stated in 1971, before SALT I was signed, that Soviet diplomacy is war. *Military Thought,* the classified journal of the Soviet General Staff, the Soviet agency most responsible for negotiating SALT, stated that "In fact, a nation's diplomatic activity becomes a part of those non-military means of policy implementation which . . . are contained within the concept of war." If the arms control process is considered an aspect of war by the Soviets, then they are guided by Sun Tzu's principle that "all warfare is based on deception."

Assistant Defense Secretary Perle has stated, "I believe we chronically underestimate the extent to which the Soviets engage in concealment and deception in order to mask programs that they have underway. . . . The Soviets have not hesitated to mislead us deliberately and all too successfully, in order to achieve their purpose." And as Perle stated to the Senate Armed Services Committee on February 20, 1985, "The Soviet Union has violated almost all of the most important arms control agreements signed since 1963."

Perle also stated to the Senate Armed Services Committee on February 20, 1985, that:

The current rash of Soviet arms control violations did not happen by accident. It resulted from the fact that our behavior vis-à-vis their noncompliance with signed agreements convinced the Soviets that they could get away with these acts. We did little in response to repeated Soviet violations of the LTBT during the 1960s and 1970s. We resolved many SALT I compliance problems by accepting Soviet behavior as legitimate. We resolved the SS-19 "heavy" missile issue by accepting the SS-19 as a "light" ICBM. There are now 2,000 warheads aimed at us on SS-19 missiles. We resolved the launch control silo issue by accepting the legitimacy of launch control facilities that are nearly identical to missile silos. We resolved the deployment of an ABM radar to Kamchatka by accepting it. We resolved the expanding pattern of Soviet concealment activities by ignoring them. During the 1970s we resolved the issue of Soviet testing of SAM missiles on the ABM mode by pretending it had stopped.

And as the President's General Advisory Committee on Arms Control (GAC) stated in November 1983, "Aspects of Soviet conduct related to about half their documentary arms control commitments were found to constitute material breaches of contracted duties."

Soviets Deceptively Sign Treaties, Intending to Violate Them

It is worth noting that the Defense Department has officially stated that "Several of these violations must have been planned by Soviet authorities many years ago, in some cases perhaps at the very time the Soviet Union entered into the agreement."

These cases of deliberate violations planned by Soviet leaders at the very time of signing the arms control agreements relate to the Soviet heavy SS-19 ICBM and the SALT I Interim Agreement of 1972, the six Pechora Class ABM battle management radars, and the SALT I ABM Treaty, the Soviet biological offensive warfare program, the 1972 Biological Weapons Convention, and the SS-16 and SS-25 mobile ICBMs and the SALT II Treaty.

Moreover, in March 1984 the Senate was told by a former member of the Joint Chiefs of Staff that twelve years before, in 1972, neither the Senate nor the Joint Chiefs of Staff were informed of vital intelligence information that the Soviet Union intended to violate the SALT I accords even before they were signed. Through an inordinate and even irrational desire to appear before the public as peacemakers and to preclude jeopardizing the chance of SALT I approval by Congress and thus electoral success, the Nixon Administration apparently withheld this essential military intelligence from our top military leaders, who, remaining in ignorance of it, supported SALT I, as did a similarly uninformed Congress.

In particular, Dr. Henry Kissinger may have deliberately misled the Senate by failing to reveal our knowledge of a Soviet plan for circumvention of the key SALT I provision limiting heavy ICBMs. If so, SALT I and the whole ensuing fabric of strategic arms control since 1972 received congressional approval at its inception under false pretenses covering up Soviet bad faith.

In any event, no one can now doubt that the USSR from the beginning of detente in 1972 planned to use the agreed limitations of SALT to freeze U.S. defenses while illegally building Soviet might. Any other interpretation ignores the facts of Soviet strategic growth and what they themselves have revealed. As the Soviet foreign policy expert, Rostislav Tumkovskiy, wrote in 1979 for internal Soviet readership only, "Signing the [SALT I] agreement was a victory of the Soviet Union in the arms race."

A full catalog of Soviet deceit shows that there are a total of over 310 major cases of Soviet arms control and other diplomatic deceptions since the Bolshevik Revolution of 1917. Fifty Soviet treaty violations involving international security have been confirmed by official Defense and State Department reports and also by Senate studies. In fact, official U.S. government documentation now fully supports the conclusion that the Soviets have violated, evaded, or circumvented virtually every international security treaty they have signed since 1917. In fact, the only significant treaty the Soviets are known to have kept was their August 1939 surprise agreement with Hitler to invade and divide Poland, the event that precipitated World War II.

Soviet Negotiating Deception

We turn now to a brief description and discussion of the highly complex subject of Soviet negotiating deception in arms control. The following are examples of Soviet negotiating deception in arms control negotiations.

Examples of Soviet Arms Control Negotiating Deceptions

1. The SS-19 heavy ICBM existence and large-scale deployment plans were concealed by Soviet leader Brezhnev. (SALT I, 1972.)
2. The Soviets concealed their SS-N-8s full range in order to gain a 3-to-2 advantage in SLBMs. (SALT I, 1972.)
3. The Soviets falsified ICBM deactivation reports from 1975 to 1981. (SALT I.)
4. The Soviets concealed thirty H Class SLBMs in their allowed 950 SLBMs in order to avoid deactivating them. (SALT I, 1972.)
5. The Soviets built mobile SS-16 ICBMs, despite Brezhnev's pledge not to. (SALT I, 1972.)
6. The Soviets lied on Stretch Yankee submarine. (SALT I, 1974.)
7. The Soviets withheld operational SS-16 mobile ICBMs from SALT II Data Base. (1979.)

8. The Soviets withheld long-range AS-3 Kangaroo missiles from SALT II Data Base. (1979.)

9. Brezhnev falsely claimed that their Backfire bomber did not have refueling capability or intercontinental range. (SALT II, 1979.)

10. The Soviets refused to agree to heavy ICBM definition, intercontinental bomber definition, or missile capability baseline data. (SALT II, 1979.)

11. The Soviets lied on Mutual Balanced Force Reductions (MBFR) negotiations troop strength data. (1978–present.)

There is extensive evidence of Soviet deception in the SALT negotiations. This evidence spans both SALT I and SALT II and relates both to Soviet negotiating behavior and to the operation of Soviet strategic forces.

The Soviets deceived the United States in May 1972 on each of the three main issues of SALT I: constraints on ICBM and silo size increases, constraints on SLBMS, and constraints on mobile ICBMs.

In SALT II, the Soviets continued to negotiate deceptively in order to avoid all effective constraints on new-type ICBMs.

Soviet SALT negotiating deception is confirmed by a highly classified 1978 CIA study by this author entitled *The Soviet Strategic Planning Process and SALT (U)*. An unclassified version of this CIA study has been published by this author as *The Bitter Fruit of SALT: A Record of Soviet Duplicity*.

In SALT I the United States fell victim to Soviet deceit and to U.S. gullibility and myopic assumptions. In essence, the United States traded off its superior ABM technology in return for what proved to be illusory constraints on Soviet offensive strategic capabilities. Carefully shrouding their ongoing and ambitious strategic programs, the Soviets negotiated ceilings that in no way compromised their force goals. They used this deception and loopholes in the SALT I agreement both to camouflage and to legitimize a thrust to strategic superiority that will endure well into the 1990s. The fact that the United States continues arms control negotiations with the Soviets despite officially confirmed Soviet violations and deceptions is an indication of the power of Soviet deception and Western self-deception.

Not only was the United States deceived by the Soviet Union in SALT I, but that deception, which has since been acknowledged by former American officials who were its victims, is compounded in the SALT II Treaty. Soviet deception has embraced not only negotiation tactics but also active concealment of offensive programs. The triumph of those tactics is a SALT II Treaty that guarantees an overwhelming Soviet strategic superiority throughout the 1990s.

The following points confirm the above examples of Soviet arms control negotiating deception. First, as the President's General Advisory Committee (GAC) report stated, "The Soviets sign and ratify arms control treaties they are planning to violate."

The GAC report added:

> The Soviet Union's actions since 1958 concerning arms control agreements demonstrate a pattern of pursuing military advantage through selective disregard for its international arms control duties and commitments. . . . The committee found recurring instances of Soviet conduct involving deliberate deception, misdirection, and falsification of data during negotiations.

Moreover, former Under Secretary of Defense Richard DeLauer testified to Congress in 1984 that:

> The Soviets in fact never slowed or even perturbed their strategic development and deployment programs in spite of detente, active arms control negotiations, or the SALT Agreements. . . . Major programs recently deployed or now late in development were generally initiated at the highest levels of Soviet leadership about ten years ago.

As noted, the Defense Department Posture Statement for FY 1985 stated that "Several of these violations must have been planned by Soviet authorities many years ago, in some cases perhaps at the very time the Soviet Union entered into the agreements."

Finally, Assistant Defense Secretary Perle testified to Congress in 1984 that "The Soviets have not hesitated to mislead us, deliberately and all too successfully."

Negotiation over arms control treaties is, to the Soviets, part of the ongoing war against the West and capitalism. We must recognize that arms control negotiations are an integral part of this ideological war. The Soviet Union has never paid any serious attention at all to its treaty commitments with any nation. The Soviets violate their own constitution and use international law and diplomacy as instruments of policy in the international power struggle. Ever since 1933, the Soviets have been flagrantly violating the basic agreement establishing the original foundation of U.S.-

Soviet diplomatic relations by engaging in revolutionary activity within the U.S.

History of Soviet Treaty
Violations and Deceptions

In April 1984 the Defense Department stated that "To the Soviets, treaties are manipulated in the manner most conducive to the interests of national policy objectives."

President Reagan, on September 2, 1983, asked these very relevant questions after the Soviet attack on Korean Airlines Flight 007:

> What can be said about Soviet credibility when they so flagrantly lie . . . ? What can be the scope of legitimate mutual discourse with a state whose values permit such atrocities? And what are we to think of a regime which establishes one set of standards for itself and another set for the rest of mankind?

A 1962 Defense Department study entitled *Soviet Treaty Violations* confirmed over fifty Soviet security treaty violations since 1917. These violations were also confirmed by a 1962 U.S. Senate Judiciary Committee study the same year.

Long before SALT began in 1969, the Soviets violated two significant arms control treaties, one in the 1920s, which entailed on-site inspection, and another in the late 1940s.

As Soviet authorities on international law have themselves stated,

> Those institutions of international law which can facilitate the accomplishment of the stated tasks of Soviet foreign policy are recognized and applied in the USSR; those which contradict these aims in any way are rejected.

According to an official U.S. State Department Soviet Affairs Note dated August 10, 1959:

> Few nations can match the USSR in vociferous protestations of loyalty to international obligations! However, such declarations which are typical of Soviet propagandists and scholars alike—diverge widely from Soviet practice. In the years since the

Bolsheviki Revolution the Soviet government, while consistently
accusing others of bad faith in international dealings, has not
hesitated to violate its own treaty obligations when such action
appeared to be in its interest.

This conclusion is well illustrated by Lenin's cold admission in 1918
regarding the March 1918 Soviet-German peace treaty of Brest-
Litovsk: "Yes, of course we are violating the treaty. We have
already violated it thirty or forty times."

The 1959 State Department analysis of Soviet treaty compliance authoritatively concluded that:

> The history of the last 40 years provides numerous examples of
> deliberate treaty violation by the Soviet regime. . . . The USSR
> has disregarded treaty provisions inconvenient to itself, has
> unilaterally denounced conventions to which it is a party, has
> threatened abrogation as a means of intimidation, and has on
> several occasions attacked fellow signatories to treaties of
> friendship and nonaggression.

It is evident that the Soviet Union places no value in abiding by
international agreements. The Soviet view is that, if an international
obligation no longer serves its purposes, Moscow has no inhibitions
about violating it. As the record of diplomatic history indicates, the
Soviet approach to its international commitments should warn us
that we must create a clear Soviet self-interest in treaty compliance;
otherwise, treaties with the Soviets are self-deceptive scraps of
paper, which are worse than worthless. In fact, treaties with the
USSR can be a positive danger if they lull us into a false sense of
security, as they have done so often in the past.

That same false sense of security has permitted the enormous
momentum of the Soviet strategic weapons buildup, which started
even before the Cuban missile crisis of 1962, and which will
continue into the 1990s, unconstrained by existing SALT treaties,
which the United States still unilaterally observes.

Former Reagan Administration Arms Control Director Eugene
Rostow has written, "The SALT I Agreements and the process of
negotiating SALT II did not prevent the worst decade of the Cold
War or the Extraordinary buildup of the Soviet nuclear arsenal."

Finally, as Richard Perle has testified, "The Soviets see arms
control negotiations not in terms of negotiating mutually beneficial
agreements to limit the risks and consequences of war, but as an

opportunity to inhibit U.S. programs, create divisions within the Western Alliance, and prevent the exploitation of advanced U.S. technology to balance Soviet quantitative advantages in military systems." Perle added that there has been almost a hundred percent increase in Soviet nuclear warheads aimed at the United States since SALT II was signed in 1979.

But the best summation of the Soviet attitude toward treaties was given by Soviet leaders themselves. Lenin stated that "Promises are like pie crusts, made to be broken."

And Joseph Stalin stated that:

Words have no relation to actions—otherwise what kind of diplomacy is it? Words are one thing, actions another. Good words are a mask for concealment of bad deeds. Sincere diplomacy is not more possible than dry water or wooden iron.

Lenin and Stalin's approach has been confirmed as the consistent Soviet approach by official U.S. government documentation from 1959, 1962, 1984, and 1985. This documentation supports the inescapable conclusion that the Soviets have violated, evaded, or circumvented virtually every international security treaty they have signed since 1917.

Americans Must Understand the Truth About Soviet Deception

In 1934 Winston Churchill challenged the British government to explain to the British people and to the world that the Germans were violating the arms control provisions of the Versailles and other arms control treaties. In the House of Commons Churchill stated, "The worst crime is not to tell the truth to the public." Unfortunately, the British government lied to the British people. Thus Britain slept until Englishmen had the choice of another world war or eventual Nazi domination.

To avoid a similar choice, we must first admit to ourselves the true result of our misguided recent history. We must acknowledge that the hypnotic fog of detente has frozen U.S. forces and brought about relative unilateral American disarmament through stagnation and obsolescence of U.S. strategic systems and a corresponding massive growth in the quality and quantity of Soviet weapons.

Additionally, countless successful Soviet deceptions and the significant practical military effects of Soviet arms control violations
have further aggravated the strategic imbalance—an imbalance that
never more urgently required the American government to take
countermeasures than it does now.

These are the concrete realities that we must face. As President
Reagan stated on March 22, 1985:

> I would like to call your attention to something that no one
> seems to be aware of—that we ourselves have cut the defense
> budgets over the last four years—our own proposed or projected
> five-year defense spending—we to date reduced those by more
> than $150 billion, and today the 1985 budget is $16 billion less
> than the 1985 budget that had been projected by the Carter
> Administration.

And as Richard Perle has stated, "To cut that [defense] budget in
the aftermath of Soviet violations, I think, would only encourage the
Soviets to the view that they can continue to violate with impunity,
without suffering the consequences that people have wrongly assumed would inevitably follow the detection of a Soviet violation."

We must recognize also that overdue remedies will not be
cheap. Carter Administration Defense Secretary Harold Brown said
in 1979 that, without SALT, the United States would be required to
spend $30 to $100 billion more on defense during the 1980s for
strategic systems.

Now that massive Soviet violations have made SALT, which
already favored the Soviet Union, a mere hollow shell, America
must accept the new reality and must implement defense programs
even, as Harold Brown said, at the additional cost of tens of billions
of tax dollars, in order to achieve any hope of catching up with the
USSR, much less regaining our lost superiority. Yet the Reagan
Administration has been forced by Congress to spend tens of
billions of dollars less on defense than proposed even by Jimmy
Carter, whose defense program relied on Soviet good faith and on
Soviet SALT compliance.

To build public and congressional support for the strategic
spending that even the Carter Administration admitted would be
needed (and that most Americans even now erroneously believe is
being expended), American leaders must come clean with the
American people and explain the effect and extent of congressional

defense budget cuts as well as the full extent and effects of Soviet arms control break-out. Otherwise, Americans could receive a highly unpleasant surprise when finally given an answer to Professor Harold Rood's question: "Can it really be true that Soviet negotiations for the Strategic Arms Limitation Treaties are nothing more than part of the preparations for war? That would place Soviet leaders in no better odor than Adolf Hitler."

Confirmation of the Failure of Arms Control

Finally, we should look back for a moment to 1971, when America was number one, still a great power, and examine how American tolerance for the Soviet strategic buildup was the basis for the failure of the arms control process. Gerard Smith, the Nixon Administration's Arms Control director, stated overconfidently in 1971:

> If, after a reasonable period, SALT negotiations prove unproductive, or if the USSR resumes land-based ICBM deployment or moves to modernize or expand its Moscow ABM system, the United States would take whatever steps are necessary to maintain its strategic deterrent.

Today we should evaluate Gerard Smith's self-confident prophecy.

First, the SALT II negotiations did not produce a ratifiable treaty, even after seven years of negotiations. Thus it is fair to say that SALT negotiations have been "unproductive."

Second, Soviet violations of SALT II and the SALT I ABM Treaty, many of which have been confirmed by the President to the Congress, prove conclusively that SALT treaties have not constrained Soviet strategic force buildup. Indeed, the Soviets have "resumed" land-based ICBM deployment, in violation of SALT II, and the Soviets are both "modernizing" and "expanding" their ABM system in violation of the SALT I ABM Treaty.

Third, despite Smith's confidence that the United States would respond to all these Soviet challenges, the United States is not taking the necessary responsive steps to "maintain its strategic deterrent."

In 1972 the SALT I ABM Treaty and SALT I Interim Offensive Agreement succeeded in killing the superior U.S. ABM program in exchange for "constraints" on Soviet forces that turned out to be completely illusory. The Soviet offensive buildup continued unchanged by SALT I and II. But since 1972 the Soviets have also completely reversed the relative position of the sides on ABM capabilities, and now the Soviets are breaking out of both defensive and offensive SALT I and II constraints. Meanwhile, the Soviets are once again trying to convince the United States to give up its Strategic Defense Initiative and defensive antisatellite program in exchange again either for nothing or for illusory offensive constraints.

As the Committee on the Present Danger concluded recently:

The adverse balance entails both political and military risks. . . . As relative Soviet power continues to increase, the Soviets expect the U.S. and its allies to move increasingly toward accommodation and *appeasement*.

Winston Churchill warned gravely after World War II:

Sometimes in the past we have committed the folly of throwing away our arms. Under the mercy of Providence, and at great cost and sacrifice, we have been able to recreate them when the need arose. But if we abandon our nuclear deterrent, there will be no second chance. To abandon it now would be to abandon it forever.

SOVIET DECEPTION IN NUCLEAR WEAPONS DEPLOYMENT

Sam Cohen

No sound and reliable agreement can be made unless it is completely covered by an inspection and reporting system adequate to support every portion of the agreement. The lessons of history teach us that disarmament agreements without adequate reciprocal inspection increase the dangers of war and do not brighten the prospects of peace.

These words were uttered by President Dwight Eisenhower during his address to the Geneva Conference of Heads of Government on July 21, 1955. They were intended to pave the way for secure arms control agreements between ourselves and the Soviet Union. They were intended to ensure that both sides would have adequate knowledge of each other's military capabilities *before* negotiating arms control agreements. First things first, the President was saying. Before we can consider the problem of verification of an arms control treaty, we must possess the knowledge that allows safely formulating one. Otherwise we are working against peace, not for it.

In his address President Eisenhower proposed an arrangement in which both sides would give to each other "a complete blueprint of our military establishments from beginning to end, from one end of our countries to the other; lay out the establishments and provide the blueprints to each other." Having such blueprints in hand would greatly facilitate the inspection process and the attainment of essential knowledge. There was no other way for us to gain such knowledge. The Soviets knew this, so they said no and continued their nuclear buildup in secrecy.

In the meantime the United States had embarked upon a program to pierce the Soviet veil of secrecy. The U-2 high altitude observation airplane was developed and began flights over the

USSR. But this came to an end when one of them was shot down in 1960. The Soviets made it very plain that they did not want us spying on them from above. We were persuaded to stop the U-2 flights.

By then, however, we had commenced orbiting our first primitive spy satellites. They would pass over the Soviet Union, taking snapshots of the earth below. When they ran out of film, they would deorbit, float down on a huge parachute, and be snagged in midair by a specially equipped aircraft. Today our spy satellites stay up almost indefinitely and have a wide variety of sensors: TV cameras, infrared photography, radars, and the like. They can pick up a truly fantastic amount of information on Soviet nuclear weapons activities. But the question is, how much is genuine information, and how much is Soviet disinformation or outright deception?

We do not know how to answer this question. However, there is a high likelihood that what we consider to be the most valuable information is Soviet disinformation. Much, if not most, of the essential knowledge we require to determine true Soviet nuclear capabilities very likely has been denied to us. We very likely do not possess the knowledge that President Eisenhower held to be indispensable for safely negotiating arms control treaties.

One person in a position to know whether we have been deceived by the Soviets into accepting false nuclear information is Viktor Suvorov, a Soviet defector. Before his defection, Suvorov had served as a Soviet Army staff officer. Although he is presently living in the United States, he is under sentence of death in the USSR.

In his recent book, *Inside the Soviet Army,* Suvorov recounts his fascination with capitalist movies. He describes one particular movie where three thieves successfully burglarized a diamond warehouse. The room containing the diamonds was ingeniously guarded by TV cameras. "But the thieves, too, were ingenious," wrote Suvorov. "They had with them a photograph of the room, taken earlier. They put this in front of the cameras and using it as a screen emptied the safes. The guards sensed something was happening. They began to feel vaguely uneasy. But looking at the television screen they were able to convince themselves that everything was quiet in the safe room." And this, according to Suvorov, is exactly what the Soviets have been doing to deceive our spy satellites:

I am sometimes told that the American spy satellites are keeping a careful watch on what is happening in the Soviet Union. They take infrared photographs of the country from above and from oblique angles, their photographs are compared; electronic, heat and all other emissions are measured, radio transmissions are intercepted and painstakingly analyzed. It is impossible to fool satellites. When I hear this, I always think of the trio behind a photograph, using it as a shield behind which to fill their bags with diamonds. Incidentally, the film ended happily for the thieves. . .

The Chief Directorate of Strategic Deception does exactly what the sympathetic trio did—they show the watchful eye of the camera a reassuring picture, behind the shelter of which the gangsters who call themselves the Communist Party of the Soviet Union, the Soviet Army, Military Industry, and so forth, go about their business. . . .

The Chief Directorate differs from our resourceful burglars in presenting false pictures not for a few hours but for decades. It has at its disposal not three crooks but tens of thousands of highly qualified specialists and almost unlimited powers in its dealings with generals, marshals, and those who run the military industries over the concealment of the true state of affairs.

Practically all of us have read about the almost unbelievable capabilities of our photographic satellites. Orbiting high above the earth, their cameras can even read license plates. Perhaps they can. However, if the car is illegally owned and the owner doesn't want some snooper in a police helicopter to read the plates, all he has to do is park it in the garage. This may be precisely what the Soviets have been doing with many of their nuclear weapons: concealing them to blend into the normal domestic scene while presenting a reassuring picture to our spy satellites to convey a false impression as to where the weapons actually are. Then, having been deceived and having deceived ourselves into believing that we know how many and what kinds of weapons the Soviets have deployed and where they are, we decide that we can realistically enter into arms control negotiations.

As a case in point, consider the Soviet intercontinental ballistic missiles (ICBMs). Some years ago, we decided that these missiles constituted the most serious threat to our nuclear deterrent. Most of them were of enormous size, far larger than our most numerous

ICBM, the Minuteman. Each Soviet missile could deliver a number of highly accurate nuclear warheads. The Pentagon estimated that the Soviet ICBM force could destroy the great bulk of our Minuteman force plus a large fraction of our nuclear bombers and submarines in a surprise attack. This was the so-called "window of vulnerability" for our strategic retaliatory capabilities, the major defense issue raised by Ronald Reagan during the 1980 election.

When President Reagan today speaks about strategic nuclear arms control negotiations designed to achieve significant reductions in Soviet nuclear arms, uppermost in mind is the need to significantly reduce the Soviet ICBM force. But the question is, do we know enough about this force to be able to negotiate realistically and safely? Most likely we don't.

Underlying the Strategic Arms Reductions Talks (START) now going on at Geneva is the assumption that practically all Soviet ICBMs are deployed in silos heavily hardened against the effects of nuclear explosions. This assumption formed the basis of the SALT I and II agreements, which placed limits on fixed ICBM launchers, where launchers were interpreted by us to be silos. Why did we make this interpretation?

The answer is really quite simple. The only concrete evidence we had on Soviet fixed ICBM launchers was their massive complex of silos—some 1,400 of them scattered around the USSR. This is what our spy satellites saw; this is what we assumed represented the Soviet ICBM force. Whether all, or even a fraction, of the silos contained missiles and what kind—this we could not possibly determine unless we were given access to the silos; that is, unless we had intrusive on-site inspection rights, which we didn't. The analogy here is the car parked in the garage; if you want to know if it's inside, you've got to go inside the garage.

Now, the Soviets are nobody's fools when it comes to deception. To allay our suspicions that the silos might be devoid of missiles, they have taken steps to convince us otherwise.

They have allowed our satellites from time to time to observe silos being loaded with missiles. Or so we presumed, for what we actually saw were missile canisters, which we presumed contained missiles. Technically speaking, the actual missile housing is the canister; the silo is a protective structure that doesn't necessarily have to be in a silo. It could be almost anyplace, like a shed, hundreds of miles from a group of silos.

Since we have long known that the missiles could be hidden

someplace away from the silos, to further allay our suspicions the Soviets may have elected from time to time to fire missiles from silo groupings. Such firings readily can be observed by our satellites; and, indeed, they have been observed. In fact, the Soviets have even gone so far as to release movies of ICBMs being fired out of silos. However, rather than suspect that these firings have been Soviet deceptions, we have held them to be hard evidence pointing to Soviet silos and missile launchers being one and the same.

As the Soviets proceeded to modernize their ICBM force, developing newer and generally larger missiles, our satellites observed that the silos were being modified, presumably, we decided, to accommodate the new missiles. In fact, one particular silo design modification was plainly in violation of a restriction imposed by the SALT I agreement. Our satellite photographs showed that the silo size significantly exceeded the SALT I constraint. Were the Soviets up to this skulduggery to gain a military advantage by storing bigger missiles than SALT allowed? Or were they trying to further deceive us into believing that their silos contained missiles?

Logic would dictate the second possibility, for a far larger advantage could be gained by deception. In fact, the Soviets almost certainly must have known that we would see the silo modification violation and complain about it. Which we did—but all we did was complain. We rarely do anything about Soviet treaty violations. So one could reason that most probably this violation was little more than a ruse to deceive us into believing that the silos were being modified, even at some risk, to actually accommodate the new missiles.

Surely, one might argue, the Soviets would never have conducted such a massive effort to construct all these silos if they didn't intend to use them. But the question is, how did they intend to use them? As ICBM launchers, constrained in numbers by the SALT agreements? Or as decoys, to force a waste of U.S. missiles, while they deployed some unconstrained numbers of ICBMs elsewhere, hidden from our "eyes in the sky"?

Logic would dictate the second possibility. Silo construction in the Soviet Union is cheap, practically as cheap as the excavated dirt. The Soviets are hardly in the habit of employing union construction workers and paying them the U.S. union scale. To construct their silos they use slave labor, of which there is a great abundance. As such, a Soviet silo represents a cost that is but a very small, even tiny, fraction of the cost to the United States to destroy the silo with a nuclear weapon. A cheaper decoy is hard to imagine. And in the meantime the real Soviet ICBM force could be deployed, hidden and thereby invulnerable, over the vast expanse of the USSR. Moreover, having no routine surveillance over these hidden missiles, our vulnerability to a surprise first strike would increase appreciably.

For the same reasons, one is hard-pressed to prove that we have firm knowledge of the Soviet ICBM force, firm enough to justify the START talks at Geneva. We do not know whether the Soviets have one thousand or ten thousand missiles, of what kinds, or where they are deployed. Not only do we lack reliable knowledge to permit safe and sensible negotiations to be conducted, we also lack a reliable target system for attacking these weapons in the event of war. Considering that the Soviet ICBMs constitute our most important target category, this is an extremely grave deficiency. It is a deficiency that we have no plans for correcting in the foreseeable future.

Another category of arms control talks underway at Geneva deals with intermediate-range nuclear forces (INF). These forces consist of nuclear weapons having ranges insufficient for conducting intercontinental attacks. They are defined as theater nuclear weapons, for use in, say, a conflict between NATO and Soviet bloc forces. Although they embrace a wide variety of bombers and missiles, so far the weapons of primary concern in the Geneva negotiations have been: SS-20 mobile ballistic missiles, on the Soviet side; and Pershing II ballistic missiles and ground-launched cruise missiles, on the NATO side.

The genesis of the INF talks stems from the deployment of the SS-20, which began in the mid-1970s. This deployment, held to be a dramatically new and particularly menacing threat to NATO, caused great consternation in the West. The result was a NATO agreement in which the United States would develop and deploy the Pershing and cruise missiles (known as Euromissiles) to counteract the ominous SS-20 buildup. Part of the NATO agreement was that the Euromissile deployments were to be accompanied by a concerted effort to bring the Soviets to the bargaining table, to try to bring these new weapons under control. The Soviets accepted, and the INF talks began.

So far, these talks have had a stormy history, accompanied by Soviet petulance and a highly divisive debate in Europe over the deployment of Euromissiles. At one juncture, when the Euromissile deployment began, the Soviets walked out of the INF talks in protest, vowing never to return. But they did return, not necessarily out of devotion to arms control. The European debate still goes on and is still highly divisive. In the meantime, the missile buildup on both sides proceeds apace, and the allegedly ominous SS-20 threat to Europe becomes more ominous with each passing week.

With this backdrop in mind, a question is raised: How have the Soviets regarded the SS-20 missile?

By no means is it clear that the Soviets have regarded the SS-20 in the same way as the United States and NATO have. In fact, the Soviets have never openly explained how they regard this missile, no more than they have bothered to explain any other nuclear weapon in their arsenal. This has never been the Soviet way of operating. They have always endeavored to enshroud their nuclear weapons development in maximum secrecy. When it has served their purpose, as in securing arms control agreements to their advantage, they have gladly accepted our version of their weapons. But they never have allowed us to verify our version.

If one examines the full panoply of theater nuclear weapons that the Soviets had under development at the same time of the SS-20 development, it becomes extremely puzzling why they would wish to consider the SS-20 a theater weapon. There were three other nuclear ballistic missiles being developed—the SS-21, the SS-22, and the SS-23—that provided very substantial coverage over critical NATO military targets. In addition, they were developing a new high-performance fighter-bomber aircraft (designated FENCER by NATO) that could be dispatched over the full range of NATO targets. And besides, certain of their ICBMs had a variable range capability, enabling them to attack Europe just as readily as they could the United States.

Adding up the capabilities of all these weapons, not only did they have full target coverage over NATO, but they represented a substantial overkill against the NATO target system. In this context, the SS-20, as just another theater nuclear weapon, would have been a wasteful over-overkill. It is most doubtful that the Soviets would have indulged themselves in any such extravagance. Perhaps they never had any such intention and from the beginning regarded this weapon primarily as a strategic missile for use against U.S., not NATO, targets.

It is not generally understood how little we know about the SS-20, nor that most of what we do know is what the Soviets have allowed us to know. And even then we have no reliable way of knowing whether much that we think we know is factual or Soviet disinformation. In fact, for the reasons just given, most likely what we believe we know about the SS-20 is what the Soviets have deceived us into believing. What this weapon really represents, only the Soviets really know, and they're not talking.

There has been a great deal of public complaint over how the Soviets have conducted their SS-20 program, over the excessive secrecy they have applied to it. They have conducted flight tests under cover of darkness. They have encoded test telemetry, thereby denying us the ability to gain information on certain key aspects of missile performance. However, if one wishes to condemn them for such secrecy, one should realize that they are not prohibited by any arms control agreement from doing so.

So long as they do not test this missile at intercontinental ranges, where they would be covered by the SALT agreements, they are free to do as they see fit in their SS-20 flight test program. The question is, what have they been doing? The answer is, unfortunately, that we really do not know, but most likely not what we think they've been doing.

The Soviets may not seem to have had valid requirements for deploying the SS-20 as a theater missile. On the other hand, they have long expressed requirements for a mobile ICBM as an invulnerable weapon to be held safely in reserve once a nuclear war has started. It is almost impossible for us to detect and destroy mobile ICBMs, which can roam around and readily be concealed over the vast expanse of the Soviet land mass.

So there would seem to be very good reasons to believe that from the very beginning the Soviets planned the SS-20 as an ICBM and then proceeded to deceive our technically marvelous but mentally gullible spy satellites into believing it was a theater missile by restricting their flight tests to theater missile ranges. Even then these test ranges have been barely—only 10 percent—below the accepted definition of an ICBM range, hardly enough to seriously reduce confidence in the missile's performance at intercontinental range.

If our knowledge of the SS-20 is so uncertain—and there is every possibility that it is not what we think it is—then why have we been in Geneva attempting to negotiate controls on this weapon? Is it possible that the Soviets, who have full knowledge of this missile, are using it as what U.S. arms controllers call a bargaining chip to negotiate controls on NATO's missiles? If one believes the U.S. estimates of how many SS-20s the Soviets have deployed, the Soviets may already possess more than ten times as many intermediate-range nuclear-force missile warheads as NATO—which means that any agreement that might be reached would be greatly to the Soviet advantage.

Putting it another way, if there is every possibility that the SS-20 is a strategic missile, why are we not including this weapon in the START negotiations? The rejoinder by our arms controllers to this question would be that we can't. We have already defined the SS-20 as a nonstrategic weapon. The Soviets simply would not accept a redefinition. Undoubtedly they wouldn't, but this hardly addresses the problem of our START negotiations being based on so little reliable knowledge. In fact, our inability to include the SS-20 in START makes those negotiations ever so much more dangerous.

Regarding the extent to which the Soviets may have deceived us on the SS-20, additional questions arise. Why have the Soviets allowed our satellites to "see" more than four hundred SS-20 missile launchers deployed at the surface on a limited number of bases in the USSR? The major advantage of mobile missiles is that they can be highly dispersed and concealed to make them invulnerable to enemy attack. This being the case, why have they elected to display them to our satellites in so vulnerable a basing mode? After all, they seem not to have done so with their ICBMs. They display these in heavily hardened silos that are not very vulnerable. Or is it possible, using Viktor Suvorov's words, that these SS-20 displays "show the watchful eye of the camera a reassuring picture, behind the shelter of which the [Communist] gangsters go about their business"?

Common-sense military logic dictates that SS-20s actually produced would be deployed with full mobility, widely dispersed, and well hidden—which the Soviets have most likely been doing with these missiles, in numbers we have no way of counting. There may only be a few hundred of these missiles concealed over the USSR; but on the other hand, there could be a few thousand. The fact is that we don't know. And if there were a few thousand of these missiles that could strike targets in the United States, our self-deception over the true purpose of the SS-20 would have been most dangerous for our national security.

When the SALT I and II agreements were being negotiated, our data on Soviet nuclear submarine construction was believed to be very accurate. As nearly as we could tell from our spy satellite observations, Soviet submarine construction was going on in shipyards in the open. This made it quite simple for us to obtain well-defined intelligence on the number and nature of these submarines, especially regarding the complement of nuclear ballistic missiles (SLBMs) they could carry. Thus we were able to sign agreements that we believed would place strict limits on the number of SLBMs the Soviets could deploy.

Today Soviet nuclear submarines are constructed under cover. In addition, massive underground berthing facilities have been built. Moreover, the newest class of Soviet nuclear submarines are of enormous proportions—the world's largest, being able to store large numbers of missiles in excess of the number of launching tubes. And there is no reliable way to determine the number of launching tubes if we can't observe a submarine's construction.

Our knowledge of Soviet nuclear submarine capabilities is becoming increasingly undependable. This gives rise to two concerns. First, the alleged advantages of the SALT I and II treaties, which were supposed to keep a lid on these Soviet capabilities, are becoming fewer and fewer for us; the direct opposite holds for the Soviets. Second, the notion of enhancing our national security by continuing with START becomes even more questionable, over and above the questions raised earlier by our lack of dependable knowledge of Soviet ICBMs.

The START dilemma becomes even more compounded when the matter of defense against nuclear attack is taken into account. Supposedly we had taken this into account in 1972 when we signed and ratified a treaty with the Soviets. This agreement prohibited both sides from deploying nationwide defenses against a nuclear ballistic missile attack. This was the heralded ABM (antiballistic missile) Treaty, which received overwhelming endorsement by the U.S. Senate, 90 to 2 in favor of ratification.

In the context of the ABM treaty, the SALT I agreement limiting the ICBMs and SLBMs of each side was held to practically guarantee a stable strategic nuclear balance. Both sides could be assured of being able to deliver such terrible retaliatory blows against each other as to make nuclear attack a totally incredible military option. In this respect the ABM treaty supposedly ensured the credibility of the U.S. Mutual Assured Destruction (MAD) nuclear policy, in which the guarantee of each side's being able to annihilate the other's population and cities represented an ironclad deterrent against nuclear war.

Just as the Soviets had seemed to accept our estimates of their

ICBM strength in the SALT I agreement on offensive strategic nuclear armaments, they seemed to accept our MAD nuclear policy as the basis for the ABM treaty. This should have made us highly suspicious, since prior to the time the Soviets seemed to accept MAD and agreed on the ABM Treaty, everything they were saying in their military writings and political pronouncements seemed to reject them out of hand. For example, in 1969 Soviet Premier Aleksei Kosygin had stated, "I think that a defensive system, which prevents attack, is not a cause of the arms race but represents a factor preventing the death of people. . . . An antimissile system may cost more than an offensive one, but it is intended not for killing people but for saving human lives." This hardly was an indication that the Soviets intended to forswear, by treaty, the right to defend their people against nuclear attack.

At the time of Kosygin's pro-ABM remarks, the Soviets had assembled and were steadily improving the most extensive nation-wide air defense system against bomber attack that the world had ever seen. This they had done for the very best of reasons: the United States had assembled the most powerful bomber force the world had ever seen. Were nuclear war to occur, the U.S. policy of massive nuclear retaliation, using this bomber force, threatened the very survival of the USSR.

Also at that time, to protect themselves against U.S. nuclear retaliation, the Soviets had assembled and were steadily improving an extensive nationwide civil defense system. This they had also done for the best of reasons—to save the lives of their citizens, especially their leadership echelon in Moscow, and to enable their country to survive.

In view of this Soviet determination to survive nuclear war—a determination that persists to this day—on what conceivable basis would they wish to sign and observe a treaty that would forbid them to defend themselves against a nuclear attack? If they really wished to comply with the U.S. interpretation of the ABM Treaty, where the populations of both sides were held hostage, why didn't they offer to enlarge the scope of the treaty to include all kinds of defense? Why didn't they choose to follow the U.S. example and disband their air and civil defense systems? Considering that they were investing perhaps half of their strategic force budget in defense, there was an enormous amount of money and effort that could have been redirected toward easing their severe economic difficulties.

Or was agreeing to the ABM Treaty still another part of the pattern of Soviet strategic deception—in which the Soviets never had any intention of denying themselves a defense against nuclear ballistic missile attack but used the treaty to stop the U.S. ABM program in its tracks while secretly continuing with their own program? One expert on Soviet deception, Viktor Suvorov, a Soviet military officer at the time the treaty was signed, believes this is exactly what happened.

In his book *Inside the Soviet Army* Suvorov states that the Soviets were determined to halt emerging U.S. ABM technology, which they regarded as a threat to their offensive missiles. This was to be accomplished by giving the United States the impression that the Soviet ABM program was moving along rapidly and success-fully, thereby making it appear that an ABM treaty would be equitable to both sides. Along these lines, according to Suvorov, the Soviets conducted a number of deceptive moves.

They displayed a huge new missile in a Moscow parade—but not in a military unit from their offensive missile force. Instead, it was in a national air defense unit and was meant to convey the impression that it was an ABM defensive missile.

They constructed in the outskirts of Moscow an enormous building having the external appearance of an ABM guidance sta-tion for controlling the launching of defensive missiles. The building was alongside the highway ringing the Soviet capital, for all foreign diplomats—including U.S. intelligence officers—to see. High-powered signals were transmitted by the station that, when analyzed by U.S. experts, were exactly the kind to be expected for such a station. "But inside," wrote Suvorov, "the building was empty, without its most essential component—a computer and command complex."

Soviet intelligence agents were ordered to cease their efforts to gain information on U.S. ABM technology. This was intended to further mislead the United States into believing that the Soviets were making out very well on their own ABM program.

"Thus," wrote Suvorov, "in the period running up to the [ABM] negotiations, every sort of attempt was made to present a picture of Soviet activity and success in anti-missile operations. After the negotiations, great pains were taken to hide activity and successes in this field, since these represented a violation of the agreements which had been reached."

It is one thing for the Soviets, many years ago, to have misled us into believing that they had embarked upon a large-scale ABM program. It is another thing, however, for them to conceal the actual implementation of such a program, whatever its true proportions originally may have been. One can parade a bogus antimissile through Red Square and construct a bogus antimissile guidance station for everyone to see and listen to, but one cannot easily hide from our satellite monitoring systems the actual testing of an ABM system. This is one area of activity where it is extremely difficult to fool us. It is also an area strictly prohibited by the ABM Treaty, where in recent years our satellites have detected definite violations of the treaty. The most worrisome part of these violations is that they seem to have upgraded the performance of their air defense system to permit a dual bomber/missile defense capability.

At present, there is very serious concern in our intelligence community over the possibility that the Soviets may be on the verge of a break-out of a nationwide ABM capability, masqueraded as an advanced antiaircraft system. Were this to be the case, our START objectives for securing reductions by both sides in strategic nuclear ballistic missiles would become even more questionable. Not only would the reductions themselves substantially favor the Soviets, but our reduced force of missiles might not be able to penetrate the Soviet ABM defenses to a degree sufficient to guarantee our deterrent strategy. So we have still another reason for questioning the wisdom of START.

The design details of our spy satellites are, and always have been, highly classified. This, of course, is the way it should be. There is no point in making these details available to anyone and everyone who might use the data in a manner adverse to our security.

On the other hand, it should be realized that all these satellites have sensors that work in accordance with the laws of physics. The scientific principles that allow the construction of spy satellites having truly fantastic intelligence-gathering capabilities in many cases can be applied to neutralize these capabilities. And in most instances such countermeasures do not call for an undue amount of imagination or effort.

Were the Soviets to deploy all their ICBMs out in the open, sooner or later our photographic satellites would find out not only how many there were and where they were, they would also find out exactly what kind they were. However, were all their ICBMs deployed under cover—in sheds appearing to be part of an industrial complex, in underground facilities, and so on—our amazing spy cameras would be oblivious of their existence. For example, last year the Defense Department issued a report to Congress showing a sketch of the Soviet SS-25 mobile ICBM parked in a shed. Were the Soviets indeed to deploy SS-25s in this manner, our satellite photography would reveal nothing to demonstrate such deployment.

Now, even the most zealous proponent of satellite observation for furthering arms control would have to admit that a camera can't see through a roof. However, very likely he would point out that satellites also have infrared sensors that see temperature patterns on earth in amazing detail. And he would then point out that an ICBM facility contains equipment generating a large amount of power, thereby generating a large amount of heat. This heat would make the facility stand out like a sore thumb in the relatively cooler earth environment. But if the missile facility were camouflaged to appear as a light industrial complex that also generates a large amount of power and heat, no matter how remarkable our infrared photography might be, it still would be unable to determine what the complex actually was. We might be darkly suspicious and worried—maybe with good reason. But beyond that, there's nothing we could do except to remain suspicious and worried—hardly a satisfactory state of affairs.

The proponent might next point out that the ICBM facility has a number of unique electronic signatures that we have been able to detect and analyze with our satellites. It must be realized, however, that these signatures may have been generated by the Soviets to mislead us into believing that they represent actual deployment signatures. This does not necessarily have to be the case. Or, if the Soviets so desired, they readily could shield these signatures against satellite detection. This same remark applies to shielding communications signals going to and from those facilities. In this age of microchip technology, closed-circuit communications can be established that cannot be monitored by spy satellites.

It is hardly surprising that those making the strongest claims for the intelligence-gathering capabilities of our spy satellites, in order to allow safe and verifiable strategic arms control agreements to be reached, are also those most likely to be strongly opposed to the United States' developing new strategic weapons. This has been especially true when defensive weapons are concerned. Most recently we have seen the spy satellite–arms control proponents in practically violent opposition to President Reagan's Strategic Defense Initiative (SDI).

Ever since the President proposed the SDI in March 1983, this group has put forth a series of countermeasures that the Soviets might take to render the SDI ineffective. Yet one is hard-pressed to find even the mildest reservations about the efficacy of spy satellites expressed by these proponents, in the light of Soviet counter-measures. And it is pointed out that countermeasures against spy satellites are far more easily achieved than against the SDI defensive weapons.

When confronted with arguments that our spy satellites can be rendered ineffective by Soviet countermeasures, these proponents are likely to respond by ignoring the arguments. Instead, they are likely to express a belief that the Soviets would not want to deceive our satellites, for it would not be in their self-interest to do so. Like ourselves, these people claim, the Soviets realize the imperative of nuclear arms control to reduce the danger of nuclear war. So why would they deliberately want to risk having their deception program discovered if this held the risk of wrecking the arms control process?

The answer to this question is very straightforward: the Soviets have never made any bones about the fact that deception is and always has been a cardinal tenet of their military doctrine. Their official military doctrinal journals long have contained statements on deception and disinformation, exemplary of which are the following:

> If it is not possible to conceal troops and facilities from hostile observation, then one can reduce their revealing features by altering their external appearance. For example, a large camp or supply base can be camouflaged as a town; a tank farm can be camouflaged as apartment houses, while individual military installations can be camouflaged as rubble, smoldering ruins, etc. Such action can be employed not only at the tactical echelon but particularly at . . . *strategic levels.*

> Strategic disinformation assists in the execution of State tasks, and is directed at misleading the enemy concerning the basic questions of State policy, the military economic status, and the scientific-technical achievement of the Soviet Union; the policy of certain imperialist states with respect to each other and to other countries; and the specific counterintelligence tasks of the organs of State Security.

As to the veracity of statements such as these, it should be appreciated that they are not expressions of Soviet propaganda directed toward us. Were this the case, they legitimately could be held to be statements of deceit and disinformation. On the contrary, these statements are directed inward to the Soviet military as basic guidance for their planning activities. And it is extremely doubtful that the Soviet military would deliberately wish to deceive and disinform themselves. Former Soviet Defense Minister Marshal A. A. Grechko explained these doctrinal statements as follows: "We have never hidden and are not hiding the basic principal positions of our military doctrine. They are expressed with utmost clarity in the policies of the Communist Party and the Soviet government, in the state of our Armed Forces."

Perhaps the Soviets are sincere about the grim necessity for arms control measures to reduce the danger of nuclear war. At the same time, however, there is no evidence to indicate that they are insincere in their stated intentions to deceive and disinform us as to the true nature of their strategic nuclear forces. Nor is there any evidence that they have regarded such practices as unduly risking the nuclear arms control process. Nor is there any evidence that almost anything they do that we may regard as reprehensible has jeopardized nuclear arms control negotiations. Just look at the record.

In 1961 the Soviets outraged the United States and all other Western nations by violating an understanding not to test nuclear weapons. This violation was followed by the most massive series of nuclear tests the world has ever seen. But several months later we were back at the conference table with the Soviets trying to negotiate a nuclear test ban treaty, which we signed and ratified the next year.

In 1968 the Soviets shocked the world by invading Czecho-slovakia when it looked as if the Czechs were attempting to gain their freedom. The next year, the U.S. initiated the SALT I negotiations and three years later signed and ratified the SALT I agreements.

In 1979 the Soviets again shocked the world by invading Afghanistan, when it looked like the Soviet puppet regime was in danger of falling. This caused an incensed U.S. Senate to refuse to ratify the SALT II Treaty, although the Carter Administration favored ratification. But three years later the Reagan Administration announced it was abiding by the terms of SALT II.

In 1983 the Soviets again outraged the United States and all other Western nations by shooting down Korean Airlines Flight 007.

But President Reagan, practically in the same breath condemning the Soviets, declared that this despicable act would have no effect on our nuclear arms control policies. Our talks with the Soviets continued.

If this series of Soviet outrages over so many years has had no appreciable effect on U.S. determination to pursue strategic nuclear arms control, on what grounds could one say that an uncovering of Soviet strategic nuclear deception would produce a different effect? And we are not referring here to the revelation of an enormous, widespread pattern of deception. Rather, it would be the discovery of probably less than a handful of instances where, due to a slipup or some violent act of nature, a nuclear weapons facility was seen by one of our satellites. Such a discovery might whet our suspicions, but it wouldn't give us even the faintest idea what the true extent of the deception really was.

Furthermore, although we might accuse the Soviets of a dastardly deed, as we did for the above-mentioned list of dastardly deeds, in no sense could we accuse them of going back on an agreement or promise not to do such things. After all, if we are to believe the avowal of Marshal Grechko, if they had made any promise at all, they had promised themselves and made it very plain to us that they would try to deceive us to the hilt. Why shouldn't they want to deceive us when we are their main enemy? And by no stretch of the imagination could it be claimed that a sincerity for deception equates with an insincerity for arms control, i.e., arms control that controls U.S. weapons.

Lenin is reputed to have once said that the Soviet quest for disarmament was to disarm the capitalist while arming the proletariat. In this respect, any nuclear weapons *reductions* treaty that might come out of START would put the United States in a position of having fewer weapons and would thus be less capable of retaliating against the Soviet Union. On the Soviet side, if they indeed had been deceiving us on a massive scale, all a reductions treaty might accomplish would be the destruction of a number of missile silos. We would have fewer missiles; the Soviets would have fewer holes in the ground. We would be less safe; the Soviets would be more safe.

This kind of arms control would of course be most appealing to the Soviets. But it may very well be the kind of arms control that we are practicing with them. So when you hear a U.S. arms control zealot say that the Soviets are sincere about arms control, don't instinctively admonish him for being naive and wrong. It's quite likely that he's being naive and right.

What evidence, besides doctrinal declarations, do we have that the Soviets may have been engaging in a massive program of strategic deception? Unfortunately there is no way to logically address this question, for the simple reason that it is not a logical question. It's like asking what evidence we have that the Invisible Man is hanging around watching us. If you can't see him, you have no evidence he's hanging around. If you could see him, he wouldn't be hanging around.

You might hear rumors that he's around. Somebody will report on some very mysterious happenings caused by someone who had managed to escape detection because he couldn't be seen. But how do you check on a story involving someone you can't see? In this connection, there have been rumors leaking out of the USSR of missiles hidden in caves, sheds, and other concealed places. Maybe they were true, but you can't determine that from space if the Soviets won't let you because it's critical for their military security not to let you. If they're bent on deceiving you, even if they've admitted to this, they're still not about to cooperate in revealing the nature and extent of their deception—which brings us to the issue of verifying nuclear arms control agreements.

What good does it do to sign a nuclear arms control treaty that we think can be verified by our spy satellites when the substance of the treaty and our knowledge of Soviet nuclear capabilities are very likely a product of Soviet deception and disinformation? What is so impressive about a satellite verification system that can count missile silos to the nearest silo and measure their dimensions to the nearest inch if the silos don't contain missiles? The point is that we have become so obsessed with what our super high-technology satellites can see to verify a treaty that we have forgotten about all that they couldn't see when they attempted to gather knowledge for negotiating the treaty. We have taken great pride in being able to check on facts when we may have had the wrong facts to begin with. Nothing could be more illogical or more dangerous to our security.

Early in 1986 President Reagan told a group of congressmen how important it was for us to get a "good" agreement in the Geneva negotiations. "I've told our negotiators," said the President, "if they don't have a good agreement, get up from the table and come on home. The only thing more dangerous than no agreement is a bad agreement." The President might have added that the only way to get a good agreement is to have good knowledge of what the other side is up to. That it does little good for our security to be able to verify adequately, or even partially, the terms of a bad agreement based on bad knowledge. And that the Soviets weren't about to provide us with good knowledge to allow us to negotiate a good treaty—that is, good for us.

If we truly wish to gain a good nuclear arms treaty with the Soviets, which we truly do, we will have to heed President Eisenhower's words of thirty years ago: "No sound and reliable agreement can be made unless it is completely covered by an inspection and reporting system adequate to support every position of the agreement." We will have to insist to the Soviets that they completely open their country to intrusive on-site inspection. This would call for bringing our spies in the skies down to earth and substituting intelligent human inspectors who can't be fooled for ingeniously designed robots that can be fooled by the Soviet Chief Directorate of Strategic Deception. There is no other way to proceed safely with nuclear arms control. If we do not make this change, we cannot negotiate responsibly—to ourselves—with the Soviets. And if they refuse to grant us full inspection rights, we should terminate arms control negotiations.

"Tell them what they want to hear," said Lenin, instructing his disciples on how to deceive the capitalists. Had he lived to see the nuclear and space ages and observed the intense U.S. desire for nuclear arms control and the beliefs that spying from space could make arms control feasible and safe, Lenin undoubtedly would have repeated himself. This time, however, since the United States wanted to see, rather than hear, reassuring things, he would have said, "Show them what they want to see." And it would have made all the sense in the world for the Soviets to show our spy satellites exactly what they have seen: ICBM silos being constructed, but not for the purpose of launching missiles; SS-20 missiles being tested at nonstrategic ranges, but for the purpose of developing invulnerable mobile strategic missiles; the apparent construction of huge underground military command centers for the Soviet leadership, but not for the purpose of the leadership occupying them and risking being bombed out in a nuclear war; and so on.

In our great and sincere desire to remedy our nuclear weapons problems by taking the path of arms control, we most likely have been offering ourselves as highly willing targets for Soviet deception and disinformation practices. With our national compulsion to rely on scientific observation rather than human inspection and to place our faith in the "logic" of arms control rather than in the truth that only knowledge can provide, we have been willing to stake our security on easily fooled spy satellites and an unfounded belief that the Soviets share our views on arms control logic. So the Soviets have shown us what we wanted to see and told us what we wanted to hear as we pursued nuclear arms control. But along the way, we have ignored the most critical element of all: the truth.

On the side of the building at CIA headquarters is the biblical expression, "And Ye Shall Know the Truth, And the Truth Shall Make Ye Free." The trouble is that we don't know the truth about Soviet nuclear capabilities. The Soviets, one of the most untruthful governments on earth in dealing with other governments, aren't about to tell us the truth or let us find out the truth—that is, unless their purposes are better served by revealing the truth. And the only way for this to happen is for them to open up their country to our on-site inspection.

Based on their consistent refusal to do this over the last forty years, it seems most doubtful that they are about to. During this period they have been most paranoid over protecting their secrecy, not hesitating to shoot down commercial foreign aircraft that come into their airspace. Rightly or wrongly, it was this Soviet paranoia that led to the destruction of Korean Airlines Flight 007. The Soviets were far more concerned about their secrecy being invaded than about their image in the world community being tarnished. For these reasons, under what conceivable circumstance would they want to open their country to a group of highly qualified U.S. nuclear inspectors who could learn the truth?

One such circumstance was reported to have been raised a few years ago by Secretary of State George Shultz. In a meeting on START the secretary reportedly said, "Someday we might see some suspicious behavior, and when we challenge them, they would say, 'Yeah, we've got twenty thousand extra missiles. What are you going to do about it?'"

Now, suppose one day our satellites did see some suspicious behavior and we did challenge the Soviet Union, threatening to stop arms control negotiations or something like that unless they realistically allayed our suspicions. And suppose that the Soviet response was to say to us, "Hey, you know, maybe it's about time we provided you with the facts on our nuclear weapons instead of letting you try to figure it out yourself. It really hasn't been fair that you people have been more than willing to give us your facts but not the other way around. So why don't you put together a team of inspectors and come on over? Anything that you have some suspicions about, based on what your spy satellites have reported, you just tell us, and we'll let in your inspectors. They can poke around to their hearts' content, and we'll try to answer all their questions as honestly as possible to their full satisfaction."

So off go our inspectors, all over the Soviet Union. There they discover, as Secretary Shultz inferred they might, that the Soviets had concealed some twenty thousand ICBMs, including thousands of SS-20 missiles, from our spy satellites; that the Soviets had produced substantially more nuclear submarines than the SALT agreements presumably allowed and that the submarines carried substantially more missiles than our spy satellites indicated; that our suspicions about their air defense network having ABM capabilities were absolutely correct; that they were on the verge of testing a particle beam defense against missile attack; that they had increased their civil defense to a degree that most Soviet citizens had protection from nuclear attack; and that what we had suspected were massive underground leadership command centers were little more than massive holes in the ground—where their leadership might go in the event of war.

Suppose that after months of poking around the USSR, we came up with these findings. And the Soviets asked, as George Shultz allowed they might ask, "What are you going to do about it?" We'll let the readers give their own answers here rather than present our own subjective opinion. However, we'll guess that most of us would find our country in an extremely uncomfortable position under those circumstances. The realistic answer to this question is not conjecture on how our government might behave under such circumstances but rather serious thinking on what we should start to do, beginning right now, toward avoiding such a frightful situation. And the answer is very simple: we must start to defend ourselves in order to be able to survive in the event of nuclear war rather than do almost everything to make sure we perish, which is what we have been doing for so many years.

If we don't know how to reduce the danger to our country by being able to find and destroy strategic nuclear weapons in the USSR, then the only option left is to be able to find and destroy them after they have been launched. In other words, we will have to undertake a drastic shift in our nuclear policies along the lines of President Reagan's Strategic Defense Initiative. However, because we do not know the truth about Soviet nuclear capabilities, it would be highly imprudent, even downright dangerous, to pursue the SDI at the present pace. As we did for the atomic bomb and radar in World War II, the SDI should be put on the highest priority footing to give us a defensive capability as soon as possible. In addition, we should place the highest priority on civil defense for the American people. The SDI alone cannot guarantee their safety; they have to help save themselves.

There is an old saying: "A little knowledge is a dangerous thing." Implied here is that a lot of knowledge would be a lot less dangerous. In an age of many thousands of nuclear weapons, for us to plan our survival policies on the basis of but a little knowledge can be terribly dangerous. But most likely this is what we have been doing, and there are no signs that this situation will change. And even if the situation changed and the Soviets gave us all the knowledge we asked for, it might have little effect on reducing the danger. It is not axiomatic that a lot of knowledge makes things a lot less dangerous if it is knowledge that shows an overwhelming Soviet nuclear superiority.

What matters most of all for our security and our survival is that the time is overdue for Americans to reread their Constitution, which imposes on the government the responsibility for the common defense of the people. Time was when we desired to protect our shores from foreign attack. The time is overdue for us to start doing it again.

SOVIET STRATEGIC NUCLEAR FORCES, AND GOALS: DECEPTION, AND SURPRISE

Dr. William R. Van Cleave

Secrecy, concealment, deception, and disinformation—Soviet *maskirovka*—are, as other chapters explain, inherent and deeply ingrained characteristics of the Soviet system and its approach to the world and to its own populace. They are also cardinal elements of Soviet strategic thought and Soviet strategy. Disinformation abounds in what the Soviet leadership tells its own people and the people of the world about Soviet strategic motivations, aims, and programs, and about U.S. ones. The former are defensive, the latter aggressive. George Orwell's *1984* explained clearly the need of totalitarian states to invent external threats in order to justify their own repression, the regimentation of their people, and the militarization of the state. In reality the Soviet concept of "security" is inherently aggressive, a rationalization for an expansive empire; and the Soviet expression "equal security" is merely a formula for military superiority. But the terms themselves, in contrast to the reality, manifest Soviet adeptness at deception.

It is standard Soviet practice to attribute their own motivations and purposes to the West, to accuse others of planning precisely what the Soviets are planning. When the Soviets deny a particular military aim or program and attribute it to the United States, it is a sure sign of what the Soviets are in fact doing.

Nevertheless, for those willing to pay attention and to look behind the thin facade of Soviet propaganda, Soviet strategic military doctrine, goals, and principles are very clear. In professional military writings and in military programs, the Soviets have made it abundantly clear that they are on a determined quest for nuclear superiority, guided by strategic doctrine, concepts, and objectives based firmly on a nuclear war-fighting and war-winning capability.

If this is not well understood in the West, it has more to do with self-deception than with successful Soviet deception efforts.

The Soviets have been surprisingly candid in their military literature. Chief Justice Oliver Wendell Holmes once observed that
candor is the best form of deception, at least when the targets are
Western democracies. If Western democracies are given the slightest
encouragement, they tend to overlook reality and favor the most
hopeful interpretation of events. Any opportunity to rationalize the
truth of Soviet military programs and intentions is seized upon.

Former Secretary of State Dean Acheson observed this
phenomenon with great frustration when he wrote over twenty-five
years ago:

> No matter how plainly the Russians talk and act, we simply
> refuse to believe what they say and to understand the meaning
> of what they do. [We insist] that the test must be deeds, not
> words. Floods of deeds follow, amply explained by torrents of
> words. Yet our leaders and, indeed, our people cannot believe
> what they see and what they hear.[1]

In other words, we ourselves enhance the success of Soviet deception and disinformation.

This chapter addresses the role of concealment and deception
in relation to the Soviet strategic nuclear threat: strategic nuclear
programs, doctrine, and objectives and the question of surprise
nuclear attack. The conclusion is that there is concealment and
deception (the extent of which we do not know) in the first; both
deception and candor in the second; and, because deception may
be critical to surprise, one should expect quite a lot in the third. A
corollary observation, however, is that much of the success of
Soviet deception should be attributed to our own penchant for
self-deception.

The Strategic Nuclear Threat

Soviet nuclear programs are conducted in the strictest secrecy. Even
internal information about them is highly compartmentalized. (It is,
for example, well known that American negotiators in SALT learned
early that senior foreign ministry officials on the Soviet delegation
had little or no knowledge about Soviet strategic arms capabilities
and programs, and what they had came from Western sources.)

Extensive measures are taken to deny the West information
about Soviet strategic programs until the Soviets have achieved the

advantage they seek or until it becomes impossible to conceal programs due to the magnitude of deployments. Soviet military research and development, in particular, are shrouded in concealment, but so is the output of Soviet military production facilities.

We do have much information on Soviet strategic forces, capabilities, and programs. An examination of the splendid Department of Defense publication *Soviet Military Power* (hereafter *SMP*) confirms that. But we certainly do not know all there is to know about Soviet strategic capabilities and programs. What we do not know may or may not be considerable. There is a smug tendency in intelligence to accept what we know, plus what we explicitly acknowledge we do not know, as all there is to know. It is acknowledged, for example, that Soviet concealment practices covering their strategic forces (encryption of missile telemetry, for example) have intensified in recent years. However, that assumes that we have identified and understand all concealment practices and attempts at deception that the Soviets have undertaken, and that is probably a shaky assumption.

Moreover, there is often a bias in what our intelligence agencies look for in the mass of data that is technically acquired. For example, our intelligence agencies for years overlooked Soviet civil defense and leadership protection shelters simply because they were not particularly looking for them. It was only when they were virtually coerced into doing so that they began to discover—going back over *old* photos and other data—the existence of a far-flung system of shelters, many of which are very large, very deep, and very resistant to nuclear attack.

What we know and publicly reveal of Soviet strategic nuclear force (hereafter SNF) capabilities is awesome enough. Too often, skeptics or Soviet apologists accuse the government of exaggerating when it reveals such information. What should be understood, however, is that intelligence released to the public is *agreed* intelligence; that is to say, it is information that has been so validated and confirmed that all participating government agencies can agree upon it. It is also only the information that can be released without compromising sensitive and valuable sources of intelligence. Therefore, it is safe and conservative, probably an understatement of reality, and incomplete. At times what is presented to the public intentionally understates reality, perhaps to disguise what we do not know so well or to protect sources, or perhaps because the information is presented according to counting rules established for the purposes of arms control.

The number of Soviet ICBMs is a very good example of this. *SMP* presents a chart showing a precise number for Soviet ICBMs: 1,398. On more careful reading, however, we see that this is not really the number of Soviet ICBMs. There are more. But we do not know how many more. *SMP* simply states, "For their ICBM, LRINF (longer-range intermediate-range nuclear forces), SRBM (shorter-range ballistic missiles), and air defense forces, the Soviets have stocked extra missiles, propellants, and warheads throughout the Soviet Union." *SMP* then reveals that the 1,398 only refers to SALT-counted silo launchers for ICBMs, which can be reloaded with these additional missiles.

Previous editions of *SMP* estimated that since SALT I in 1972, when Soviet ICBM launcher numbers reached their peak, the Soviets have produced 200 to 250 ICBMs per year. Over ten years, that is up to 1,000 more ICBMs than we count ICBM launchers. One thing that *SMP* does not tell the reader is that Soviet ICBMs come in their own self-contained canisters, which undoubtedly contain the essential launch equipment, so that those ICBMs do not have to be "reloaded" into those silo launchers in order to be fired. Hence, on every score the launcher number cited may be virtually meaningless; it tells us very little about the Soviet ICBM force.

What we do know, unfortunately, is enough to make us somber, if not justifiably hysterical. The Soviets have not concealed the possession and continued development of a first-strike capability against the preponderance of U.S. nuclear deterrent forces with a fraction of Soviet forces, leaving an overwhelming and secure reserve force.

President Reagan has openly acknowledged to the American people on more than one occasion that the Soviets have acquired a dangerous strategic superiority over the United States. On one occasion, he said, "The truth of the matter is that on balance the Soviet Union does have a definite margin of superiority—enough so there is risk, and there is what I have called, as you all know, several times, a window of vulnerability." On yet another occasion, the President candidly reported that "Today, in virtually every measure of military power, the Soviet Union enjoys a decided advantage."

This advantage continues to grow alarmingly, despite the highly publicized (and exaggerated) Reagan Administration strategic force modernization program. Charts published by the Joint Chiefs of Staff over the last two years contain curves showing Soviet strategic superiority as far ahead as projected, which happens to be twelve to fifteen years after Mr. Reagan's election. Significantly, a comparison of those charts with similar ones published during the Carter Administration shows the situation worsening, not improving.

According to the 1985 issue of *SMP,* the Soviets have added over two thousand strategic nuclear warheads since SALT II was signed alone, and that only counts those warheads on weapons in SALT-counted launchers. On June 26, 1985, an unclassified Central Intelligence Agency report to Congress showed a marked increase in Soviet strategic nuclear warheads over what was reported in the March 1985 issue of *SMP.* This report stated that the Soviet intercontinental attack force, counting only those warheads on weapons on SALT-counted launchers, consists currently of "over 9,000 deployed warheads," a number that will grow in the near future to "over 12,000," even if the Soviets stay within SALT II limitations (which they are not).[2] This number, far in excess of the number for comparable U.S. systems, is remarkable because only a few years ago, many pundits were insisting that despite Soviet superiority in every other measurement one could name—launchers, missiles, throw weight, megatonnage, equivalent megatonnage, hard-target kill capability, relative force size, and so on—what mattered was that the United States still had the advantage in the number of deployed warheads. That advantage, like others held in the past, has vanished.

Today, not only is the Soviet ICBM force far larger than that of the United States, but so is the Soviet strategic nuclear submarine force. Even the Soviet intercontinental bomber force is now larger than that of the United States.

The gap will continue to grow. The CIA report warned that Soviet strategic nuclear warhead numbers are increasing: "new Soviet Typhoon and Delta-IV submarines, Bear H bombers, and SS-24 ICBMs will carry many more warheads than the systems they are replacing." Bear in mind that the systems being "replaced" are relatively new systems themselves, and rather than being phased out they may be added to the store of "additional missiles" held in reserve.

Moreover, Soviet systems are newer and more modern than their American counterparts. Seventy percent of Soviet strategic nuclear weapons are on delivery vehicles no more than five years old, while 77 percent of U.S. strategic nuclear weapons are on delivery vehicles over fifteen years old. Since SALT I was signed in 1972, the Soviet Union has deployed about twenty new or substantially modified strategic ballistic missile systems. It has deployed variants of three new ICBMs (excluding the SS-16, the number of which *SMP* lists merely as "undetermined"). The *smallest* of those ICBMs is the size of the MX. The Soviets are now beginning deployment of two new solid-fuel ICBMs, the SS-24 and SS-25, the second of which is a violation of the SALT II limitation of "one new type." Both of these will have mobile versions, one on railroad and the other on a self-contained mobile launcher, nearly identical to the SS-20. The SS-20, officially listed as an intermediate-range ballistic missile with a five-thousand-kilometer range but with intercontinental capabilities in certain configurations, has now reached a deployment of about 420 launchers, each with one or more refire missiles, each missile with three warheads. (The SS-20 warhead numbers are *not* included in the preceding numbers of intercontinental attack warheads!)

In airbreathing systems, the Soviet Union has over 250 modern Backfire intercontinental bombers operational (a number, it might be noted, that equals the current total U.S. heavy bomber force), in addition to older Bison and Bear bombers. It is beginning production of the Blackjack bomber, an aircraft both larger and faster than the B-1B, and is producing a new, large cruise missile carrier bomber-aircraft. The Soviets also have operational three new cruise missiles with ranges greater than those the United States is deploying. These are in addition to the hundreds of nuclear-capable cruise missiles already operational with Soviet forces.

Soviet superiority over the United States in strategic offensive forces is clear, just on the basis of what the Soviets have not concealed from us. In strategic defensive forces that is also the case. The Soviets, however, have engaged in extensive concealment and deception practices covering their strategic defensive activities, from underground shelters to ABM programs to antisubmarine warfare capabilities. Our knowledge is consequently far from complete. What we do know is that the so-called U.S. Strategic Defense Initiative is, in fact, a strategic defense *response* to a Soviet Strategic Defense Initiative already in progress for many years. To illustrate, it is useful to compare the two sides on the basis of the following categories:

1. Existing ABM Systems: The Soviet Union has the only operational ABM system in the world, covering Moscow and the surrounding region. But it also has air defense surface-to-air missile (SAM) systems possessing ABM capability. These are

operational and are still being deployed nationwide. The Soviets have in place what *SMP* calls "the world's most extensive early warning system for both ballistic missile and air defense." This nationwide network of large phased-array radar is the foundation for what the President has identified as the base for a rapidly deployable nationwide ABM defense.

2. Modernization of Existing ABM: The Soviets have a major program to modernize and upgrade the capabilities of its current ABM systems, including the ABM SAMs. New SAMs—the SA-10 and particularly the SA-12—have such inherent ABM capability as to blur any distinction between air defense and ballistic missile defense. The United States, having no existing ABM capability, clearly has no modernization program.

3. ABM Research and Development: President Reagan has inaugurated the SDI, or SDR, program for research and development in ABM, with emphasis on the long range and new technologies. The Soviets have had such a program for many years and are spending annually far more than the United States proposes to spend. As a result, according to official congressional testimony, they are already a decade ahead of the United States in this area. They have active research and development, and test programs on every ABM-laser technology that the United States considers interesting, as well as programs on laser technologies that the United States has not yet seriously considered. The Soviets, in fact, have prototype ABM-laser systems *already* operational at their ABM test center at Sary Shagan, and these systems already have serious anti-satellite potential. The Soviet particle beam weapons program has existed for well over a decade, and the Soviets are conducting research and development on a number of other advanced ABM technologies. Overall, in this category the Soviets have a full-scale, high-priority program, compared to which the United States has an anemic, tenuous studies program.

4. Air Defense: The Soviet Union has some twelve thousand surface-to-air missile launchers for continental air defense, most of which are reloadable with refire missiles. These are supported by over six thousand air defense radars and about four thousand interceptor aircraft. An entire branch of service is devoted to the air defense of the Soviet Union. In the United States, there is not even an official mission of continental air

defense for the military services—only warning of attack. The warning would be of little help since there is very little defense, consisting of a few interceptor aircraft, most of which are old. In the middle 1970s the United States phased out its last operational SAM systems, phased out two-thirds of its active military air defense aircraft, and changed NORAD'S mission to early warning.

5. Civil Defense and Wartime Sheltering of Leadership: Again, there is virtually none in the United States, while in the USSR, according to SMP:

> Soviet passive defense preparations have been underway in earnest for some 30 years and have, over time, expanded from the protection of such vital entities as the national Party and government leadership and Armed Forces to embrace the territorial leadership, national economy, and general population. The Soviets regard passive defense as an essential ingredient of their overall military posture and war planning.

SMP reports a massive Soviet program "to ensure the survival and wartime continuity" of political-military leadership, command and control, war-supporting services and industry, essential elements of the work force, and as much of the population as possible. What this amounts to is far more than the Western expression "civil defense" connotes. It amounts to "extensive planning for the transition of the entire State and economy to a wartime posture" and continuity during wartime.

6. Space Programs: Soviet disinformation would have the world believe that the Soviet space program is civilian, scientific, and peaceful in nature. In fact, as the Defense Intelligence Agency reports, "The Soviet space program is not only overwhelmingly military in nature, but the civilian scientific and economic aspects of the program are entirely subordinated to the military functions."[3] The Soviets conduct about six times as many space launches per year as does the United States, 80 percent of which are clearly identifiable as solely military in nature. Soviet space expenditures are about $28 to $30 billion per year, twice as much as those of the United States.

Soviet space programs are covered with deception, but Soviet plans and doctrine for the military use of space are known to U.S. intelligence. The Defense Intelligence Agency summarized them for Congress. According to Soviet plans:

The Soviet Armed Forces shall be provided with all resources necessary to attain and maintain military superiority in outer space sufficient both to deny the use of outer space to other states and to assure maximum spaced-based military support for Soviet offensive and defense combat operations on land, at sea, in air, and in outer space.

Deception and Soviet Military Doctrine

"The West has inflicted certain psychological wounds on itself which have no parallel in the Soviet Union. I have especially in mind the anti-nuclear propaganda of the Western left . . . [which] has a debilitating impact on the NATO countries and especially on the United States. *Cui Bono?* The answer is obvious. No such accounts of the horrors of nuclear war ever reach the Soviet public, because the whole area of military planning is banned from discussion. This means that in the vital field of psychological confrontation the balance is strongly tilted in favor of Soviet interests."[4]

This statement, while referring particularly to propaganda of the Western left, in fact draws attention to perhaps the greatest success of Soviet deception and disinformation: the nuclear fear factor in the West, which has a paralyzing tendency and interferes both with Western nuclear arms programs and with Western understanding of Soviet military doctrine.

Soviet propaganda at home and abroad denies the very tenets and objectives of Soviet military doctrine and ascribes them to the United States. Richard Shultz and Roy Godson's book *Dezinformatsia: Active Measures in Soviet Strategy* analyzes *Pravda* and the Soviet weekly *New Times*. It shows a long-standing theme that it is the United States that has "the twin goals of nuclear superiority and a first strike capacity," that believes a nuclear war winnable, and that is engaged in preparing for nuclear war. The United States is of course described in such Soviet publications as aggressive, imperialistic, and militaristic. In reality, this is a deception meant to camouflage Soviet plans, doctrine, and programs. In fact, it is not Soviet threat perception at all. The Soviets understand the United States politically; they can analyze American weapons systems and capabilities. The dichotomy even comes through in Soviet writings, as Shultz and Godson point out:

> While the United States persistently was characterized as the
> major threat to world peace, careful analysis of Soviet
> propaganda indicates that in reality the Kremlin did not per-
> ceive any direct threat or challenge to its security interests
> emanating from alleged U.S. aggressiveness and militarism.[5]

Soviet doctrinal writings, aimed internally for the consumption of
the professional Soviet military, although frequently elliptical, are
very different. Concealment and deception, they make clear, are
key elements *of* Soviet doctrine, but there is little concealment and
deception *about* that doctrine.

Deception and disinformation concerning Soviet military
doctrine, and particularly the Soviet view of nuclear war, have been
more successful in the West than should be warranted, given the
candor of professional Soviet writings on doctrine. Unfortunately,
few in the West bother to study such writings. Most are eager to
mirror-image Western views, and the Soviets have often played on
this tendency with success.

During the 1960s American officials and intellectuals firmly
believed, with assistance from Soviet disinformation, that Soviet
views about nuclear war and deterrence were identical to those
prevailing in the United States. Soviet military writings were seldom
studied or translated into English, with the exception of Sokolovski's
Military Strategy, which was widely misinterpreted, particularly as
conveying a nonnuclear emphasis. The classified journal of the
Soviet General Staff, *Voyennaya Mysl'* ("Military Thought"), was
available to U.S. intelligence agencies but was ignored. More emphasis was placed on Soviet public statements, including professed
Soviet fear of nuclear war and interest in nuclear arms control.
Consequently, Soviet military doctrine was portrayed and accepted
in the West as conventional with emphasis on the theater level and
on assured destruction deterrence on the intercontinental level at the
very same time that the Soviets (as *Voyennaya Mysl'* and other
military professional materials clearly show) were working out the
elements of a nuclear war-fighting strategy, including detailed operational and tactical plans.

This deception extended into the 1970s, largely through the
medium of arms control exchanges, until two developments. More
students of the Soviet military began paying serious attention to
Soviet doctrinal writings, and Soviet nuclear force developments
and civil defense began giving far less ambiguous evidence of

Soviet doctrine. The two—written expressions of Soviet doctrine and force developments—became clearly congruent. By 1976–77, both Department of Defense and Central Intelligence Agency reports had identified the principal elements of Soviet military doctrine pretty accurately. The Soviets clearly rejected American concepts of parity, stability, and mutual deterrence and instead based their doctrine and military preparations on the view that nuclear war could be fought successfully and damage to the Soviet Union could be limited. Soviet doctrine heavily emphasized strategic counter-force capabilities and damage limiting—the importance of negating each element of Western nuclear power. Soviet doctrine also rejected the concept of deterrence based upon second-strike retaliation and instead emphasized the importance of striking first at the enemy's military forces and C^3 (communications, command, and control).

Publicly, however, Soviet disinformation efforts continued. In fact, after it became clear to the Soviets that their own professional military writings were being studied in the West, elements of deception and disinformation began creeping into some of them, allowing those who would mirror-image to select passages from Soviet military writings to support their case.

This deception has recently enjoyed success even in professional Western military and intelligence interpretations of Soviet military doctrine, some of which, for example, now describe a new "conventional emphasis" to Soviet theater warfare doctrine on land and sea. (If the Soviets, while continuing to place heaviest emphasis on nuclear combat operations, could lead the West to believe that theater war with the Soviets would be nonnuclear and to prepare accordingly, the benefits to the Soviets would be clear: NATO would be preparing in peacetime for the wrong type of war, investing heavily in forces for nonnuclear combat, and increasing its own vulnerabilities to nuclear attack.) In fact, however, Soviet doctrine has not changed in that direction, as Soviet force developments and two recent major publications from the Frunze Military Academy—*Tactics* and *Tactical Maneuver*—make clear.

Soviet military doctrine determines the nature of theater and intercontinental forces developed and deployed. Soviet doctrine emphasizes the importance of surprising the enemy, of seizing the initiative, of striking first, of not allowing an enemy to strike first. The forces they deploy reflect those goals. Nuclear weapons and modern means of delivery, according to Soviet literature, magnify the importance and feasibility of these principles. Soviet doctrine, accordingly, emphasizes the "use of nuclear rocket weapons as a decisive means of armed conflict" in the opening stages of combat.[6]

Surprise Attack

Both U.S. strategic nuclear force and NATO theater force postures are based upon the assumption of strategic as well as adequate tactical warning.[7] It is an article of faith that the only possibility of a Soviet attack would be after a period of intense political crisis, during which Western nuclear forces would be placed on advanced stages of alert. Surprise, accordingly, is denied.

Yet our nuclear deterrent posture, both in the United States and in Western Europe, is critically vulnerable in the event of a surprise attack, and Soviet strategic thought clearly assigns the highest value to surprise. Logically, it must be expected that the Soviets would strive to achieve surprise in any attack on the West and would use both political and military deception and concealment to do so.

The incentive for any Soviet attack on U.S. strategic forces to be based on surprise is increased by the large difference in U.S. retaliatory capabilities, between a day-to-day posture and a "generated alert." U.S. strategic deterrent forces are appreciably more robust if on generated alert, such as might (but not necessarily) be expected during a confrontation with the Soviet Union.

For example, the U.S. bomber force carries a large fraction of U.S. megatonnage. In a day-to-day posture, only about one quarter of the bomber force is on rather relaxed *ground* alert, loaded with nuclear weapons, and concentrated on very few bases (most near the coasts and highly vulnerable to submarine-launched ballistic missile attack). In generated alert, however, perhaps 75 percent or more of the bombers might be ready, loaded, and dispersed to a larger number of inland bases. Crews would be vigilant and reaction time, for base escape, would be compressed.

In generated alert, U.S. C^3 and the National Command Authority would be at the peak of readiness, at least for the initial launching of forces on tactical warning, and the NCA would have thought through and planned immediate responses to such warning, including perhaps the difficult decision of whether to launch a portion of the alert ICBM force on a particular type of attack warning. Normally, about 50 percent of U.S. ballistic missile submarines are in port; during generated alert a much larger portion would be at sea. U.S. ICBMs, of course, are now thoroughly vulnerable to the type of attack the Soviets are capable of launching, whether in day-to-day or in generated alert. Their only prospect of use for the time being is by launching them *early* at the first signs of attack warning, and that is highly unlikely.

Many of the systems we depend on—for observance of Soviet activities, for warning of missile attack, and for sorting, confirming, routing, and evaluating any such signals—are fragile, vulnerable to a variety of disruptive measures, and distressingly undependable. False alarms and periods of lost communications are not exceptional. Real warning signals might be lost, ignored, or checked and rechecked until too late in the event of an actual attack.

Some believe (e.g., the Scowcroft Commission) that a coordinated attack on bombers and ICBMs would be too difficult due to timing. Unfortunately, it is possible, as Harold Brown warned when he was Secretary of Defense:

> It is equally important to acknowledge, however, that the coordination of a successful attack is not impossible, and that the "rubbish heap of history" is filled with authorities who said something reckless could not or would not be done.[8]

A well-executed Soviet surprise attack could well destroy the ICBM force, the bomber force, and at least the 50 percent of the submarine force in port, as well as the warning, command, control, and communications systems necessary for any use of whatever forces survive the attack—for that matter, U.S. warning satellites and radars. Very few in number could be destroyed first, as well as the few critical C^3 nodes. (A high-yield nuclear weapon in a Soviet satellite with a perigee at the right altitude over the center of the United States could produce EMP—electromagnetic pulse—and blackout much of U.S. C^3.) The benefits of a surprise attack, as compared to one with ample warning, are clear.

What about the Soviet view? We know that the Soviets have been engaged in a massive, methodical, and determined effort to develop a first-strike counterforce capability against Western deterrent forces. Strikes with Soviet ICBMs, or in the theater with the SS-20, can be made without visible preparation. So can SLBM strikes from the increasing number of Soviet submarines at sea. Moreover, Soviet military writings make clear that the Soviets perceive the benefits of surprise *and that they believe it possible to achieve surprise.*

On the latter, *Voyennaya Mysl'* observed, "The opinion exists that the capabilities for detecting an attack being prepared are sharply decreased at the present time and that the probability of achieving surprise is increased, and we agree with this." Even more recently, Marshal of the Soviet Union N.V. Ogarkov, at the time he was head of the Soviet General Staff, argued in a Soviet defense White Paper, *Always in Readiness to Defend the Homeland,* that surprise is today "a factor of the greatest strategic importance." The Soviet manual *The Basic Principles of Operational Art and Tactics* emphasizes that "the importance of surprise steadily rises with the development of means of armed conflict. . . . Surprise permits forestalling the enemy in delivering strikes, catching him unawares, paralyzing his will, sharply reducing his combat effectiveness, disorganizing his control, and creating favorable conditions for defeating even superior forces."

There are many similar authoritative Soviet views candidly expressed on this subject, e.g.:

> The side achieving surprise can obtain a decisive advantage. . . . Surprise nuclear attacks are capable of changing the correlation of forces sharply in short periods of time and thereby exerting a decisive influence on the course and even the outcome of military operations.
>
> Colonel Tyushkevic

> The role of surprise in combat has become considerably more important under present-day conditions. With the unexpected employment of new weapons, and nuclear weapons in particular, it is possible . . . to inflict on the enemy irrecoverable losses in a short period of time.
>
> Colonel Chervonobab

> Surprise makes it possible to inflict heavy losses upon the enemy in short periods of time, to paralyze his will, and to deprive him of the possibility of offering organized resistance.
>
> Soviet *Dictionary of Basic Military Terms*

That Soviet "dictionary" goes on to emphasize that among the ways decisive surprise is achieved is "by unexpected use of nuclear weapons."

To achieve surprise, the Soviets emphasize concealment, deception, and conditioning of the enemy. *Strategic* surprise, according to the Soviets, "is derived from concealing intent and time of onset." Surprise, according to a *Voyennaya Mysl'* article, "is achieved by deluding the enemy as to one's own intentions," coupled with "bold actions."

Another article in *Voyennaya Mysl'* stated:

> In modern conditions, surprise action is of importance for the successful execution of strategic missions and subsequent achievement of strategic goals. The concealed execution of all preparatory measures and thoroughly planned, active supply of misinformation to the enemy side about the true plans catch enemy troops unaware . . . and ensure the successful execution of the mission.

The Soviets demonstrated deception and surprise in Hungary in 1956, in the invasions of Czechoslovakia in 1968 and Afghanistan in 1979, and in their preparation of the Egyptians and Syrians for the Yom Kippur attack on Israel in 1973. And the West has demonstrated many times its own capacity to be surprised.

The United States might be surprised without large-scale Soviet deception efforts, but deception to achieve surprise is standard Soviet theory and practice, and skillful use of it would certainly enhance the likelihood of surprise.

Warning, in fact, may not matter. It would have to be interpreted correctly and with such clarity that the critical decision would be taken to move to generated alert (in full knowledge that this very action could precipitate or escalate a crisis). Due to our very disbelief in a nuclear attack, warning signals indicating a Soviet attack would be resisted strongly by U.S. and Western governments. They would conflict strongly with the prevailing views of reality and of Soviet intent.[9]

This has been the norm in U.S. historical experience from Pearl Harbor to Korea to the Soviet invasions of Czechoslovakia and Afghanistan. A study of U.S. surprise first at the North Korean attack on South Korea and then at the entry of Chinese forces into the war, despite many warning signals, concluded:

It was not the absence of intelligence which led us into trouble
but our unwillingness to draw unpleasant conclusions from it.
We refused to believe what our intelligence told us was in fact
happening because it was at variance with the prevailing climate
of opinion.[10]

Another study, entitled "Surprise Despite Warning: Why Sudden
Attacks Succeed," concluded, "there is always some warning . . . yet
surprise seldom fails."[11]

Soviet deception, in preparation for a surprise attack, would
likely be both political and military. Political deception would be
designed to temper the international political atmosphere in a way
to make war seem remote; detente overtures, calls for nonaggres-
sion agreements, arms control negotiations, and high-level political
visits and exchanges with the United States would all play to
American inclinations and suppress American expectations of conflict. These deceptive acts could even be employed to defuse a
crisis situation, and if that crisis were so intense that the United
States had put its deterrent forces on generated alert, the Soviets
would have even more to gain from such measures.

*It should be expected that any Soviet preparations to attack the
United States in time of crisis would include political deception
designed to lower U.S. vigilance and readiness.*

Military deception could take the form of "conditioning" the
United States not to become alarmed by Soviet military actions
prior to an attack. Prior to both the Czechoslovakian and the
Afghan invasions, the Soviets used military maneuvers to mask
preparations and intent. These "non-stop maneuvers . . . served as a
form of deception by desensitizing the Czech leaders to a military
invasion."[12] The United States was desensitized, too. The three top
NATO officials were away from their posts; General Polk, commander of the Seventh Army, first heard about the Soviet attack
from an Associated Press dispatch, and President Johnson was
informed by Ambassador Dobrynin, not by U.S. intelligence.

The Soviets have already been conducting increasingly comprehensive and realistic military exercises involving their strategic
nuclear forces, including actual launches of missiles from operational silos and coordinated launches of offensive and defensive
strategic forces. In 1982 the Soviets destroyed a Cosmos satellite in
orbit with a co-orbital ASAT as the start of a simulated nuclear war
exercise. ICBMs were launched from operational silos, an SS-20 was

launched (in a northerly ICBM-like direction), an SLBM was fired from a Delta class SSBN, ABM interceptor missiles were fired, submarines were surged, bomber aircraft moved, and all actions were tightly linked through effective command and control.[13] Such exercises may be repeated and enlarged and could have the effect of conditioning the United States not to be alarmed by such events.

Conditioning of an opponent, as Roberta Wohlstetter has warned, "may create a normal pattern by a sequence of exercises or penetrations of the warning system before the attack."[14]

Not unreasonable scenarios, for the Soviets' achieving surprise in any nuclear attack can easily be constructed for either peacetime (noncrisis) or crisis situations.

For the former, a careful and possibly lengthy time of preparation could be involved, wherein the United States and the West would be exposed to both political and military deception. The Soviet Union could desensitize the United States to ever-increasing levels of military exercises while fostering a climate of detente. The Soviets could appear to pursue arms control agreements vigorously, while blaming U.S. nuclear arms programs and U.S. "nuclear war preparations" for the lack of progress. Meanwhile, coordinated Soviet strategic force exercises, increasingly involving space systems, would become frequent occurrences. Surge "exercises" for Soviet nuclear submarines would become normal, as well as patrols along the U.S. coasts and in the Caribbean. While such events might initially be alarming, the peaceful aftermath along with Soviet assurances of peaceful intentions and the unthinkability of nuclear war would condition the United States to accept them as not menacing. As the SS-24 and SS-25 became deployed in large numbers (a mobile and largely unlocatable force), test firings of SS-18s and SS-19s from operational silos might be conducted. While reaffirming their allegiance to the ABM Treaty, the Soviets could proceed to create a nationwide ABM capability based on the "tactical" ABM-X-3 and SA-12 systems.

Mr. Gorbachev, naturally, would be publicly emphasizing his role as a pragmatic reformer intent on his first priority of bolstering the Soviet economy and agriculture. The mutual benefits of trade and other exchanges would be stressed. Soviet support for worldwide terrorism might be noticeably lessened.

In the United States strategic force modernization would remain forestalled by the promise of arms control, the fervor of nuclear freeze movements (catered to by politicians), and a bipartisan emphasis on robbing defense to maintain government nondefense spending programs or to balance the budget. U.S. Presidents, however, would continue to argue the need for a stronger defense and to express the firm conviction that their programs were "closing the window of vulnerability" and erasing Soviet military advantages. The Soviets might be led to feel that, in such event, the peak of their strategic advantage over the United States had been reached; and, in any case, that the costs of such massive nuclear arms programs were becoming less and less endurable.

The basis for strategic surprise would exist.

A Soviet surprise attack might begin with the destruction of U.S. early warning satellites and attacks on U.S. C^3 and the National Command Authority (by a combination of EMP attacks, SLBMs, and *spetznaz* special forces pre-emplaced in the United States; such forces with light rocket launchers might also ensure that U.S. bombers did not take off before the arrival of SLBM warheads). A wave of SLBMs would attack bomber bases and pin down ICBMs, which would be unlikely to launch before Soviet ICBM warheads detonated anyway. U.S. tactical warning would be degraded, fragmented, and uncertain. The fact and nature of the attack could not be confirmed in time to complete all necessary communications and preparations. Surviving U.S. forces would consist of a very few submarines at sea, and these would be subject to Soviet attrition over time; their capabilities would be overwhelmed by the Soviet strategic reserve.

Such a surprise attack scenario would not necessarily vary greatly in the context of a crisis situation. If the Soviets believed war inevitable as the result of a crisis, it is quite likely, given the importance the Soviets assign to surprise, that they would make every effort to "defuse" a crisis, lead the West to come off of generated alert, and then strike (similar to the techniques used before the Czech invasion and the Yom Kippur War). U.S. forces coming off generated alert after a period of such alert would be even *less* ready and capable than they are on a day-to-day peacetime posture: more bombers would be down for maintenance, crews would be exhausted; more SSBMs would be in port for rotation of crews and maintenance; and the energy and alertness of key political and military personnel would be decreased.

The Soviets might induce such a stand-down from crisis by any number of political overtures, indications of reasonableness and desire to negotiate differences, and apparent moderation of objectives. Simultaneous expressions of anxiety and warnings about the crisis getting out of hand would increase the inclinations of Western leaders to reduce military preparations. The Soviets could contribute to this trend of relaxation by troop pull-backs and standdowns (while carefully keeping first-strike strategic forces secretly on the highest alert). With skillful deception, Western leaders could be led to believe that the risk of war and chance of Soviet attack had passed.

No one can say how probable or improbable such scenarios or the likelihood of such a Soviet attack might be. What can be said with some reasonability is that Soviet doctrine and strategy place the highest priority on surprise, and that—given current nuclear deterrent postures—the benefits to the Soviet Union of such surprise would be very great. What can also be said is that the probability of an attack can be increased or decreased by the weakness or strength of our own nuclear deterrent forces and particularly by their vulnerability or survivability to attacks that the Soviets are capable of launching. The answer, of course, would be to assign the highest priority in the United States and NATO to reducing the vulnerability of our nuclear deterrent forces to a Soviet first strike, and to return to the standard of force sufficiency in the event of a well-executed surprise attack. There is today too much dependency on strategic warning and on the irrationality of an attack being perceived by the Soviets. As Roberta Wohlstetter concluded from her well-known study of Pearl Harbor:

> One major practical lesson emerges . . . We cannot count on strategic warning. We might get it, and we might be able to take useful preparatory actions that would be impossible without it . . . However, since we cannot rely on strategic warning, our defenses . . . must be designed to function without it.[15]

Notes

1. Dean Acheson, *Power and Diplomacy*. (Harvard University Press, 1958; republished in paperback by Atheneum Press, 1962), p. 9.
2. Robert M. Gates and Lawrence K. Gershwin, "Soviet Strategic Force Developments." Joint Session of the Subcommittees on Strategic and Theater Nuclear Forces of the Senate Armed Services Committee.
3. Defense Intelligence Agency, *Soviet Military Space Doctrine*. (Washington, D.C.: U.S. Government Printing Office, May 1984).

4. "A Conversation with Milovan Djilas." *Encounter* (December 1979).

5. Richard H. Shultz and Roy Godson, *Dezinformatsia: Active Measures in Soviet Strategy.* (Washington, D.C.: Pergamon-Brassey's 1984), p. 101.

6. See, e.g., Joseph Douglass and Amoretta Hoeber, *Selected Readings from Military Thought (Voyennaya Mysl').* (Washington, D.C.: U.S. Government Printing Office, 1982), and the series of Soviet doctrinal writings translated by the U.S. Air Force, *Soviet Military Thought.* (Washington, D.C.: U.S. Government Printing Office, 1986).

7. As Army Major Don Mercer observed for NATO, "The standard planning assumption is that NATO would acquire clear warning of Warsaw Pact intentions to attack, would begin its mobilization and deployment within a few days after the Warsaw Pact and would have time to build up its defenses. General Haig, former supreme allied commander, Europe, stated that NATO could count on 8 to 14 days warning time." The former planning standard for U.S. strategic nuclear forces was that they should be able to absorb even a "well-executed surprise attack" and still be adequate to carry out assigned retaliatory missions. This is no longer the case.

8. *U.S. Department of Defense Annual Report to Congress,* Fy 1980, p. 81.

9. One might conjecture reasonably that ample *strategic* warning has already been received (although not as to the timing or precise events leading up to an attack). If a thoroughly unconditioned newcomer—the canonical "man from Mars" or, even better, a Belisarius, Caesar, or Napoleon from the past—were to appear on the scene and be exposed to intelligence on Soviet nuclear programs, he would likely conclude that the Soviets are preparing for nuclear war. He would conclude that strategic warning for this exists. He would be dumbfounded that the United States has not prepared for that contingency and has not believed the seriousness of the Soviet preparations and, indeed, that the mere suggestion of the possibility of a Soviet nuclear attack is nearly unanimously regarded with the utmost incredulity as the most extreme kind of fanaticism.

   Given that situation, is there really any strong doubt that the Soviets could achieve surprise, even in a time of crisis, with reasonably adroit deception?

10. H.A. DeWeerd, "Strategic Surprise in the Korean War." *Orbis* (Fall, 1962), p. 439.

11. Richard K. Betts, "Surprise Despite Warning: Why Sudden Attacks Succeed." *Political Science Quarterly* (Winter 1980–81), p. 553.

12. Jiri Valenta, "Soviet Use of Surprise and Deception." *Survival* (March/April 1982), pp. 53–54.

13. "Soviets Stage Integrated Test of Weapons." *Aviation Week and Space Technology,* June 28, 1982.

14. Roberta Wohlstetter, "The Pleasures of Self-Deception." *The Washington Quarterly* (Autumn 1979), p. 54.

15. Roberta Wohlstetter, *Pearl Harbor: Warning and Decision.* (Stanford University Press, 1962).

THE TRUCE OF THE BEAR

The Truce of the Bear

But (pay, and I put back the bandage)
  this is the time to fear,
When he stands up like a tired man, tottering
  near and near;
When he stands up as pleading, in wavering,
  man-brute guise,
When he veils the hate and cunning of his
  little, swinish eyes;

"When he shows as seeking quarter, with
  paws like hands in prayer,
That is the time of peril—the time of the
  Truce of the Bear!"

Over and over the story, ending as he
  began:—
"There is no truce with Adam-zad, the Bear
  that looks like a man!"

Rudyard Kipling
1898

THE
TREATY
TRAP

Dr. William R. Kintner

The 1985 resumption of U.S.-Soviet arms control talks in Geneva is being widely hailed as both necessary and a harbinger of more normal relations between the superpowers. President Reagan set the stage for another round of arms control talks in a speech to the United Nations on September 24, 1984:

> We are ready for constructive negotiations with the Soviet Union.
>
> We recognize that there is no safe alternative to negotiations on arms control and other issues between our two nations, which have the capacity to destroy civilization as we know it. I believe this is a view shared by every country in the world and by the Soviet Union itself.[1]

On Thanksgiving Day 1984, National Security Adviser Robert McFarlane stated, "The United States and the Soviet Union have agreed to enter into new negotiations with the objective of reaching mutually acceptable agreements on the whole range of questions concerning nuclear and outer-space arms."

In January 1985, Secretary of State George Shultz met with the foreign minister in Geneva and agreed to new arms control negotiations. On January 14, Deputy Secretary of State Kenneth W. Dom commented:

> The accord reached in Geneva is, of course, only a beginning. While Secretary Shultz and Foreign Minister Gromyko were successful in working out a basis for new negotiations, their discussions made clear that there are major differences of substance between us. There is a long road ahead. With patience, determination, and flexibility on both sides, the process set in motion last week in Geneva can successfully lead to a more stable peace.[2]

The U.S. and the USSR agreed to conduct three sets of negotiations simultaneously. Each nation's negotiating team will be divided into three subgroups. One will discuss long-range missiles and strategic weapons: nuclear warheads carried by intercontinental missiles or launched from submarines or bombers. The second will bargain about intermediate-range weapons, primarily Soviet SS-20 missiles targeted on Western Europe and U.S. Pershing II and cruise missiles deployed by NATO countries. The third group will grapple with the most contentious issue of all: defensive systems, including Star Wars, antisatellite (ASAT) weapons, and such Soviet ground-based systems as antiballistic missiles, radars, and antiaircraft devices.

In a statement before the Senate Foreign Relations Committee on January 31, 1985, Secretary of State Shultz said, "My meeting in Geneva with Soviet Foreign Minister Gromyko was a constructive beginning of what the United States hopes will be a fruitful negotiation." He then talked of new defensive technologies and a period of transition that "could lead to the eventual elimination of the nuclear arms, both offensive and defensive. A world free of nuclear arms is an ultimate objective to which we, the Soviet Union, and the other nations can agree."

These developments were warmly endorsed by many who believe that we can negotiate our way to better relations with the Soviet Union. According to Leslie H. Gelb and Anthony Lake, senior officials in the Carter Administration:

> Nineteen hundred and eighty-five begins as a year of promise in world affairs. The Soviet Union has returned to the bargaining table with the United States after a year's hiatus. . . .

> Nineteen hundred and eighty-four marked a passage of sorts for the Reagan Administration. After three years of stifling rhetoric and inaction, the White House and the State Department returned to more traditional diplomatic forms—moderate words that allow for compromise, and actual engagement with adversaries previously shunned.[3]

Finally, the death of Konstantin Chernenko and the accession to power of Mikhail S. Gorbachev was widely interpreted as bringing new vigor into the Kremlin, which could lead to improvements in Soviet-American relations. In his acceptance speech on being named General Secretary of the Communist Party, USSR, Mr. Gorbachev said the Soviet Union sought a "real and major reduction in arms stockpiles, and not the development of ever-new weapon systems, be it on space or on earth." Subsequently, President Reagan told a group of magazine publishers that he believed the Soviet leaders were "really going to try and, with us, negotiate a reduction in armaments."[4]

Such euphoria deserves to be dashed with cold water drawn from the well of Laurence W. Beilenson's book *The Treaty Trap*.[5] This book is a carefully documented history of the dismal performance of treaties by the United States and European nations including Russia, now the Soviet Union. Much of our experience of negotiations with the Soviet Union has been in the realm of arms control. President Reagan has publicly praised Beilenson's book for the valuable lessons it provides policymakers.

The United States, in particular, has tended to rely on treaties as the most effective way of disposing of, if not resolving, complicated and thorny issues such as the U.S.-Soviet nuclear confrontation. This American penchant for negotiating treaties—which is in contrast to the realism of the Founding Fathers—has not been diminished by evidence that treaties are nearly always breached and that nations have regularly broken treaties on the basis of their changing national interests. According to George F. Kennan:

> The most serious fault of our past policy formulation [lies] in something that I might call the legalistic-moralistic approach to international problems. This approach runs like a red skein through our foreign policy of the last fifty years. It has in it something of the old emphasis on arbitration treaties, something of the Hague Conferences and schemes for universal disarmament, something of the more ambitious American concepts of the role of international law, something of the League of Nations and the United Nations, something of the Kellogg Pact, something of the idea of a universal "Article 51" pact, something of the belief in World Law and World Government. But it is none of these, entirely. Let me try to describe it. It is the belief that it should be possible to suppress the chaotic and dangerous aspirations of governments in the international field by the acceptance of some system of legal rules and restraints.[6]

Beilenson has made a unique contribution toward a clearer understanding of the efficacy of treaties as an instrument of state policy. In *The Treaty Trap* he looked at every important political treaty (as distinct from those of a purely economic or commercial nature) negotiated by European nations and the United States over the past three hundred years. With painstaking care he examined each treaty to determine whether it was broken by one or more of the signatories; why it was broken or honored; and what the result was in relation to the treaty's objectives. By analyzing various types of treaties, he sought to determine whether there has been any consistent pattern of behavior in relation to the treaties. He found that there was. Beilenson contends that:

> Peace treaties have walked hand in hand with war. Yet such is the magic of labels that treaties for peace are subconsciously associated with peace and their absence with war. This has led some commentators to assert that since war has become so suicidal, logic dictates dependence on treaties to prevent it. The conclusion, however, does not follow from the premise. Nuclear war would be a calamity, but only historical experience is a guide to whether treaties will prevent war. Before a nation relies on new promises, good sense suggests a scrutiny of the promises previously made.[7]

If relied upon, Beilenson argues, "a treaty can be a snare." Machiavelli, whose name connotes duplicity, once said, "One prince of the present time, whom it is not well to name, never preaches anything but peace and good faith, and to both he is most hostile, and either, if he had kept it, would have deprived him of reputation and kingdom many a time."[8]

The Founding Fathers of the United States were idealists in their love of liberty for their own land, but they had no illusions about foreign affairs. Richard Oswald, the English agent who negotiated with John Jay for peace in the Revolutionary War, reported that Jay said "he would not give a farthing for any parchment security whatever. They had never signified anything since the world began, when any prince or state, of either side, found it convenient to break through them."[9]

This observation sounds incredibly like a much-quoted utterance of Joseph Stalin, who considered diplomatic deceit and dishonesty quite normal: "With a diplomat words *must* diverge from acts—what kind of diplomat would he otherwise be?" Stalin asked in 1931. "Words are one thing and acts something different. Good words are masks for bad deeds. A sincere diplomat would equal dry water, wooden iron."

In the postwar period the treaty-making malady among American leaders became almost incurable. With the invasion of Czechoslovakia in August 1968, the Soviet Union and four other Communist nations each violated the collective United Nations treaty to keep the peace, a Warsaw Pact alliance, and a bilateral alliance with Czechoslovakia. Two months later, both major candidates for President of the United States said they would ask the Senate to ratify the Nuclear Nonproliferation Treaty, of which the invading nations were prominent signatories.

Now that the United States is back on the negotiating track with the Soviet Union, hopes are being expressed that the Geneva talks could break the Cold War climate that supposedly characterized President Reagan's first term.

President Reagan had opposed virtually all Soviet-American arms pacts for almost two decades. His basic position was that Moscow has acquired nuclear superiority for a decade and has been using arms control as a way of lulling the American people into a false sense of security and thus helping undermine support for a U.S. military buildup that would reestablish a nuclear balance. Because of the defense programs, he now maintains the United States has regained equality and is in a position to negotiate seriously and from strength. In particular, he wants to convince Moscow of the virtues of his proposed space-based defensive weapons.

Moscow maintains that there is now overall nuclear parity between the two superpowers. Soviet leaders claim they want a gradual reduction of offensive nuclear arms while keeping limits on defensive systems in accordance with the ABM Treaty of 1972.

In addition to arms control agreements and treaties with the Soviet Union, the most important single accord reached by the United States with the Kremlin was the Helsinki Final Act, signed by President Ford at the Conference on Security and Cooperation in Europe (CSCE) at Helsinki in 1975. The Final Act created a framework for the thirty-five participating states to work to resolve the humanitarian, economic, political, and military issues that have divided Europe.

Soviet compliance with arms control agreements and their implementation of the Helsinki Final Act should provide a way to judge the utility of the new round of arms control negotiations at Geneva. Evidence shows that the Soviet Union is continuing its buildup of strategic weapons, including space defense systems. Public outcry against the strategic arms race, especially against U.S.

efforts, has been rampant on both sides of the Atlantic and especially in favor of the unilateral "nuclear freeze" movement. No issue
was more widely discussed in the 1984 political campaign.

But one development has brought this issue to its present
international prominence. This is a capability of the United States to
build an effective space defense system. Once this system is in
place, it will entirely change and reduce the danger of Soviet
nuclear strategy.

The prospect of this development by the United States was
undoubtedly one of the main factors leading the Soviet Union to
reopen a dialogue on arms control with the United States.

The Soviet leaders and the Soviet press have repeatedly stated
their opposition to Star Wars, or the Strategic Defense Initiative.
Does a renewal of discussions with Washington indicate a desire on
the part of Moscow to really negotiate on this issue, or will the new
talks prove to be another Soviet attempt to split the United States
from its NATO allies? How useful is Winston Churchill's famous
dictum that "jaw-jaw is better than war-war" in relation to the
renewed arms negotiations? While anything is better than nuclear
war-war, the question is whether the superpower jawers have a
common interest and whether the jawing is accompanied by a
shared sense of behavior. "Linkage" is a fact of political life; we
cannot separate Soviet international behavior from arms negotiations.

The Soviet record of treaty breaking is well documented. In
1955 the Senate Judiciary Committee, under the chairmanship of
James O. Eastland (D–Miss.), compiled a study on Soviet treaty
violations. The study found that the Soviet government "had broken
its word to virtually every country to which it ever gave a signed
promise." In thirty-eight years, from 1917 to 1955, the Soviet Union
broke over 110 treaties.[10]

In 1961 Thomas E. Morgan (D–Penn.), chairman of the House
Committee on Foreign Affairs, released hearings on Soviet violations of treaties. Those hearings document Soviet violations of
virtually every major treaty made with over twenty countries. The
report included a quote from Lenin himself: "Yes, of course, we are
violating the [Brest-Litovsk] treaty; we have violated it thirty or
forty times." Chairman Morgan concluded that the results of those
hearings "should give pause to those who believe that agreements
with the Soviet Union will assure peace."[11]

On October 10, 1984, the Reagan Administration released to

Congress, pursuant to congressional amendments to the fiscal 1985 Defense Authorization Bill, a report on Soviet violations of treaties and declarations bearing on arms control and disarmament. The report was prepared by the bipartisan General Advisory Committee on Arms Control and Disarmament, which has been studying the subject for more than three years.[12]

In an earlier report to Congress (January 23, 1984) on Soviet noncompliance with arms control agreements, President Reagan said that:

The United States Government has determined that the Soviet Union is violating:

1. the Geneva Protocol on Chemical Weapons,
2. the Biological Weapons Convention,
3. the Helsinki Final Act, and two provisions of SALT II,
4. telemetry encryption, and
5. a rule concerning ICBM modernization.

In addition we have determined that the Soviet Union:

6. has almost certainly violated the ABM Treaty (SALT I),
7. probably violated the SALT II limit on new types (ICBMs),
8. probably violated the SS-16 deployment prohibition of SALT II,
9. and is likely to have violated the nuclear testing yield limit of the Threshold Test Ban Treaty.

The report substantially increased the number of named violations—still holding in reserve a large number of violations that were not listed in the declassified version of the report given to Congress and the public.

In transmitting the report[13] to Congress, President Reagan noted:

The Administration continues to be seriously concerned about Soviet behavior with regard to compliance with arms control obligations and commitments. We are actively pursuing several such issues in confidential discussions with the Soviet Union and are seeking explanations, clarifications, and corrective actions.

The report of the General Advisory Committee is the first comprehensive United States study of all Soviet practices under arms control obligations since World War II. It studies 26 documentary agreements along with numerous unilateral Soviet commitments. The committee noted that in most cases of alleged Soviet violations, the Soviets readily could have shown that the allegations were false—if they had been false. In summing up its findings, the committee said:

> The Committee has determined that the Soviet Union's practices related to about half of its documentary arms control commitments have raised no questions regarding compliance. Soviet practices related to the other half, however, show material breaches—violations, probable violations, or circumventions—of contractual obligations.

The areas of apparent Soviet compliance were confined to agreements where it was clearly in the Soviet interest to comply or where non-compliance involved no important benefit to the Soviet Union—e.g., the Hot Line Agreement of 1963 (amended 1971), the Nonproliferation Treaty of 1968, the Convention on the Physical Protection of Nuclear Material (U.S.S.R. ratification 1983), the Antarctic Treaty of 1959, and the Outer Space Treaty of 1967.

Among the more serious charges made by the GAC report were the following:

- The Soviets had breached the unilateral commitment not to send offensive weapons to Cuba, thus precipitating the Cuban missile crisis of 1962.
- The Soviets had on numerous occasions violated the prohibitions contained in the Limited Test Ban Treaty of 1963 by testing underground nuclear devices that vented radioactive debris beyond the borders of the Soviet Union.
- In the settlement of the Cuban missile crisis, the U.S. had committed itself not to invade Cuba, in return for which the Soviet Union had committed itself not to base offensive weapons in Cuba. From 1970 to 1974, however, the Soviets had deployed and tended nuclear weapons submarines in Cuban waters.
- The Soviet Union has systematically violated the provisions of the SALT I Interim Agreement barring the use of concealment and missile test encryption to impede verification of compliance by national technical means.
- The Soviet Union has failed to dismantle ICBM launchers as SLBM launchers became operational—as called for by the SALT I Interim Agreement.
- The Soviet Union has probably violated the SALT II Treaty of 1979 by continuing to produce and deploy SS-16

mobile ICBMs. (Although the SALT II Treaty has not been ratified, both sides claim to be observing it.) In addition, the Soviet Union has probably violated the clause of the SALT II agreement which permits each party to develop only one new type of ICBM.

Under the SALT I treaty of 1972, neither side is allowed to develop a nationwide system of antiballistic-missile defenses.

By 1983 American spy satellites had spotted a huge construction project near Krasnoyarsk in central Siberia. It seems to be a giant radar station that would be useful for providing early warning against a missile attack and could also help shoot down the incoming warheads with ABMs. Its location deep inside the USSR would make it a clear-cut violation of SALT if it is used for early warning, since the ABM Treaty says that such facilities must be near the periphery of the country.

The Soviets claim that the radar, which will not be completed until 1988 or 1989, is not for looking outward toward the Pacific Ocean for enemy missile warheads, but for looking upward to track satellites and manned vehicles in space, a function permitted by SALT.

In concluding its report the GAC said:

> The Soviet Union's actions since 1958 concerning arms control agreements demonstrate a pattern of pursuing military advantage through selective disregard for its international arms control duties and commitments.
>
> The committee found recurring instances of Soviet conduct involving deliberate deception, misdirection, and falsification of data during negotiations.
>
> Soviet denial activities significantly increased over the last quarter century and today are challenging U.S. verification capabilities despite improvements in U.S. verification technology. Deliberate Soviet efforts to counter U.S. national technical means of verification strongly indicate a Soviet intention to persevere in circumventing and violating agreements.[14]

In testimony before Congress on February 25, 1985, Assistant Secretary of Defense Richard Perle urged the United States to end a "double standard" on arms pacts that tolerates Soviet violations while the United States adheres to them to the letter.

Richard R. Burt, Assistant Secretary of State for European and Canadian Affairs, who also testified, agreed with Mr. Perle that the Russians had committed violations of past accords. He said the Soviet Union's failure to live up to the terms of previous accords demonstrated the difficulty of cooperating with Moscow on arms control without harming our own interests.[15]

One must place Soviet violations of arms control agreements in a wider perspective if serious treaty traps are to be avoided. Here the views of Andrei Sakharov are important:

> I am convinced that international trust, mutual understanding, disarmament, and international security are inconceivable without an open society with freedom of information, freedom of conscience, the right to publish, and the right to travel and choose the country in which one wishes to live. I am also convinced that freedom of conscience, together with other civic rights, provides both the basis for scientific progress and a guarantee against its misuse to harm mankind.[16]

The United States signed the Final Act of the Conference on Security and Cooperation in Europe in Helsinki in 1975. In part, the Helsinki accords were intended by the West to help open up Soviet society.

The Helsinki signing came some twenty years after the Soviets launched the idea in the closing hours of the 1955 summit meeting in Geneva. Soviet objectives for the holding of such a conference varied over time. At one stage the Soviet purpose of such a conference had become the exclusion of the United States from Europe:

> The United States of America believes for some reason that Europe cannot do without its presence and guardianship, without American bases on European soil, without American soldiers in the streets of European cities, without American planes in European skies. . . . The peoples of Europe are having and will continue to have their say on this score.[17]

In June 1970 the Soviet Union conceded explicitly that Canada and the United States were to be participants. Two months later, in August, the Soviet Union and the Federal Republic of Germany festively signed the Moscow treaty. The treaty achieved some of the objectives that had been projected by Moscow into the agenda of the proposed security conference: namely, Bonn's formal acceptance of the status quo in Europe via the recognition of existing borders.

For the USSR, the proposed Conference on Security and Cooperation in Europe would reconcile one profound Soviet dilemma: how to satisfy East European desires for expanding relations with the West without forfeiting Soviet control over such contacts. The security conference, by creating an institutional forum for East-West relations in which the Soviet Union could expect to play a dominant role, could be one solution to that dilemma.

Yet Soviet defensive motives are contradicted by the history of Soviet endeavors to intimidate the countries of Western Europe. If the Soviets desired tranquillity on their Western flank, they already had it. No Soviet planner, no matter how pessimistic, could make a plausible case for aggressive intent in NATO against the Soviet Union or her security position in Eastern Europe.

What the Soviets achieved at Helsinki was universal acceptance of the status quo in Europe and recognition of the existing international boundaries between East and West that the Soviet Army had established by force in the closing days of World War II. The result was a significant expansion of Soviet control over Eastern Europe.

In exchange the Soviets promised some opening of contacts between its empire and the West. The Helsinki Final Act recognized that follow-up meetings were essential for maintaining the Helsinki framework as a vigorous means of addressing problems in Europe. The first meeting was held in Belgrade. The second CSCE review conference was held in Madrid from November 11, 1980, until September 9, 1983. At both meetings the United States was ably represented by Ambassador Max M. Kampelman. In the seventeenth semiannual report by the President to the Commission on Security and Cooperation, a general assessment was made of the implementation of the Helsinki Final Act and the Madrid Concluding Document. The Soviet record was dismal.[18]

The President's report stated:

> Once again, the continuing deterioration of the Soviet Union's already poor record of compliance gave the greatest cause for concern. The Soviet authorities continued to amend the legal code to outlaw independent forms of expression and to sever contacts between Soviets and foreigners.

In the international arena, the Soviet Union has continued to violate basic principles guiding relations among states by waging war against Afghanistan, supporting the Vietnamese occupation of Cambodia, and defending the September 1983 downing of a civilian Korean airliner that accidentally strayed into Soviet airspace. Domestically, the Soviet authorities continued to introduce new amendments to the legal code to strengthen their hand against independent forms of expression and lend a certain fictitious legality to their campaigners. In this respect, a new decree establishing fines for Soviet citizens who provide broadly defined material support to foreigners represents a continuation of the effort to tighten legal restrictions that were begun under the previous review period.

Persecution of individuals who attempted to express themselves outside the framework of state-controlled organs continued at an alarming rate in the 6 months under review. Human rights monitors, religious believers, proponents of greater cultural and political rights for ethnic minorities, and peace activists were all subject to arrest and imprisonment. Renowned human rights activist Yelena Bonner was sentenced by a Gorky court to 5 years of internal exile while her husband, Andrei Sakharov, who began a hunger strike on her behalf in May, was forcibly separated from her and placed incommunicado in a medical facility. Anatoly Shcharansky was placed on a strict regimen in the prison where he is being held, and Yuriy Orlov remained isolated in his remote place of exile in the Far East. Dissident activist Yuriy Shikhanovich was sentenced to a term in a labor camp for compiling information on the status of political prisoners and Yelena Sannikova and Lina Tumanova awaited trial on similar charges. Soviet persecution of religious activists took on an ominous hue with the arrests of Hebrew teachers Aleksandr Kholmianskiy and Yuliy Edelstein, the arrest of Odessa *refusenik* Yakov Levin, and the sentencing of Riga *refusnik* Zakhar Zunshaine to labor camp. These arrests were part of what appears to be an intensified crackdown on Jewish cultural activists. Psychiatric abuse has also not abated, as witnessed by the recent sentencing of Catholic activist Aleksandr Riga to indefinite treatment in a special psychiatric hospital and the death of Alexey Nikitin in a psychiatric hospital.

Despite commitments under the Helsinki Final Act to facilitate family reunification, the rate of emigration from the Soviet Union continued to decline below the disappointing figures of early 1984 and has come to a virtual standstill. Some 423 Jews left the Soviet Union from April 1–August 30; 356 ethnic Germans left in the same period, and 46 Armenians from April 1–September 30. The abysmal level of Jewish emigration was accompanied by an alarming increase in the level of official anti-Semitic propaganda.

The Soviet authorities continued to exercise tight control on travel outside the country, allowing only 786 Soviet citizens to make private visits to the United States during the past 6 months. Only 93 Soviet citizens received exit permission to join relatives in the United States.

The Soviet authorities maintained their traditional strict control of information media, denying Soviet citizens access to all filmed, printed, and broadcast information which might call into question the tenets of Marxism-Leninism or the official line of the Communist Party. Jamming of Voice of America and Radio Liberty native language broadcasts continued.

Soviet violations of arms control agreements and noncompliance with the Helsinki Final Act do not hold promise for the United States' ever obtaining any benefit from future negotiations with the Soviet Union. In 1979 the House Committee on Foreign Affairs published volume one of a report on Soviet diplomacy and negotiating behavior.[19] In an abstract of the concluding chapter on *Soviet Strategic Deception*, the report stated that Soviet diplomacy and negotiations are characterized by:

An obsessive concern for security continues that is rooted in history, doctrine, and the prevailing concern for war in the Nuclear Age. This obsession may never diminish. . . .

Soviet style in diplomacy is geared to the exigencies of the times: Hostility, arrogance and intransigence in time of stress and cold war, a diplomacy of weakness; conciliation, congeniality and traditionalism in times of detente and accommodation.

The report endorsed the course suggested by Philip Moseley, over a quarter century ago, of monitoring the nation's strength and holding out the option of negotiations, suggesting a posture where risks for the Soviets to seek unacceptable advantages in the strategic balance and in Third World would outweigh the possibilities of gain, while keeping open the option of resolving differences through negotiations. Moseley's hope that time might moderate Soviet ambitions has yet to be realized.

Up to the present it should be apparent that the Soviets do not view diplomacy as a means for settling disputes but as another tool to manipulate to their advantage in the East-West struggle.

Soviet diplomacy presents a fundamental challenge to the Western democracies. The United States seeks negotiations with the Soviet Union to resolve disputes, since every effort must be made to avert military conflicts. On the other hand, optimistic expectations regarding the outcome of negotiations have no basis in reality. So long as the Kremlin believes that fundamental East-West differences are irreconcilable, negotiations are a palliative, not an answer.

Beilenson sums up the Soviet penchant for treaty busting this way:

The motives for Soviet breaches of all classes of political treaties have stretched national and ideological interest. In a broad sense they have merged, since the Soviet Union has identified its own interest as the base for and the leader of world revolution with that of Communism. But both Soviet world-side subversion and the breech of Soviet treaties against subversion have been pushed far beyond the requirements of security for the homeland, and with little hope of territorial or material profit. The rationale by which the Soviet leaders have supported the dictatorship they still practice is helped by the ideological wellspring of the world revolution and of preserving its base. That has forced the leaders to emphasize the ideological motive in all actions abroad. Even publicly they have not disowned it. And in the fighting for the crown of leadership, if a wearer should be tempted to forgo actions in favor of Communism elsewhere, his ambitious comrades near the throne would soon try to deprive him of his crown.

In observance and breach of alliance treaties, the USSR has merely equalled the pattern of the West. Considering the short history of the Soviet Union and the even shorter period when it considered it safe to break treaties to keep the peace, it has at least equalled its precursors. In breaches of treaties not to subvert, it has made a new high. Overall, the average of breach per year by the USSR probably entitles it to the championship. If this accolade be thought unfair to some other nations, the Soviets have at least staked a joint claim to the crown.[20]

Regarding disarmament treaties, Beilenson concludes that they "have been unreliable and ineffective."

The Potential Geneva Treaty Trap

Despite the Soviet record of treaty breaches and its avowed hostility, the United States will seek to negotiate arms agreements at Geneva. Yet how can the United States overlook the Soviet aim to destroy all opposing systems? This goal was clearly stated by Andrei Gromyko in April 1984: "Peaceful co-existence is a specific form of class struggle against capitalism. This struggle is going on and will continue . . . because the world outlooks of the two social systems are opposite and irreconcilable." Henry Kissinger wrote in 1957, "The emphasis of traditional diplomacy on 'good faith' and 'willingness to come to an agreement' is a positive handicap when it comes to dealing with a power dedicated to overthrowing the international system."

Nevertheless, we are going to Geneva, according to Kenneth Adelman, director of the Arms Control and Disarmament Agency (ACDA), because "the passion for 'an agreement' is barely resistable. Paul Nitze, acknowledging "a sharper contrast between the way the U.S. approaches foreign policy issues and the way in which they are approached by the Soviet Union," concluded that "this does not mean we should not negotiate."

Until Western publics obtain a clearer picture of the nature of the Soviet adversary, negotiations will be demanded and politicians will seek some sort of a deal with Moscow.

In his first public statement after being named to head the Geneva bargaining team, negotiator Max M. Kampelman told the Senate Foreign Relations Committee on February 26 that although the Soviet Union was a "repressive" and "aggressive" society, the United States "dares not and cannot blow the Soviet Union away.

"We cannot wish it away," he said, arguing for the necessity of pursuing negotiations. "It is here, and it is militarily powerful. We share the same globe. We must try to find a formula under which we can live together in dignity. We must engage in that pursuit of peace without illusion but with persistence, regardless of provocation."

Kampelman appeared with his fellow Geneva negotiators, former Senator John G. Tower, Maynard Glitman, and Paul Nitze, the senior arms control adviser.

Nitze said it was important to prepare the public "for a long process" in the negotiations because "there are major substantive differences between the approaches of the two sides."

He said the Russians continued to insist that it was impossible to achieve an agreement in one arms control area without agreement in the others. "This is part of their effort," he said, "to bring about an end to American research into space defensive weapons, even though the Russians already have devoted considerable resources into this field."[21]

Committed as we are to playing Russian roulette at Geneva, what criteria should guide the U.S. delegation? First, we can never get a good arms control agreement unless we are fully prepared to live without one. Others include a sound negotiating strategy, incentives to the Soviets, linkage, precision, and verifiability. In the past the United States also needed to be careful of the ego factor—chief negotiators often acquired a personal stake in a successful outcome of negotiations, regardless of their impact on U.S. national security. Yet Max Kampelman's performance at both the Belgrade and the Madrid CSCE meetings can put this fear to rest. At the close of the Madrid meeting Kampelman issued a "warning against euphoria" and denounced the Russians for continuing violations of human rights.

"Signatures on a document do not necessarily produce compliance with its provisions," said Kampelman.

The Soviets replied with a blistering attack on Kampelman. His response took a longer view of optimism, as he explained why the United States had signed the accord at a time of what he said were the worst Soviet human rights abuses in years. "It is because the pursuit of peace is too vital, the need for understanding too indispensable," he said, to "permit us to be discouraged by the task or the obstacles we face."

At Geneva, Kampelman will place U.S. security interests over agreement for agreement's sake. Two experienced, former high-level U.S. officials put this issue squarely. According to Zbigniew Brzezinski, "comprehensive arms control . . . is likely to be the victim of the bloody-mindedness of the present Soviet leadership and of the dynamics of the technological revolution." And Henry S. Rowen, chairman of the National Intelligence Council, 1981–83, was even more blunt: "There is no important U.S. objective related to the balance of nuclear forces, or the role of these forces in discouraging Soviet moves abroad, which is obtainable through any remotely feasible arms control agreement. . . . If we want a better protected and more discriminate nuclear force—and, if possible, a less costly one—we will have to get it on our own."

The chances of any positive results coming out of the Geneva arms control talks are slim indeed. According to a news report:

> "The Soviet Union is entering the talks with an honest striving to achieve practical results," Gorbachev said in a speech reported by the official news agency TASS, before he became the successor to Chernenko. "Regrettably," he continued, "this cannot be said about the approach of the Washington administration. Activities have been launched in the U.S.A. on the eve of the talks that breed doubts over the true intentions of the U.S. side."[22]

This same negative theme was reiterated by Nikolai Shishlin, a consultant to the Secretariat of the Communist Party's Central Committee, in an op-ed piece in *The New York Times*. Rather than reaching an agreement on reducing nuclear armaments:

> Washington has another objective in mind. The American defense budget for 1986 has beaten all records. America continues to modernize its strategic triad. The timetable of missile deployments in Western Europe is being strictly observed. The so-called Strategic Defense Initiative, which envisions militarization of space, has become a pet project of the Administration.

Shishlin then mentioned American support for:

> the counter-revolutionary forces in countries that want to decide their own destinies. This applies to actions with regard to Nicaragua, South Africa, the Middle East and Afghanistan. All this has nothing to do with the Geneva talks, but such actions are not conducive to improvement in Soviet-American relations.

After this exercise in reverse linkage Shishlin turned to the topic of alleged Soviet violations of Arms Control Agreements:

> It is no coincidence that America sparked such speculation shortly before the opening of the talks. It appears that the aim of that campaign is to question the need to continue any agreements with the Soviet Union, or even to conclude new ones.

Shishlin saved his major broadside for his last:

> The Soviet Union prepared for Geneva seriously and is deter-
> mined to do everything to work out mutually acceptable solu-
> tions to the problems that will be discussed there. However, the
> United States has created quite a few problems that will make
> negotiation difficult. This particularly applies to the "Star Wars"
> plan whose implementation would destabilize the international
> situation as a whole and open up new channels for an uncon-
> trolled arms race.[23]

If one views the past Soviet record, the prospects for success in the
Geneva talks are most dismal. How could they be otherwise? The
Soviet Union views arms control negotiations as a theater to be
manipulated in their overall struggle against freedom.

The outcome of the Geneva talks are almost as predictable as
the sun's rising tomorrow. After all the chaff is blown away, the
Soviets will finally demand that the United States abandon its
Strategic Defense Initiative. President Reagan will not give in. The
Soviets will walk out, denouncing U.S. provocation and intran-
sigence.

The European peace movement will erupt into a storm of
anti-American frenzy. The U.S. freeze-niks will march on Washington
and demand that President Reagan be impeached.

The world, however, will not come to an end. Creative minds
will search for other ways of coping with the "Evil Empire."

As negotiations, for a while, take a backseat, more attention
will be paid to the exit line in Beilenson's book:

> Jack Benny, a lifetime success as a comedian, once remarked
> that in comedy the important thing is to know what not to do.
> In relying on treaties, the short guide is simply "don't." In
> making treaties, the passwords for the guide are "selectively,"
> "sparingly," and "cautiously," and when in doubt, "don't." If the
> United States writes those guides upon its gates in such large
> letters that it must see them before it embarks on a treaty
> venture abroad, it will avoid falling into "the treaty trap."[24]

A Postscript

Since the initial writing of this chapter, additional rounds of arms
control negotiations have been held in Geneva with no signs of
progress.

Moscow complained of an American "smokescreen of empty words and indefinite promises," and the chief Soviet delegate, Viktor P. Karpov, said he was still waiting for new proposals.

In contrast, Washington said it had heard new Soviet ideas for reducing strategic weapons, but suggested that they may have been as bad as no ideas at all. The concepts are vague and designed to maintain a Soviet advantage in land-based missiles, United States officials said.[25]

Obviously, the Soviet Union is concerned that the SDI may ultimately render nuclear offensive arms strategically useless. In June 1984 the United States successfully tested a land-based antiballistic missile (ABM). It tracked a dummy ICBM and hit and destroyed it one hundred miles before it would have reached its target. The Soviets, afraid that their hundreds of billions of rubles invested in offensive ICBMs might be wasted, agreed to come back to the bargaining table.

Their aim is to scuttle all U.S. defensive systems, particularly the revolutionary antiballistic missile, which can be deployed under the 1972 ABM Treaty. The United States should move ahead with the new ABM as a separate program from any future space-based systems. This decision is not to be subject to negotiations. We should propose, however, that we mutually agree to amend the 1972 ABM Treaty to permit unrestricted deployment of ABMs by both sides. This proposal would again test Soviet intentions. If they turn it down, it would reconfirm what we already know—that they are committed to a first-strike "win" strategy. We should then exercise the right to withdraw from or ignore the treaty in order to proceed with our own defense.

We simply must recognize, both in our leadership and our public sector, that ever since Lenin, the Soviet Union has been in a state of permanent war against democracy and freedom. For this reason, negotiations at Geneva are unlikely to succeed. We must not forget that past negotiations have served Soviet strategic interests, not ours. Whether the current Geneva talks succeed or fail, we must move quickly to create a balanced defensive-offensive nuclear deterrent so as to convince the Soviet leaders that their archaic empire cannot face the risk of war.

Notes

1. President Ronald Reagan, "Reducing World Tensions." *Current Policy* 615 (September 24, 1984), p. 4.

2. "Geneva and Beyond: New Arms Control Negotiations." *Current Policy* 647 (January 14, 1985.)

3. Leslie H. Gelb and Anthony Lake, "Four More Years: Diplomacy Resolved." *Foreign Affairs* (Spring 1985.)

4. *The New York Times*, March 15, 1985, p. A7.

5. Laurence W. Beilenson, *The Treaty Trap*. (Washington, D.C.: Public Affairs Press, 1969). Foreword by William R. Kintner.

6. George F. Kennan, *American Diplomacy 1900-1950*. (The University of Chicago Press, 1951), p. 95.

7. Beilenson, op. cit., p. 1.

8. Quoted in Ibid, p. 3.

9. Ibid, p. 18.

10. *Washington Alert*, Leadership Foundation, Vol. 3 (February 1985), p. 1.

11. Ibid.

12. American Bar Association, Standing Committee, Law and National Security Intelligence Report, November, 1984. (Chicago: American Bar Association, 1984), p. 1.

13. Ibid, p. 2.

14. Ibid, p. 8.

15. *The New York Times*, February 26, 1985, p. A12.

16. *Current Policy* 650 (January 31, 1985), p. 7.

17. *Pravda*, April 13, 1966. Translated in *Current Digest of the Soviet Press*, May 18, 1966. Address to the Twenty-Third Party Congress of the Communist Party of the Soviet Union.

18. Department of State, Special Report No. 119 (April 1, 1984–October 1, 1984.)

19. Special studies series on foreign affairs issues, Committee print.

20. Beilenson, op. cit., p. 190.

21. *The New York Times*, February 27, 1985, p. 3.

22. *The Philadelphia Inquirer*, February 21, 1985, p. 13A.

23. Nikolai Shishlin, "Soviet Arms in Geneva." *The New York Times*, March 15, 1985, p. A27.

24. Beilenson, op. cit., p. 221.

25. *The New York Times*, July 21, 1985, section 4, p. 1.

SOVIET DECEPTION IN THE UNITED STATES

David Martin with John Rees

Within the past five years, two new terms from the Russian language have entered the vocabulary of those who write about Soviet affairs: *active measures* and *disinformation*. Only recently has the first full-length treatment of Soviet disinformation and active measures (*Dezinformatsia: Active Measures in Soviet Strategy* by Richard H. Shultz and Roy Godson) appeared.[1]

In 1959 a full-fledged Disinformation Department was set up in the Soviet KGB. The principal target of this operation was and remains the United States, its government, and its people. It is not to be concluded from this that disinformation and active measures are new instruments of Soviet foreign policy. Actually, both terms, in more direct English, mean "deception"—and deceptions on a massive scale have been characteristic of international communism ever since the Bolsheviks seized power in the Soviet Union and gave themselves a power base from which to carry on subversive activities directed against every country in the non-Communist world.

In carrying out their repeated campaigns of deception, the Communists have taken advantage of the infinite capacity for self-deception and wishful thinking that is characteristic of democratic peoples. Over and over again, the American people have learned the hard way that the Soviets are the world's foremost liars, jailers, and mass murderers. And just as often they have, within a matter of years, been persuaded by a new round of Soviet propaganda that the Soviets are basically the same as ourselves and that the Soviets desire nothing more than to live and let live in peace.

Thus, when the Soviet government under Lenin introduced the New Economic Policy (NEP) in 1920, it was used to persuade the Free World that the Soviet Communists were becoming more moderate and more respectful of private property, and that, among other things, the Soviet Union welcomed investment by Western

business. Many Western political leaders and businessmen fell for
this line. As Lenin cynically put the matter, when the time comes to
hang the capitalist class, the international capitalists will compete
with one another to sell the Soviets the rope with which to accomplish the hanging.

Thus, too, after U.S. recognition of the Soviet Union in 1934,
the Soviet Union, while continuing its subversive activities in other
countries, underscored the propaganda theme that it was possible
for communism and Western democracy to live side by side in
peace. It called for a "united front" against fascism. Many Western
intellectuals were caught up in such "united front" activities—until
the Soviet Union dashed their illusions by signing the Hitler-Stalin
Pact and collaborating with the Nazis in the dismemberment of
Poland. The theme of "peaceful coexistence" then took hold, despite
the fact that the Soviets, to the dismay of government bureaucrats
who were hardheaded enough to realize what was going on, used
their new relationship to pull off "the largest programmatic theft in
history, cleaning out the capitalists' larder and paying for it with a
bad check."

The Hitler-Stalin Pact brought the American people back to
sober appreciation of the historic villainy of the "Evil Empire." But
almost overnight the Nazi invasion of the Soviet Union converted
the Soviets into a Jeffersonian democracy.

The Soviets once again used deception on a strategic scale and
put at rest any misgivings Western governments might have about
postwar Soviet intentions when they disbanded—or said they had
disbanded—the Communist International and made noises that convinced both Roosevelt and Churchill that the Soviet Union after
World War II would be a restrained and cooperative partner.

The Soviet Purchasing Commission in Washington, during our
wartime alliance, "abused and exploited every extension of good
faith and trust by Americans who were anxious to aid the Allied
cause. . . . Industrial processes, entire turnkey refineries, strategic
raw materials, scientific instruments, radio manufacturing plants . . .
and thousands of designs, drawings, patents and proprietary secrets
sluiced out to the USSR by air and sea."

The ultimate result, as everyone knows, was the employment
of the Red Army to incorporate the countries of Eastern Europe
into the empire of the Iron Curtain.

In their strategic campaigns of deception the Soviets have been
helped immeasurably by the Western media. For example, Walter

Duranty, the Moscow correspondent for *The New York Times* during the 1930s, was a close friend of both Stalin and Roosevelt. On repeated visits to Washington he briefed Roosevelt at length about the situation in the Soviet Union. In print he vehemently denied rumors that Stalin's man-made famine in the Ukraine had cost the lives of several million farmers. But in an offhand manner on a *New York Times* elevator, he admitted to John Chamberlain, then also a member of the *New York Times* staff, that there had indeed been a man-made famine and that it had cost the lives of some three million Ukrainian peasants. When Chamberlain incorporated this information into a book review, Duranty denied that he had made the statement attributed to him. However, Simeon Strunsky, a *Times* columnist who had been on the elevator with Chamberlain and Duranty, confirmed Chamberlain's account. Malcolm Muggeridge, who knew Duranty in Moscow, described him as "the greatest liar of any journalist I have met in fifty years of journalism." Not surprisingly, Duranty was awarded the Pulitzer Prize in 1932 for his Moscow reporting.

Before Castro's accession to power, Herbert L. Matthews of *The New York Times* played a similar role by deceiving the American people and selling Castro to the American government and to the American public as a combination of Robin Hood and Thomas Jefferson.

In situation after situation, the Soviets have deceived the leaders of the United States and other Western governments, the Western media, and, to a large extent, Western public opinion as a whole. In a disturbing number of situations, the Communists have been able to manipulate Western governments into pursuing precisely those policies that best serve the ends of Soviet expansionism.

More recently, as a result of statements made both by important Vietnamese defectors and by officials of the North Vietnamese government, we have learned something of the nature and scale of the deception practiced on the Vietnamese people and the U.S. government at the time of the Vietnam War.

Al Santoli, the Vietnam War veteran who wrote *To Bear Any Burden*,[2] quotes Le Duc Tho, the chief North Vietnamese negotiator at the Paris peace talks in 1972, as saying, "For the fifth time we have declared clearly that the DRV government [Hanoi] and the PRG [Viet Cong] have never wished to force a Communist government on South Vietnam."

Santoli also quotes Truong Nhu Tang, minister of justice in the shadow Viet Cong government from 1960 until the end of the war, as saying:

> Our aim was to present ourselves to the world as a large representation of the South's population. And the American media is easily open to suggestion and false information given by Communist agents. The society is completely hypnotized by the media. . . .
>
> The tragedy was that the PRG (Viet Cong) told international and Vietnamese public opinion that our movement is a nationalist movement, with our end to create a democratic Vietnam. And that our political regime would not be Communist. . . .
>
> In South Vietnam, religious organizations, like Buddhists or Catholics, protested the regime. But behind them were always some political activists who were Communists. This is a tactic we call "the watermelon"—green on the outside and red on the inside. . . .
>
> We were not so much looking for supporters, but rather for opponents to the American and Saigon regimes in order to create a crisis among allied governments of the free world. And paralyze them so that they cannot act. And to isolate the U.S. government from its people.

The Communists practice deception at two levels: overt and covert. Overt deception usually involves propaganda conveyed by media under Communist control and diplomatic initiatives. Covert measures include forgeries, "black" propaganda, and front organizations, nominally acting independently but in reality under tight Soviet control. The astonishing success of their front operations has been made possible by thousands of woolly-headed sympathizers in every country and the even greater numbers of those who lend themselves to manipulation because of their commitment to a single issue like "peace" or "disarmament." These react with indignation to the accusation that they are Communist sympathizers—but they nevertheless play the Communist game. These are the so-called "useful idiots," to employ a term that Lenin made famous. The tragedy is that quite a few of the "useful idiots" are really highly intelligent people who can nevertheless be manipulated because of their political naiveté.

Why do so many intelligent people lend themselves to political manipulation? In October 1982 the Leadership Foundation monitored an International Awareness Day at Mary Baldwin College at Staunton, Virginia. The program featured six Soviet "average citizens," members of the World Peace Council, who ostensibly were acting on their own in visiting the United States because of their intense personal commitment to "peace." They were presented as traveling under the auspices of the United Church of Christ and the World Council of Churches. Apparently the president of the college was unaware that both organizations had played major and consistent roles in fronting for Soviet-controlled "peace" movements. The Leadership Foundation monitor reported that "from the very outset, the leader of the Soviet group took gentle but absolute control of the meeting. He immediately achieved a rapport with his audience through his laid-back, kindly manner. . . . The presentation made by the Russian delegation was extremely effective, to the point that even I found myself wanting to believe them."

One of the principal reasons for the success of this Soviet propaganda mission was the basic honesty of the American people. There is a great tendency to impute a similar degree of honesty to visitors from other countries. Thus, the young women at Mary Baldwin College found it difficult to believe that a group of Soviet citizens, free of all control from their own government and sponsored by two ostensibly reputable church organizations, would come over to the United States for the express purpose of lying to them. Taking advantage both of the basic ignorance of their audience and of the predisposition of this audience to believe the best about the Soviet guests, the Soviet propagandist troupe gambled successfully on their ability to get away with gross factual inaccuracies and glaring omissions in their presentation on the nuclear freeze.

The young women at Mary Baldwin, for example, were unaware that Lenin had taught that "war is simply a continuation of politics by other means." Nor were they aware that more recently, Brezhnev, at the Twenty-Fifth Congress of the CPSU in 1976, had said:

> Bourgeois politicians . . . raise a howl over the solidarity of Communists and the Soviet people with the struggle of the peoples for freedom and progress. This is either naiveté or, more likely, deliberate obfuscation. . . . Peaceful coexistence . . . does not in the slightest abolish, and it cannot abolish or alter, the laws of class struggle.

At the time Brezhnev spoke these words, the Soviet Union, through its program of massive military aid to North Vietnam, but primarily thanks to its propaganda and deception activities, had succeeded by proxy in bringing about the first military defeat of the United States since the founding of the Republic. (No combat unit of the U.S. Army was ever defeated by a Vietnamese force during the entire war in Vietnam. But the Communist takeover after the Paris peace agreement of 1973 represented a major defeat for U.S. policy objectives.)

Since that time, Department A of the Sixth Directorate of the KGB, which is responsible for orchestrating deception measures, has moved from one anti–United States campaign to another, hardly stopping to catch its breath.

First, there was the campaign against the neutron bomb in 1977–78, which finally had the effect of constraining President Carter to call off his planned production and deployment of the neutron weapon.

Then in quick order there were the campaign against the B-1 bomber, the campaign against Pershing and cruise missiles, the campaign against the Strategic Defense Initiative (nicknamed Star Wars by the media in an effort to make the project look silly), and the campaign against new binary munitions for chemical warfare. Where the rearmament of America is involved, the Communists and the World Peace Council (WPC) and their numerous satellites can always be counted on to take the opposition—and tens of thousands of innocents will always follow them. The Communists, the WPC, and their satellites can also be counted on to support Soviet aggression, as they did in Budapest and Prague and Afghanistan and Kampuchea, and to excoriate all attempts by the United States to respond to the Soviet threat, even in its own backyard in Central America.

In May 1982 Vladimir Bukovsky, the famed Soviet dissident, wrote:

> There is a term in party jargon coined by Lenin himself: a useful idiot. . . . The Soviet rulers have scored a spectacular victory: they have recruited millions of useful idiots to implement their bankrupt foreign policy. . . . We are into only the second year of a planned ten-year "struggle for peace." Within a few years, the whole earth will be trembling under marching feet of the useful idiots, for their resources are inexhaustible.[3]

A month after this article appeared, the "peace" movement in the United States was able to mobilize an estimated 700,000 "marchers for peace" in New York City.

The Soviet campaign of deception has been targeted not only against the U.S. defense establishment but against political objectives essential to the strategic defense of the United States. For example, the Soviet Union has been actively involved in a campaign to bring about "disinvestment" in South Africa. Soviet defectors have warned the Western nations for years that the Soviet Union places priority on the conquest of political power in South Africa and Southwest Africa, both of them treasure houses of rare mineral deposits. If they achieve this, the Soviets will be able to deny the United States access to minerals that are of critical importance to our defense industries.

The active membership of the Communist Party in the United States (CPUSA) probably numbers no more than ten thousand. But this strength is multiplied tenfold when one adds to it the numbers of fellow travelers and demi–fellow travelers and the numerous Marxist groups who have differences with the Communist Party but who almost invariably unite with them when it comes to opposing the foreign policy of the United States or our defense buildup. And the actual political influence of the Communist Party undergoes another major increase when one adds to their power, again, the truly staggering number of decent, patriotic citizens who are deceived and manipulated on issues like the nuclear freeze, often taking the lead from basically patriotic and religious organizations that are similarly prone to manipulation.

The Soviet Forgery Offensive

Before we go on to deal with the Soviet "peace" campaign, it would be appropriate at this point to devote a few paragraphs to the Soviet forgery offensive because it helps to demonstrate the Soviet penchant for dishonesty on a criminal scale.

The Soviet forgery offensive was the subject of three reports put out by the Department of State in 1981, 1982, and 1983. A review of these three documents reveals how widespread, indeed, how commonplace, these Soviet forgeries have become. Most of them are surfaced through the international press. Some of them are fed to foreign governments in order to create or intensify frictions with the United States. In the following paragraphs, we shall briefly discuss several of the numerous identified forgeries that the Soviets have used to make mischief in the Western world. In each case the forgery was designed to serve either the Soviet peace campaign or some other current objective of Soviet anti-U.S. policy. The following items are taken from the State Department round-ups:[4]

Spain: In November 1981, at a time when negotiations were going on to bring Spain into NATO and when the Conference of Security and Cooperation in Europe (CSCE) was meeting in Madrid, journalists in Madrid and delegations to the CSCE mysteriously received copies of what purported to be a personal letter from Ronald Reagan to the King of Spain urging him to crack down on *"Opus Dei* pacificists" and other left-wing elements with a view to smashing the anti-NATO opposition. The letter, which was written on White House stationery, bore a remarkably good facsimile of Ronald Reagan's signature. It was a complete fraud.

Nuclear weapons: In 1967, for the first time, the Soviet disinformation apparatus surfaced a doctored U.S. military planning document showing supposed U.S. nuclear targets in Western Europe. The document was promptly denounced as a fraud. Since first being printed in the Norwegian magazine *Orientering,* the document and charges based on it have resurfaced more than twenty times in various countries, most recently in Austria in December 1982.

Falkland Islands: In May 1982, at the time of the Falklands crisis, the Communist disinformation apparatus came up with a fraudulent Pentagon press release reporting on comments that had never been made by Secretary of Defense Caspar Weinberger. The purpose of the press release was to exacerbate relations both with Great Britain and the Latin American countries. On the one hand it said that U.S. support for Great Britain will lead to the establishment of a U.S. military base "from which we will assert our control of the whole of the Latin American continent." On the other hand it spoke of "the stubborn policy of Argentina, Peru, Venezuela, and Brazilia [sic]."

India: In February 1983 the Communist disinformation apparatus in India surfaced a fake speech by UN Ambassador Jeane Kirkpatrick on U.S. policy toward India and the Third World. According to the speech, the United States was in favor of "balkanizing" India. The Soviet press as well as that of the other Communist countries gave this completely phony speech extensive coverage—as did the Indian press.

Ghana: In March 1983, basing itself on forged West German documents, the government of Ghana accused the United States of plotting to overthrow the government of President Rawlings.

Nigeria: In April 1983 a forged U.S. Embassy document had Ambassador Thomas Pickering ordering the assassination of a principal Nigerian presidential candidate in a mythical "Operation Headache."

KGB, the World Peace Council, and the World "Peace" Machinery

Soviet active measures involve the cooperation of several major departments of the Soviet government. While the guidance of the Communist parties worldwide and of their various international and national front organizations falls under the International Department of the Central Committee of the CPSU, it is the First Directorate of the KGB that orchestrates the entire disinformation program.

Also heavily involved, although it is limited to active measures of the overt kind, is the International Information Department of the Central Committee, which has responsibility for Soviet broadcasts, for TASS and *Izvestia*, and for other components of the news media complex. It commands an international program of formidable magnitude that apparently keeps on expanding and expanding. In contrast the U.S. Congress is reluctant to add to the facilities of the Voice of America or Radio Free Europe or to inaugurate a "Radio Liberation" aimed at Cuba to combat Soviet world propaganda. For example, in 1960 the Soviet broadcasting effort internationally totaled just over 1,000 hours. A decade later this figure had doubled to 2,155 hours. By 1980 there had been another major increase that brought the total hours of broadcasting to 2,762 a week, in over eighty languages. In comparison, the current combined figures for the Voice of America, Radio Free

Europe, and Radio Liberty stand at approximately two thousand hours per week, in forty-six languages.

In its manipulation of the "world peace movement," Moscow relies much more heavily on its front organizations than it does on the Communist parties in separate countries, although the Communist parties operate as conduits and coordinators. At the forefront of these organizations is the World Peace Council (WPC), which was established in 1949, and its affiliate, the U.S. Peace Council (USPC), established in 1978. Although the WPC has involved many thousands of non-Communist Westerners in its activities, and although WPC delegations have sometimes been fawned upon by the American media and American politicians, there can be no question that the entire operation is owned and controlled, lock, stock, and barrel, by the Soviet Union.

In 1981 the WPC applied for Category 1 Consultative Status with the UN Economic and Social Council (ECOSOC). ECOSOC, to its credit, demands publicly audited financial statements from organizations granted Consultative Status. This was a condition that the WPC could not and would not meet. The ECOSOC report of March 16, 1981, said that WPC accounts:

> are not submitted to an independent audit. . . . The financial statement submitted to the committee covered only a fraction of the WPC's actual income and expenditures. . . . In its application, the World Peace Council also stated that it does not receive contributions from any government. . . . But the representative of the organization [Romesh Chandra] carefully avoided answering specific questions put to him by members of the committee on that point. It is clear, however, that the World Peace Council has received large-scale financial support from government sources, and has gone to great lengths to conceal the fact from the committee.[5]

Not very surprisingly, the WPC withdrew its application. The Soviet press, moreover, has been very frank about income received by the WPC from Soviet sources. Thus, it announced that the Soviet "church officials" contributed three million rubles, and the Soviet Peace Fund $200,000.

There have also been numerous confirmed instances of KGB involvement in World Peace Council activities in individual countries. In connection with activities conducted under the umbrella of the WPC, Soviet Embassy officials were declared persona non grata in

Norway, in Denmark, in Switzerland, in France, and in other countries for "unacceptable interference" in the internal affairs of these nations. The Soviet officials expelled were in most cases identified as KGB agents, and a number of nationals in the countries affected were arrested.

The WPC has the distinction of never differing with Soviet policy. In this respect its record is far more slavish than that of the European Communist parties, most of which have differed on one or more issues with Moscow. Thus, a conference convened by the WPC on the heels of the December 1979 NATO decision to counter the growing force of Soviet SS-20s targeted against Western Europe not only avoided all criticism of the Soviet Union but did not even discuss or mention the growing force of SS-20s, which now numbers over 414 missiles, each with three warheads.

Run down the issues dividing the Soviet Union from the United States issue by issue, and you will find the WPC on the side of the Soviets one hundred percent of the time—whether it is the false charge that the Americans waged germ warfare in Korea, or opposition to the Vietnam War, or opposition to the MX missile, the neutron bomb, and the B-1 bomber.

Romesh Chandra, president of the WPC and a leading Indian Communist, justifies the WPC's unbroken record of support for the Soviet Union in these terms: "The Soviet Union's military policy fully corresponds to these goals [peace and opposition to imperialism]. It is of a purely defensive character." On another occasion, Chandra said that the World Peace Council "positively reacts to all Soviet initiatives in international affairs."

In its campaigns, the WPC is automatically assured of the assistance of the other major Soviet international fronts, including the World Federation of Trade Unions (WFTU), the Afro-Asian Peoples Solidarity Organization (AAPSO), the International Union of Students (IUS), the International Institute for Peace (IIP), the International Organization of Journalists (IOJ), the Christian Peace Conference (CPC), the Women's International Federation (WIF), and the International Association of Democratic Lawyers (IADL). There are at least a score of other international fronts, but these are the principal ones.

Given the fact that its greatest strength is in the Communist countries where cooperation with the WPC is somewhat less than voluntary, it is not surprising that the WPC was able to present the Secretary General of the United Nations on one occasion with a petition signed with 400 million signatures, and on a more recent occasion with a petition on which they claimed 700 million signatures.

The Campaign Against the Neutron Bomb

In early 1977 it was revealed that the U.S. government planned to complete the research and development on the neutron bomb and to deploy this weapon in Europe.

The neutron bomb, a concept developed by nuclear physicist Sam Cohen, is a modified nuclear device that accomplishes its effect, not by blast or heat as conventional nuclear bombs do, but by an intense emission of uncharged particles of matter called neutrons—particles so tiny that they can penetrate up to several feet of concrete. It does not leave large tracts of land radioactive and uninhabitable, as our hydrogen bomb tests at Bikini did. Sometimes called an "enhanced radiation weapon," its burst of neutrons lasts for only thousandths of a second. It does not kick up clouds of radioactive debris, because the blast effect does not reach the ground; indeed, it produces so little lingering radioactivity that the area where it has been used can be entered almost immediately.

Its range is roughly from one-quarter of a mile to one mile. It can therefore be used in the vicinity of built-up areas with a degree of discretion designed to save civilian life impossible with other nuclear weapons. All of these qualities make it the ideal weapon for use against the massive Soviet tank formations. The crewmen inside the tanks would not be protected by their armor and would immediately become incapacitated and die within a day or several days. The tanks would remain unharmed. (Those who received a nonlethal exposure, however, would far more often than not, recover without any adverse effects.)

Whether the Soviets had tested the neutron bomb or not at the time they launched their campaign against American production of the bomb is not known. What is known with certainty is that the Soviets had been familiar since the early 1960s with the basic theory behind the bomb and had been working on it. Descriptions of war with the West in Soviet military theoretical publications have always assumed that the Soviets would triumph quickly in a blitzkreig campaign, spearheaded by thousands of tanks, in which the Soviets have an enormous superiority over the combined NATO forces.

Not very surprisingly, therefore, the Soviets opposed the neutron bomb or, to be more precise, opposed U.S. manufacture of the neutron bomb, with all the energy at their disposal.

The bomb was called a typical "capitalist weapon" that spared property but destroyed people.

In their effort to force the United States to reverse its decision, the entire machinery of the U.S. and world peace movements was mobilized and given the full support of the Soviet propaganda apparatus. Indeed, in broadcasts in many languages from July 25 to August 14, 1977, fully 13 percent of news and commentary items broadcast by Moscow was on the subject of the neutron bomb. The events that followed pointed to a carefully integrated plan of action.

During the week of August 1 to 7, according to the CIA, the Soviet media repeatedly called attention to the international "week of action" against the neutron bomb, planned by the World Peace Council for August 6–13.[6]

The Communist bloc nations of Eastern Europe followed suit, with heavy press, radio, and television attention focused on the issue and with demonstrations and organized petitions and letter writing.

All over the world, even in backward countries where one would not expect the populace to be knowledgeable or interested in such exotic weapons as the neutron bomb, Communist propaganda was able to whip up a highly voluble and organizationally successful campaign of hysteria directed against the neutron bomb. There were demonstrations in India, in Pakistan and Japan, in Bonn and in Frankfurt, in Stuttgart and in Dusseldorf and protests from Tanzania, Istanbul, and Lima. Indeed, everywhere one turned people seemed to be protesting against the neutron bomb.

As an immediate reaction to this outcry, Secretary of Defense Harold Brown announced that President Carter would not approve production of the neutron bomb until the other NATO nations agreed to deploy the weapon.

The Bureau of the Presidium of the World Peace Council, meeting in Berlin from September 9 to 12, welcomed "the world protest against the neutron bomb—a torture weapon being cynically presented as a so-called 'clean' bomb by the United States Administration." The Bureau urgently called "for worldwide actions during the fortnight October 1 to 15, under the slogan: '*Against the Neutron Bomb and All Other Weapons of Mass Destruction*.'" It appealed for meetings, mass rallies, demonstrations, petitions, use of the media, and "letters of protest, especially to the President of the United States, against the development of the neutron bomb."

Communist front organizations, needless to say, were prompt to join the campaign. But Moscow propaganda endowed the neutron bomb with such scary qualities that scores of thousands of ordinary people in the Western European countries joined the protest. Even the moderate and conservative West European press, generally pro-NATO, was infected by the hysteria.

During the week of January 22–28, 1978, the bureau of the World Peace Council met in Washington, D.C., to review the campaign against the neutron bomb.

On February 1 in Mexico City, there took place the Second Continental Latin American and Caribbean Conference on Peace and Sovereignty. The Conference, jointly sponsored by the WPC and its satellite the Mexican Peace Movement, joined the international hysteria that had been whipped up against the neutron bomb.

In Geneva on February 27, 1978, the WPC, acting through an ad hoc group called the Special Nongovernmental Organizations Committee on Disarmament, staged a much larger meeting of 126 representatives of "peace" organizations from fifty countries. Romesh Chandra also presided over this meeting.

On March 18–20, 1978, the Dutch Communist Party played a role of central importance in organizing an "international forum against the neutron bomb." Sympathizers from all over Europe were brought in by car and train and by air for the conference, which wound up on March 19 with a demonstration of some forty thousand persons in Amsterdam.

As a result of its campaign of untruths and half-truths and the widespread ignorance of the real nature of the neutron bomb, the Soviet propaganda assault was successful to the point where, as one Italian source indicated, it was impossible to tell left from right on the bomb issue. The result was that the Carter Administration, battered from right, left, and center, announced on April 4, 1978, that it had decided to postpone production and deployment of the neutron weapon—despite the fact that Chancellor Helmut Schmidt of West Germany had agreed to deploy it over strong opposition from his own party.

The Communists did not hesitate to identify the central role they had played in the fight against the neutron bomb. In September 1979 the chief of the International Department of the Hungarian Communist Party, Janosz Berecz, wrote:

The political campaign against the Neutron Bomb was one of the most significant and most successful since World War II. . . . It was a good program that the European Communist and Workers' Parties adopted in Berlin three years ago, but we think it is in our common interest to make greater efforts than so far for the implementation of this program and for strengthening the anti-imperialist unity.[7]

During the first days of August 1981, the Reagan Administration announced that it planned to produce a quantity of neutron bombs but that they would be retained in the continental United States instead of being stationed in Europe. The Soviet propaganda apparatus reacted with predictable hysteria to this announcement. *Pravda,* on August 11, said that the "horrendous decision to produce the neutron weapon is the latest step in the present Administration's adventuristic policies, for the neutron bomb is one of the most refined and barbaric means of mass destruction. It is a weapon which produces an exceptionally high level of radiation, directed not against military targets or hardware, but against human beings."

On August 13 a Soviet English-language transmission quoted a TASS commentator as saying, "The ruling circles of the United States are in the grips of dangerous insanity. This is the only way to assess President Reagan's decision on the production of neutron weapons and the motives by which he is guided."

On August 18 TASS reported that the representatives of the German Democratic Republic, Hungary, Czechoslovakia, Mongolia, Cuba, and Romania to the UN Disarmament Committee had joined the Soviet representatives in strongly condemning "the decision of the U.S. Administration to start full-scale production and stockpiling of the neutron weapon. They described it as a blow to international security and the process of disarmament talks as a whole."

Despite the sustained and vicious nature of the attacks that were made on the United States as a result of the Reagan decision, President Reagan did not reverse himself or falter or, for that matter, "bat an eyelash."[8]

The WPC condemned "in the strongest possible terms" Reagan's decision to assemble a quantity of neutron weapons. In a statement issued in September 1981, it appealed for continued agitation against the neutron bomb, urging its followers to write to President Reagan and members of Congress, to newspapers and other mass media, and to organize referenda and ballot initiatives. "Remember, no matter how insignificant or small an activity you undertake may seem to you," said the WPC, "it adds to the weight of the national and international campaign."

The clamor did not die down for some time. But President Reagan refused to give an inch. Ultimately, no doubt because the Soviets realized that they were fighting a losing battle, the campaign tapered off to the point where the neutron bomb merited no more than a casual and occasional mention in Soviet propaganda. This does not mean that the Soviet propaganda apparatus and the WPC became quiescent. On the contrary, without pausing, they launched into a series of new campaigns—the nuclear weapons freeze campaign, the campaign against deployment of the MX missile, and the campaign against the emplacement of cruise and Pershing missiles in Europe.

The WPC and the United States

Until 1979 the WPC was content to let the CPUSA coordinate its activities in this country. In late 1979, however, the WPC and the International Department of the CPSU decided that it would be advantageous to have a U.S. Peace Council (USPC) that could act in its own name on the national theater. Following the pattern established by the World Peace Council and its affiliates in other countries, the two top leadership positions were given to prominent members of the CPUSA, Sandra Pollak and Michael Myerson. (Since that time, peace councils have been organized in many of the fifty states.)

The memorandum on "Soviet Active Measures Relating to the U.S. Peace Movement," issued in March 1983 by the FBI Intelligence Division, noted that the CPSU International Department had instructed the CPUSA to place high priority on the issue of arms control, disarmament, and the peace movement, and that the CPUSA had responded with fervor to the Soviet request. It had organized symposia, conferences, and demonstrations and had distributed quantities of publications. It had sponsored tours of major American cities by high-level WPC delegations. And it had been able on various issues to assemble a national coalition of organizations of formidable strength.

In this activity it had been given important assistance by another Soviet front organization, the National Council of American

Soviet Friendship (NCASF). On paper, the NCASF is supposed to be an independent organization. Its purpose, ostensibly, is to promote friendship, understanding, and cultural and educational exchanges between the peoples of the United States and the Soviet Union. In practice, however, the NCASF works unremittingly to advance the political and foreign policy objectives of the Soviets.

The FBI Intelligence Division noted that during April–June 1982 the NCASF had sponsored three separate Soviet delegations on tours of the United States. Two of these delegations had made propaganda tours of cities on the West Coast, promoting the U.S. peace movement and attacking U.S. positions on nuclear disarmament and other disarmament issues. The impact of the Soviet delegation was maximized because of the great attention they received from the local media and from radio and television talk shows. The third Soviet delegation conducted a parallel propaganda operation in cities on the East Coast.

At the third national convention of the NCASF, which took place in Madison, Wisconsin, from September 11 to 13, 1981, two Soviet representatives addressed the assembly and participated actively in workshop discussions. They were Vadim Gorin, Deputy Secretary General of the USSR–USA Friendship Society in Moscow, and Vladimir Zolotukhin of the Soviet Embassy in Washington, D.C. Needless to say, they presented the Soviet position, sparing no criticism of U.S. government policy. Conversely, Soviet peace proposals were praised to the skies.

Not very surprisingly, the NCASF convention called on the U.S. government to abandon its plans to manufacture and deploy the neutron bomb and endorsed the Soviet call for a freeze on production, research, and deployment of nuclear weapons. Delegates were instructed to organize petitions to senators, especially to the members of the Senate Foreign Relations Committee, to congressmen, and to President Reagan and to conduct local campaigns to persuade mayors and city councils and state governments to adopt resolutions calling for a nuclear freeze.

The FBI Intelligence report of March 1983 noted that "the Soviets systematically used the NCASF-sponsored tours to promote Soviet policies and propaganda concerning peace and disarmament to the American people and to conduct covert active measures." The report further noted that a twenty-one-member Soviet "tourist" group that arrived in Los Angeles from Mexico City on April 29, 1982, was taken under the wing of the NCASF for a twelve-day tour of Los Angeles, San Francisco, and San Diego, as was a sixteen-member Soviet "tourist" group that arrived in San Diego a month later, in June 1982. In both cases the NCASF was successful in maximizing the presence of the Soviet visitors by arranging meetings, press conferences, radio, and television interviews for them.

Apart from the U.S. Peace Council and the National Council of American-Soviet Friendship, there are numerous organizations and "scholarly" institutes in the United States that are militantly opposed to U.S. national security and foreign policy and whose positions on an array of issues are identical, or virtually identical, to those of the Moscow and Castro governments. Not very surprisingly, these organizations are all heavily involved in the U.S. "peace" movement.

For example, the Institute for Policy Studies (IPS) in Washington, D.C., functions as the principal think tank of the left wing in this country. The IPS has managed to achieve a surprising degree of respectability, thanks to the attitude of the media and of a number of members of Congress. While there may not be the kind of hard proof that there is in the case of the World Peace Council to establish that the IPS is a Communist front organization, there can be no doubt where the IPS really stands. Let us examine five of the most revealing criteria:

First, where there are sharp disagreements between Castro's Cuba and the United States, the IPS is invariably on the side of Cuba.

Second, the IPS displays a uniform enthusiasm for Third World terrorists and revolutionary movements, including the Palestine Liberation Organization.

Third, the IPS has been heavily involved in anti-U.S. intelligence activities, including the publication of *CounterSpy* and collaboration with CIA defector Philip Agee.

Fourth, it has been directly involved in the creation of subversive cells in the U.S. armed forces and has talked about creating a mass soldier organization with a view to "crippling military effectiveness."

Fifth, its publications and spokesmen have expressed jubilation over Communist victories and American humiliation in Vietnam, Cambodia, and Laos. Several IPS spokesmen defended the murderous Pol Pot regime in Cambodia against the charge—supported by the testimony of thousands of refugees—that it had killed somewhere between one million and two million Cambodians to establish Democratic Kampuchea in that sad country.

With the help of organizations like the IPS, which bat close to one hundred percent in support of the Soviet line, and of numerous other organizations that, although not quite as orthodox, support the Soviet-WPC line on "peace" and on other issues, the World Peace Council and the U.S. Peace Council have made themselves a formidable destructive force in American politics.

All of the earlier activities came together on June 12, 1982, when a coalition of the U.S. Peace Council and numerous other American organizations brought out almost 700,000 people (according to New York City police estimates) from across the country to demonstrate for peace, disarmament, and a nuclear freeze in front of the United Nations. The demonstration was timed to coincide with the Second U.N. Special Session on Disarmament (SSOD II).

In November 1981 a high-level delegation of the World Peace Council sat in on the second National Conference of USPC. Romesh Chandra, president of the WPC, gave a characteristically pro-Soviet presentation and called on the delegates to thwart U.S. plans to modernize theater nuclear weapons.

Of course, the 700,000 people who turned out at the UN rally were not all Communists or under Communist control. As the FBI report was careful to note:

> Based on the information available to us, we do not believe the Soviets have achieved a dominant role in the U.S. peace or nuclear freeze movement, or that they control or manipulate the movement. The Soviets, however, do not view direct control or manipulation of a movement as a necessary prerequisite or condition for a successful active measures campaign. The Soviet peace campaign, for instance, is designed to focus public attention on new American nuclear weapons systems and to help create the impression that the Soviet Union is more interested than the United States in serious arms control and disarmament negotiations. This campaign does not require direct Soviet control or manipulation to be effective. The Soviets believe they can achieve these objectives through a planned series of arms control and disarmament proposals that play on the sentiments of the Western peace movements in concert with the systematic use of the Soviet worldwide propaganda apparatus, international fronts, and local communist parties, and trusted contacts and agents.[9]

In covering the release of the FBI Intelligence report, the American media concentrated heavily on the first sentence in the above paragraph and glossed over or ignored the rest of the paragraph and, for that matter, the rest of the report.

They ignored, for example, the fact that the CPUSA had held an Extraordinary Conference in Milwaukee, Wisconsin, in April 1982 to plan their participation in the New York rally, and that it placed representatives on the June 12 committee in addition to the two representatives that the USPC already had on it. As the FBI Intelligence report notes:

> Soviet-controlled organizations participated at the highest levels of the June 12 committee and exerted pressure to influence the June 12 committee to focus on U.S. nuclear weapons policies as opposed to Soviet policies.

An article by Ronald Radosh in *The New Republic* at the time stated that the U.S. Peace Council made vigorous efforts to "tone down the official rally call so that it was not equally addressed to the United States and the Soviet Union." The official call—which must be considered an outcome of the unequal struggle between the hard ideological determination of the Communist minority and the disunity and flabbiness of the non-Communist majority—was a clear victory for the CPUSA-USPC group. The official call said:

> The demonstration addresses all governments which have developed nuclear arms and which compete in the international arms race, but its primary focus is on the United States government. Possessing more nuclear bombs than all other countries combined and leading the technological, first-strike weapons race, the U.S. government is the least willing to stop its nuclear insanity. The demonstrators are absolutely clear that only when there is a strong citizen's movement to reverse and end the arms race will the U.S. government change its policies regarding first use, first-strike and nuclear deterrence. The June 12th Rally reveals once again that the disarmament movement in the United States is rapidly growing and increasingly powerful.

The dismal compromise that this wording represented really constituted a near-total victory for the Soviet position loudly proclaimed here in our own country. It was a major deception of the non-Communists involved as well as all other Americans affected.

Active Measures: The Case of South Africa

As we write these lines, U.S. governmental sanctions of some kind are about to be imposed on South Africa. Toward the end of last year the case of South Africa became headline news in the American press. Under the overall management of TransAfrica, a steady stream of VIPs, Republicans, Democrats, clergymen, and professionals demonstrated outside the South African Embassy. The demonstrators deliberately crossed police lines in order to get themselves arrested, and the press was quick to print photos of various dignitaries being led away in handcuffs.

The goal of this protest movement was, on the surface, a freer, more dignified life for the people of South Africa. To achieve this goal the demonstrators urged legislation that would result in withdrawal of all investment in South Africa and other economic sanctions, including an embargo on shipments of oil.

The great majority of those who participated in these protest demonstrations were not by any stretch of the imagination Communists or Communist sympathizers. They simply took the professed goals of the managers of the demonstrations at face value.

There can be no question about the political sympathies of Randall Robinson, the leader of TransAfrica, or about precisely how the campaign against South Africa plays into the hands of the Soviets.

Randall Robinson and TransAfrica have been consistent and vociferous supporters of Marxism in African countries, both in those countries that already have Marxists in power—Angola, Mozambique, the Brazzaville Congo, Zimbabwe, and Ethiopia—and in those countries where the Marxists are contending for power—primarily South Africa and Southwest Africa. They have also been consistent opponents of the black African freedom movements that have been fighting the Marxist governments of Angola and Mozambique and that would almost certainly have come to power if it had not been for the thirty thousand Cubans in Angola and for the many thousands of East-bloc personnel in Mozambique. They have also been consistent admirers of Fidel Castro, of Libyan dictator Muamar Qaddafi, and of slain Grenadan Marxist Prime Minister Maurice Bishop. Robinson has featured Sam Nujoma, the head of the Marxist-Leninist South West People's Organization (SWAPO), and Oliver Tambo, the head of the African National Congress (ANC)—an adjunct of the South African Communist Party—at TransAfrica functions in different parts of the country. Both of these organizations have engaged in bloody acts of terrorism and are under complete Soviet control.

The political goals of both the ANC and SWAPO were the subject of a heavily documented report put out by the Senate Subcommittee on Security and Terrorism in November 1982. Among those who testified was Bartholomew Hlapane, a former leader of both the South African Communist Party (SACP) and the ANC. Hlapane said, "No major decision could be taken by the ANC without the concurrence or approval of the Central Committee of the SACP. Most major developments were in fact initiated by the Central Committee." In late December 1982, Senator Jeremiah Denton informed the Senate that both Bartholomew Hlapane and his wife were assassinated in Soweto on December 16, 1982.

As the State Department has pointed out, South Africa has made some dramatic moves to dismantle apartheid in recent years. Indeed, it has made more progress in the past four years than in the entire preceding era.

By all means let America use its great moral authority to persuade and assist the South African people to move toward policies that properly respect human rights. But let's do so independently of those who, speaking in the name of "liberation," really plan to fasten a far more pernicious form of servitude on the South African people as a whole. Let us not be deceived by Soviet-controlled activists in the United States.

In shaping our foreign policy, we cannot forget that the United States is heavily dependent on South Africa for a number of critical minerals. South Africa possesses 83.6 percent of the world's chrome, 80.8 percent of its platinum, 70.8 percent of manganese, 47.1 of all vanadium, and considerable reserves of other minerals that are in short supply internationally. Nor must we forget that South Africa is vitally important to the United States strategically; twenty-five thousand ships a year pass around the Cape of Good Hope, including the majority of the supertankers carrying oil from the Middle East and Indonesia to the United States.

The Plans of the U.S. "Peace" Movement

As we write these lines, the U.S. "peace" movement is gearing up for another series of major efforts.

The December 14, 1984, issue of the authoritative *Information Digest* (a highly professional, limited-circulation intelligence report on subversive and anti–national security activities) carried an exceptionally detailed article about the fifth national conference of the Nuclear Weapons Freeze Campaign (NWFC) in St. Louis on December 7–9, 1984. The report contained a partial list of the organizations represented at the conference. We list these organizations below so that the reader will have a better idea of the remarkable range of front organizations and non–front organizations composed of "useful idiots." (In the original, the name of each organization was followed by a one-paragraph characterization and history. Regrettably, we do not have room for this here.)

American Friends Service Committee (AFSC)
Church Women United (CWU)
Clergy and Laity Concerned (CALC)
Committee in Solidarity with the People of El Salvador (CISPES)
Fellowship of Reconciliation (FOR)
Interreligious Task Force on Central America (IRTFCA)
Methodist Federation for Social Action (MFSA)
Mobilization for Survival (MFS)
National Network in Solidarity with the Nicaraguan People (NNSNP)
National Network in Solidarity with the People of Guatemala (NISGUA)
Nuclear Weapons Freeze Campaign (NWFC)
Pax Christi
SANE
Southern Christian Leadership Conference (SCLC)
War Resisters League (WRL)

The above-listed organizations constitute only a partial listing of the organizations active in the U.S. "peace" movement. An expanded list would include all of the several Marxist-Leninist organizations such as the Communist Party, the Socialist Workers Party (Trotskyite), the Revolutionary Workers Party, the Communist Party Marxist/Leninist, the Progressive Labor Party, and numerous smaller organizations. It would also include left-wing think tanks like the Institute for Policy Studies (IPS), the Trans-National Institute (TNI), which works closely with the IPS, the North American Congress in

Latin America (NACLA), the Pacific Study Center (PSC), the Center for Defense Information (CDI), the Center for National Security Studies (CNSS), and numerous lesser think-tank operations. It would also include religious organizations like the World Council of Churches and many of its U.S. affiliates, the American Friends Service Committee, Clergy and Laity Concerned, United Church of Christ, New York Riverside Church, and other organizations, both national and local. It also includes organizations ostensibly concerned with civil and constitutional rights such as the Center for Constitutional Rights, the Emergency Civil Liberties Union, and the National Lawyers Guild. The latter organization, which has been identified in Congress as a legal front for the Communist Party, is affiliated with the Soviet-controlled International Association of Democratic Lawyers, which performs on the international arena the same function performed by the NLG in the United States.

How many such organizations are there? The number runs to at least several hundred, large and small, and according to some estimates it exceeds a thousand. Of course, not all of these organizations conform to the Communist line one hundred percent of the time. But 80 percent of the time, 60 percent of the time, 50 percent of the time, or even less can still serve the Soviet propaganda and deception campaign in highly important ways.

There has been a noticeable growth over the past several years within the Nuclear Weapons Freeze Campaign in the strength of the advocates of confrontation and direct action.

At the December 1983 conference the Direct Action Task Force was established "to develop a national direct action strategy to complement other aspects of the freeze strategy."

On November 12, 1984, the Direct Action Task Force reported to a joint meeting of the NWFCs Strategy and Executive Committees in the following duplicitous terms:

> While we recognize nonviolent civil disobedience as a part of any movement for social change, we believe that the National Freeze Campaign should not take on nonviolent civil disobedience as a part of its strategy at this time. Nevertheless, we encourage and support local groups and individuals who do choose to organize or participate in nonviolent civil disobedience, and we have directed the National Staff to distribute information about such actions through the Local Organizer Mailings.

Although the NWFC has not given its backing to the full inventory of Soviet foreign policy positions, on Central America its position is indistinguishable from that of the Communist Party and the World Peace Council. Thus, it has participated in the Emergency Response Network, which was set up to oppose U.S. support of freedom in Nicaragua and El Salvador. The Emergency Response Network has been gathering signatures to a "Pledge of Resistance" by "nonviolent direct action at U.S. Federal Facilities, including U.S. Federal buildings, military installations, Congressional offices, offices of the Central Intelligence Agency, the State Department," and so on.

All the organizations listed above are also involved in the Emergency Response Network. But roles of prime importance are played by the Committee in Solidarity with the People of El Salvador, the U.S. Peace Council, and the Institute for Policy Studies, all of which have undeviating records of support for Soviet-Castro policy in the Americas and opposition to U.S. policy.

The European and U.S. "Peace" Movements: A Comparison

The majority of the estimated 700,000 people who marched in New York, as well as those who participated in parallel demonstrations at the Hollywood Bowl, in San Francisco, and elsewhere were not, as we have stated, Communists. Neither were the organizations that brought most of them out. But the non-Communist organizations that marched for peace can learn a lesson or two from the far less pliant examples set by component organizations of the European "peace" movement.

Thus, while the European "peace" movement has undergone sometimes violent dissension between its pro-Moscow elements and independent pacifist organizations like the German Greens, the U.S. organizations, although they may have differences with the Communists, have generally suppressed their differences or arrived at unsatisfactory compromises after discussing them in Executive session. What is more, as has been noted by Rael Jean and Erich Isaac, the major American pacifist organizations—the AFSC, the Fellowship for Reconciliation (FOR), the War Resisters League (WRL), and the Women's International League for Peace and Freedom (WILPF)—"are centers of radicalism whose relation to nonviolence is highly problematical since in practice they condone violence to achieve the goals of what the left defines as 'liberation movements.'"[10]

The Isaacs note that most of these pacifist organizations had openly supported the Palestine Liberation Organization and that a spokesperson for the WILPF had said that her only regret was that "more of us could not be there to come to understand why the struggle of the Palestinian people must continue."

Although pro-Moscow elements have exercised an influence far exceeding their numbers in the European "peace" movement, the non-Communist elements in this movement have from time to time exhibited a degree of partial independence from Communist control. For example, in May 1982 the Inter-Church Peace Council in the Netherlands walked out of the Conference of Religious Workers for Saving the Sacred Gift of Life when it was not permitted to speak on the SS-20 and the repression of the Solidarity movement in Poland. The German Greens, at a conference in Bad Godesberg in 1982, accused the Communists of trying to take over and manipulate the peace movement in their own interest. It was suggested that the peace demonstration projected in Bonn would be more persuasive if some reference was made to the invasion of Afghanistan and the suppression of the Solidarity movement. Even the European Communist Parties have on certain issues digressed from the Moscow–World Peace Council line. For example, *Humanité*, the organ of the French Communist Party, denounced nuclear weapons development by both superpowers, and the rally that was held in Paris on October 25, 1981, demonstrated under banners that read, "Neither Pershing nor SS-20, but Disarmament."

But the so-called pacifist organizations involved in the "peace" movement in this country have thus far proved resistant to the example of independence, or partial independence, established by non-Communist organizations adhering to the European "peace" movement. At the time of the Stockholm "peace" campaign in the early 1970s, the Fellowship of Reconciliation, for example, was wary of becoming involved. "Communist-inspired 'peace campaigns' are not genuine," said the Fellowship of Reconciliation. They lead "to building up the Communist Party rather than pacifism or peace."

Alas! Such common sense observations are now muted in the "higher" interests of the unity of the "peace" movement.

If one can fault the non-Communist organizations that belong to the U.S. "peace" movement for their excessive civility to the Communist viewpoint, what is one to say about the eager-to-help attitude of so many of our political leaders when a nine-member

WPC delegation came to this country in 1975 to promote their Second Stockholm Peace Petition? The Isaacs have chronicled some of the events that took place. In New York City, Ambassador Angier Biddle Duke, acting on behalf of Mayor Abraham Beame, presented Bicentennial medals to the members of the delegation. In Los Angeles and Milwaukee there were mayoral proclamations honoring the delegation. In Detroit the delegation was given a sheriff's escort and the keys to the city. In South Bend, Indiana, again, they were given the keys to the city, and the Chamber of Commerce hosted a luncheon in their honor. And all of this happened, it is important to remember, before the "bad years" of the Carter Administration. It is difficult to escape the conclusion that someone in the Department of State put out the word that the WPC delegation was to be accorded such honors by the communities they visited. Since the WPC had long been identified as the number-one Soviet front internationally, the next questions that have to be asked are: Who? And why?

What Can Be Done?

What can be done to frustrate and expose Soviet deceptive measures aimed at the U.S. public and policymakers?

First of all, there is the basic requirement of public awareness. An aware public is an educated public. One of America's greatest political weaknesses today is the fact that there is no public education at the secondary-school level on the nature and meaning and tactics of communism and, conversely, on the vital advantages of democracy and personal freedom and government under the rule of law. If such a program of education could be launched on a national scale, directed in the first instance to senior high school students, we would, within a decade, enjoy a public opinion that is much more resistant to Soviet manipulation.

The U.S. public, from the man on the street to members of Congress, must be made aware of the fact that Soviet deception does exist, that its purpose is to influence or manipulate public and official opinion, and that there are few people so wise and so resistant that they cannot be manipulated indirectly by pressures that seem to originate spontaneously but that can be traced back to the Soviet apparatus of disinformation and deception.

In order to achieve this degree of public awareness, it is

essential that the Department of State, the FBI, and other concerned government agencies continue to make available concrete original data on Soviet deception activities in the United States and targeted against the United States. The three reports of the Department of State dealing with the Soviet forgery offensive and the several reports dealing with Soviet involvement in the "peace" movement are dramatic examples of what can be done.

It is also of critical importance that the U.S. media identify Communist or radical activists and organizations when these are involved in demonstrations for "peace," or against apartheid, or for other ostensibly laudable causes.

It is an affront to objectivity when an organization like the Institute for Policy Studies is identified simply as a "think tank" or as a "research institute" instead of being identified as a "consistently leftist anti-U.S. think tank," and it is equally an affront to objectivity when a man like Randall Robinson is identified simply as an "anti-apartheid activist" without any mention of his totally consistent record of support for Soviet foreign policy positions in Africa, even when these involve opposing the aspirations for freedom of black Africans in Mozambique and Angola.

We have a right to ask this much of our media. And if our media will not immediately comply, the chances are that they will ultimately be influenced by a flood of letters from indignant U.S. citizens.

With all due respect to the Fourth Amendment, it does appear that constitutional rights reserved for U.S. citizens are being stretched to the point of imperiling national security when these rights are interpreted as meaning that we must give Soviet officials and other known Communists identified with the WPC free access to our country to agitate against the national security policies of our government. The attorney general has the right, although rarely invoked, to deny the admission of people whose presence in the country is deemed harmful to the national security. It seems to us that the American public would overwhelmingly support a more restrictive handling of foreign propagandists for the WPC.

Next, in order to know what the enemy is up to, it is imperative that we break completely with the restrictive intelligence guidelines imposed on the FBI by Attorney General Levi in 1976. These guidelines, in effect, made the collection of long-term domestic intelligence impossible without proof that a crime had been committed or was in the process of being committed. In 1974 the

FBI opened or reopened over fifty-five thousand cases on "subversives and extremists," according to a GAO report. Two years later the GAO reported that "as of early October 1977, 17 organizations and approximately 130 individuals were under domestic intelligence investigation." By August 1982, FBI Director William Webster informed Senator Denton that the FBI had active domestic intelligence investigations going on four organizations and ten individuals.

The guidelines introduced by Attorney General William French Smith in 1983 represented an improvement, but they still retained the strict prevention of long-term investigations. Obviously, there have to be guidelines to insure that the constitutional rights of citizens are not violated. But where the national security of the country is at stake, these guidelines have to be drafted in a manner that gives the FBI the maximum of flexibility with a minimum of encumbrance.

Finally, there is the eminently sensible suggestion made in *The Washington Times* for April 11, 1985, by Joel Lisker, currently counsel for the Senate Subcommittee on Security and Terrorism and formerly in charge of enforcing the Foreign Agents Registration Act for the Justice Department. Lisker suggests that organizations like the Committee in Solidarity with the People of El Salvador (CISPES) and the World Peace Council be obliged to register under the Foreign Agents Registration Act and that, in order to police this operation, the Justice Department be given "civil investigative demand authority akin to administrative subpoena power."

These are some of the things that can be done to increase public awareness of Soviet deception measures designed to influence American policy. It is imperative that we act at once because the present degree of ignorance of the scale and workings of Soviet deception activities constitute an open invitation to more Soviet manipulation and control of the political life of America.

Notes

1. Richard H. Shultz and Roy Godson, *Dezinformatsia: Active Measures in Soviet Strategy.* (Washington, D.C.: Pergamon-Brassey's, 1984.)
2. Al Santoli, *To Bear Any Burden.* (New York: E. P. Dutton, 1985), p. 165.
3. Vladimir Bukovsky, "The Peace Movement and the Soviet Union." *Commentary* (May 1982.)

4. "Soviet 'Active Measures': Forgery, Disinformation, Political Operations," *Foreign Affairs Note*. (Washington, D.C.: Department of State, October 1981); "Soviet Active Measures: An Update," *Special Report No. 101*. (Washington, D.C.: Department of State, July 1982); "Soviet Active Measures: Focus on Forgeries," *Foreign Affairs Note*. (Washington, D.C.: Department of State, April 1983); and "Soviet Active Measures," *Special Report No. 110*. (Washington, D.C.: Department of State, September 1983.)

5. "The World Peace Council's 'Peace Assemblies,'" *Foreign Affairs Note*. (Washington, D.C.: Department of State, May 1983.)

6. Permanent Select Committee on Intelligence, U.S. House of Representatives, *Soviet Covert Action (The Forgery Offensive)*. Hearings before the Subcommittee on Oversight of the Permanent Select Committee on Intelligence. House of Representatives, Ninety-Sixth Congress, Second Session. (Washington, D.C.: U.S. Government Printing Office, 1980), p. 75.

7. Annex to Testimony of CIR before House Permanent Committee on Intelligence, April 20, 1978, p. 554.

8. Permanent Select Committee on Intelligence, op. cit., p. 75.

9. Herbert Romerstein, *The World Peace Council and Soviet "Active Measures"*. (Washington, D.C.: The Hale Foundation, 1983.)

10. Rael Jean Isaac and Erich Isaac, "The Counterfeit Peacemakers: Atomic Freeze." *The American Spectator*, Vol. 15 (June 1982.)

POLITICAL PILGRIMS

Selected by David Martin

There is no end to the number of outrageously silly statements about the Soviet Union made by people of standing and intellect in the Western world covering all aspects of Soviet society. This was true particularly during the 1930s, when the massive Soviet deception operation, especially tailored for Western intellectuals, was in full swing. In the pages that follow, we reproduce a small number of these statements. The utter inanity of these statements is perhaps best exemplified by the quotations having to do with the Soviet system of justice and the Gulag archipelago, the cruelest and most murderous punitive apparatus in recorded history.

For most of the quotations reproduced below, we are indebted to the unrivaled collection put together by Paul Hollander in *Political Pilgrims,* paperback (New York, Harper and Row, 1983), hardcover (New York, Oxford Univ. Press, 1981.)

> In England a delinquent enters [the punitive system] as an ordinary man and comes out as a "criminal type," whereas in Russia he enters . . . as a criminal type and would come out an ordinary man but for the difficulty of inducing him to come out at all. As far as I could make out they could stay as long as they liked.
>
> George Bernard Shaw

> On good behavior, which is easy in Soviet jails, as easy as in Soviet schools, the sentence is pared down. Constant amnesties on the occasion of revolutionary holidays bring further reductions. During the period of confinement criminals experience no other hardships than the enforced separation from home. Unless they violate the light discipline that they must observe they never are made to feel the yoke of the stigma of prison life.

171

There are no chain gangs. There are no severe compulsions. There is no lockstep. There is no striped or any kind of uniforms. There are no limitations to the amount of literature or correspondence they may receive. Indeed the prison exists not for punishment but for ministration.

Maurice Hindus

The prisoner . . . must live a full and self-respecting life. All prisoners do normal industrial work, and they all receive wages. They have the right to a vacation; they receive a generous allowance of visits; their privilege of writing and receiving letters is practically unlimited and uncensored. . . . No one who has seen a Russian prison, and compared that experience with a visit to one in England, can doubt that the advantage is all on the Russian side. The prisoners with whom I talked were . . . men who were conquering themselves. . . . They had not been disciplined into machines. They had learned the value of regular labor. They had not been made to feel that they were cut off from the outside world. They had no sense of being under the continuous supervision of an unfriendly eye. There was neither furtiveness nor fear about them. I think, on any showing, that these are great gains which say much for the theory which underlies their treatment.

The degree to which prisoners are put on their honor has also an excellent effect. The unaccompanied holiday at home, the uncensored correspondence, the right to receive visitors without supervision, all remove that constant sense of being humiliated which I believe to be one of the most destructive features of our own system.

Harold Laski

The really fundamental thing is a change of attitude towards human nature in general. The Communist view of human nature seems to be far more inspired by Faith, Hope and Charity than our own. To them the prime cause of evil . . . is the poison of wealth which stultifies men's natural instincts of fellowship. Once a State is delivered from this perversive influence acting on any of its citizens, and granted also a certain degree of education, all can be trusted to receive equal rights. Their confidence in unspoilt human nature forbids the Communists to believe in self-interest as the indispensable motive by which alone the economic machine can be kept going.

As an example of the new order of incentives, the self-denying ordinance of the Communist Party in the matter of salaries is significant. . . . The simple unostentatious life of Russia's rulers represents a notable advance in *real* civilization—real because based on a more enlightened interpretation of human nature, both of its needs and capacities; an interpretation which incidentally is also a more Christian one.

D.F. Buxton
English Quaker leader

One gradually comes to realize that, though the people's clothes are dreary, there is little, if any, destitution; though there are no swell parts of the city, there are no degraded parts either. There are no shocking sights on the streets: no down-and-outers, no horrible diseases, no old people picking in garbage pails.

I was never able to find anything like a slum or any quarter that even seemed dirty.

Edmund Wilson

I went around the Soviet Union in those rather rough, primitive and casual days when one saw very much of the difficulties . . . [in 1931]. And yet there was no mistaking the sense of purpose and achievement . . . in those days of trial. It was grim but great. Our hardships in England were less; theirs were deliberate and undergone in an assurance of building a better future.

J.D. Bernal
British scientist

I came to the Soviet Union from countries where complaints are the general rule and whose inhabitants, discontented with both their physical and spiritual conditions, crave change. . . . The air which one breathes in the West is stale and foul. In the Western civilization there is no longer clarity and resolution. . . . One breathes again when one comes from this oppressive atmosphere of a counterfeit democracy and hypocritical humanism into the invigorating atmosphere of the Soviet Union. Here there is no hiding behind mystical, meaningless slogans, but a sober ethic prevails.

Leon Feuchtwanger

Perhaps we should have called Soviet old folks the second privileged class. [Children were the first.] Every possible care and comfort is given those who have retired from active life. The fear of poverty in old age has been completely banished by pensions for all. For the sick and infirm there are rest homes and sanatoriums in beautiful surroundings. For those who still feel young in body and mind there is leisure to enjoy the infinite variety of experiences that abound in the vigorous new land of the Soviets.

No color lines, no "dirty foreigners," no filthy overcrowded slums, no unattended sickness, no criminal vice and prostitution, no lifelong toil shadowed forever by insecurity. . . . The Soviets abolished all these evils.

Dyson Carter
Canadian scientist

There is something about a Russian train standing at a station that thrills. . . . The little locomotive is human. . . . The dingy cars are human.

Waldo Frank

No nation in history has ever done so much so fast. If the Soviet leaders tell us that the control of information was necessary to get this job done, we can afford to take their word for it for the time being. We who know the power of free speech, and the necessity for it, may assume that if those leaders are sincere in their work of emancipating the Russian people they will swing around toward free speech—and we hope so soon.

Life editorial
1943

The experiment which is being worked out in a sixth of the earth's surface is founded on a new organization of economic life based on clearly defined principles which are thoroughly understood and gladly accepted. . . . Our system lacks moral basis. . . . It gives rise . . . to that fatal divergence between principles and practice of Christian people, which is so damning to religion. . . . Such is the moral aspect of contemporary economic society. Its scientific aspect is the wholly irrational wastage of wealth, the artificially induced shortage, the poverty amidst plenty. . . . In opposition to this view of the organization of economic life is that of the Soviet Union, where cooperation replaces competitive chaos and a Plan succeeds the riot of disorder. . . . The community rather than the self-seeking individual stands in the centre of the picture. The welfare of the whole and of each individual within it replaces . . . the welfare of a select class or classes. The elimination of the profit-motive makes room for the higher motive of service. . . . A new attitude towards human life is the natural counterpart of the new economic morality. Individuals, all individuals, become ends as well as means. The development of the human potentialities of each individual receives fullest opportunity and encouragement.

Dr. Hewlett Johnson
Archbishop of Canterbury

Paul Hollander tells of the visit of Henry Wallace and Owen Lattimore to Magadan, "One of the most notorious places of detention and forced labor." They were shown around by Ivan Feodorovich Nikishov, the KGB officer in charge of this complex of forced labor camps. Mr. Nikishov, Lattimore pointed out, had "just been decorated with the Order of Hero of the Soviet Union for his extraordinary achievements. Both he and his wife have a trained and sensitive interest in art and music and also a deep sense of civic responsibility."

Mr. Wallace talked of his meeting with Nikishov: "We went for a walk in the taiga. . . . The larch were just putting out their first leaves and Nikishov gamboled about, enjoying the wonderful air immensely. . . . The Kolyma gold miners are big, husky young men, who came out to the Far East from European Russia. I spoke with some of them."

Elinor Lipper, a young Swiss radical who was caught up in the Gulag archipelago, wrote of her experiences in a book, "Eleven Years in Soviet Labor Camps." Of the visit of Wallace and Lattimore to Magadan while she was a prisoner there, Elinor Lipper said: "He [Wallace] does not mention, or does not know, that this city [Magadan] was built solely by prisoners working under inhuman conditions. . . . He does not say—or does not know—that this highway [which Wallace had repeatedly admired] was built entirely by prisoners and that tens of thousands gave their lives in building it."

SOVIET
PEACE
DECEPTION

Ambassador Paul H. Nitze

First, we have to consider how the Communists think that policy should be analyzed. They start with the proposition that there are certain fundamental theses that distinguish the Communist approach to the world from that of others, particularly from that of the capitalist world. Among these theses are the primacy of class struggle and the continuing fight against "imperialism" in the formerly colonial world. These theses they hold to be unchangeable.

They also have a somewhat more flexible view with respect to strategy. They think that strategy should, from time to time, be altered to reflect changes in the "correlation of forces." In the correlation of forces they include not only military forces, but economic, political, and psychological factors as well. When the correlation of forces is favorable to their ends, their doctrine calls on them to exploit that favorable correlation by moving forward. When the correlation of forces is negative, the doctrine calls upon them to hold or to retreat while they attempt to reverse the adverse trends. With respect to tactics, the Communists believe there should be great flexibility. The guiding thoughts should be deception and surprise.

They also hold that it is important at all times to decide upon what they call "the general line." By this they mean that it is necessary at all times to identify correctly the group that constitutes the major threat to their ability to carry their program forward. During the early years after the October 1917 Revolution, the general line called for concentrating their attack on the social democrats within the Soviet Union, that being the group having the greatest potential appeal to workers, the class the Communists claimed to represent but were in fact less close to than the social democrats.

Later, after their victory in the civil war, the general line called for concentrating their attack on the social democrats in other countries, particularly Germany. In 1946 Stalin made it clear that he saw the United States as the principal potential opponent, even at a time when President Truman and his advisers were striving hard to preserve in peacetime the wartime collaboration between the United States and the Soviet Union. Today the general line focuses directly on the United States (and particularly on President Reagan) as being at the heart of the only potentially effective opposition to the Soviet program.

A further Soviet Communist precept is not to let emotion interfere with what they call "scientific realism." One should never let anger influence one's judgment, although it may be advisable from time to time to show anger. For some time before 1960 we were flying U-2 reconnaissance aircraft over the Soviet Union, but the Soviets could not shoot them down. During that period they showed no anger. The moment they were able to shoot down a U-2, Khrushchev put on a tremendous show of anger and beat his shoe upon his desk at the UN meeting of that year, 1960. I doubt that there is merit in the common thesis, prominent from time to time, that the Soviet leadership is "angry" at the United States. More likely, Soviet propagandists tell the Politburo that it is astute to create that impression.

There is a sharp contrast between the way the United States and other countries in the West approach foreign policy issues and the way they are approached by the Soviet Union. Much of our experience in negotiating with the Soviet Union has been on arms control. Arms control is not an end in itself, but a means. The object of arms control negotiations is to support foreign policy and security policy by negotiating agreements that will contribute to reducing the risk of war, primarily the risk of nuclear war. Many other purposes are discussed in the immense literature that now threatens to engulf the subject of arms control and make it incomprehensible. These other purposes—stopping the arms race, saving money, increasing stability, assuring predictability, providing the foundation for a better East-West relationship—may well be desirable, but they are desirable only if they contribute to the more important goal of reducing the risk of war and strengthening the prospects of peace.

At the heart of the matter are the twin concepts of peace and war. It is in one's understanding of these linked concepts that thought about arms control must be grounded. I am convinced that much of the difficulty that the United States has had in getting along with the Soviet Union stems from contrasting meanings and connotations of the word *peace*. In the West, internally, it means a state of domestic order; externally, it means equilibrium and an absence of war.[1] The Russian word for peace—*mir*—means something quite different, however, particularly as used by the Soviets since the October Revolution.[2]

Let me draw on another illustration from my visit to Moscow after the 1955 summit meeting in Geneva. Ambassador Chip Bohlen took me to a session of the Supreme Soviet, at which Khrushchev and Bulganin were reporting on the "Spirit of Geneva," as the Western press had christened the apparent spirit of cooperation that resulted from that summit conference. Khrushchev and Bulganin took turns making the presentation. As Bohlen translated for me, I found it fascinating to watch the faces of their delegates and their reactions to what was said. Whenever the speakers dwelled on the Geneva conference, its apparent success, and "the Spirit of Geneva," the audience was dead; people yawned, and some actually fell asleep. Whenever Khrushchev or Bulganin launched into an impassioned description of Western faults, errors, and shortcomings, the necessity for *mir,* and the actions the Party proposed to take to achieve *mir*, the audience became animated and broke into loud applause.

I asked Bohlen for an explanation of this apparently contradictory behavior. He said that the primary dictionary meaning of *mir* was "the world and those who live on it" and that "concord among peoples and nations and absence of war" was only a secondary meaning. He explained that, as the Soviets used the word in Party statements and writings, it meant a condition in the world in which socialism, the first stage of communism, had triumphed worldwide, class tensions had been removed, and the conditions for true peace under Communist leadership had come to pass. The reaction of the members of the Supreme Soviet to Khrushchev's and Bulganin's remarks therefore indicated a lack of interest in the relaxation of tensions exemplified by the "Spirit of Geneva" but enthusiasm for the continuing struggle for *mir*.

Thus the essence of the Soviet concept *mir* is quite different from what we in the West understand by *peace*. Two Dutch authors have described the Soviet concept:

In the Soviet view, the masses in non-socialist societies are exploited and repressed; there is no class basis for *mir* and no real peace. Therefore, the source of all wars is "capitalist imperialism" which seeks to prevent the peaceful socialist world system from fulfilling its holy mission. The Soviets, indeed, believe in such a mission—*missiya*—to establish *mir* in all other societies, the populaces of which are believed to be longing for liberation and genuine peace.[3]

This is a peculiarly Leninist concept. Marx had developed no real concept of international relations, for after the proletarian revolution and the "melting away" of the socialist governments, there would be no need for international relations in the accepted sense. Lenin, of course, was confronted by a situation not anticipated by Marx: the revolution was limited to one country. Thus, he had to elaborate a doctrine of the role of peace and war in Soviet policy, a doctrine that became a central part of Marxist-Leninist thought. This doctrine in large part reflected the problems and aspirations of the newly formed Soviet state, the single socialist entity in a world of capitalist states that were, by their very nature, hostile to it. Lenin's contention was that only a proletarian society could enjoy *mir*; it could be attained only with the establishment of socialism, the first phase of communism. At times, *mir* could only be achieved through "wars in defense of the fatherland." The Soviet encyclopedia states that the historical mission of communism is to end war and bring about everlasting *mir* on earth.

Thus, the Soviet concept of peace (*mir*) has come to mean a continuing struggle rather than a state of equilibrium, as *peace* is often defined in the West. *Mir* takes as a given that there is a natural and irreconcilable conflict of interest between the socialist and nonsocialist worlds. In the long run international equilibrium cannot be guaranteed in a world of competing social systems. True *mir* can be achieved only through the establishment of a worldwide classless Marxist society, which, given the nature of capitalism, will be achieved only through revolutionary struggle. Thus, over the long run the pursuit of *mir* will come into conflict with the pursuit of international equilibrium.

That being said, it should be noted that Marxist-Leninist thought permits, indeed strongly encourages, unlimited tactical flexibility in the pursuit of *mir*. Moreover, Lenin counseled caution and calculation. International order based on equilibrium is not good in itself because it is a hindrance to the struggle to achieve a worldwide classless society. However, it may be an acceptable temporary policy objective if the prevailing circumstances dictate—that is, if the "correlation of forces" is unfavorable or if the interests of the Soviet State will be served by abatement of international conflict or tension.

The Soviet interpretation of *mir* is related to the strategy of "peaceful coexistence," which was formulated by Lenin in 1917 at a time when the Soviet Union desperately needed peace with Germany. This strategy stressed the avoidance of direct armed conflict with the capitalist states while pursuing Soviet interests through other means, when the "correlation of forces" was adverse. Before World War II, Stalin continued to consider the Soviet Union weaker than its potential enemies. In 1927 he said:

> Hence our task is to pay attention to contradictions in the capitalist camp, to delay war by "buying off" the capitalists and to take all measure to maintain peaceful relations. . . . Our relations with the capitalist countries are based on the assumption that the coexistence of the two opposing systems is possible. Practice has fully confirmed this.[4]

In other words, caution and calculation prevailed; the circumstances permitted—and required—acceptance of an equilibrium with the principal European countries.

During the 1960s, when the United States enjoyed nuclear superiority but the principal European states were in the midst of the difficult process of dismantling their former colonial empires, the Soviet strategy of "peaceful coexistence" was further elaborated. A typical Soviet statement from those days was:

> Peaceful coexistence of states with different social orders does not mean the end of the class struggle. Peaceful coexistence not only does not exclude the class struggle but is itself a form of the class struggle between victorious socialism and decrepit capitalism on the world scene, a sharp and irreconcilable struggle, the final outcome of which will be the triumph of Communism throughout the entire world.[5]

During this period, emphasis was placed on supporting terrorism, guerrilla warfare, and wars of national liberation, while direct confrontation with the United States was avoided.

Some in the West argue that, whatever the Soviet ideologues assert, the ruling group in Moscow no longer truly believes in the

Marxist-Leninist dogma. Almost certainly, many in the Soviet leadership have serious doubts about various aspects of the doctrine. But what counts is that the Soviet rulers believe in their dogma in various ways. Former Soviet Chief of Staff Marshal Nikolai Ogarkov, for example, believes in its utility as a rationale for keeping Soviet society bound to an unmatched level of effort in directing resources to the accumulation of military might. A Soviet counterpart of mine in the INF (intermediate-range nuclear forces) negotiations, though a thorough cynic, found it necessary to believe in the efficacy of the doctrine if he was to advance in his career. One of my Soviet scientist friends was frank in expressing his disbelief in many important aspects of Marxism-Leninism, but he is loyal and believes in the contribution Soviet science can make to knowledge and to the security of the state; he sees no alternative but to support the system. Foreign Minister Gromyko reiterated the dogma with force and clarity in an article published in Moscow this past spring entitled "Lenin's Peace Policy."[6]

This is not to say that Russian nationalist drives have had no role in forming Soviet policy. During World War II patriotism for Mother Russia was officially invoked by Stalin and became a strong and unifying force in checking and then defeating Hitler's armies. But immediately after the defeat of Hitler Stalin quickly reestablished the primacy of the Party and Marxist-Leninist-Stalinist doctrine.

The objective situation has changed over the past forty years. Internal opposition is weaker, but dissatisfaction with the regime is widespread. The Soviet Union's control has expanded over some 110 million additional people in Eastern Europe, with both the advantages and the strains that such control brings. Soviet influence in remote areas of the world has increased, but the attractiveness of its image as a model for emulation has eroded. Its military power has grown immensely. The mix of these factors in turn has had a bearing on the evolution of Soviet policy.

Marxist-Leninist ideology continues nevertheless to have an important influence on Soviet policymaking. Soviet leaders are schooled in that philosophy; it provides the prism through which they view the outside world. All of them believe in that dogma in the sense of ascribing to it efficacy and indispensability in underpinning the regime's hold on power. Concessions or compromise on the dogma would be suicidal for the regime; the effects throughout the realm of Soviet domination would be shattering and incalculable.

The Soviet rulers believe in the Marxist-Leninist dogma because it is the linchpin of the system; it alone gives the system legitimacy. Chip Bohlen once said that Marxist-Leninist doctrine is the fig leaf of the Soviets' respectability; without it they could not live with the reality of the crimes committed in its name.

These Soviet concepts and beliefs inevitably clash with our own. The experience of World War II reinforced the ideas, not only in America but also in Europe, that peace must be the norm, that an international order should be based on equilibrium, and that war had become potentially so destructive as to be virtually unacceptable. But initially we hoped we would not be called upon to do much about it. Surely other states, including our wartime ally the Soviet Union, must similarly see the unacceptability of war.

As early as the spring of 1946, Stalin made it evident that he saw it otherwise. He proclaimed that the Marxist-Leninist doctrine of the struggle for *mir* was to be continued into the indefinite future and that the United States was to be viewed as the center of the opposing capitalist world, whose very existence made true *mir* impossible. By 1947 it became clear that Britain and the other Western countries that had formerly carried the Western burden of world politics and strategy had been too weakened by the two world wars to continue to carry that burden. The United Nations had proved itself ineffective in the face of great power disagreements. The United States had to take the lead or see the world accommodate to Stalin's view of the future.

Under this impulse the great shifts in U.S. foreign policy of the late 1940s and early 1950s took place. At first, emphasis was placed on helping to create a world economic system based on the Bretton Woods Agreements, the World Bank, and the International Monetary Fund, backed by the ordering of trade arrangements through the General Agreement on Tariffs and Trade. That work was supplemented by U.S. aid programs, notably the Marshall Plan and Point Four. Germany, Japan, and Italy were returned to the family of nations as free nations. A serious but unsuccessful effort was made to bring the atom under control through the Acheson-Lilienthal Plan and the Baruch Proposal. The United States later participated in the construction of a network of collective defense treaties intended to enhance security against aggression.

The point of all this effort was to help extend from the United States to the world the concept of a just and reasonable order—a condition of peace. A place in this structure was offered to the

Soviet Union. That offer was consistently rebuffed; for the Soviets to have accepted a permanent position in that order, however favorable the circumstances, would have been in diametric opposition to the very concept of the struggle for *mir*. Stalin and all of his successors have rejected such a concession based on their ideology, and the opposition between the two concepts—peace and *mir*—continues to this day.

Indeed, I observed it at first hand. The failure of the INF negotiations to date to reach an equitable and mutually acceptable solution can be seen as grounded in this clash of concepts. U.S. positions were designed to enhance the balance and equilibrium that we see as being basic to international order. The Soviet approach, on the other hand, was based on efforts to preserve and, if possible, enhance a "correlation of forces" that favored them. While exploiting available pressures in an attempt to cause us to accept an unequal and destabilizing agreement at the negotiating table, the prime Soviet interest in the INF negotiation was in using them to achieve wider purposes: to sow division within NATO, particularly between the United States and Europe, and to create tensions within individual countries, especially the Federal Republic of Germany. A NATO thus weakened would be less prepared to resist the expansion of Soviet influence, a situation that would both enhance the position of the Soviet state and contribute toward the future achievement of what it considers true peace, or *mir*.

It was the hope of U.S. policymakers during the late 1940s that the use of force in international affairs, or even the threat to use force, could be avoided. But just as in assuring internal tranquillity the resort to force cannot be wholly avoided, so in support of order in international affairs deterrence through the threat of force—and on occasion the actual use of force—cannot be avoided. To paraphrase Clausewitz, the use of force exists for the benefit of the defender; the aggressor will always prefer to enter your country unopposed. The point is that the use of force, whether used internationally or internally, should be based on principle and a process giving it legitimacy.

The question then is, which set of principles and which process of legitimization should be supported: *peace* in its normal meaning—the absence of anarchy, terrorism, and civil war internally and, externally, an international system of order leading to the absence of war between nations—or *mir*, the support of terrorism and guerrilla warfare in other countries under the banner of "wars of national liberation" leading to an increased risk of international war—what the Soviets would call a "just war"—followed by a worldwide regime of structured violence calling itself *mir,* which would parallel the continuous process of intimidation that now characterizes the Soviet regime domestically.

On this question it is possible to be too impartial. There have been obvious shortcomings in the way the concept of peace has been carried out in practice by all countries, including the United States. Perfection is not obtainable in the real world. But imperfections in implementation do not invalidate a valid idea. Failure to choose between peace and *mir* can result in a Hamlet-like inability to act until it is tragically late, perhaps too late. It can lead to confusion, uncertainty, and chaos, the very conditions most apt to lead to an unintended war. A clear and timely choice should be made.

Let us assume, for the moment, that there is in fact a consensus, not only in the United States but also in the rest of the world not controlled by Moscow, in support of peace in its normal meaning. What then should be the proximate aim of policy? I suggest that the key phrase describing the aim of policy be "live and let live." The Soviet phrase "peaceful coexistence" means exactly that to non-Communist ears. This is not the meaning Khrushchev and Brezhnev gave it, but for once let us take a phrase of theirs and give it the meaning we believe it should have.

"Live and let live" has been the actual aim of American policy toward the Soviet Union since the end of World War II. From time to time we did adopt a different declared policy of "rollback," for example in the early 1950s. But our action policy has consistently been "containment"; in other words, let the Soviets be as they are if they will likewise let others be. In contrast, Soviet declared policy since 1945 has been "peaceful coexistence," which has given the impression of "live and let live"; but in fact to Communist ears it calls for an action policy of successive takeovers wherever and whenever this is possible without excessive risk. Whether "live and let live" can be fruitfully pursued as a policy for both sides therefore depends on whether there is any prospect for a change in Soviet action policy.

Notes

1. For a discussion of Western views of peace, see Michael Howard, "The Concept of Peace." *Encounter* (December 1983), p. 18.

2. In pre-October Revolutionary Russia, there were two words, spelled MNP and MIP in the Cyrillic alphabet, both pronounced in the same way. In 1918 the Cyrillic alphabet was simplified; I was abolished and became N. Thereafter, there has been a single word *MNP*, transliterated as *mir* in our alphabet. Prior to 1918, *MNP* meant "peace." *MIP* had two meanings: "universe" or "world," and its historical meaning, the village commune of elders that from time to time reallocated the cultivation of the village communal land among individual members of the village. (Isaiah Berlin, in *Russian Thinkers*, points out that for the pre-Marxist Russian revolutionaries and authors who created the foundations of the Russian populist, revolutionary socialist movement in the 1840s, 1850s, and 1860s—such as Herzen, Belinsky, Chernyshevsky, and Turgenev—"the village commune was the ideal embryo of those socialist groups on which the future society was to be based.") Thus, *mir* (*MNP*) now has three meanings: "world," "commune," and "peace."

3. Dr. J.A. Emerson Vermaat and Dr. Hans Bax, "The Soviet Concept of 'Peace.'" *Atlantic Community Quarterly* (Winter 1984), p. 326.

4. Stalin, "Political Report of the Central Committee to the 15th Congress of the CPSU (B)," December 3, 1927. Cited in Richard Allen, *Peace or Peaceful Coexistence*. (Chicago: American Bar Association, 1966), p. 78.

5. Khrushchev, Speech at the plenary meeting of the Central Committee of the CPSU, June 21, 1963. Cited in Richard Allen, op. cit., pp. 86–87.

6. *Moscow News*, April 29–May 6, 1984, p. 5.

SOVIET
DECEPTION
THROUGH WORDS

Raymond S. Sleeper

"The most important weapon in my arsenal is the dictionary. Let me choose the words . . . by which you think and I will tell you what and how to think."[1]

The Soviet Union and the nomenklatura conspiracy that runs it have been deceiving the West ever since Lenin's seizure of dictatorial power in the Soviet Union in 1917. This deception is very broad, consisting of the historical Russian theme of secrecy and deception together with the use of Marxist-Leninist concepts that are subversions of well-accepted Western ideas. As a matter of fact, many Soviet "active measures," acts of "disinformation," and acts of "deception" are intentionally rooted in double-meaning language. This is surely one of the major reasons Soviet leaders consistently use Marxism-Leninism as their ideology and as their main strategic thrust worldwide.

When Lenin began to organize his revolutionary conspiracy, he found that the main ideas of communism were already or could be expressed in terms of Western ideas so cleverly that the average citizen of the West (as well as the average citizen of the USSR) would not see the trick—the inherent deception of communist ideas. To the contrary, the average citizen understood *genuine democracy* and *economic freedom* to mean what they had always meant, the right to vote, the right to own property, the right to travel, the right to work where he pleased—in short, freedom.

The Leninist subversion of Western ideas and the wide use of double-meaning concepts—one meaning being the accepted Western concept and the other meaning being the opposite or subverted meaning that was the true Marxist-Leninist meaning—helped the plotters escape the network of tsarist censorship as well. Of course, such double-meaning concepts also served the very useful purpose of not immediately alarming the established government, which

191

Lenin had to deceive, confuse, and destroy in order to capture political power in Russia.

This secret or deceptive language has served the Soviet conspiracy well. It still serves them well. Soviet leaders are of course fully aware of their deceptive use of language. Stalin wrote several times on the importance of language in the world revolution.

Nikita Khrushchev was especially adept at using double-meaning concepts. Examples from his speeches and writings are some of the most colorful and clearly expressed deceptions. In the early 1950s, when the Western allies were attempting to establish the four-power agreements on the administration of Berlin, Khrushchev commented on the process and openly stated that the Soviets used words differently than the West did. Khrushchev referred to the double meaning of Marxist-Leninist words: "You know that the heads of government of the four powers met there later. Great efforts were made to achieve agreement, but the results were very small so far. This happens because we understand the same words differently."[2] This "different understanding" is designed and employed to deceive non-Communists. Some examples follow.

General Concepts

By "genuine democracy" the Soviets mean communism. By "economic freedom" they mean communism. The idea is that the elimination of capitalism destroys the upper and middle classes, and those who make profit from workers are eliminated. This, according to the Communists, "frees" the worker from the exploiting class. In truth, what happens under communism is that all democracy is eliminated. All freedom is eliminated, and complete dictatorship enforced by the police and the military is the result. Thus, we see the total subversion and reversal of the expressions "genuine democracy" and "economic freedom," as well as other widely accepted Western concepts. (See A Lexicon of Marxist-Leninist Semantics for a representative sample of subverted terms and concepts.[3])

It is a popular misconception (encouraged by Soviet propaganda) that communism is dead or dying in the Soviet Union and the rest of the world. President Jimmy Carter made the mistaken judgment in his well-known Notre Dame speech that we no longer had to fear communism. Some people think that the Soviet leaders are embracing the more "mature" concepts of the West, and that as communism "matures," the Soviet leaders will think more and more like Western people. This is the mirror-image syndrome.

The arguments that the vigor of communism is fading, that Communist philosophy is maturing, and that Soviet leaders are more like Western leaders are deceptions. However, the average U.S. citizen expects his representatives, State Department executives, foreign service officers, and the ambassadors in charge of negotiating with the Soviets to know the fundamental characteristics of Soviet leaders and to know that communism is not fading.

Yet on January 4, 1985, Ambassador Max Kampelman addressed the Standing Committee on Law and National Security of the American Bar Association on the lessons we can learn from the Madrid Conference on the Helsinki Final Act, a treaty signed by thirty-five nations, including the USSR. Ambassador Kampelman handled the negotiations so well that he was propelled into his present position as head of the U.S. negotiating team in Geneva on nuclear weapons. To the members of the American Bar Association he stated that he was surprised "to find the degree of commitment to Leninism that I actually did find in the heads of the Soviet delegation. . . . I was surprised by the degree of commitment to Leninism that existed in the leadership of [the Soviet] delegation.

"These are serious people," Ambassador Kampelman continued. "They're well trained. The training is vigorous. At the outset, it is very much a theoretical training with an emphasis on basic principles. Those who undergo this training understand that it is not safe to deviate from these principles:

"I am also convinced that this is probably the most deadly and most serious adversary that we have faced in our long history—and this for many reasons.

"First is the question of their intent. . . . The extent to which they are permeated with Leninist ideology and the extent that they do not know us strengthens . . . an attitude which believes in (a) an inevitable victory on their part because they are riding the wave of history and (b) a feeling on their part that there is a kind of corruption in the West which undermines will and intent and which has within it the seeds of its own destruction. They believe this; the leadership, I am convinced, believes this. The system depends on this belief—indeed I think it is this kind of conviction which permits the system to survive its difficulties.

But despite these difficulties, we cannot ignore the faith in their own ultimate victory."

What is the intent to which the Soviet leadership is dedicated? It is expressed, as Ambassador Kampelman stated, in the Leninist ideology to which the Soviet leadership continually refers.

Lenin expressed Soviet intent many times and in many ways. He once wrote, "Communists should know that the future belongs to them; therefore, we can (and must) combine the most intense passion in the great revolutionary struggle with the coolest and most sober estimation of the frenzied ravings of the bourgeoisie. But in all cases and in all countries communism is becoming steeled and is spreading, its roots are so deep that persecution does not weaken it, does not debilitate it, but strengthens it."[4]

In another instance Lenin spoke of liberation: "Let your brothers in the West know tomorrow that you on your banners are bringing them not war, but peace, not enslavement, but liberation." But of course liberation is the freeing of the people from the "yoke of capitalism" and the installation of Communist totalitarian dictatorship!

Thus the Pol Pot Communists "liberated" Cambodia by killing some two to three million Cambodians. They then established the Democratic Peoples Republic of Kampuchea. Kampuchea became "democratic"! This is democracy? Obviously it is not. Yet every Western news media reference to Democratic Kampuchea extends the propaganda that Cambodia has been liberated and is "democratic." South Vietnam's subsequent invasion of Cambodia to remove Pol Pot modified the regime some, but it is still a totalitarian dictatorship that is called in the Western press "Democratic Kampuchea."

Khrushchev expressed Soviet intent over Radio Moscow in 1962: "Yes," he said, "we are firmly convinced of the full and final triumph of communism. This conviction rests on the knowledge of the laws of development of human society which were discovered by Marx, Engels, and Lenin and which possess a force similar to that of the laws of nature, because they too operate objectively."

Ambassador Kampelman is correct when he emphasizes the dedication and the conviction that Soviet leaders have that victory will be theirs. He is also correct that great changes are rapidly increasing Soviet military power. Kampelman is wrong, however, when he implies that the vitality of Marxism-Leninism is dead or dying. It is not. True, the invasion of Afghanistan, the inhuman genocide tactics employed in Afghanistan, the destruction of Korean Airlines Flight 007, the assault on the Pope, and similar actions have pretty well alerted the world to Soviet repression and brutality. Nevertheless, Soviet-Cuban-Nicaraguan-supported guerrillas still wage vigorous "revolution" against the legitimate government of El Salvador and succeed in deceiving some U.S. senators and congressmen to the point where they refuse to fund anti-Communist activity in Nicaragua, and they even participate as propaganda tools of the Sandinistas on U.S. TV.

The Soviet leaders' vision of world victory is a strong motivation for Marxist-Leninists worldwide. Their goal is well expressed in very idealistic terms in the world bible of communism, *The Fundamentals of Marxist-Leninist Philosophy*:

> The victory of communism on the world scale will provide the necessary material and intellectual preconditions for the merging of nations. A communist economic integration never known before will gradually be formed throughout the world. There will emerge a common moral code which will absorb all that is best in the character of each nation. There will be a common language, a common means of communication for all people. Mankind will become one united, fraternal community completely free of antagonism.[5]

And what language will this utopian Communist world speak? *The Soviet Literary Gazette* of January 1949 predicted that the world language would be Russian:

> No one who does not know Russian and cannot read the works of the Russian intellect in the original can call himself a scholar in the full and true sense of the word. It may be seen in the history of mankind how in the course of thousands of years the world languages succeed one another. Latin was the language of antiquity and early middle ages. French was the language of feudalism, English became the language of imperialism, and if we look into the future, we see the Russian language emerging as the world language of socialism (communism.)

How well are the Soviet leaders achieving their goals? Are they making progress toward world communism? In their own eyes they are making good progress. They repeatedly tell us so. Khrushchev, in the quotation above, told us that communism would triumph worldwide. Dr. Michael Voslensky shows elsewhere in this volume that Communist leaders in the USSR form a conspiracy not to establish communism as specified by Marx, but a conspiracy of total dictators who have learned that their concepts work. They now use these concepts, based on increasingly great military force, for the establishment, the exercise, and the expansion of their power.

On October 26, 1973, in a speech in Moscow, Leonid Brezhnev gave the world his assessment:

> We are deeply convinced that the current changeabout from cold war to detente, from military confrontation to a more solid security and to peaceful cooperation is the main tendency in present-day international relations. How has this become possible? The main factor, we are certain, is the general change in the correlation of world forces—a change . . . in favor of the forces of peace and progress [i.e., the USSR.]

"The correlation of forces on a world basis" is a special Soviet concept involving all the major elements of conflict between the two world systems ("the Soviet world socialist system" and "the United States world capitalist system"). This concept, the correlation of forces, is central to Soviet world strategy. It involves an analysis of the relative power of the two systems in military forces, economic forces, and political, psychological, scientific, ideological, cultural, and sociological forces.

By employing this total systems conflict concept backed by growing military force and constant use of deception, the Soviets have made major headway in achieving world communism.

There are 159 nations in the United Nations. There are now thirty-seven Marxist-Leninist countries in the world. It is true that not all of these (China, for example) are under Soviet control, but it is perfectly clear that they are Marxist-Leninist, or "Socialist," and they do cooperate with the USSR when conflicts with the West are involved. (China, for example, cooperated with the USSR in the Vietnam War.)

More recent Soviet statements demonstrate that they believe that Marxism-Leninism is making great progress against the U.S.-led Western capitalist forces. In 1978 Marshal Nikolai Ogarkov told a group of U.S. congressmen visiting Moscow, "Today, the Soviet

Union has military superiority over the United States. Henceforth, the United States will be threatened. It had better get used to it." And the January 1980 *Red Star*, the Soviet military journal, stated, "With respect to the military balance, the correlation of forces has shifted—once and for all and irrevocably."

Meanwhile, as the Soviets built substantial military supremacy and deceived the West that they were pursuing "peace and progress," our own leaders—McNamara, Kissinger, Nixon, Ford, and Carter especially—pursued policies that in the end have helped the USSR. The establishment of a "just peace" in Vietnam and "detente" with the USSR are examples. Both concepts were deceptions. The "just peace" in Vietnam resulted in a Communist victory, followed by hundreds of thousands of Vietnamese boat people who fled "democratic" Vietnam.

In a similar manner we were deceived by "detente." The Western meaning of *detente* is a mutual relaxation of tension between two or more nations, an attitude of live and let live. But the Marxist-Leninist meaning of *detente* is quite different. Their meaning is simply that Western forces do not oppose Communist takeovers. Brezhnev assessed detente in a 1973 speech to Communist leaders in Prague: "We are achieving with detente what our predecessors have been unable to achieve using the fist. . . . By 1985 we will be able to extend our will wherever we wish."

In 1974 Brezhnev again assessed "detente":

> Over the past few years something truly great and important has been achieved. This is a turn in the development of international detente and the affirmation of the principles of peaceful coexistence between countries with different social systems. Clearly this is a victory for the Leninist foreign policy of our party and the consistent efforts to carry out the Peace Program advanced by the 24th CPSU Congress. This is the result of our united action with the fraternal countries of the socialist community, the communist and workers' parties, and all progressive forces throughout the world. And, of course, this is the result of a certain realism displayed by top political leaders in a number of capitalist countries.

By "realism" Brezhnev meant Western acquiescence to Soviet power. We would call it "appeasement." Brezhnev expressed it in a collection of his speeches published in Moscow, June 14, 1974:

A struggle between representatives of aggressive forces and *supporters of realism* is taking place in practically all the bourgeois countries. But whatever acute forms the struggle may assume we are confident of one thing; the future is not with the advocates of cold war. [emphasis added]

Thus it becomes "realistic" to acquiesce to "socialist" power in Vietnam, "socialist" power in El Salvador, in Nicaragua, and wherever else Soviet-backed "socialist" power attacks the West.

Thus, while Robert McNamara successfully suppressed U.S. Department of Defense weapons systems programs to give the Soviets time to match (and exceed) our military power, while Henry Kissinger initiated and advocated detente, the Soviets rapidly built military forces to persuade Western peoples to acquiesce to Soviet advances.

Religious Deception

Surely one of the most important and most powerful worldwide Soviet deception and manipulation programs involves world religions. Why this program has been and still is so successful is strange because Lenin was crystal clear that Marxism-Leninism is against religion and is in fact actively atheistic. (See Dr. William Fletcher's essay in this volume.)

Lenin's repetition of Marx's famous dictum, "Religion is the opium of the people," is the foundation of understanding the status of religion in the Soviet Union and its use of world religions. Lenin went on in 1909 to say, "This dictum of Marx's is the cornerstone of the whole Marxist view of religion. Marxism has always regarded all modern religions and churches and all religious organizations as instruments of bourgeois [non-Communist] reaction that serve to defend exploitation [by the capitalists] and to drug the working class."

Early efforts to destroy religion completely in Russia failed. Religious beliefs held on, however difficult it was for the "believer," as he is called in Russia, to practice his beliefs. Churches were closed, and religious meetings were prohibited. Yet many continued to practice their beliefs—to read the Bible, to meet in secret, and to pray.

Official Soviet policy changed—not to permit religion freely to exist and flourish, but to manipulate it and use it for the regime's purposes. Some churches were authorized, and some religious activity was permitted—under strictly controlled conditions.

The Soviets took control of the Russian Orthodox Church, promoted the theology of liberation worldwide, supported and infiltrated the World Council of Churches, and in general penetrated several of the major world religions.

In South Vietnam the Marxist-Leninists penetrated the Buddhist churches and used them for sanctuaries for Communist forces and to promote the North Vietnamese takeover of South Vietnam.

In the Western Hemisphere the Marxist-Leninists have penetrated many of the denominations. They have been especially successful in promoting an entirely new philosophy of religion, "the theology of liberation," and they have enlisted deceived bishops, priests, nuns, and Catholic laymen into action to overthrow established churches, established religious bodies, and established governments.

The Maryknoll Order in the United States; Father Robert F. Drinan, the renowned Communist priest-activist; the Reverend William Sloane Coffin, the well-known Communist sympathizer at the Riverside Church in New York; and many other "religious people" have joined the Marxist-Leninist forces or are, in fact, supporting Communist activities. The Pittsburgh Theological Seminary, Catholic University, and several other divinity schools in the United States teach Liberation theology as if it were a bona fide Christian philosophy. Pope John Paul II has made some progress in combating this theology in the Catholic Church, but the struggle still is sharp and vicious.

Liberation theology has as its main thesis the idea that many Marxist-Leninist methods can help the Church produce social change and lift up the poor and downtrodden who are being oppressed and exploited by traditional religions and their governments. This is a blatant deception of the people.

The Church of God in Christian concepts thus becomes the Church of the People under Liberation theology. Christ becomes, not the son of God as he is in Christian doctrine, but "the son of the People" in Liberation theology.

The continuity between early Leninist attempts to eradicate religion and more recent efforts to use and manipulate churches and their members is demonstrated in the following quotes.

Lenin, in his treatise *Religion*, stated, "The fight against religion must not be limited nor reduced to abstract ideological preaching.

This struggle must be linked up with the concrete practical class movement: its aim must be to eliminate the social roots of religion."[6]

When it developed over the years that religion was most difficult to eradicate, the Soviet leaders took control over the churches they did permit and organized them to serve the building of communism. Thus, in 1976 Brezhnev defined the role of religious forces. (One should remember that the Soviet constitution guarantees freedom of worship.)

> The ever more extensive Catholic forces and the representatives of other religious communities and believers of other faiths play an important role in the struggle for the rights of the toilers, for democracy and peace. The communist and workers' parties realize the need for a dialogue with these forces and for joint action, this being an integral part of the fight to develop Europe in a democratic spirit [Communist] and advance toward social progress [communism.]

Soviet success in controlling the churches in the USSR is understandable. But Soviet success in infiltrating the Quaker movement (especially the American Friends Service Committee, which appears in almost every Communist controlled operation,) the Catholic Church through Liberation theology, and the Protestant churches, especially through Communist influence in the World Council of Churches, is phenomenal.

Large sectors of Catholics, especially in Latin America, have embraced Liberation theology, as mentioned above. This is so serious that the Vatican issued a grave "Instruction on Certain Aspects of the Theology of Liberation" that severely chastizes the continuing oppression of the poor by the rich in Latin America, clearly supports the theme of Christian liberation, elaborates on the biblical meanings of *liberation*, and exposes the Marxist subversion of these meanings. The most brutal and clearly non-Christian concept in Liberation theology is the adoption of the Marxist idea that violence to overthrow the oppressive rich, including killing, is fully justified.

The Vatican "Instruction" thus rightly charges that Liberation theology's adoption of "class struggle," which is a cornerstone of Marxism, is evil, not good, and thus not Christian. The Vatican instruction concludes that truth about Christ and truth about God are the key—not "the theology of liberation."

Peace, Soviet-Style

Andrei Gromyko, minister of foreign affairs of the USSR, described Soviet "peace" policy as based on Lenin's "peace" policy. He told the world in the April 29–May 6, 1984, *Moscow News* that Lenin himself wrote the "Peace Decree," which was the "Soviet States' first foreign policy act."

If peace and peaceful coexistence are really fundamental principles of Soviet foreign policy, why does the West see the USSR as a threat? To answer this question, it is necessary to ask what the Soviets mean by *peace* and *peaceful coexistence*.

Lenin said, "We cannot wiggle out of an imperialistic war, we cannot have a democratic peace, but only a *peace imposed by violence,* until we overthrow the power of capitalism."[7] *Peace,* in the Soviet view, means the overthrow of the West by violent means and the imposition of a Communist system; then there will be peace.

Gromyko also stated in his *Moscow News* article that "socialist internationalism" is the supreme form of relations between socialist (real communist) countries and the unity of action of the national detachments of the victorious working class and their Marxist-Leninist vanguard." Gromyko was using communist concepts that need to be translated here.

"Socialist internationalism" is the Brezhnev Doctrine, wherein the USSR will intervene to preserve communism in a country if it is threatened internally or externally.[8] Similarly, Gromyko stated that the Soviets will intervene in other countries to protect the vanguard of the victorious workers—which is the Communist Party—in those countries.[9]

By "peaceful coexistence," Gromyko meant, as Lenin, Stalin, and Brezhnev meant, that "outstanding issues between countries must be settled not by force, not by war, but in a peaceful way. . . . But peaceful coexistence does not extend to the struggle of ideologies."[10]

Thus, a government such as El Salvador's will embrace "peaceful coexistence" with Nicaragua or Cuba; then the Communists may move in and take over with guerrilla forces supported by Nicaraguan, Cuban, and Soviet "socialist internationalism."

If one reads Gromyko's paper with an understanding of the double meanings of Communist concepts, one sees that "peaceful coexistence" is a specific form of socialism's class struggle against capitalism. This struggle is going on and will continue in the field of economics, politics and, of course, ideology, "because the world outlooks . . . of the two social systems are opposite and irreconcilable."

Then Gromyko stated, "There is no hope of the West's settling such struggles by force because the Soviets are now too strong." He continued:

> Introducing the principle of peaceful coexistence into relations between the socialist [Communist] and capitalist [Western] countries is connected, directly and immediately, with the growth of the might of socialism [communism] as a social system. World socialism's [communism's] increased might and cohesion, its active peace policy, its strengthening alliance with all the progressive [Communist] and antiwar [fellow traveler] forces, as well as the increasing realization by the sober-minded leaders of the bourgeois world [the West] that there are no grounds for planning to settle the historic argument between capitalism [the West] and socialism [communism] by force of arms. . . . Following Lenin's behests, the USSR remains as before an advocate of peace and an opponent of predatory wars. As before, it also advocates disarmament, international detente, and settling of disputed questions by peaceful means.

But what do these concepts mean? In the first place, Gromyko means "a Soviet peace," which means the worldwide defeat of capitalism and the conversion of Western societies to Communist societies.

"Predatory wars" are wars involving Western forces. All wars involving Communist forces are "just wars" or "wars of national liberation." The Afghanistan war, where the USSR is systematically murdering the Afghanistani people, is a "war of liberation." The truth is, however, that it is systematic genocide.

"Disarmament" means simply the disarmament of the West. *There is no mutual disarmament in the Soviet meaning.*

In a speech in Moscow on June 7, 1969, Brezhnev stated, "To force disarmament on the imperialists [the West] means to shake the positions of the instigators of another war [the West] . . . and to strengthen world peace [under communism]."

The rest of Gromyko's article on Lenin's peace policy is equally deceptive. He spoke of the "nuclear freeze," which of course means the West freezes while the USSR continues to build; he spoke of "reducing strategic arms," which means for the West to reduce while the Soviets continue to build; he spoke of "preventing the militarization of space," which means preventing the West from military operations in space while the Soviets develop the military forces to control space and enforce "peace"; and he spoke of "banning and liquidating chemical weapons," which means the West bans and liquidates their chemical weapons while the Soviets build more chemical weapons, tests them against the Afghan, Southeast Asian, and other peoples and deploys chemical weapons to their own military forces for use against the West if war begins.

In short, this article by Gromyko is a catalog of Soviet strategic and tactical campaigns worldwide while appearing to be a major Soviet statement in support of world peace. It is a typical high-level Soviet deception. It is a compendium of lies.

The Need for Truth

In his excellent presentation to the American Bar Association referred to above, Ambassador Kampelman made a significant point of the Soviet Union's leaders' facility in using language differently from the way we do. "They have the ability to use language," he said, "in a way which is designed to confuse people like ourselves and undermine our will. This they do professionally and effectively. They take a noble word like *democracy* and adopt it as their own— as you know, they frequently call their systems 'people's democracies.' This is a total corruption of the term.

"Words," he continued, "have different meaning. The Communists are able to use these differences to promote their own appeal, which they then use as an instrument of expansionism or aggression. Their ability to use 'people' and to use 'democracy' is an example of this talent. The Communist appeal is essentially a humanitarian appeal. They talk about 'justice' being the end result. . . . In their propaganda they identify themselves and ally themselves with efforts to achieve humanitarian goals such as 'freedom' or 'justice.'"

Ambassador Kampelman concluded that Soviet excesses have neutralized much of their ideological appeal, but "what they do have going for them now is massive military power."

The basic point is that the "different use" of words the Soviets have is much more than a talent—it is an instrument of subversion, of disinformation—an instrument of deception.

There is thus an urgent need for understanding the Soviet use of language. Whose responsibility is this? When he was awarded the Nobel Prize for literature, Alexander Solzhenitsyn stated, "The simplest act of an ordinary brave man is not to participate in lies. . . . But it is in the power of writers and artists . . . to defeat the lie." It is time for the media to exercise its right and its power to tell the truth.

The government of the United States can help by setting a pattern. It is crucial that the President tell the people the truth about Soviet lying. This applies to Soviet lying in treaties, Soviet lying in the arms control process, and Soviet lying in all aspects of internal affairs and international relations.

The government should establish a facility, perhaps related to the Joint Publication Research Service, which translates foreign documents. This facility should further translate the "Communese" in their documents into plain English. This function is needed in the Administration, but it is also needed in the U.S. news media.

The U.S. and all Western news media should develop a code of examining Soviet and Communist news for disinformation, misinformation, propaganda, and deception. This effort should similarly translate Soviet ideological "Communese" into plain English, French, or German, whatever the language may be.

Finally, there should be a major effort to introduce courses in translating "Communese" into plain language in our schools and universities.

If Americans do not understand these subverted concepts, there is danger that under the star-spangled banner they will embrace a "nuclear freeze" to stop the U.S. "war-mongering" arms buildup and will face a call for world peace that results in the "liberation of America" and the establishment of a "peoples' democracy" in the United States, a "dictatorship of the proletariat."

To alert readers to important Marxist-Leninist concepts, many of which are subversions of accepted concepts, Figure 1 lists concepts that the Soviets use worldwide to deceive people.

Figure 1

Important Marxist-Leninist Terms

absurdity and truth	aim, common
aggression	anticommunism
agitator	Army, Soviet, superiority of
agrarian reform	atheism, obligatory

basis and superstructure
bourgeoisie
camps, two
capitalism, crisis of
church
citizen, free
civil defense
class struggle
class struggle, armed
coexistence
collectivism
communism
CPSU, its leadership
CPSU, world Communist movement, vanguard of
competition, economic
contradictions, taking advantage of
correlation of forces
counterrevolution
Cuba
defense of socialism
democracy, genuine
democratic centralism
detente
developed socialist society
dictatorship of the proletariat
disarmament
ebb and flow
economics, decisive battlefield
economy, planned
education of the masses
education, religious
end justifies the means
enemy of the whole world
epoch, our
ethics, Communist
force
forces, armed
forces, peace-loving
foreign policy, Soviet
fraction
fraternal bond
freedom
fundamental principle of communism

future belongs to communism
globe, transforming of
goal, ultimate
God, belief in
hatred for the capitalist
ideological advance
imperialism
international solidarity
justice, socialist
language, Russian
love and hatred
man, new Soviet
Marxism-Leninism
Marxism-Leninism, doctrine, integrated
Marxism-Leninism, and religion
mass action
masses
might, Soviet need
militarization, Soviet
military might
morality
movement, liberation
multiparty system, use of
national liberation
national liberation, wars of
NATO
negotiations
neutralism
nuclear weapon, uses of
opposition, suppression of
organization, weapon of proletariat
overthrow, forcible
ownership
parliament, Communist role in
party
peace, just
peace, lasting world
peace-loving forces
peace program
peace struggle
peace struggle, class war, form of
peaceful coexistence

peaceful coexistence and class
  struggle
people's democracy
private, eradication of word
progressive
proletarian internationalism
property, private, abolition of
realism, support of
religion, fight against
religion, opium of the people
religious forces, role of
revolution, agrarian
revolution, Communist
revolution, socialist, principles
shelters, USSR
slogans, revolutionary
socialism and capitalism
socialist internationalism (Brezhnev
  Doctrine)
solidarity
Soviet Union, role of
Soviet Union stands guard over
  peace
space, conquest of
states, socialist, cohesion of
strategy, of the party
strike
struggle, between two social systems

struggle, legal, and illegal
superiority, military-technical
surprise attack, frustration of
tactics
terror, rule by
three revolutionary streams
truth, concealment of
truths, eternal, abolition of

underground Communist
united action
united front
United States, advancing to
  communism

vanguard of the working class
victory
violence

war
war, just
warfare, ideological
work, ideological
world, capitalist, obsolete
world Communist movement,
  unity of
World Peace Council
world socialist system

youth, Communist
zig-zags, and communism

Discussion of the meaning of these terms would require more space than is available in this chapter. The best meanings are contained in quotations used by prominent Communists, by Lenin, Stalin, Brezhnev, or a current leader. This list is not complete, but it covers a significant portion of the core terms used by Marxist-Leninists. This list was drawn from *A Lexicon of Marxist-Leninist Semantics*.[11] However, they can be found in many lexicons and dictionaries of Communist terms. An understanding of these terms as used by world Communists is very helpful to the understanding of the activities of world Communists. Some of these concepts are defined in lengthy detail in *A Dictionary of Scientific Communism* (Moscow, Progress Publishers, 1980, English translation, 1984).

Notes

1. J. Stalin, *Words*, np., n.d.
2. N. S. Khrushchev, "Speech." Radio Moscow Broadcast, November 23, 1955.
3. *A Lexicon of Marxist-Leninist Semantics*, Raymond S. Sleeper, ed. (Western Goals, 1983.)
4. V.I. Lenin. *Selected Works*, vol. 2. (New York, International Publishers, 1937), p. 57.
5. *The Fundamentals of Marxist-Leninist Philosophy.* (Moscow, Progress Publishers, 1974), p. 406.
6. V.I. Lenin, *Religion.* (New York, Little Lenin Library, n.d.) Vol. 7, p. 14.
7. Sleeper, op. cit., p. 202.
8. Sleeper, op. cit., p. 256.
9. Ibid., p. 313.
10. Ibid., p. 209.
11. Ibid.

SOVIET
STRATEGIC
DECEPTION

Dr. Joseph D. Douglass, Jr.

Strategic deception differs from what normally comes to mind when the word *deception* is used. Usually we think of *The Man Who Never Was*, the Overlord feint used to divert German attention away from the Normandy invasion, and, more recently, *The Sting*. Soviet strategic deception is different from these examples because it is long-term, often extending over ten, twenty, even fifty years. It involves a myriad of techniques and tactics that are designed to influence the way we think about the Soviet Union. They are strategic, as opposed to tactical, and are an integral part of Soviet grand strategy.

Most important, in the case of Soviet deception, *we* are the target, not the bad guys. None of us likes to admit that we may have been deceived or that our policies and strategies may be based on assumptions that are false, assumptions that are the product of long-term Soviet deception. This helps explain why so little attention is focused on Soviet deception—better to study U.S. and British deceptions in World War II, where the studies are unlikely to attack our sensitivities or sensibilities.

Moreover, the "we" is an all-inclusive "we"—the government, academia, the news media, the right wing and left wing alike, industry and finance, even the public. All special interests are targeted by carefully designed Soviet deceptions, which is why we all need to be concerned. The problem is not just an intelligence problem or a national security community problem.

Although deception is an integral part of all Soviet activities, "Soviet deception" is rarely discussed in print in the Soviet Union. Deceptions and deception strategy are among the most closely guarded State secrets. Still further, officially, deception is not practiced by the Soviets. "Deception" is a dirty capitalist pursuit, beneath the dignity of the Soviet Union. Hence, when speaking of deception

211

in print, a variety of euphemisms are employed, such as "the political plan," *maskirovka,* or "strategic disinformation."

Soviet strategic deception, as explained in an official KGB training manual, is, first of all, for use in "the execution of State tasks." That is, it is an important tool of the top Party leadership, which is the meaning of *State* in the Soviet Union. It is "directed at misleading the enemy concerning the basic questions of State policy, the military economic status, and the scientific-technical achievement of the Soviet Union." It is also designed to mislead states, especially "Western imperialist states," about the policies of other imperialist states, which means, for example, to turn the United States against Europe and the European states against the United States and against each other. Finally, the KGB manual points out, strategic disinformation is designed to mislead us all about "specific counterintelligence tasks of the organs of State Security," which includes the whole Soviet worldwide police-state operation.

One of the best examples of the Soviets misleading the West is arms control. The Soviet advocacy of arms control goes back sixty years. They are forever proclaiming their peaceful intentions and crying out for complete disarmament. What we in the West fail to comprehend is that, in the Soviet dictionary, *peace* is synonymous with "world socialist republic." There can be no peace as long as capitalism exists. In a similar vein, *arms race,* as defined by the Soviets, refers only to arms manufactured by imperialist (i.e., Western) states. And arms control itself is viewed as a mechanism that is to be used to "disarm the bourgeoisie" while arming the proletariat; that is, to disarm the West, not the East.

And that is precisely what has taken place over the past quarter-century. The Soviet Union has used arms control to debilitate Western defense planning, to encourage unilateral disarmament, to enable the Soviet Union to come from far behind and achieve substantial military superiority over the West, and to do so not only with the West's acquiescence but with its assistance as well. In 1973 British Intelligence tried to warn U.S. officials about what was happening. The British reported details of a speech that the Soviet Communist Party boss, Leonid Brezhnev, gave to high-level East European party officials. In the speech Brezhnev explained that detente was really a ruse designed to enable the Soviets to gain superiority. Not only did the report fall on deaf ears, it was buried in the United States because what it had to say ran counter to U.S. concepts of detente.

Why are the Soviets apparently so successful and Westerners so easily misled? Understanding this question and its answer is fundamental to understanding Soviet deception and the threat it poses to the West. The simple answer is that deception is a natural characteristic of the Soviet system. The State needs deception to survive, and all those who live in the Soviet police state need deception to survive. The Soviets are simply experts, as a natural by-product of their system.

The Communist organization, with its centralized control mechanisms, is ideally suited to orchestrate complex deceptions in ways that go unnoticed in the West because of the West's decentralized, uncoordinated, often fragmented character. This is especially evident in the planning process. Soviet strategic deception is formulated as part of their long-range plan that projects over twenty years into the future. But there is no place in the U.S. government where Soviet long-range planning is studied or where apparently diverse Soviet actions are compared and assessed as they contribute to a long-range plan. Hence there is no concept of Soviet deception as an integral part of a long-range plan.

In contrast, in the United States the emphasis is on freedom and knowledge. All instruments and agencies in the West are open and available for use by the Soviets in weaving their webs of deceit. Our news media are open, our schools are open, the public is freely available, and government and private sector officials are available, including high-priority targets such as congressmen. Soviet writings and statements are reported in the news media as they are received. It is rare for such news items to carry a "consumer beware" caveat. This lack of attention to the deceptive content of Soviet statements also applies to most national security analysts studying Soviet Strategy. Little regard is given to the possibility that Soviet statements are designed to communicate what they want us to believe, which more often than not stands in stark contrast to reality.

People in the United States tend to have an optimistic view of life. People are seen as inherently good with similar needs and drives, independent of where they are located. There is almost no appreciation of what the closed Soviet totalitarian society is like. We incorrectly mirror-image our own value system, wants, and desires when trying to understand the Soviet system, and we look for similar entities—for example hawks, doves, and moderates. In a sense, we are very naive.

Conversely, the Soviets recognize the value of propaganda and disinformation and are organized to take advantage of the openness of Western societies. In 1982, the CIA estimated that the Soviets spent upward of three billion dollars each year on such activities. In this process, all Soviet agencies are involved and carefully controlled. The overall effort is directed from the top, by the Communist Party chairman, who is himself one of the key operational instruments.

The Soviets have adopted a basic tactic that thrives on this Western naiveté. It was set forth by Lenin in his famous deception guidance to the first chief of Soviet state security: "Tell them what they want to believe." The simplicity of this tactic may well be the factor most responsible for the success of Soviet deception.

These two different approaches—the Soviet deception orientation and the American sense of freedom and desire to live in an orderly and peaceful world—are the crux of the problem. The United States simply wants to believe, and the Soviets feed this desire with the greatest care and understanding. Perhaps the best way of showing how this works is with a variety of illustrations—case studies of where our perceptions of the Soviet Union are being very deliberately manipulated.

Perhaps the most important continuing Soviet deception is the notion that the Soviet Union is not a lethal threat. This deception has many components, such as the notion that the Soviet Union is only defensive, that it is only reacting to aggressive moves by hostile enemies such as Afghanistan, and that it only wants peace. The historical record completely disproves these basic themes, and Soviet actions themselves continue to demonstrate how false the themes are. But one very special component of this deception serves to rewrite or negate this history and enables people to continue to swallow the basic deception, that the Soviet Union is not a lethal threat. This most critical component is the idea that the Soviet Union is changing, especially now under Gorbachev's new policies of openness.

Do not concern yourself with the past, the Soviet Union is changing, we are told. Their ideology is dead. Nobody believes anymore. The system is merely driven by bureaucratic momentum. As soon as the old leadership dies off, a new moderate element will take power. It is important for the United States to play to these moderates and not be too tough. Give their new policies and desires for peace a chance to take root and grow. Their economy is a disaster, and the government is rotten with nepotism. The younger moderates know this, and their first priority is to implement changes. The West should see that internal pressures make reform inescapable, and it should encourage its implementation by providing a fertile climate for change—a relaxation of tension and an increase in trade—in which the moderating influences can grow.

This sounds eminently logical, precisely what we would like to believe is the case. Only one problem: It is totally wrong. It is a very effective Soviet strategic deception, one that dates back many years—well over half a century.

Consider the proposition that the ideology is dead. The problem with ideology is understanding all that it encompasses and distinguishing what about it is dead and what is alive and well. Ideology has two sides, simply stated: what it promises and how it operates. What it promises has been dead or understood as only a deception to those enslaved or in power for well over thirty years—in many cases, over fifty years. But to the unwary and unsuspecting, the promises are alive and still effectively used, for example, in Third World and underdeveloped countries and against youth wherever the Communists control or have infiltrated the educational process. A good example of this is in the papers taken from Grenada. These papers clearly show that Grenadian Communists were believers. Morever, the promises have become an integral part of the dogma. And the dogma of Communist ideology is alive and well and practiced. It is evident in every published Communist paper. It is still used with effect to channel people's thinking, and it is clearly very much alive.

The other side of ideology is the operational side. Here, ideology is used with great effectiveness to steer the Communist system. In its operational mode, ideology controls the Communist movement. It sets the goal, which is world domination, and the morals, in which anything that advances the movement is moral; it provides the basis for discipline and control, whereby all decisions are "unanimous": there is no dissent, party unity is absolute, and all activities are organized to advance the movement. In this regard, the ideology is more alive and well than it has ever been. It is in control, and there is no evidence of any deviation in its objectives or diminution in its force.

The need for the West to support moderate elements is another deception that furthers the notion of change in the Soviet Union that has been around for many years. The problem is, there are no moderates. There is little disagreement, if any, among the leadership regarding objectives. Debates are about how best to achieve the objective, world domination. To suggest that there are hawks and doves in the Soviet leadership, as one finds in the West, is false mirror-imaging. How false it is is perhaps best illustrated indirectly by the manner in which the Soviet leadership internally refers to hawks and doves in the West, which is as "the eagles and the pigeons." Doves and moderates do not survive in the Communist system. There are only hawks, with varying types of deceptive colorations applied from time to time.

Stalin referred to himself as a moderate in seeking concessions from the West to pacify the "hawks" in the Supreme Soviet with whom he had to contend. In more recent times an equally absurd ploy, and one readily picked up in the Western news media, was to characterize Andropov as a "closet liberal" just a few months before his predecessor, Brezhnev, died. And illustrating how the West never learns, Gorbachev, the instant the Chernenko deathwatch began, traveled to London, sipped tea politely, and was accorded by the press the image of the "Gucci kid," a gentleman with whom Margaret Thatcher believed she could work in harmony!

And as for the economy, to suggest that the Soviet economy is on the rocks and that the leadership is concerned or that agricultural problems may help motivate change is wishful thinking, oblivious to the past. The Soviet economy and agriculture have been disasters for over fifty years, and this has caused no changes, only efforts by the West to "help" the Soviets and thereby encourage change. This totally ignores a regime that forced tens of millions to starve in the process of collectivization. The Soviet economy is no worse now than it was in 1920 or 1930 or 1950. If anything, it is better.

A good illustration of how the deception that the Soviet Union is changing is successfully foisted upon the West was provided by Jan Sejna, a high-ranking Czechoslovakian official who sought political asylum in the West in 1968. He provided a firsthand description of Khrushchev's strategy as it was explained by Khrushchev to a group of high-level Czechoslovakian officials in mid-1954.

Speaking informally over cocktails to Czech officials, Khrushchev explained that Stalin's policies needed to be changed. The Soviet Union and Eastern Europe had not progressed since World War II. They were still in a war economy. Khrushchev's solution was to end the Cold War specifically to make Western technology and economic assistance available to the Soviet Union. The Cold War was to be replaced with "peaceful coexistence," which continues to this day as the main contemporary Soviet foreign policy deception. As Khrushchev described peaceful coexistence to Sejna, the Communist world was simply placing its arm around the shoulders of the West—not in friendship, but rather to lead the West to the grave more quickly.

To end the Cold War, he believed that the West—specifically the West's intellectual middle class—had to be convinced that the Soviet Union had changed. The only way to accomplish this, Khrushchev explained, "was to lay the blame for the past on the shoulders of the only person who could carry the burden"—that is, on Stalin.

This was one of the major motivations for the de-Stalinization campaign that was initiated with Khrushchev's famous "secret speech" at the 1956 Party Congress, in which Stalin's crimes were first revealed and decried. "Peaceful coexistence" had begun to emerge in Soviet speeches the preceding year, and this secret speech was the key play in the deception to sell "peaceful coexistence" to the West. Following the speech, numerous examples of change were introduced to show a rise of pluralism and democratic processes and a cutback in cultural suppression.

Was it successful? Within one month following Khrushchev's secret speech, the concept of change in the Soviet Union was front-page news. For example, as analyzed by Harrison Salisbury on March 25, 1956, in *The New York Times*:

> It is no longer possible to discuss what is happening in Moscow since the death of Stalin in terms of "tactical change" or "strategic" maneuver. . . . Perhaps a word like revolution is still too strong to use. Perhaps not. In the Soviet Union itself they are beginning to talk of the changes in terms comparing them to the spring breaking-up of ice on a Siberian river.

What a delightful way to describe the end of the Cold War!

Similar views were also expressed in *The Washington Post* by Chalmers Roberts, who wrote, "Many observers believe it may, in fact, further the idea of a great change in Russia." These views were subsequently restated by Secretary of State John Foster Dulles.

Only a few news commentators cautioned that perceptions of change in the Soviet Union were premature. After all, such change was exactly what people wanted to believe and still want to believe—most importantly the media, which are probably the foremost target of Soviet deception, and the Western leadership, both political and business.

The Western desire to see what it wants to believe is especially evident in assessing Soviet nuclear war strategy and intentions. Basic Soviet nuclear strategy and intentions and the associated deception were formulated in the mid- to late 1950s; the principal detailed work took place from 1957 to 1959. This was when the basic principles were established (May 1957) and implementation plans developed and approved (September 1959).

In analyzing these and other Soviet decisions, it is important to recognize that deception is an integral part of each. When a decision is made, the manner in which the decision is to be implemented and controlled (oversight) and a deception plan to ease its implementation are also decided on. Thus, as the Soviets were deciding on a national strategy in which nuclear weapons would be the foremost and decisive weapon to use in their war against the West, an accompanying deception plan was developed, one that would play on the West's fear of nuclear war and mislead the West regarding true Soviet intentions. This deception was incorporated into the policy of "peaceful coexistence," and continues today in nearly its original unmodified form.

How nuclear war and nuclear strategy entered into the "peaceful coexistence" deception is very simple. Nuclear war was to be made as awful appearing as possible; hence the image of radioactive deserts. Also, the possibility of nuclear war was to be made realistic—for example, via the "irrational" behavior of Khrushchev and more recently by Andropov—as a counter to Reagan's anti-Soviet rhetoric and plans to modernize the U.S. nuclear deterrent.

The conclusion the West was persuaded to reach was that the only alternative to nuclear war was "peaceful coexistence." Nuclear war was to be used as a club to cause the "realistic" elements in the West to pull together and triumph over the hawks, or radicals, and at the same time to hide the true nature of Soviet intentions, which continue to be portrayed as only defensive. The Soviet approach to nuclear war would be put forth as a countervalue approach, both to support those fears and to cover their principal aim, which was a real military war-fighting counterforce strategy.

As the Soviets worked hard to use nuclear war to get the West to accept "peaceful coexistence" and forgo preparations for nuclear war, they also worked hard to build up their own nuclear war capability, which they saw as decisive in the East-West battle—decisive in war and in peace. The essence of their philosophy is very clear. As stated in official publications, "superiority accelerates the process of the physical and moral defeat of the enemy and makes it possible to operate more daringly and decisively and to impose one's will on the enemy and to attack him more successfully."

The basic Soviet objective is obvious. Military power is relative; so are preparations. What counts is not only how much one nation prepares but also how little (or how incorrectly) another nation prepares. The Soviet forces are far more powerful if those of the United States are decreased. Accordingly, the Soviets strive to hide important indications of their true capability, intentions, and preparations from the enemy (that is, the United States) and simultaneously to influence the enemy to neglect to prepare for war, or better still to see nuclear war as impossible and to unilaterally disarm.

One element of Khrushchev's nuclear war deception in the early 1960s was revealed in an American and British "intelligence coup"—the case of Colonel Oleg Penkovskiy. Colonel Penkovskiy had recklessly pushed to be recruited upon President Kennedy's election in November 1960. He began spying for the West formally in April 1961, the result of his forcing the issue, and it continued until his arrest in October 1963 following the Cuban missile crisis.

If one accepts that the CIA book *The Penkovskiy Papers* is a reasonably accurate account of what Penkovskiy had to say (and the alternative possibility raises serious, if not damning implications concerning CIA deceptions directed against the U.S. people, and our national security community.) It provides an excellent illustration of the manner in which deception is used. Penkovskiy warned that Khrushchev was preparing for war and that many were afraid he might unleash such a war. However, most of the Soviet generals opposed him and believed nuclear war was impossible and could not be fought. The Soviet Union had many technical problems and was far, far behind the West. Their strategy was countervalue, and by 1964 they would have completed their nuclear buildup. (In retrospect, the enormity of this lie is obvious; 1964 was the "take-off" point rather than the "tapering-off" point in the Soviet buildup.) And after Khrushchev, the Soviets would return rapidly to conventional war capability.

Aside from a number of valid "trees" that are present in the Penkovskiy material, perhaps designed to impart a measure of credibility, the image of the overall Soviet nuclear forest as presented by Penkovskiy was false and deceptive in almost all important aspects.

Beginning in the early 1960s, U.S. national security policy became almost wholly dependent on what analysts and decision makers wanted to believe. Although slightly diminished in recent years due to the growth of Soviet nuclear capabilities beyond all expectations, even beyond those of the hardest-line Western hawks, U.S. policy is still based on what people would like to believe and is fed by appropriate Soviet disinformation rather than by what the data indicate the likely situation is. How much of this is due to the success of long-term Soviet deception and how much is simple self-deception is difficult to assess. There has been tremendous pressure to want to believe, and this still is the case.

The effectiveness of the two—self-deception to support policy desires and Soviet deception—can be seen with ease in various intelligence assessments—for example, those contained in the 1969 Board of National Estimates study on Soviet strategic nuclear capability. This intelligence estimate argued as follows:

> We believe that the Soviets recognize the enormous difficulties of any attempt to achieve strategic superiority of such order as to significantly alter the strategic balance. Consequently, we consider it highly unlikely that they will attempt within the period of this estimate (ten years) to achieve a first-strike capability, i.e., a capability to launch a surprise attack against the U.S. with the assurance that the U.S.S.R. would not itself receive damage it would regard as unacceptable.
>
> For one thing, the Soviets would almost certainly conclude that the cost of such an undertaking along with all their other military commitments would be prohibitive. More importantly, they almost certainly would consider it impossible to develop and deploy the combination of offensive and defensive forces necessary to counter successfully the various elements of U.S. strategic attack forces.
>
> Finally, even if such a project were economically and technically feasible, the Soviets almost certainly would calculate that the U.S. would detect and match or overmatch their efforts.

It is quite apparent now that the Soviets did "significantly alter the strategic balance"—and deception appears to have played an important role. While they probably did not achieve an unquestionable first-strike capability in the time frame of the analysis, they do appear to have come disconcertingly close, and the extent of damage they would receive in return from a U.S. retaliatory strike has become highly uncertain. By the late 1970s a successful Soviet decapitation strike had become a real possibility.

The cost of their efforts, which also included a large investment in civil defense, command and control, conventional forces, and theater nuclear forces was far from "prohibitive." And most analysts both in the government and outside are now concerned that the Soviets are in the process of conducting a defense breakout—civil defense dispersed national ABM defense with the SAM-10 and SAM-12, and Pechora Class battle-management radars.

While one cannot say how the Soviets calculated the possibility that the U.S. would detect the Soviet efforts and respond, what is perhaps more important are the efforts the Soviets undertook to cover what they were doing, to deceive the United States regarding their intentions, and, through a wide variety of active measures, to debilitate the U.S. capability to detect and respond.

As described by a former KGB officer, Soviet use of disinformation decreased under Stalin but was given new life as a major pillar of Soviet strategy by Khrushchev. It was so successful that the KGB portion of the effort was intensified and elevated in importance: first in 1959 with the creation of Department D (for dezinformatsia); second in 1967, when General Agayants took command of the operation; and again in 1971, when the "department" became a "service." The expansion in 1971 probably was part of the integrated and intensified Soviet "peace" deception program that was initiated with great fanfare at the 1971 party conference. The effort was designed to capitalize on U.S. arms control fever and desire for detente. The Soviet flags of peace, disarmament, and noninterference were waved while they proceeded to accomplish blatant takeovers of numerous Third World countries and leapfrog ahead of the United States in nuclear strength.

The use of the Soviet media as an instrument in this deception in the 1970s and the performance of their strategic leadership in spreading the deception provide a valuable case study of the successful application of Soviet techniques and tools. A rejuvenated Soviet effort to mislead the West concerning their superiority and first-strike intentions emerged roughly in 1972 and reached a peak about 1976. At that time, even Soviet General Secretary Leonid Brezhnev played in the charade when he emphasized in a major foreign policy address delivered on the eve of President Jimmy Carter's inauguration that they were not out to achieve military superiority and that the aim of delivering a first strike was not and never had been a part of Soviet policy. Simultaneously, the Soviets introduced a new theme into their propaganda: that there was a balance, and that this balance should and would be preserved, and that should it try to upset the balance, the West would only be initiating a new arms race.

It should be noted that this increased Soviet disinformation in the mid-1970s did succeed in influencing U.S. perceptions of what was happening. One of the best examples is a series of Foreign Broadcast Information Service (FBIS) analyses of high-level Soviet pronouncements in the mid- to late 1970s. FBIS reached such conclusions as: "Since 1974, the USSR has come to recognize the limitations of military power and the benefits of military balance with the West in achieving national security."

This particular 1979 analysis by the FBIS concluded by quoting the following excerpt from a 1977 Brezhnev speech as an indication of the progress in the evolution of Soviet thinking: "Maintaining the existing equilibrium is not an end in itself. We are in favor of starting a downward turn in the direction of the arms race and gradually scaling down the level of military confrontation."

This is one of the many examples of the failure of analysts to consider the internal Soviet literature, Communist ideology, the possibility that the Soviet public remarks are part of a disinformation campaign, alternative motivations, or even what the Soviets mean when they use words like *balance* or *arms race*. The analysts fail to comprehend Soviet ideology—and why should they even try to understand it if ideology is dead!

When the Soviets use the word *balance*, they do not use it in the sense of "equivalence," as the West does. Rather, it is used in the sense of "the comparative distribution or correlation of forces," or as "a balance of ingredients in a patent medicine," which certainly do not imply equivalence.

When the Soviets speak of "balance," they generally mean a balance that strongly favors the Soviet Union. Consider, for example, the Soviet statement, "The military balance, *which we have now*, is a decisive factor that will be used to eliminate military activity of imperialism throughout the whole world and will be used to prevent any attempt by the United States to *change the balance*" (emphasis added).

In the case of *arms race,* when the Soviets use the concept, it has nothing to do with Soviet arms production and deployment. As defined in a recent Soviet dictionary, *Political Terms: A Short Guide* (Novosti Press, 1982), "Arms race is the arms manufacture on an ever increasing scale carried out by aggressive circles of imperialist states."

These FBIS errors in analysis and the resultant effectiveness of Soviet deception techniques are not unusual. They almost always result when Soviet words are read without regard for what they mean, for what their ideology is, or for how they operate to achieve Soviet objectives. One of the most disturbing examples of this process is an analysis by a Washington-area defense contractor in 1977 undertaken for the U.S. government to assess the intentions of the Soviet military and political leadership. The analysts restricted their analysis to statements contained in the open press. Again, no use was made of Soviet internal literature, ideology, Communist definitions of words, or deception practices or objectives. The conclusions reached during this study were:

> The Soviet leadership believes that the only alternative to nuclear war is peaceful coexistence.
>
> Soviet statements of military intentions are primarily defensive and reactive to a perceived growth in Western military power.
>
> A first-strike goal is denied.
>
> The goal of Soviet strategic intentions is parity.
>
> There is no evidence that the Soviet Union is seeking either a first-strike or second-strike capability.
>
> Fighting and winning a next war is not an issue to which the Soviet political and military leadership examined devotes much attention.

What the analysts failed to comprehend was that this was precisely the image the Soviets were trying to project as part of their long-range strategic deception. Each and every one of the above conclusions is totally false. The problem here is serious, because these same false impressions appear to be influencing U.S. policy. For example, an analysis of statements of U.S. policy in a variety of public documents covering the same period of time as the above analysis of Soviet statements, undertaken by the author to understand what assumptions of Soviet intentions were behind U.S. policy, yielded the following U.S. policy model of Soviet intentions:

- The Soviets are deterrence oriented.
- They are interested in stopping the arms race.
- Their goal is retaliation.
- The arms buildup is a reaction to U.S. programs.
- They are unlikely to plan to use their nuclear forces.
- They are not interested in achieving a disarming first strike.
- The Soviets are not a nation of superplanners.
- Communism must change, is changing, has changed.
- The political and military moderates will triumph.

Although the two analyses were performed at the same time and with neither's knowledge of the other's study, the results correspond remarkably and regrettably well. This model of Soviet intentions is a false model. What is worse, it is still the dominant model driving U.S. policy—for two reasons: It is what the Soviets and their agents tell us over and over, and it is what we want to believe.

How successful Soviet deception is is difficult to say. The FBI and CIA would have us believe it is not very successful, that the decisions of our leadership have not been influenced to our detriment by Soviet deception, and that the media are seldom misled. This, however, does not explain the above beliefs that seem to underlie U.S. policy. It does not explain the acknowledged deception of U.S. negotiators in SALT I and SALT II. This does not explain the continuing gross misestimate of Soviet doctrine, intentions, capabilities, strategy, and activities around the world. This does not explain a media that is forever critical of statements from the U.S. government yet accepts Soviet statements at face value.

Another example that many people will recognize is the Soviet dislike for war as a result of their suffering so many casualties in World War II. Twenty million is the most common figure. This figure is used by all Soviet dignitaries to show graphically how fervently they hate war and desire peace. On the other hand, to place the number and Soviet concern in perspective, the best estimate on the number of Soviet citizens and military killed by self-inflicted collectivization of agriculture and purges just prior to World War II is 50 to 70 million! And if the number of human sacrifices in other Communist countries—China, Eastern Europe, Southeast Asia, Afghanistan, Cuba, Nicaragua, Ethiopia, everywhere the Soviets sow their seeds of peace—are added in, the figure—over 150 million—becomes even more appalling and, along with it, Soviet statements about their concern for human rights, the proletariat, and peace.

A very interesting example of how subtle Soviet deception works was recently identified by a Czechoslovakian emigré, Dr. Igor Lukes. The heart of this deception is a war memorial the Soviets built in Khatyn, near Minsk, to commemorate a German atrocity. The memorial is a black granite statue of a man holding his lifeless son and a re-creation of a village the Nazis had destroyed in World War II. But rather than a shrine to warn posterity of the horrors of war, the memorial, Dr. Lukes points out, is actually an Orwellian "memory hole," designed to confuse and destroy the historical record.

On September 17, 1939, the Soviet Union, an ally of Hitler's Germany, attacked Poland, and some fifteen thousand Polish officers were taken prisoners of war. They were detained in three separate camps (Ostashkov, Kozielsk, and Starobielsk). A great deal is known about what was going on there because the officers were allowed to correspond with their families via the Red Cross.

Then, in the spring of 1940, all but a handful of the prisoners were forced into boxcars and taken to Katyn, near Smolensk. There, in the forest surrounding a large recreation area of Soviet security forces, the Poles were executed one by one and buried in mass graves. It was later determined that many prisoners had been forced to climb onto the graves and position themselves so that the graves would accommodate more bodies. Irrefutable evidence of these facts can be found in numerous publications and was presented before the U.S. Congress in 1952.

Following the war, the Soviets brought Eastern Europe under their control, including Poland. Suddenly, the dead in the Katyn forest became an unpleasant memento of an era Moscow now wanted erased from history. Soviet disinformation experts know that silence or flat denials are passive and weak when contradicted by hard evidence. Therefore, "deception by substitution" has been invented. In order to erase the record of the Soviet atrocity in Katyn, a monument has been erected to commemorate a German atrocity in Katyn.

This latter has been turned into a show war memorial, and Western delegations are bused around with amazing frequency. Even President Richard Nixon went there during his last trip to the

Soviet Union. He was apparently unaware that his presence at Katyn and the subsequent publicity the place achieved had been well thought out by his Soviet hosts.

The Soviet deception activities against the West are best described by the people who know them best—ex-Communist officials who were part of the process. One of the most expert is former KGB officer Anatoli Golitsyn, who studied and was trained in deception, among other activities, before he defected to the West in 1961. He has now experienced life in the West for twenty-five years. His description of Soviet deception is now conditioned by many years of observation of the West and of our vulnerability. Communist disinformation, he explains, "has engendered a state of crisis in Western assessments of Communist affairs and therefore, a crisis in Western policy toward the Communist world. The meaning of developments in the Communist bloc is misunderstood and the intentions behind Communist actions are misinterpreted."

In trying to provide an assessment of long-range Communist deception and the threat it poses to the West, Golitsyn leaves no doubt that the threat is more serious, its scope is wider, and its culmination is more imminent than scholars and politicians in the West realize. These people accept at face value what the Communists choose for them to see and hear. While they accept the existence of Communist tactical disinformation—for example, forgeries and simple covert political actions—they fail to appreciate the problem of strategic disinformation. "Even those who recognize the dangers of disinformation cannot conceive that it can be practiced on so grand a scale and with a subtlety so disarming. They forget—or perhaps have never fully realized—that their predecessors were similarly deluded in the 1920s, and they fail to take into account that Communist penetration of Western governments and intelligence services provides an accurate early warning and monitoring service of Western reactions to disinformation."

This same basic message has been presented over and over, most recently by Alexander Solzhenitsyn and Andrei Sakharov. Unfortunately, however, the message never seems to get absorbed, and Soviet deception continues to confuse and confound U.S. policymakers, academics, intelligence analysts, press, and businessmen. The West continues to see only what it wants to see and hear only what it wants to hear.

Andrei Sakharov, Soviet physicist and nuclear weapons designer turned dissident and peace activist, described his view of the problem in a letter to the West published shortly after his exile to

Gorki. The West and the developing countries, he explained, "are filled with citizens who by reason of their positions are able to promote Soviet influence and expansionist goals." He identified four such groups of people. The first group is motivated by ideas; these are people who do not consider Communist ideology as a complete fraud. The second group are people "who conduct themselves in a 'progressive' [i.e., Communist] manner because they consider it profitable, prestigious, or fashionable." The third group consists of "naive, poorly informed or indifferent people who close their eyes and ears to the bitter truth and eagerly swallow any sweet lie." Finally, there is the fourth group, "people who have been 'bought' in the most direct sense of the word, not always with money. These include some political figures, businessmen, a great many writers and journalists, government advisors, and heads of the press and television. Overall, they make up quite a group of influential people."[1]

There is not much comfort for us in the idea that the Soviet system will change—as described above. The possibility of change in Soviet intentions and ideology, "peaceful coexistence," and arms control are all parts of a significant and long-running Soviet strategic deception. It was present in Lenin's time. It is present today. And its nature has been made abundantly clear. One of the best examples was a British Intelligence report sent to U.S. intelligence in 1973, the heyday of detente. The report detailed remarks by Brezhnev to East European leaders in which he explained that detente was really a ruse designed to enable the Soviets to gain superiority. "Trust us, comrades," Brezhnev counseled. "By 1985, as a consequence of what we are now achieving with detente, we will have achieved most of our objectives in Western Europe. We will have consolidated our position. We will have improved our economy. And the shift in the correlation of forces will be such that, come 1985, we will be able to exert our will wherever we need to." This report was scorned and suppressed by high-level U.S. officials because it ran counter to their detente and arms control policies.[2]

Notes

1. Andrei D. Sakharov, "Sakharov Urges Europeans to Join U.S. in Standing up to Soviet Expansionism." *The Washington Star,* June 9, 10, 11, 1980.
2. William Beecher, "Brezhnev Termed Detente a Ruse, 1973 Report Said." *The Boston Globe,* February 11, 1977.

SOVIET
DECEPTION IN
LATIN AMERICA

Charles B. Dickens

SE
HABLA
ESPAÑOL

The United Front Movement

This chapter focuses on three countries in which the Soviet Union invested a great deal of material and human resources to surround the United States on its southern flank. Its notable disinformation successes were Cuba and Nicaragua. Its notable failure, about which little is heard, was Venezuela.

When Fidel Castro and his fellow *barbudos* rolled into Havana on January 8, 1959, to a rapturous welcome by the Cuban people and the general plaudits of Americans and the Free World, Premier Nikita Khrushchev probably was duplicating the triumphant jig performed by Adolf Hitler in Paris some twenty years before.

Castro's entry into Havana was the culmination of thirty-six years of painstaking subversion in Cuba, which employed the full range of Soviet overt and covert actions to which the Soviets now refer as "active measures."

When the mysterious figure of Fabio Grobart (aka Abraham Simkovitz) walked off the gangplank of a ship from Poland to disembark at the port of Havana in 1922, his Soviet masters could not have imagined that they had set off a train of events that would lead to the establishment of a Soviet bastion ninety miles from U.S. shores. Nor could they have foreseen that, using the same process, they would, twenty years later, be able to implant on the American Continent another bastion—in Nicaragua.

Using the same techniques, they tried to take over Venezuela but failed in 1963; similar efforts that are now underway in Argentina, Brazil, Chile, Uruguay, Colombia, Peru, Bolivia, Guatemala, the Guianas, and El Salvador have yet to be successful. For a time they had success in Grenada, but they were thwarted when the U.S. armed forces freed that island nation.

The deception that had been perpetrated on the Cubans and the world was not fully revealed until Castro, in a speech on December 2, 1961, said he had been a Marxist since his student days but could not admit to it earlier because he would have lost his appeal to the Cuban people and to his *Fidelista* supporters and would never have been allowed to come to power.

Just after taking power, Castro showed his disdain for the United States during a tumultuous visit to New York City, well before his long and deep-seated hatred for the United States became clear. Before leaving for New York, Castro instructed Felipe Pazos, the president of the National Bank of Cuba, and Rufo Lopez Fresquet, minister of the treasury, who accompanied him, that under no circumstances would they bring up the possibility of receiving financial assistance from the United States; further, they would reject any offers that might be made.

Later, Fresquet was to say, "When Castro finally told us that we were not to ask for aid, we were indeed surprised. . . . I believe that it was never Castro's intention to ask for aid. If the U.S. had helped Cuba, he would never have presented the Americans as an enemy of the revolution."

What is clear from Castro's anti-U.S. prejudices formed during his youth and from his unwillingness to be indebted to the U.S. financially from the very beginning is that he was not driven into the hands of the Soviets by President Eisenhower, as is argued by Castro apologists. In fact, the events that led to Castro's total control of Cuba show that Castro was in the Soviets' pocket before his 1956 landing with eighty-one followers on the southeastern coast of Cuba.

Cuba was not neglected by the Soviets when they began to send Comintern agents around the world in the 1920s. The whole panoply of Soviet "active measures" used by them in their drive for world domination could not begin without preparing the groundwork through the recruitment and indoctrination of the native populations of the countries to become their victims.

Throughout Latin America Comintern agents helped form national Communist Parties loyal to Moscow and then sent the most promising of their recruits to the Soviet Union for specialized training in propaganda, agitation, recruitment, and terrorism. In the 1950s guerrilla training began to receive emphasis.

The popular or united front tactic, which was successful in Europe following World War II, through which, with the help of the Red Army, Czechoslovakia, Hungary, Poland, and Romania were forced into the Soviet orbit, took a different tack in Latin America. Whereas the united front tactic in Eastern Europe used political subversion with the Soviet Army as the enforcer, in Latin America their tactics employed violence, urban terrorism, kidnapping, and guerrilla forces to provoke government repression, the suspension of civil guarantees, and the declaration of a state of seige, which unified all the forces opposed to the government in violent revolt. Then the tightly disciplined and well-organized Communist militants would take or attempt to take control of the "revolutionary" government. Their duped tactical allies were then dealt with swiftly, through exile, defamation, imprisonment, or execution. Castro was an excellent Soviet disciple and leader of the united front tactic in Cuba. He also excelled at ridding himself of his opponents by firing squad.

When the Pole Fabio Grobart, agent of the Soviet Comintern, arrived in Cuba, he became involved immediately in the indoctrination of any who would listen to him. His ability to recruit and indoctrinate showed him to be skilled in the Soviet activist training that he had received and employed earlier as a member of the Communist Party in Poland. His propagandizing activities became most fruitful among the Cubans, and he was one of the founders of the Communist Party of Cuba on August 17, 1925.

One of Grobart's most faithful disciples was Eduardo Corona, overtly a member of the Ortodoxo Party but in reality a secret and dedicated Communist. Corona and Fidel Castro were members of the 1947 abortive attempt by the "Caribbean Legion" to invade the Dominican Republic and overthrow the dictator, Rafael Leonidas Trujillo. Interestingly, Grobart was a behind-the-scenes manipulator in this plot.

Supporting evidence of Castro's early links to the Soviets is the fact that Grobart's secret Communist, Eduardo Corona, was one of the founders of the July 26 Movement, which became vital in mobilizing urban support for the guerrilla action in the hills by Castro and his men during 1957 and 1958. The July 26 Movement was an important step in creating an informal united front movement in those same years. It was established while Castro was still in jail for leading the July 27, 1955, abortive attack on the army barracks in the town of Moncada.

Through the recruitment of labor leaders, the Cuban National Confederation of Labor had been taken over by the Communists at the time when the Sergeants' Revolt of 1933 brought Fulgencio Batista to prominence.

During the first period of Batista's rule, the labor unions of Cuba remained under the control of the Communist Party of Cuba, and when Castro came to power in 1959, the top labor echelon was Communist.

And what was Fidel Castro doing during his formative revolutionary years? In 1948, while a student at the University of Havana, he travelled to Bogota, Colombia, with a Cuban Communist, Alfredo Guevara, to agitate there during the Pan American Conference of Foreign Ministers.

Moments before Fidel Castro was to keep an appointment with Jorge Eliecer Gaitan, Colombia's Liberal Party demagogue, that popular leader was assassinated, an act that provoked the worst riot of Bogota's history. Hundreds were killed and wounded, and property losses were in the millions as a result of the ensuing violence. In the midst of the rioting many incitements to violence were broadcast over a Bogota radio station. One such statement was, "This is Fidel Castro. This is a Communist revolution."

As a student at the University of Havana, Castro studied Marxism, as he stated later, and he was involved in a continual struggle for student leadership, resulting often in gunplay. This period was the time of Castro's gangsterism, which involved him directly in at least two killings and one attempted killing of rivals.

The second regime of Fulgencio Batista was exceedingly corrupt and unpopular. Castro thought he could exploit the situation, and he led an irrational attack with a handful of pitifully armed supporters on the military barracks at the town of Moncada on July 26, 1953.

The ill-planned and poorly executed attack failed miserably, but it was the spark that in three years would ignite a united front movement in Cuba, although never formalized, against Batista.

At his trial on October 16, 1953, Castro made a speech in justification of his action, which established his socialist and anti-U.S. credentials.

On May 15, 1955, Fulgencio Batista made the mistake that three and a half years later would turn Cuba into a Soviet satellite. An amnesty law brought the release of Fidel and Raul Castro and eighteen of Fidel's followers. In July Fidel left for Mexico, where he had a fateful meeting with Ernesto "Che" Guevara, an Argentine expatriate, wanderer, adventurer, and Marxist.

Che Guevara, Fidel, and a former general of the Spanish Republican government that was overthrown by Francisco Franco, General Alberto Bayo, began training Fidel's followers in Mexico. It is to be remembered that the Spanish Republican government came to power in 1936 through a Popular Front election campaign, in which the Communist Party of Spain was an active participant. As a result of their effective work, the Communists gained two ministries in the First War Cabinet of the Spanish Republican government.

What brought General Bayo, with his experience and background, together with Fidel Castro? A clue could be a personal card found on Fidel Castro when he was arrested by Mexican authorities on July 24, 1956, for his guerrilla training activities. The card they found was that of a Soviet diplomat, Nicolai Leonov.

Leonov was accredited to the Mexican foreign ministry as "cultural attaché." Actually, he was an officer of the Soviet KGB and was one of the new breed of Soviet spies—talented, suave, cultured, impeccably dressed, and speaking almost unaccented Spanish. He stood out from the other KGB officers and other Soviet diplomats in Mexico who were still wearing voluminous trousers that flapped around their ankles as they walked. There is little likelihood that Castro's contact with this KGB sophisticate was merely casual.

When the Mexicans released Castro, he set up camp in another area. After subsequent raids on various training sites, during which significant arms were seized, the Mexicans finally made clear to Castro that he and his band of men were no longer welcome in their country.

Before leaving Mexico Castro began his plans for a united front movement. In April 1956 he had a conversation with one of his old university friends, Justo Carrillo, a leader of the Cuban Directorio Revolucionario, which was anti-Batista. In his talks with Carrillo about united action with the Directorio against Batista, Castro proposed an alliance with the Communist Party of Cuba, but in his effort to reassure Carrillo, he said, "The Communists will never be in a majority though their strength will grow in this struggle; you also, like I, will prevent them from dominating." A deliberate false reassurance, if only in terms of Castro's well-grounded knowledge of what had happened in Spain and Eastern Europe.

Carrillo and the Directorio later were to play an important role in the overthrow of Batista, but Carrillo and his organization were shunted aside as soon as Castro came to power; they then took up arms against him.

On the night of November 24–25, 1956, Fidel, Raul, Che, and seventy-nine of their followers left Tuxpan, Mexico, near Veracruz, for their seven-day voyage to Eastern Cuba on the one hundred-foot yacht *Granma*. Delayed by poor navigation, they landed in a swamp at Playa de los Coloradios (ironically, Beach of the Reds) near Bahia, Oriente Province, which required a three-hour slog to dry land.

By December 19, as a result of disarray, discovery, and attack by the Cuban Army, only fifteen of the original party were able to make it to the mountains of the Sierra Escambray.

Looking back at what was happening in Cuba while Castro was preparing his men in Mexico as early as December 1955, the groundwork for a popular or united front movement had begun. The calamitous strike of sugar workers, numbering 500,000, began then. It had the support of the Communist Party (then known as the Partido Socialista Popular), of the Directorio Revolucionario, and of some members of Castro's July 26 Movement.

By late December 1955 students of the July 26 Movement were detonating bombs throughout Cuba. Some caused blackouts in several towns in the province of Oriente and provoked reprisals by the Batista government, which resulted in the deaths of about fifty, including members of the Ortodoxo and Autentico political parties. Two terrorists were hanged, and their bodies were left hanging outside the city of Holguin.

The Batista government was condemned by the Cuban press for the violent repression of terrorism.

The July 26 Movement exploded bombs on New Year's Eve 1956, including a sensational bombing at the Tropicana nightclub, popular with well-to-do *habaneros* and U.S. tourists. Thereafter, the Cuban army killed three men in Oriente and two others in Las Villas Province. Further brutality by the Cuban police resulted in a protest march in the city of Santiago by five hundred women dressed in black.

It was in the midst of this early united front atmosphere, in which Cuban Communists played a critical role, that Fidel landed in Oriente.

His raiding party reduced to fifteen men, it appeared that all was lost for Castro. News reached Havana that he had been killed, and the attacks on Santiago and the Castro landing seemed of little consequence to most Cubans. But Castro, schooled in the value of international publicity, knew he had to reinspire his supporters and create among the Cubans a sense of his eventual triumph.

Fidel sent word to his followers in Havana that a U.S. journalist should be brought to interview him. In Havana it was decided that the journalist should be Herbert Matthews of *The New York Times*. How that decision was made has never been uncovered, but given the significance of that decision, one cannot but wonder if it was arrived at solely by the leaders of the July 26 Movement in Havana.

In any event, within a few days, on February 17, 1957, Herbert Matthews reached Castro in the Sierra Maestra. On February 24 the world and Cuba knew that Castro was still alive, and Matthews's report of his interview with Castro established the fiction that Castro's force numbered a few hundred well-armed men thriving in the hills and well prepared to defeat the Cuban army. This was the beginning of Matthews's outrageous pro-Castro reporting that carried so much weight in the Department of State, where he was considered infallible. He was considered such an expert that he was called in by the State Department to brief Ambassador Earl E.T. Smith before he left for his new post in Havana.

On March 13, 1957, members of the Directorio Revolucionario attacked the Presidential Palace in a futile attempt to assassinate President Batista. Reprisals were swift, and parents, relatives, and friends of the Directorio attackers joined the opposition to Batista.

Matthews's reports breathed new life into the opposition, and the ranks of the ragtag guerrillas in the mountains began to swell, initially mostly with dissatisfied peasants.

At about this time a front organization for the July 26 Movement was created, the Civic Resistance, and through this tactic other opponents of Batista drew together.

Though Herbert Matthews continued to laud the successes of Fidel Castro, by December 31, 1957, Castro described his own situation as "position desperate." Meanwhile, Ambassador Smith recognized that the opposition to Batista was so general that he recommended to the Department of State in February 1958 that the United States begin steps to negotiate the departure of Batista and help establish a caretaker government. His recommendations were not supported by Roy Rubottom, assistant secretary of state for American Republics affairs.

The war in the mountains continued, but of greater significance was the campaign of urban terrorism and the repressive counteraction of Batista's forces. In response to the heightened action and repression, in March 1958 the United States cut off military assistance to the Batista government, an action repeated disastrously almost twenty years later in Nicaragua, when aid to Somoza was cut off.

In his hope to subdue the rising revulsion of the Cuban people, Batista decided to hold presidential elections. The July 26 Movement responded with an operation to intimidate the Cuban people, which included death threats made to the candidates.

In a rigged election Andres Rivero Aguero, Batista puppet, was elected on November 1, 1958. Too late, a worried Eisenhower Administration sent William Pawley, an American businessman who had served as ambassador to Brazil, to talk Batista into stepping down in favor of a civic-military junta, essentially Ambassador Smith's original proposal. Pawley failed, since Assistant Secretary Rubottom denied him the authority to say that the United States would support its own proposal.

Pawley's mission having failed, Washington instructed Ambassador Smith to order Batista to leave the country, a scenario that was repeated tragically just short of twenty years later in Nicaragua.

Before the November election, in mid-1958, the Pact of Law Mercedes was signed with Castro. Members of the Communist Party of Cuba (PSP) then joined Castro in the Sierra Maestra, where they were given important positions. This reinforcement also took place in the Second Front of the Escambray. Members of the Directorio had earlier joined the fighting in the hills.

A long process of deteriorating military morale had set in, much of it caused by the widespread civilian dissatisfaction resulting from the violent nature of the army's response to the guerrillas and terrorists. Some of Castro's successes were due to this deteriorating morale and his ability to bribe key military officers who were supposed to deploy troops against him.

By December 1958 Batista had lost confidence in the loyalty of his key officers, and he left the country hurriedly. With the military in complete disarray, Castro quickly ordered two of his lieutenants, Camilo Cienfuegos and Che Guevara, to rush to Havana to seize the key posts of Camp Columbia and the La Cabana fortress, thus beginning his successful program to isolate the members of the informal united front and install only those of proven personal loyalty in positions of power in the revolutionary government, headed by his puppet, Manuel Urrutia, as president.

It was then that the mysterious figure of Fabio Grobart reappeared suddenly in Havana to form a shadow cabinet that later became the Integrated Revolutionary Organization.

Beginning in January 1959, cadres formed by Communist Party members working with the protection of the revolutionary government took control over youth, labor, and women's groups. Not neglected were the many local, neighborhood, and national associations. From them the notorious block committees were formed, which became one of Castro's main instruments for controlling and repressing the Cuban people. From the beginning, Castro's G-2, chief of intelligence, became his most important arm of repression. Then the National Directorate of Intelligence (DGI) was organized. A KGB general became the Soviets' controlling force, and the DGI became a direct arm of Soviet espionage throughout the world.

Castro consistently followed a path to take the Cuban people into the Soviet camp, even to the point of discarding the July 26 Movement. In 1959, on the anniversary of the Moncada attack, Fidel installed an old-time Communist, Oswaldo Dorticos, in the place of President Urrutia.

The first Latin American united front takeover was successful beyond all the Soviets' expectations. By patient work in laying the ground for a disciplined Party, which the Soviets did through Fabio Grobart; by working, when able, through the legal political process, open propaganda; by taking control of labor and at the same time not neglecting their subversive capabilities; by political action through agents of influence, unattributable propaganda, terrorism, and guerrilla warfare, the Soviets used a classic two-track policy that bewildered U.S. policymakers in the late 1950s and again in 1961 and 1972 (the Bay of Pigs fiasco and the Cuban missile crisis).

During the immediate aftermath of the Communist regimes' coming to power in Cuba, State Department leadership was concerned that if the United States acted severely toward Fidel Castro, it would antagonize all the other Latin American countries—the same argument used during the Carter Administration to win the approval of the American public and of Congress for the surrender of the Panama Canal to Panama, and the same justification for the abandonment of Somoza of Nicaragua.

After Cuba the Soviets believed that they had taken the measure of the Americans and had found us wanting. They had seen in us a propensity for rationalization that tended to immobilize us. They have since used that knowledge in Central America, in the Caribbean, and in the rest of the world rather effectively.

On July 9, 1960, Khrushchev rattled Soviet rockets in defense of Castro to intimidate the Eisenhower Administration. He said, "The Soviet Union . . . extends its hand of assistance to Cuba. . . . The Monroe Doctrine has died a natural death." Notwithstanding Eisenhower's reply, the Monroe Doctrine has been treated as if it were moribund. It must be revived. Eisenhower's response was, "Nor will the United States, in conformity with its treaty obligations, permit the establishment of a regime dominated by international communism in the Western Hemisphere." Well, the United States did just that and did it again in Nicaragua, although President Reagan is at this late date now trying to reverse the policies dealing with Nicaragua.

In the Seventh Annual Message to the U.S. Senate and House of Representatives, President James Monroe included a friendly reference to relations between the United States and the European powers, but at the same time he acknowledged the differences in our political systems. He went on, "We owe it, therefore, to candor and to the amicable relations existing between the United States and those powers, to declare that we should consider any attempt on their part to extend their system to any portion of this hemisphere as dangerous to our peace and safety." What came to be known as the Monroe Doctrine, spoken on December 2, 1823, served the American people in good stead for almost a century and a half but also served as a bulwark that preserved the freedom from European conquest of the other young nations of the hemisphere.

In following the united front tactic in Cuba and elsewhere in the world, the Soviets were following guidelines laid down by Stalin for the "proletariat" working with another "class" to achieve power ("a special form of alliance"). He wrote, "This special form of alliance has its basis in the fact that the guiding force of this alliance is the proletariat and that the leader in the state—the leader in the system of the dictatorship of the proletariat—is one party, the party of the proletariat, the party of the Communists, which *does not and cannot* [emphasis added] share that leadership with other parties." Stalin also warned, "From this logically follows the provisional character of our tactics to 'strike together' with the bourgeoisie, and the duty to carefully watch 'our ally as if he were an enemy.'"

The Soviets found it convenient and advantageous to conceal the nature of the "special alliance" with Castro. In December 1956 the Communist Party of Cuba president, Juan Marinello, went so far as to write the Secretary General of the United Nations to disclaim any connection between the Party and the July 26 Movement. Marinello then noted, "Nevertheless, though it fights with incorrect tactics, it is doing so for a laudable objective."

Notwithstanding the clarity of the "special alliance" tactic, the gullible West continues to be deceived, just as it was in 1959 about Cuba; now, more dangerously, many are deceived about the self-declared Marxist-Leninist Sandinistas ruling Nicaragua, who came to power through a clearly organized united front movement just twenty years after the Soviets took control of Cuba through their puppet, Fidel Castro.

The rambunctious Castro, exhilarated by his success in 1959, immediately set about sending forces to Panama, the Dominican Republic, and Nicaragua, suffering defeat after defeat.

Although the Soviets may have been somewhat uneasy about Castro's adventurism in the Caribbean, they saw no fatal consequences for his brash actions and came to recognize his future usefulness as their stalking horse. That "plausible denial" ability has been so effective that Soviet subversion in Latin America is rarely so identified in the U.S. media and even within the U.S. government and in Congress. If any subversion is recognized at all, it is called Castro or Cuban subversion, not Soviet.

Besides being a convenient Soviet stalking horse, Cuba has become an extraordinary training ground for Soviet diplomats and intelligence officers, who are later assigned to other Hispanic countries. This has been one of the most important elements of Soviet subversion in Latin America.

The training of foreign nationals in subversion, which had exclusively been done in the Soviet Union until the 1950s, has also been farmed out by the Soviets. Cuba has become one of several foreign training countries. Such trained subversives are now once removed from the Soviet Union. This dispersal improves the Soviets' ability to deny responsibility for Soviet-directed actions. It is the foundation of the Soviet claim that they do not interfere with local revolutions.

The United Front Tactic in Venezuela

The united front tactic was tried twice by the Soviets in Venezuela; it succeeded partially in 1958 and failed in 1963.

The Communist Party of Venezuela (PCV) was founded in Caracas in 1924. Among the founders were the brothers Gustavo

and Eduardo Machado, the latter to become a KGB agent. Of the
two, Gustavo was the best known as a party ideologue and or-
ganizer and as the more charming; but Eduardo has the most
interesting history, some of which he recounted on the floor of the
Venezuelan Congress in the 1960s. In discussing his early escapades,
he boasted about his 1931 arrest in the United States for advocating
the violent overthrow of the U.S. government. He claimed that this
resulted when he led a strike of "500,000" Mexican workers in the
United States, which ended in some strikers being killed. Eduardo
said that he avoided being deported to Venezuela by protesting that
he would be killed there. He said that instead he was deported to
the Soviet Union.

During the regime of Venezuelan dictator Marcos Perez
Jimenez, the Machado brothers were in exile in Mexico, where they
maintained close ties with the Soviet Embassy.

Gustavo, at the age of sixteen, was imprisoned by dictator Juan
Vincente Gomez, and Eduardo was involved in a plot with dissident
Venezuelan military members to overthrow that same despot and
later helped in the overthrow of Marcos Perez Jimenez.

Although founded in 1924, the PCV remained an inconsequen-
tial party until World War II. The legitimacy that the Soviet Union
gained as an ally of the forces fighting Nazi Germany provided the
PCV with sufficient prestige to bring about a wartime collaboration
between the government of President Medina and the Party and, in
turn, opportunities for the penetration of the Venezuelan government.

The united front movement to overthrow Marcos Perez Jimenez
was cofounded in July 1957 as the Patriotic Junta by Guillermo
Garcia Ponce, the leading Communist not in exile, and by an
extreme leftist journalist, Fabricio Ojeda. Although the three leading
Venezuelan political parties became linked to the Patriotic Junta,
the Communists took the ideological leadership of the Junta and
control of the organizational work in Venezuela's cities, especially in
the capital, Caracas.

By 1957 some opposition to Perez Jimenez had begun to
develop among the military, but it was unorganized; a feeble
attempt at his overthrow on January 1, 1958, barely got off the
ground. The Patriotic Junta remained the focus of opposition to
Perez Jimenez, and demonstrations against him were joined by
professionals, businessmen, labor, student, and women's groups.
These demonstrations were suppressed violently, and many

prominent Venezuelans were jailed. Still, the Venezuelan military remained passive.

When the Patriotic Junta called for a general strike to begin on January 21, the police responded brutally. By the second day of the strike, the Venezuelan military decided to act, and Perez Jimenez fled Caracas on January 23, 1958.

The short span of the Patriotic Junta's effort to rid the country of Perez Jimenez did not gain the prominence for the Party in Venezuelan political life that its Soviet masters had hoped for. Nevertheless, the PCV did all it could to exploit the political relationships with individuals in the other parties that were made in that united front.

Romulo Betancourt of the Accion Democratica Party (AD) was elected president in 1958, and PCV leaders won a few seats in the Venezuelan Senate and Chamber of Deputies.

Having failed in their efforts to gain influence and power through the candidate the PCV supported, Admiral Wolfgang Larrazabal, the left-leaning provisional president during 1958, the PCV received new orders from Moscow: to resume the attack, to cause chaos, and engage in sabotage and terrorism to undermine the fledgling democratic government.

The effort to provoke government repression and re-create a united front opposition seemed plausible to Moscow because of threats to the stability of the new president from Venezuela's extreme right. The plotters included some elements of the Venezuelan military and right-wing extremists in the Venezuelan business community. The belief was strong among these elements that Betancourt remained a Communist. They argued that his youthful Communist experimentation and his role, while in exile in Costa Rica, in founding the Communist Party there represented an ideology which remained unchanged in the president. These men had difficulty being persuaded that sometimes the most able and effective anti-Communist fighters are the disillusioned who have been steeped in their tactics and strategy.

The right-wing extremists were supported by dictator Rafael Leonidas Trujillo of the Dominican Republic, who was convinced that Betancourt had a role in the Caribbean Legion attempt to invade his country in 1947, and he was outraged by the nightly radio broadcasts from Venezuela that encouraged the Dominicans to overthrow him.

Trujillo provided the Venezuelan plotters with sophisticated technology in the field of explosives. The bomb that exploded on June 24, 1960, missed killing President Betancourt by a fraction of a second. Those in the front seat of his limousine were killed when the car bomb they were passing exploded. Betancourt and his companions were severely burned by flaming gasoline, with the president's hands so severely burned that he was not able to use them for weeks.

The first PCV response to Soviet orders to undermine Betancourt was to organize large-scale and violent demonstrations of the unemployed in Caracas. A series of riots began in August and September 1959; with mobs taking control of the streets in the center of Old Caracas and around the Venezuelan Congress, the police were overwhelmed and fled for their lives in sheer panic.

It took the disciplined troops of the army and Guardia Nacional to restore order in Caracas, which they accomplished under strict orders from President Betancourt to avoid violence. This they succeeded in doing; nevertheless, their restraint emboldened the PCV to engage in more severe actions.

Moscow also believed the moment was propitious, and the PCV was ordered to provide its best young militants for training in the Soviet Union in agitation, urban terrorism, and guerrilla warfare.

By late 1959 a campaign of terror by PCV militants began. First they used noise bombs (to gradually introduce some of the inexperienced into the terrorist field), which were quite frightening to the Caracas populace. They then robbed banks to build a war chest, just as the Bolsheviks had done early in the Russian Revolution. Sporting goods stores were raided, and weapons were seized. When the Soviet trainees returned, serious bombings began, as well as the killing of lone policemen.

Attackers committed their acts of terror and raced back to the sanctuary of the Central University of Caracas, by tradition free from all government intervention. They then began a well-planned, sophisticated, and sustained campaign to disrupt the country's economic base by sabotaging oil pipelines, power plants, and petroleum installations.

By 1960 the Soviets had recognized that Fidel Castro would be a useful pawn in their campaign to disrupt the Betancourt government, and Cuban-inspired slogans and propaganda were everywhere. It wasn't long before PCV members started traveling to Cuba for training.

A few days after an aborted coup by exiled Venezuelan Colonel Castro Leon, which took place on April 20, 1960, Salvador Allende, the Chilean Marxist senator, lectured students at the Central University of Caracas. His inflammatory speech received a noisy and enthusiastic response from the students, and the ominous cry heard so often in Cuba right after Castro's victory was now heard: "*Al paredon, al paredon*" (literally, "to the firing squad," or "to the wall"). The cry went on and on: "*Castro Leon, al paredon! Castro Leon, al paredon!*" The demagogic talents and Marxist ideology of that future Chilean president were clearly evident.

Beset by attacks both from the extreme right and from the Communists and other extreme leftist elements allied with them, the president continued to maintain restraint in the handling of his violent opponents, and the united front movement that Moscow had hoped to organize never developed.

Within the Venezuelan Congress, guillermo Garcia Ponce (so important in building the united front movement against Perez Jimenez), the Machado brothers, Jesus Faria, and Pompeyo Marques were the important Communist leaders who pursued the "democratic" road to increase the influence of the PCV and eventually bring the Party to power. But the Soviets certainly had not neglected their two-track, converging tactic. In fact, it became somewhat entangled in Venezuela.

Communist congressmen were directly involved in supporting the terrorists, confident that their congressional immunity, together with the inadequacy of the fledgling intelligence service, the National Directorate of Police (DIGEPOL), would protect them.

They were so successful in disguising their involvement with the terrorists that as late at 1962 Carlos Andes Perez, then acting but later officially minister of the interior, to whom the DIGEPOL was subordinate, believed that there were two distinct wings of the PCV, the legal party and the subversive one, with no links between them. (Perez, in December 1973, was elected Venezuelan president—propitiously for the Communist Sandinistas of Nicaragua, as it turned out.)

Eventually, DIGEPOL was able to prove to the minister of the interior that he was wrong. A DIGEPOL raid on the home of Senator Jesus Faria in May 1962 revealed it as one of the headquarters from which PCV terrorists operated and provided complete documentary evidence that there was no separation between the so-called legal and subversive wings of the Party. On October 17,

1962, President Betancourt asked the Supreme Court to outlaw the PCV and the far-left Revolutionary Movement of the Left (MIR), its ally in some of the PCV's terrorism and sabotage.

Prior to that time, however, on January 23, 1962, a PCV terrorist, celebrating the fourth anniversary of the overthrow of Perez Jimenez, carried high explosives on his person into the U.S. Embassy in Caracas. Miraculously, because of the extent of destruction to the Embassy and because the explosion happened during office hours, no one was killed or injured.

The success of that act of terror was particularly significant as a morale booster for the PCV terrorists, as well as for their confidence building, simply because they had outwitted U.S. Marine Guard security measures. It started heightened terrorist activity by the PCV, eventually leading to the burning of the headquarters of the U.S. military mission on June 6, 1963, while the deputy commander, Lieutenant Colonel Chenault, and several enlisted men were held at gunpoint. The U.S. military suffered the additional indignity of being forced to remove their trousers, a supreme reflection on the victims' manhood in Latin American terms. On November 28, 1963, Lieutenant Colonel Chennault was kidnapped by the Communists, though eventually he was safely ransomed. Again, the Soviets had succeeded in increasing disrespect for the United States.

The PCV and the MIR were associated with military rebellions in Carupano in May 1962 and in Puerto Cabello the following month.

By 1963 the Armed Forces of National Liberation (FALN), which included PCV and MIR terrorists, saboteurs, and guerrillas, was engaged in outright rural guerrilla warfare. The FALN stated that it would campaign to thwart the holding of the presidential election that December.

The discovery of an arms cache positively identified as coming from Cuba on the coast of Venezuela in November 1963 became a cause célèbre. In July 1964 the Organization of American States (OAS) found the Castro government guilty of subversion and aggressive action against Venezuela and was expelled from the OAS. Mexico became the only Latin American country maintaining diplomatic relations with Castro.

Heightened terrorism and guerrilla warfare united the people in support of the government and strengthened the will of the people to go to the polls in the December national election. It was the most honest and free in Venezuela's history, and President Betancourt's successor, Raul Leoni, was peacefully elected. The orderly transfer of the presidential sash in early 1964 was followed by three others, and democracy became a tradition for the first time in Venezuela.

That Romulo Betancourt was the first civilian elected president in Venezuela to even complete a single year in office and that he was then able to complete his full five-year term seems near miraculous, especially given the thorough nature and commitment of human and material resources by the Cubans, Soviets, and Venezuelan Communists to bring him down.

Betancourt's skill in courting the Venezuelan military negated the opposition from the extreme right, and his knowledge of Communist tactics kept him from overreacting to the violence of the PCV and the FALN, thus denying them the ability of reforming the united front against him. The risks of his restraint were great, but when the Venezuelan people finally had their fill of Communist violence, they supported the 1963 government crackdown.

Betancourt is the patriarch of Venezuelan democracy, but his success was also a tribute to the growing political maturity of the Venezuelan people. The critical role played by the U.S. government to help the democratic process remains unsung.

The Interval

Castro and his Soviet masters did not neglect to attempt to subvert other governments in the Western Hemisphere. Argentina was the greatest victim of such subversion. "The Switzerland of the Americas," Uruguay, suffered Tupamaro violence (which Castro supported) to such a degree that the military were provoked into taking control, only recently restoring democracy there. In 1965 U.S. troops and an OAS peace-keeping force had to rescue the Dominican Republic from a Soviet-Cuban–supported military uprising.

The ill-fated Che Guevara expedition into Bolivia in 1967 discouraged Castro from further direct involvement of Cuba in military adventures there. When the bewildered and then wounded Argentine-Cuban Communist was captured and executed by the Bolivian army on October 8, 1967, Castro decided to regroup, and the Soviets saw the wisdom of letting him do so. But then he turned his sights away from the Western Hemisphere to act as their foreign legion in Africa.

The irony of the direct resumption by the Soviets in 1977 of their expansionist goals in the Western Hemisphere is that their ambitions were reawakened by the distorted human rights policies of the Carter Administration. A further irony is that the Soviets finished what Fidel Castro had started in Nicaragua early in 1959.

The United Front Tactic in Nicaragua

Nicaragua first came into Castro's sights immediately after he came to power. It was natural that in early 1959 Che Guevara trained the Castro-sponsored guerrilla force that was ordered to land in Nicaragua. Che, in 1947, had known in Mexico surviving veteran officers of Luis Sandino's guerrilla campaigns against the U.S. marines in Nicaragua, and he was a great admirer of Sandino. Sandino's mountain guerrilla tactics, which used small units, was learned by Che from the Sandino veterans. That was the method used for the initial thrust of the Castro attack against the Batista army in Cuba in 1957.

The combined Nicaraguan-Cuban guerrilla force, trained and armed at Fidel Castro's order, infiltrated Honduras on its way to Nicaragua. There it was joined by a Nicaraguan Marxist, Carlos Fonseca, a student from the Autonomous National University of Nicaragua. He had been deported from Nicaragua by the Somoza government for his agitation and propagandizing among the university students. Fonseca was to become a "martyred" Sandinista hero, killed during a later guerrilla action.

The guerrilla band was surprised in Honduras and defeated by Honduran army elements. Fonseca was wounded but escaped; then he managed to make his way to Cuba, where he met Fidel and Che. When Fonseca returned to Nicaragua, he was well prepared to lead the early skirmishes against the Somoza family.

The Somozas were *caudillos*—chieftains—in the Latin American tradition, and Nicaragua was a fiefdom rather than a totalitarian state. They were not admirable, yet they were not despots. Under the stepped-up attacks from Soviet-Cuban–supported guerrillas and terrorists, the relative charitableness with which they had dealt previously with even their violent opponents disappeared. The Soviet tactic to cause government repression and the subsequent abhorrence of that government by the people, encouraging a united front revolt, was run by the textbook in Nicaragua, benefiting from the earlier experiences in Cuba and Venezuela—a triumph and a failure, respectively.

Between 1944 and 1967 the Somoza dynasty was assailed with regularity through small invasions, conspiracies, attempted coups, strikes, and student demonstrations. The founder of the dynasty, Anastasio Somoza Garcia, was assassinated on September 21, 1956. Implicated among the plotters were Tomas Borge (now minister of the interior of the Communist Sandinista government) and Pedro Joaquin Chamorro (of the family that owns Nicaragua's leading daily, once editor of that paper). Both men were jailed, but Chamorro was able to escape; he then led a Conservative Party invasion force into Nicaragua in May 1959, which was defeated. Interestingly, Chamorro had appealed to Castro for support but was refused, no doubt because it coincided in its timing with Che's own guerrilla activity.

Tomas Borge was released in 1960 and made his first pilgrimage to Cuba. Borge and Carlos Fonseca were members of the Soviet-aligned Communist Party, the Nicaraguan Socialist Party (PSN), and they established the first Marxist cell at the National University in the mid-1950s. The PSN was founded in Nicaragua on July 3, 1944, in an atmosphere not entirely unfriendly, because the Soviet Union was one of the Allied Powers fighting Nazi Germany, just as the Venezuelan Communist Party was able to make inroads in that country.

Fonseca returned clandestinely to Nicaragua in July 1960, but his presence was exposed to the Somozas by the PSN, whose leadership did not then support the idea of an armed struggle for which the Cubans had trained him during a year in Cuba. Deported to Honduras, he was reunited there with his old friend Borge. Together they founded, on July 23, 1960, the National Liberation Front, with the name *Sandinista* added two years later, making it the FSLN. This was the beginning of the two-track converging policy advocated by Stalin, with the FSLN taking the violent road and the PSN the political route. The PSN joined forces finally with the FSLN in the fateful year 1979.

In the period 1944 through 1967 the violence that assailed the Somozas included some twenty-five serious incidents, ranging from guerrilla actions and invasions, to bank robberies to finance the FSLN war chest, to massive student demonstrations. These actions provoked a gradually increasing rate of repression by the Somoza forces, largely confined to those involved directly in serious violence. By the end of 1967 the urban organization of the FSLN was practically destroyed; its leader, Daniel Ortega (now president of the Sandinista government), was captured, and Borge and other leaders fled for Cuba.

Of early significance to the eventual establishment of a united front movement was the founding by Carlos Fonseca in May 1962 of the student arm of the FSLN, the Revolutionary Student Front (FER).

Continued guerrilla actions by the FSLN resulted regularly in heavy losses for them, and the period that followed between 1968 and 1974 was relatively quiet, a period of changing plans, a period of regroupment and new alliances.

Nevertheless, critical ingredients that led to the formation of the united front movement in Nicaragua came together as early as 1966; by then the early efforts of the Somoza government to contain incidents of violence had become more determined.

In November 1966 the relatively dormant National Opposition Union (UNO) was revived. It had the encouragement of the Moscow-aligned PSN and was made up by the four leading opposition parties.

About two months after UNO's revival, on January 22, 1967, it organized an anti-Somoza rally in Managua of about sixty thousand persons. When the UNO leader made the mistake of attempting to incite the Guardia Nacional (the Nicaraguan army) to desert the Somoza government, the rally was broken up by gunfire. Reportedly, two hundred demonstrators were killed. Fernando Aguero, the UNO leader who also headed the Traditional Conservative Party, had been previously involved in an attempted assassination of Anastasio Somoza Garcia.

The Sandinistas then began to build an infrastructure with the assistance of the Soviet-aligned PSN. Organizational work was among the urban poor, under the guise of obtaining improved living conditions, through work to organize the peasants into peasant unions. This work proved too tedious for the impatient FSLN leadership, and the Asian "prolonged-war" tactic was then adopted.

Interestingly, at the time that the new tactic was adopted, it was judged by one FSLN leader to be in accord with Che Guevara's call in Cuba for "one, two, three Vietnams," a strategy designed to disperse U.S. military forces around the world. The new FSLN prolonged-war tactic began in late 1966, coinciding with Che's failed guerrilla campaign in Bolivia.

The FSLN suffered another disastrous defeat, which brought about the next phase of the Sandinista revolution; they began with a reassessment of their abilities. It was then that the leadership that became the nine *comandantes* who head the FSLN today, began to emerge, with Tomas Borge, Humberto Ortega, and others beginning to eclipse Carlos Fonseca in the new national directorate of the FSLN.

Shortly thereafter, the FSLN goals were made clear through a pronouncement that reflected strongly anticapitalist and anti-U.S. attitudes and declared an alignment with "Third World anti-imperialist movements." The declaration included appropriate language about freedom of religion, women's rights, elimination of corruption, distribution of land, the ending of unemployment, and the elimination of illiteracy.

The pronouncement did not neglect to mention the Nicaraguan Guardia Nacional, which was to be replaced by an "ideologically committed army and militia, to defend against the inevitable counter-revolution." Prophetic words—today's Nicaragua has exactly that, an army and militia loyal to the Sandinista Party, not to the nation, Nicaragua.

The united front movement gained a great deal of momentum following the disastrous earthquake of December 1972 that leveled most of the buildings in the old part of Managua. Flagrant corruption by Somoza, his family, and associates in the handling of relief funds, principally from the United States, caused hostility toward the Somozas, which was well exploited by the FSLN and the PSN in building effective and broad-based opposition to the Somoza government.

The decision of the FSLN to resume the armed struggle brought a swift response from the Guardia Nacional. Carlos Fonseca was killed in action, and Tomas Borge was captured. In the process peasants in the guerrilla areas who were believed to support the FSLN were killed, possibly two thousand of them. Although that FSLN campaign was defeated, Somoza had played into Soviet hands through the excesses of the Guardia and had provided another link in the forging of a united front movement.

The critical element in forming a broad united or popular front emerged in 1975. Carrying the message of the classic Leninist tactic of working with the bourgeoisie was Humberto Ortega, now Sandinista defense minister and brother of the present Sandinista President, Daniel Ortega.

Humberto Ortega, the brighter of the brothers, had spent a number of years in Cuba between 1970 and 1975 before returning to Nicaragua. The Soviets had seen, with the fall of Batista, the practicality of using Stalin's temporary alliance tactic elsewhere in Latin America, and Humberto Ortega's instructions were clear. Upon his return to Nicaragua, Humberto called for outright civil war in the cities of Nicaragua, and his successful appeal to the non-Communist opposition to the Somozas created the mass movement that eventually brought down Anastasio Somoza, Jr.

Although there had been continued concern among the FSLN leadership (no doubt a reflection of Soviet-Cuban worries) that the FSLN struggle could provoke U.S. intervention in Nicaragua, by 1975 the Soviets had read correctly the temper of the U.S. Congress, and the call for an immediate civil war in Nicaragua became the new FSLN watchword. Humberto Ortega spoke optimistically of "a favorable world correlation of forces," indicating his belief that the Sandinistas would be able to count not only on the Soviets and Cubans but also on the influence of the Socialist International in Europe and Latin America as well as liberals in the United States.

Just as Fidel had warned Salvador Allende, when he was in Santiago for the Marxist Chilean President's inauguration, Castro warned the Sandinistas to proceed cautiously so as not to antagonize the United States. Consequently, Marxist rhetoric was dropped from FSLN pronouncements, and the FSLN leaders accepted that a post-Somoza government should not be seen immediately as being Marxist-Leninist.

A few months before coming to power, when the revolt was at its height, Humberto Ortega wrote:

> The fact that we [cannot] establish socialism immediately after overthrowing Somoza does not mean that we are planning a capitalist type social-democratic or similar development policy; what we propose is a broad, democratic and popular government which, although the bourgeoisie has participation, is a means and not an end, so that in its time it can make the advance towards a more genuinely popular form of government, which guarantees the movement towards socialism.
>
> Without slogans of "Marxist orthodoxy," without ultra-leftist phrases such as "power only for the workers," "toward the

dictatorship of the Proletariat," etc., we have been able—without losing at any time our revolutionary Marxist/Leninist Sandinista identity to rally all our people around the FSLN.

In having the FSLN carry out an appeal to the Nicaraguan bourgeoisie, the Soviets also recognized that a united front would be able to gain for the FSLN the kind of international support that would make a U.S. intervention less likely. Consequently, in early 1977 a secret Sandinista supporter was ordered to create a political front for the FSLN. The "Group of Twelve" was then established in Mexico, among whom were a Nicaraguan leftist intellectual and writer, Sergio Ramirez, the secret FSLN member who received the order to assemble the political front and who later became a member of the Sandinista junta, and Miguel D'Escoto, a member of the Maryknoll order of the Catholic Church in the United States, also a secret FSLN member, who is now Sandinista foreign minister.

With the political front in place, the FSLN sought a broader international appeal; with the addition of the perennial anti-Somoza guerrilla fighter, Eden Pastora, the FSLN became acceptable to the social democrats in Europe and to President Carlos Andres Perez of Venezuela.

In late 1974, when Humberto Ortega took the lead with the Soviet-proposed broad or united front strategy, he spoke about waiting for the proper moment in which an "armed insurrection of the people" could destroy the Somoza government. That moment began on March 4, 1977, when President Carter's Department of State, in implementing Carter's human rights policies, openly attacked the human rights record of Anastasio Somoza, Jr. The Soviets immediately seized upon that moment to gain an even more important foothold in the Americas than Cuba, and the FSLN was given full rein.

President Carter made respect for human rights the cornerstone of his foreign policy as soon as he took office in 1977. In fulfilling a punitive policy toward countries not abiding by his criteria, he cut off military credits and economic aid to Somoza on June 23, 1977.

When a U.S. President tampers with the internal affairs of a friendly country without thought for the outcome, legitimate concerns for human rights can easily become transformed into dangerous, though unintended, mischief making, particularly when what is said and done is publicly threatening to a chief of state, which it was for Somoza. It was the critical factor in undermining him, for it gave the green light to the Soviets and their Cuban and Nicaraguan cohorts. It provided them with the confidence that the United States would not intervene militarily. It also encouraged the non-Communist opposition to unite with the FSLN in a united front against Somoza.

What also happened when President Carter threw down the gauntlet so publicly to Somoza is that he ensured that later efforts to negotiate his resignation in favor of a national reconciliation government would be rejected by an autocrat whose pride had been cruelly wounded.

The Soviets did have those remaining concerns—that the U.S. President would not so easily play into their hands and that arrangements for a substitute government were already in place. The leader most likely to be the U.S. choice to succeed Somoza in the Soviet view was the popular Pedro Joaquin Chamorro, editor of *La Prensa,* previously involved in several attempts to oust the Somozas.

The Soviet-Cuban-Sandinista concern about the United States implanting a reformist government in Somoza's stead ended on January 10, 1978, when Chamorro was assassinated. The impact of Chamorro's death on the consolidation of a united front movement was tremendous. Chamorro's partner, Pablo Cuadra, said, "His death was the spark."

Notwithstanding the general belief among the Nicaraguans that Chamorro was killed by order of Somoza, one of Chamorro's sons insists to this day that Somoza did not order his father's killing. At the time, Somoza said that Chamorro's death was the last thing he could have wanted.

Chamorro's death was a twofold blessing for the Sandinistas: It coalesced the opposition forces, and it eliminated the figure most likely to head a possible reform government—an alternative to their triumph that the Sandinistas dreaded.

Wherever it could, the FSLN attempted to exploit the moderate opposition to Somoza. The most important of this combined opposition was the Broad Opposition Front (FAO), established in 1978 and headed by Alfonso Robelo, an advocate of a democratic alternative to Somoza. The FAO represented almost all the legitimate opposition forces and was also supported by the influential Superior Council of Private Enterprise (COSEP).

With the consent of Somoza, ten members of the Group of Twelve returned to Nicaragua. Their first action on setting foot in

Nicaragua was to declare themselves Sandinistas; their second was to join the FAO.

The FAO had participated in organizing the business-supported strike in January 1978, which demanded the resignation of Somoza for his presumed guilt in the killing of Pedro Joaquin Chamorro.

It was in this favorable atmosphere that Humberto Ortega, Moscow's most able strategist in Nicaragua, ordered Eden Pastora to do what he had longed to do for some time—attack and take over the Nicaraguan National Palace, seat of the Nicaraguan Congress. On August 22, 1978, wearing Guardia Nacional uniforms, the Pastora force of twenty-five was able to surprise the few sentries, capture the Palace, and seize about fifteen hundred hostages, including members of the Chamber of Deputies, government officials, and one of Somoza's sons. Conditions for the freeing of the hostages were carried out, and Eden Pastora secured the release of Tomas Borge and about sixty other prisoners; then he led them triumphantly through cheering crowds in a motorcade to the airport and freedom.

One of the significant conditions for the release of the hostages that was complied with by Somoza was the reading over the radio of an FSLN manifesto. It was an appeal to all Nicaraguans, including "capitalists," to join in the removal of Somoza.

Eden Pastora's daring and successful attack appealed to the Nicaraguans, who seemed very willing to accept his assurance that the Sandinistas were more Christian than Marxist-Leninist.

The raid also galvanized Somoza's opponents. The FAO general strike, supported by business and labor alike, followed on the heels of Pastora's departure for Panama and was accompanied by serious rioting and the capture by the FSLN of the city of Matagalpa. The recapture of Matagalpa involved elite Guardia Nacional troops and aerial bombardment and furthered the ever-growing hatred of Somoza and the Guardia.

Managua and three other cities also were attacked; the latter three were held temporarily under FSLN control. The FSLN was heavily armed with mortars, bazookas, and heavy machine guns, some from Cuba, some captured from the Guardia. It was estimated that between fifteen hundred and five thousand were killed during that insurrection. The return to martial law and the suspension of civil liberties also fed anti-Somoza passions.

Although the united front movement was well established, it took direct intervention by Fidel Castro on December 4, 1978, to overcome the rivalries within the FSLN leadership. The carrot that Fidel offered to bring about unity was the promise of providing important military material, which heretofore had been provided on a piecemeal basis, although the training in Cuba of FSLN warriors had been a constant process and Cuba had provided a haven regularly after each guerrilla defeat.

The result of Castro's pressure was the creating of the nine-man Combined National Directorate (DNC), eventually referred to as the Nine Comandantes, who today control Nicaragua's destiny. Humberto Ortega continued as effective commander of the Sandinista Army, although Eden Pastora, because of his international fame, popularity, and influence in socialist circles, had been named in October as the chief of the FSLN army.

Weapons, including light artillery for the final offensive, poured into Nicaragua from Cuba by way of Panama and Costa Rica. The major military support from Venezuela, which had started on September 15, 1978, was stopped in early 1979 when Carlos Andres Perez completed his term as president.

Omar Torrijos, strongman of Panama, then became the third most important supporter of the FSLN in the Western Hemisphere, behind Fidel and Jimmy Carter, although the latter had not yet realized the significance of what he was doing. Torrijos, besides being a critical conduit to disguise the shipment of arms to Nicaragua from Cuba, encouraged men and officers of the Panamanian Guardia Nacional to join the FSLN secretly.

The last important united front group created before the fall of Somoza was the National Patriotic Front (FPN), when leftists separated from the FAO in October 1978 to join the United People's Movement (MPU), which had been formed as an earlier FSLN maneuver to attract leftist opponents of Somoza. Significantly, the MPU was created in July 1978, just when the Soviets determined that the two-track, convergent tactic had succeeded. It was then that the prospects were so great for a FSLN victory that the Nicaraguan Socialist Party (PSN—the Moscow-aligned CP) publicly joined with the FSLN by becoming a part of the MPU. The Communist Party of Nicaragua (PCN, splintered years before from the PSN) also joined the MPU.

On February 8, 1979, Jimmy Carter compounded his 1977 cut-off of military assistance to the Somoza government by canceling U.S. military agreements with Nicaragua, placing a moratorium on future economic aid, and cutting the size of the staff of the Embassy in half. This action was Carter's answer to Anastasio Somoza's refusal to resign, which was the U.S. President's mediation position. Carter also prevailed upon the Israeli government to stop arms shipments that were en route to Somoza.

On May 20, 1979, Somoza's fate was sealed with the beginning of the FSLN "final offensive." It is hardly a coincidence that it was also the date when the Mexican government broke diplomatic relations with the Somoza government and that Castro had been in Mexico to talk to President Lopez Portillo just days before the break.

On June 4 the Organization of American States rejected a Nicaraguan resolution invoking the Rio Treaty against Costa Rica for permitting the FSLN invasion from that country. It was the last time that the Rio Treaty was invoked, although there has been a greater reason to have it involved in the case of the Sandinista aggression against El Salvador, which began as soon as the *comandantes* came to power.

Throughout June there were pitched battles cross the country, with heavy casualties on both sides and with newly arrived Soviet artillery from Cuba significantly contributing to FSLN successes.

On June 16 the FSLN announced the existence of the Junta of the Government of National Reconstruction (JGRN), and Venezuela, Colombia, Ecuador, and Peru granted belligerent status to the FSLN.

On that same date Omar Torrijos, in what proved to be a fruitless hope of having some benign influence on the forthcoming Sandinista government, extended Panamanian recognition to the JGRN.

In a last-ditch effort to save the game on June 21, the Carter Administration proposed to the OAS Consultation of Foreign Ministers that Somoza be replaced by a national reconciliation government, with an OAS peace-keeping force, similar to that employed so successfully in the Dominican Republic in 1965, to be landed in Nicaragua to act as the reconciliation government's guarantor. The desperate move had no credibility and was rejected.

The major assault on Managua was begun on June 19, and in other parts of Nicaragua the Guardia Nacional suffered defeat after defeat.

By a resolution of the Seventeenth Meeting of Consultation of the Ministers of Foreign Affairs of member countries of the Organization of American States, that body took the unprecedented step of withdrawing recognition from a sitting president. The resolution asked that the Somoza government be "immediately and definitely" replaced. The conditions for a new "democratic" government were outlined: pluralistic, representing the principal opposition groups; respect for human rights; and free elections as soon as possible, leading to a "truly democratic government that guarantees peace, freedom and justice." The Venezuelan-submitted resolution was approved on June 23, 1979.

In response the Sandinista JGRN promised respect for human rights, enforcement of civil justice, free elections, and freedom of speech, religion, and organization. The Communist Sandinistas have since decided they need not honor any of those promises but have feigned to honor some of them.

Although the die was cast, in an attempt to salvage the situation a new U.S. ambassador was sent to Nicaragua by Jimmy Carter for the sole purpose of persuading Somoza to resign. Ambassador Lawrence Pezzullo arrived in Managua on June 27, the day after the Brazilians broke diplomatic relations with the Somoza government. The ambassador's assignment was a follow-up to a visit by Lt. General Dennis McAuliffe, commander of the U.S. Southern Command, who had been sent by Carter to Managua on December 21, 1978. Somoza had been so hurt by Carter's public attacks and policies that he even rejected the appeal from a fellow West Pointer.

Of interest, Pezzullo and McAuliffe had been teamed up before to pressure the military government of Uruguay to improve respect for human rights. At the time Pezzullo was ambassador to Uruguay, and McAuliffe was dispatched to Montevideo to reinforce the pressure that Pezzullo was exerting.

On July 17, 1979, Somoza resigned in the expectation that the United States would ensure an orderly transition, with the Guardia Nacional remaining intact, as he had been assured. That did not happen.

On July 19 Managua was occupied by troops of the Northern Front of the FSLN and the Combined National Directorate of the FSLN—the Nine Comandantes took over.

The Soviet formula for Cuba, much more formalized, with the Communist-led revolutionary forces fighting in Nicaragua a more disciplined army than that faced by Castro, was repeated successfully.

Regardless of the critical role played by Castro and by the Soviets, immediately after the Sandinista triumph Castro acknowledged "gracefully" and publicly that if it had not been for Jimmy Carter, Somoza would never have been defeated.

On July 25, 1979, a Sandinista delegation traveled to Havana to thank Castro for his support and to help him celebrate the July 26 anniversary.

Confident that they had fully consolidated Sandinista rule in Nicaragua, Humberto Ortega, Tomas Borge, and two other *comandantes* dutifully flew to Moscow in March 1980 to sign a party-to-party agreement between the FSLN and the Communist Party of the USSR.

The Soviets accomplished their goal in Nicaragua, and although the military installations built in Nicaragua through vast Soviet expenditures are not yet thronging with Soviet combat troops, airmen, or sailors, Nicaragua has joined Cuba as a Soviet bastion in the Western Hemisphere. The installations are there for the Soviets to use when they believe that conditions are appropriate.

In September 1961, before the Cuban missile crisis, Roscoe Drummond wrote prophetically in *The Christian Science Monitor*, "What confronts the U.S. today is not a deteriorating Castro dictatorship but a powerfully armed Soviet satellite which the Kremlin can now use, in its own way, at its own will, for its own purposes." Roscoe Drummond then called on the Kennedy Administration to "liquidate Soviet penetration in the Western Hemisphere."

To our sorrow no one listened then, and the U.S. people and the Free World are paying the price for their own easy and repeated ability to rationalize that national security interests are not at stake as the Soviets encroach on other lands.

Today it is recognized that the principal Soviet objectives in Central America and the Caribbean have been to weaken U.S. influence and access to the rest of the hemisphere; to force the United States to draw down its resources; and to erode our ability to support NATO in a time of crisis. The Soviets have established Cuba as a base for long-range Soviet reconnaissance bombers. They have built a Soviet naval installation at Cienfuegos. They have armed Cuba to the teeth with two hundred jet fighters, principally the MIG-21 but including the nuclear-capable MIG-23; frigates, submarines, and fast missile-torpedo patrol boats; 950 tanks; and an armed force of 160,000 active duty military personnel, plus up to 135,000 well-trained and experienced reservists. The Soviets have built Cuba into a growing threat that can delay significantly rein-forcements to NATO in the event of a conventional Soviet invasion of Western Europe.

Soviet efforts to take control of Venezuela would have placed it in a position to block the sea land between Venezuela and Grenada, one of the most important routes for foreign oil imported by the United States. Their failure to take over Venezuela and add it to Cuba as a control point over the vital Caribbean outlets to the Atlantic Ocean made Grenada the logical alternative. It literally fell into the Soviets' lap. Nicaragua was the next step to control move-ment through the Panama Canal, and it has all the potential of another Cuba, serving Soviet strategic interests throughout the hemi-sphere.

These extraordinary Soviet gains, weakening our capability to defend the United States and the Free World, have all been ac-complished by their sophisticated deception techniques. The pas-sivity of successive U.S. governments to Soviet worldwide encroach-ments, particularly to those next door, have proven to the Soviets the validity of their highly financed and heavily staffed disinforma-tion effort. Our gullibility only encourages the Soviets to enhance and magnify the "active measures" operations. We can expect more and better of the same if we remain so gullible.

SOVIET
SPACE
DECEPTION

James E. Oberg

Routinely, the TASS news agency in Moscow releases a news bulletin. "The Kosmos-1999 satellite was launched today in the Soviet Union for the further exploration of outer space," the brief report usually starts. "Onboard the satellite is scientific apparatus and radio equipment," continues the dispatch, followed by the altitude and other orbital characteristics of the spacecraft.

And it's usually a pack of lies. Crammed into these brief bulletins is more deception and distortion than average, even for Soviet official statements.

The satellite is probably a military vehicle, most likely a spy in the sky. It could be a military navigation or communications satellite, or a weather observer. It might even be a weapons test. The least likely possibility is that it actually carries the "scientific apparatus for the exploration of space" alleged by the official cover story.

In the area of spaceflight, Soviet deception has reached literally astronomic dimensions. Several major themes are involved: I have designated them the Peace Deception, the Perfection Deception, and the Primacy Deception.

In addition, there are traditional Soviet deceptions about geography, personalities, and illustrations. They insist, for example, that their spaceport (called Baikonur) is hundreds of miles from its actual location (just north of the town of Tyuratam, east of the Aral Sea), and they tried for years to keep another northwestern Soviet spaceport secret, even though nighttime launchings were frequently seen from the streets of Moscow and Leningrad. (The government let the eyewitnesses think they had seen "flying saucers from outer space.") The people who really run the space program used to be kept hidden and anonymous; those who appeared in public were usually minor bureaucrats, retirees, or play actors. (There has been some relaxation of this rule in recent years.) Soviet space propagandists continue to rely on stealing Western spacecraft art, painting on a few red stars and CCCPs, and releasing them as Soviet products. But these "tricks of the propaganda trade" are widespread beyond just the space field.

Peace, perfection, and *primacy* also appear elsewhere in Soviet propaganda, but in space, as noted earlier, they have literally reached new heights.

The Peace Deception

The Peace Deception is by far the central theme. Essentially, it portrays the Soviet space program as entirely peaceful and scientific in nature, allegedly in gross contrast to the frantic militarization of space occurring in the United States. And it warns that the USSR "will not stand idly by" in the face of American "provocations."

For example, Soviet statements on antisatellite weaponry (ASATs) are marked by deliberate deception and propagandizing. Moscow denies having any and denounces American plans to develop one. Yet in reality, the Soviets have possessed an operational killer satellite of high reliability for more than a dozen years.

Despite this, when then Premier Yuri Andropov met with U.S. senators in August 1983, he vowed that the USSR "would never be the first to put any kind of antisatellite weapons into space." His proposal that "existing systems" be dismantled was taken by some of his visitors to mean that Soviet systems would be dismantled—except that officially the USSR has nothing to dismantle, so the "promise" was null and void.

Konstantin Chernenko's May 21, 1984, reply to yet another "peace-in-space" plea from American scientists Carl Sagan and Robert Garwin typified this persistent falsehood. Wrote Chernenko, "Deployment of antisatellite weapons would result in sharp destabilization of the situation, to an increased threat of sudden attack, and would undermine the efforts for ensuring trust between nuclear states." These phrases must seem hollow, coming as they do from a regime that deployed such weapons a dozen years ago. Added Chernenko, evidently expecting to be taken seriously by at least some people, "There must be no place for propaganda tricks or for attempts to gain for oneself temporary advantages." But the current space war advantage clearly lies with the country that has a monopoly on orbital weaponry: Chernenko's motherland, the USSR.

Soviet defense ministry spokesman Colonel General Nikolay Chervov told a *Novosti* military correspondent in May 1984 that "it is far better to come to an agreement at the very beginning, even before testing, than to do so later, after these [antisatellite weapons] have been developed, produced, and introduced into equipment." This from a military establishment that has been testing such systems for fifteen years and has had combat-ready equipment for most of that period!

Chervov, who appears repeatedly in the Soviet media spouting made-up statistics about American "war satellites," defended an ASAT moratorium late in 1984 with the false assertion that a space weapons balance already exists. "A moratorium will give us no advantage at all," he told a Moscow TV audience. "Washington is seeking superiority [with the new ASAT missile]." How can that be? Chervov insisted that the old nuclear armed Thor missile system on Johnston Island "can be quickly rebuilt in case of need" and that, in addition, "shuttle-type spacecraft, the ABM complex at Grand Forks, and the complex of Titan missiles at Vandenberg all possess anti-satellite capabilities." Chervov, who toured the United States with a Soviet political delegation in March 1985 without even once being accused of being a professional liar, displays imagination sufficient for a great career as a science fiction author: the Thor system is defunct (and nuclear warheads have been deemed inappropriate for space combat anyhow), the ABM complex was scrapped more than a decade ago, the shuttle is too expensive and too inflexible to serve as a weapon, and there are no Titan combat missiles at Vandenberg.

Izvestia on April 8, 1984, quoted Stanislav Kondrashev: "The creation of antisatellite weapons means at least to deprive the other side of the necessary means of observation, its space eyes and ears, and thereby to increase its vulnerability to a possible enemy nuclear attack. This undermines the principle of equality and identical security." This in a country that for a decade has had a monopoly on space attack weapons and that has thus wielded a distinctly "nonidentical" threat over American space "eyes and ears" without any counterbalancing and equalizing capability.

On May 10, 1984, TASS military observer Vladimir Bogachev blasted the U.S. ASAT system:

The implementation of Reagan's plans to create antisatellite systems will sharply destabilize the military and political situation in the world and will intensify the threat of nuclear war. The plans . . . are a violation of the spirit and the letter of international agreements which ban even putting obstacles in the way of the activity of the other side's surveillance satellites. . . . Violating the agreements already concluded on the limitation of military activity in space, the Reagan Administration is commiting a heinous crime against mankind, the consequences of which can be compared to the creation and use by the United States of nuclear weapons in 1945.

If the American plans alone are a treaty violation, what then should we make of the deployed Soviet killer-satellite system?

At the meeting of the UN Committee on the Peaceful Uses of Outer Space in Vienna in June 1984, Soviet delegation leader Oleg Gazenko, a leading space scientist, was confronted with a question about the existence of a Soviet killer-satellite program. Replied Gazenko, the official Soviet spokesman, "My general knowledge is that I do not have any facts in my hands that we have such a system in our country. Quite the opposite."

This deception continued into 1985 and the new Gorbachev regime. In April, Leonid Simyanin, chairman of the Supreme Soviet's foreign affairs panel, toured West Germany and denounced the stories about Soviet killer satellites as "pure provocation." Insisted Simyanin, "Our satellites have a peaceful purpose. We are for the peaceful, and only the peaceful, use of space." In May, the new Soviet defense minister, Marshal Sergey Sokolov, deftly dodged the same question. "Trying to place strike weapons in outer space," Sokolov explained, "U.S. leaders, in contradiction to facts, maintain that the USSR has allegedly been engaged in an arms race in space. This is not true." Sokolov did for the first time confess what Free World experts had long known, that some Soviet satellites were for communications, navigation, early warning, and even reconnaissance. "We conduct scientific research work, including in the military sphere," he admitted. But he insisted, "We are not creating strike space weapons. . . . The USSR does not have weapons in space at the present time." The Soviet space weapons, of course, are poised at launch pads in Soviet Central Asia, ready for orbital combat within a few hours' notice. So much for Sokolov's official posturing of "peaceful heart and open hands."

These false Soviet denials of their own orbital weapons are coupled with a smear campaign against practically all U.S. space activities, particularly the Space Shuttle and the planned 1990s space station.

In August 1983 cosmonaut Georgiy Grechko told a Soviet television audience that "we know that sights for laser weapons have already been tested on the first shuttle craft—and there are plans to deploy antisatellite systems in space." Grechko evinced great concern over these developments and struck an emotional chord among his viewing audience by appealing to the United States, "as a cosmonaut and a father," not to darken the skies with space weapons.

A similar attitude was reflected in a statement attributed to General Vladimir Shatalov, three-time spaceflight veteran and commander of the Soviet space pilot corps. Shortly before the first Space Shuttle mission, Shatalov said, "We Soviet people, in particular cosmonauts, are pained to hear that some people in the United States are trying to use space technology for military purposes."

Shortly before the first launch of the *Columbia* in April 1981, the Soviet press began a cry of alarm over the background of copilot Robert Crippen. He was "a representative of a new profession—'military astronaut,'" complained TASS. "The inclusion in the crew of a specialist of this type is added evidence of the big attention shown by the Pentagon," TASS continued. Other sources have attacked Apollo moonwalker Jack Schmitt for being a "space warmonger."

Another Space Shuttle astronaut attacked by name in the Soviet press is Jack Lousma, commander of the third mission and a veteran of the Skylab program in 1973. Lousma, since retired from space flying (and almost elected to the Senate from Michigan in 1984), was quoted as approving the development of the U.S. antisatellite missile system—which he had indeed said, in response to a journalist's question, with the understanding that the U.S. system had been first provoked by the Soviet "killer satellite" program. The *Novosti* news agency writer who reported this interview pretended to be horrified, while carefully excising any reference to the Soviet killer satellite. "How can a space pilot say such an irresponsible thing?" the Russian demanded. "And he's a mission commander, too!" And Lousma has been repeatedly quoted as saying, "From space we [the United States] can hold the whole world in fear," when what he really said was that without U.S. countermeasures, a Soviet monopoly on space weapons would allow *them* to hold the whole world in fear! Obviously the Soviet audience was being warned to watch out for such "dangerous astronauts"—and to approve of any "defensive" violence directed at them.

The most dangerous astronauts so far, if the Soviet-bloc media are to be believed, are Ken Mattingly and Hank Hartsfield of the Defense Department's (DOD's) STS-4 mission in mid-1982. Both men commanded later DOD-related missions; Hartsfield's crew deployed a navy communications satellite, and Mattingly's, a new generation of electronic "ferret" payload, according to press accounts. During their seven days in orbit in 1982, the Soviet press raised horrified alarms over the laser weapons that they were supposedly testing in space (they weren't); after Mattingly's second shuttle mission in January 1985, Moscow again alleged that laser weapons had been aboard. Their 1982 "warmongering cargo of destruction and death" was compared to "purely peaceful" Soviet space activities—except that the USSR had tested a killer satellite only a few weeks before and then lied about it.

In contrast, Soviet cosmonauts have been repeatedly trotted out to testify to their own love of peace—and to their opposition to U.S. space activities. Cosmonaut Aleksey Leonov, speaking at the launching of a trio of Soviet space pilots in April 1983, pontificated:

> The Soviet space program has always been aimed at resolving peaceful scientific and national economic tasks. I, who participated in the Soyuz Apollo program, well remember meeting U.S. scientists and astronauts. During the meetings the Soviet side repeatedly underscored the fact that space must never be allowed to be used for deploying weapons. This position meets the aspirations of all the peace-loving forces of the planet. In sharp contrast to this background are the efforts by the current U.S. administration for the forced militarization of space.

Later, in a congratulatory telegram to Sally Ride, Russia's first spacewoman Valentina Tereshkova announced her desire that space "should remain peaceful for all times, free of any kind of weaponry"—like the Space Shuttle, presumably. The cosmonauts were omitting mention of many years of Soviet tests of orbital H-bombs and killer satellites, although it's hard to believe that they had never heard of them.

Other cosmonauts have obediently taken up the refrain. In the June 1983 issue of *Aviation and Cosmonautics*, three-time space veteran Colonel Valeriy Bykovskiy wrote an emotional appeal. He denounced the "insane plans" of the U.S. militarists "who want to rule the universe" and continued, "Truly, war in space is much more dangerous than on Earth, since its consequences can lead via un-avoidable processes to the end of life on our planet. Wherever is that common sense of which Americans pride themselves? Why does their president not think about the future of his nation, about the children?" Bykovskiy then denied that the Soviet space program had any military purposes. Indeed, according to cosmonaut Vladimir Dzhanibekov, the U.S. Space Shuttle program "responds to a great extent to the interests of war, not peace," and any transfer of space technology for military purposes is "pernicious."

Particularly ironic was an appeal from cosmonaut Boris Volynov in August 1981: "The resolution of many global problems directly depends on successes in the exploration and large-scale use of space—but, I stress, only for peaceful purposes." In 1976 Volynov had been the commander in the Salyut-5 space station, generally considered in the West to have been largely a military reconnais-sance vehicle. Even photographs and drawings of it are still military secrets in Moscow.

"Large-scale preparations are being made for a possible use of shuttle-type ships in combat," claimed TASS in March 1982. An official Soviet booklet, *Whence the Threat to Peace* (issued in 1982 in response to a Pentagon booklet on the Soviet military threat), states, "The Pentagon plans to use manned Shuttle spaceships as a space attack system. Various reconnaissance facilities and weaponry to hit space targets, including lasers, are being developed for them."

Writing on the "Strategy of Space Madness" in the Soviet Army newspaper *Krasnaya Zvezda* ("Red Star"), Colonel Engineer M. Rebrov referred to the "madman's delusions of the Pentagon maniacs"—"Military bases above the human planet, bunkers among the lunar craters, powerful laser guns aimed at Earth, satellites in orbit, blinding flashes, lethal particle beams, the destruction of all living things. . . . This is an everyday matter in the Pentagon's militarist preparations." Rebrov goes on: "In connection with the first flights by *Columbia* and *Challenger*, the Pentagon is already elaborating the most delirious and inhuman plans, a fever of made ideas. . . . The task of preventing an arms race in space is becoming more and more acute, to halt the unbridled maniacs of space war."

Moscow's *International Affairs* magazine (November 1981) was explicit: "With the Space Shuttle, the U.S. Air Force can diversify the means of combat actions for striking targets in outer space, in the air, and on land. Equipped with nuclear weapons, they will act as a sort of outer space bomber."

The USSR armed forces journal *Sovietskiy Voin* ("Soviet Warrior") told its readers, "The predatory looks that the American military clique is now turning to space are nothing but an attempt to use the greatest achievements of human intelligence to unleash new thermonuclear war for world supremacy. Using their new space weapons, the malignant people in the Pentagon intend to roll back the pages of history."

The Soviet response can be considered menacing in light of their trigger-happy response to lost airliners and camera-carrying army officers. "Pentagon militarists ought not to count on the USSR allowing them to turn outer space into a U.S. testing range for conducting preparations for war against socialist countries," intoned TASS military commentator Vladimir Bogachev in 1982. In *Izvestia*, analyst A. Krasikov wrote, "It is quite obvious that the USSR will not permit the United States to become the military master of space." In mid-1982, Brezhnev had warned, "The USSR will find the ability to rapidly and effectively meet any challenge hurled at us." Andropov made the same warning about space a year later: "All attempts to gain military superiority over the USSR are in vain. The Soviet Union will never allow this; it will never find itself unarmed in the face of any threat."

The accusations are false, but the rationalization foundation has been laid for the Soviets to resort to violence in space—all the fault of the United States, of course!

Of particular value to the Soviet diplomatic goals is the campaign against the NASA space station. Extensive European and Japanese participation is being solicited, and positive responses are coming in from these nations' space agencies. However, Moscow has branded the project "the keystone to Star Wars" and has whipped up domestic leftists to demonstrate against their national participation in the project. Any such difficulties will be bound to make the final project more expensive and less technologically sophisticated—extremely beneficial results in the Soviet worldview. Again, the propaganda is totally at variance with reality, since the Pentagon has in fact shown no interest in the project and has even voiced opposition to it.

Against the reality of the Soviet space program, however, all such complaints rank as cosmic hypocrisy.

Space specialists beyond the reach of Soviet coercion are

convinced that at least 70 to 80 percent of all Soviet space shots serve purely military purposes—the same purposes at which Moscow propagandists feign horror when done by U.S. spacecraft. (The balance consists of civil applications, concealed failures, and even a few genuine scientific probes.) But in addition, the Soviets have engaged in weapons-related space testing that has no parallel in the U.S. military space effort.

With about a hundred successful space launchings every year, the USSR puts about 120 to 130 payloads into orbit. Their total weight, according to Pentagon estimates confirmed by private experts, exceeds 600,000 pounds, the equivalent of twenty Space Shuttle missions.

While it has been true that Soviet satellites have weighed more than U.S. probes with similar capabilities and have tended to have much shorter operational lifetimes, both these U.S. advantages have been steadily evaporating. While not letting up at all on the ferocious launch rate, the Soviets have been keeping their spacecraft operational for longer and longer periods, with more and more sophisticated electronics. Additionally, the high launch rate gives the Soviets a built-in advantage when it comes to quickly replacing losses in any hypothetical orbital combat scenario: U.S. photoreconnaissance could be blinded for six months by an attack on just two or three satellites; the Soviets would recover from such losses in a matter of days. And recent Soviet tests of "parking" reserve spy satellites in orbit for several weeks prior to activating them for a normal mission appear aimed at developing the capability to "surge" a fleet of prestationed replacement satellites in a precombat situation. These frightening tests, which began in mid-1984, only make sense as preparations for orbital combat.*

Foremost among the Soviet military space vehicles, of course, is the killer satellite, an orbital weapon capable of blinding American reconnaissance satellites—a feat that Moscow has signed a treaty not to do. Soviet false denials of their possession of such a system have already been described at length.

In the late 1960s the Soviets repeatedly tested an orbital thermonuclear warhead, the Fractional Orbit Bombardment System (FOBS), even though the 1967 Outer Space Treaty clearly outlawed

*Ed. Note: Soviet military space doctrine is to "attain and maintain military superiority in outer space to deny the use of outer space to other states...." Soviet Military Space Doctrine, D.I.A., Aug. 1, 1984.

the use of such first-strike weapons. As early as 1965 Moscow propagandists had begun to boast about giant Soviet rockets capable of attacking any point in the world along "orbital trajectories." A nuclear-armed U.S. ASAT system was quickly set up to deal with this very real threat. But the boasts were dropped when the treaty was signed. The space-to-earth thermonuclear attack system continued in service, however, until at least the early 1970s. In the 1979 SALT II agreement, the Soviets explicitly agreed to dismantle eighteen Fractional Orbital Missile Launchers, an official admission of their former existence. It had earlier become evident that the system was not going into advanced development or wide deployment, and so the counterforce U.S. ASAT system was also dismantled; its nuclear warhead made it a plausible weapon against enemy nuclear warheads.

And the Soviet nuclear-powered radar ocean reconnaissance satellites—the RORsats—are ready to guide tactical attacks against U.S. naval task forces and—just perhaps—against submerged missile submarines. (When such reactors fall out of the sky, the Soviets are forced to admit it but still insist the satellites were purely for peaceful research.)

Other types of military space activity includes missile early warning and electronics intelligence ("ferrets"). A defecting Soviet military officer recently made the amazing but believable claim that a Soviet military counterintelligence agency runs its own electronics eavesdropping spy satellites against Soviet targets! The purpose is to enforce strict rules against accidental transmissions that could be picked up by similarly designed U.S. satellites; reportedly, careless Soviet violators are dealt with harshly.

In the Soviet manned program, military influence has been significant. All Soviet unmanned spy satellites are modified man-capable vehicles in the Vostok and Soyuz series. In the mid-1970s, the Soviets launched two manned space platforms that appeared to be primarily military in nature and gave them the same cover name—Salyut—as the research outposts in an entirely distinct program. To date, photographs and drawings of these vehicles have not been released, presumably for military security. Meanwhile, this mid-1970s spy space station design appears to have been modified to act as a mid-1980s add-on module to the standard twenty-ton core Salyut spacecraft.

Direct military activities of Soviet manned space stations reportedly exist, but they are probably not the main mission. The

station seems to have been used as an instrumented practice track-
ing target for a Soviet antisatellite laser system at Sary Shagan on
Lake Balkhash. ("Make sure you have your goggles on," the crew
was warned during several passes near the site.) Observations of
military maneuvers and of world trouble spots like the Iran-Iraq
border have also apparently been made.

If the tactical military value of the Salyut has sometimes been
overrated, it remains true that its long-range military value is
profound. Since its announced purpose is to better map the country's
resources and advance its electronics industry, its successes in these
pursuits will greatly enhance the USSR's military potential. Any new
metal ore deposits will probably go into tanks and aircraft carriers,
not sports cars; any new high-capacity computer chips will wind up
in missile guidance systems, not video game arcades. Few major
projects are funded in the USSR if there isn't some measurable
military gain, and the cosmonaut program is no exception. These
gains may be long in coming, but they will be sensational when they
finally arrive.

The Perfection Deception

The propaganda campaign about Perfection has led to numerous
cover-ups of failures, while U.S. difficulties receive dispropor-
tionate press coverage. Particularly ironic were stories in late 1983,
when a shuttle mission nearly suffered "burn-through" in the nozzle
of one of its rocket engines. *Pravda* exulted that "An Explosion
Nearly Occurred" and gave the post-flight NASA admission twice
the column inches the original launching had gotten. What the
Soviet public was not told—for obvious reasons—was that only a few
weeks before, an explosion actually *had* occurred on a manned
spacecraft, but it had been a Soviet one! On September 26, two
cosmonauts barely escaped with their lives when their booster
caught fire and detonated on the launch pad at Tyuratam. (Their
capsule's escape tower flung them free with only seconds to spare.)
No whisper of this near-tragedy ever reached the Soviet public,
which was simultaneously being deluged by accounts of how dangerous the U.S. manned space program was!

The Soviet press is characterized by continual carping on any
breakdowns aboard U.S. spacecraft, however trivial. There is one
amusing exception to this policy: The prudish Soviet censors could

not allow any mention of the incessant and annoying problems with the Shuttle toilet on some of the early missions. That was judged too embarrassing a topic for tender Soviet ears!

One of the most amusing aspects of Soviet deception is how clumsy it often is. It is a common practice to retouch group photographs of cosmonauts (as it is with practically any kind of Soviet photograph) to remove "failed" trainees from association with true Soviet heroes. Unfortunately, such photographs are often released in different books in different forms!

One notorious case that I discovered personally involved a photo taken in May 1961 at the Sochi resort on the Black Sea. In the back row stood four trainee cosmonauts, three of whom would eventually fly in space. One book, published for an overseas audience, had all four—but the domestic version had only three men in the back row! When I published both photographs side by side about a decade ago, the Soviets were prompted to release official excuses about the man being dropped "for medical reasons" (Had his heart stopped?), and the photo-forgers went back to work on the crudely retouched group portrait. In 1984 they rereleased it, unfortunately once again in two different editions: one artist had painted a staircase into the spot formerly occupied by the purged cosmonaut, while another had filled in the artificial blank with a flowering shrub!

Other photographs from the same resort visit have had up to five failed cosmonauts airbrushed out. Observers are justified in wondering what they did—or had done to them—to deserve the enforced anonymity of the forgery lab. The official Soviet accounts have been ambiguous at best!

In another sequence of photographs, one of the purged trainee cosmonauts is first seen peering over Yuri Gagarin's shoulder on the bus to the launch pad. A later edition of the picture retains the mystery man's body, but his face has become an unrecognizable smudge. A final version has the entire background—mystery body, smudged-out face, and all—totally blacked out, suggesting perhaps that Gagarin's bus had encountered a power failure in a dark tunnel on the drive across the steppes!

To conceal the existence of a tremendous folded-optics spy camera on the Salyut-1 space station in 1971, Soviet artists carefully retouched a cutaway drawing of the spacecraft. Almost all of the intervening wall was folded back, revealing the craft's interior, except that in the station's midsection a large flap of wall suddenly protruded up from the bottom to conceal "something" large. I dubbed it the "fig-leaf effect." Later editions of the photograph had the offending flap removed, along with whatever had been behind it; only a clumsily erased white smudge remained.

The biggest Soviet "big lie" of space history involves the cover-up of the other side of the "moon race." Throughout the 1960s Soviet space engineers strove to carry out manned lunar flights ahead of the vigorously accelerating Apollo program. When their efforts failed and Apollo-11 won the race, the Soviets secretly dropped out and adopted the public stance that they had never been in the race at all—otherwise surely they would have won if they had tried! But the hard evidence for their multibillion-ruble program slipped out in the ensuing year and convinced serious space historians that the man-to-the-moon race—and the Soviet loss—had in fact been quite real. The USSR's postloss rationalizations and excuse-making were for domestic effect and also to deceive ideologically inclined Western newsmen into downplaying the epochal importance of the U.S. lunar victory.

Another preference for image over reality came up in the Apollo-Soyuz program in 1975. Following disastrous losses in the races to send men to the moon, to host crews aboard space stations, and to land robot probes on Mars, the Soviets finagled their way into a joint space mission, on which they got half the glory while the United States did nine-tenths of the work. Having lost on all tracks, they climbed up onto the winners' stand nevertheless, to pose as "equals."

Although many U.S. citizens criticized the program as a "Wheat Deal in the Sky" ("Togetherness in space," snorted one cynic, "with our arms around their shoulders and their hands in our pockets"), hindsight indicates that the greatest information flow was toward the United States, not away from it. The program was a windfall bonanza for U.S. technical intelligence agencies, allowing them an absolutely unique window into many key areas of advanced Soviet aerospace technology. Such observations led to calibrations of earlier estimates of Soviet military capabilities. As for the Soviets, in later years they showed no evidence of having acquired any U.S. manned space flight technology—they continued to use and develop their own homegrown systems. Visiting Western space officials confirm this surprising fact; a similar conclusion was voiced in a report by the Library of Congress's Congressional Research Service, which told the Senate International Relations Committee that "there has been no evidence to date of any harmful effects from any technological giveaway to either side from these [space biology, planetary and Apollo-Soyuz] joint space efforts." Soviet acquisition of weapons-related technology, a genuine problem, seems to pass through other channels.

The Priority Deception

The Priority Deception also involves rewriting space history with distortions (once Moscow had lost the ability to write space history with deeds) as proof of Soviet superiority and big-power status. The phrase "first in the world" kept ringing out, sometimes with justification but often not. For example, Soviet history books record that their country was first with probes to Venus and Mars but ignore the reality that these probes all went dead en route and that the first spacecraft to reach and report on both planets were U.S. spacecraft.

For the sake of world records, actual space events have been distorted. In 1961, when Yuri Gagarin became the first man to orbit the Earth, he followed standard procedures on his descent, which called for bailing out and making the final landing on personal parachute. But international aviation regulations required a would-be record setter to complete the mission inside his craft—bailing out was specifically forbidden. So Moscow just announced that Gagarin had done exactly this. But in later years the spur-of-the-moment lie was forgotten and follow-up announcements made it clear that Gagarin had really bailed out (and had really deserved the record anyway).

Sometimes the political push for firsts has led to pure orbital stuntsmanship. Such motivations were behind the decision to send a "typical Russian woman" into space in 1963, to do so again in 1982 just in time to upstage the first flight of an American woman, and to have the woman make a spacewalk two years later, only weeks before the announced plan to have another U.S. woman perform such a feat. Similarly in 1976, when NASA announced plans to have West European scientists fly aboard Spacelab missions (since the European Space Agency was building and paying for that module), Moscow initiated its own program for allowing one each Soviet-bloc representative to ride into space aboard routine resupply missions to Salyut space stations. Since Cuba was one of the nations eligible for this program, the specifications called for the world's first black man in space to be aboard one of these "guest cosmonaut" orbital milk runs. (So in character was this decision that I predicted it in print three years before it happened.) The purely arbitrary nature of these flight selections was underscored by the fact that the second group of guests was launched sequentially in strict Cyrillic alphabetical order!

Since their return to Earth, the guest cosmonauts have performed the propaganda functions planned for them from the beginning. The Polish cosmonaut became a figurehead member of the military junta that took over to crush Solidarity; the Cuban cosmonaut tours South America, preaching that the United States plans to wipe out the planet with space weapons; the Hungarian cosmonaut recently aborted a planned East European religious speaking tour by ex-astronaut Jim Irwin when he claimed Irwin was a liar to say he had encountered God in space. The Vietnamese backup cosmonaut, not so lucky as his colleague to get only ceremonial assignments, was sent back to an air combat unit, where he was killed in an undescribed "accident."

Such political directives for creating artificial space spectaculars have been known to cause disasters, but this mainly happened in the early years of the "space race." In late 1960 as many as a hundred people died when a balky rocket blew up on the launch pad while it was being inspected; the safe procedure of slowly draining its fuel was skipped under orders from Khrushchev's representative, who knew his boss would brook no such delays. In 1967, following the defection of Stalin's daughter Svetlana Alliluyeva, a planned Mayday space spectacular was ordered launched prematurely, even though the project engineers had concluded the new spaceships were still not fully certified. The Soyuz-1 subsequently crashed to Earth, killing its pilot and thus scoring an unwanted "space first" for Russia.

This vast array of hard examples should make it clear that Soviet statements on their space activities are made without any regard for reality. Propaganda necessities are the leading considerations. Trivial details such as truthfulness have not seemed to restrict the public statements.

While such a policy has long been considered standard in many other aspects of "Soviet reality," the leading feature of the space arena is that documented examples are common and indisputable. For those who wish to believe otherwise, the Soviet "lies in the skies" demand they face the reality of Soviet deception as a way of life.

The naked reality behind the screen of deception was described in *Soviet Military Space Doctrine,* a scrupulously documented Defense Intelligence Agency study released in mid-1984. By careful analysis of changes in the treatment of military publications, the report underscored the relevance of the traditional Soviet belief in the decisiveness of attack in war, on Earth and in space as well. Matched against such a doctrine, Moscow's hollow public pronouncements were deemed particularly hypocritical: "Insisting that only the United States possesses [space] weapons and systems, when the USSR either has or is actively developing all of them, stretches the bounds of credibility too far: how can statements of Soviet peaceful intentions regarding outer space be taken seriously when Moscow so duplicitously distorts the actual situation?"

In a recent radio broadcast, a Soviet commentator named Igor Dmitreyev unwittingly posed a damning question: "Can one sincerely seek arms reductions on Earth," he demanded, "and simultaneously conduct military experiments in outer space?" It's an excellent question, but Moscow has been asking it of the wrong side. Westerners have every right—nay, the duty—to turn it around and demand an answer from the Soviets. Against such an incessant, repetitive drumbeat of Soviet "lies in the skies," how can any negotiator be expected to take them seriously or to trust their word on any agreement that might be reached?

The Soviet answer is to continue the strategy of cosmic deception. Routinely, the TASS news agency in Moscow releases a new bulletin on yet another "scientific" satellite launched "for the further exploration of outer space" or issues another thunderous tirade against the danger of U.S. space militarization. And the pile of lies reaches into the heavens.

DECEPTION
IN THE ATTEMPT
ON THE POPE'S LIFE

Herbert Romerstein

The unsuccessful attempt on the Pope's life by a Turkish terrorist, Mehmet Ali Agca, shocked the world. No less shocking were the allegations in the Italian and world press that Agca had committed the crime under the direction of the Bulgarian (and therefore the Soviet) intelligence service. The Soviet response to these charges was an extensive and well-orchestrated campaign of overt and covert disinformation and deception.

The Soviet propaganda machine was described in 1983 by Konstantin Chernenko in the following terms:

> Comrades, our entire system of ideological work should operate as a distinctive voice and lead its theme, while harmony is achieved by skillful conducting. . . . Propaganda is called upon to embrace every aspect of social life and every social group and region and to reach every individual.[1]

The "orchestra" plays in three modes: white (overt), black (covert), and gray (lightly concealed). The influence operations carried out by the "orchestra" are called by the Soviets "active measures."

According to the CIA, "The Soviet term active measures is used (primarily in an intelligence context) to distinguish influence operations from espionage and counterintelligence," but this term is not limited to intelligence alone. Rather, Soviet "active measures" involve activities by virtually every element of the Soviet Party and State structure and are regarded as a valuable regular supplement to, and are closely coordinated with, traditional diplomacy. Soviet "active measures" include:

- Manipulation or control of the media
- Written or oral disinformation
- Use of foreign Communist Parties and front organizations

- Clandestine radio broadcasting
- Economic activities
- Military operations
- Other political influence operations

Ultimate approval for the use of "active measures," like all major decisions affecting Soviet foreign policy, rests with the highest level of the Soviet hierarchy, the Politburo and the Secretariat of the Central Committee of the Communist Party of the Soviet Union. Most decisions concerning implementation are carried out by the KGB in close coordination with two elements of the Soviet Party bureaucracy, the International Department and the International Information Department. The extensive participation of these two powerful party components in "active measures" indicates both the importance attached to such activities by Soviet leaders and their appreciation of the policy implications of such activities.[2] The world-wide network is summarized in Figure 2.

The Soviet response to press allegations of their involvement in the attempt to assassinate the Pope used three deception themes. These themes appeared in all of the "active measures" modes; white (in overt Soviet and Bulgarian propaganda); gray (through the international Soviet fronts and local Communist Parties), and black (through KGB forgeries and other covert activities).

The three themes were: 1. The Soviets and Bulgarians had no involvement with Agca or his attempt to murder the Pope; 2. All of the allegations against the Soviets and Bulgarians were concocted by the U.S. government, particularly the CIA; and 3. The real culprit was the CIA.

Theme 2 is clearly contradicted by the fact that the U.S. government consistently stated that they would not comment or reach conclusions about the evidence. The United States expressed complete reliance on the Italian courts. Indeed, Paul Henze and Claire Sterling, American journalists who have written about the case, have been critical of the U.S. reluctance to draw conclusions.

Theme 3 is the usual Soviet propaganda line that the CIA is to blame for all the evils in the world. In this case the theme serves a second purpose, to exonerate the Soviets and Bulgarians. Themes 2 and 3 have that as their main purpose.

Radio Moscow, in an English-language broadcast on January 11, 1986, provided a lengthy attack on the CIA, blaming the Agency for a variety of violent and natural deaths of prominent individuals.

Soviet Organizational Structure for "Active Measures"

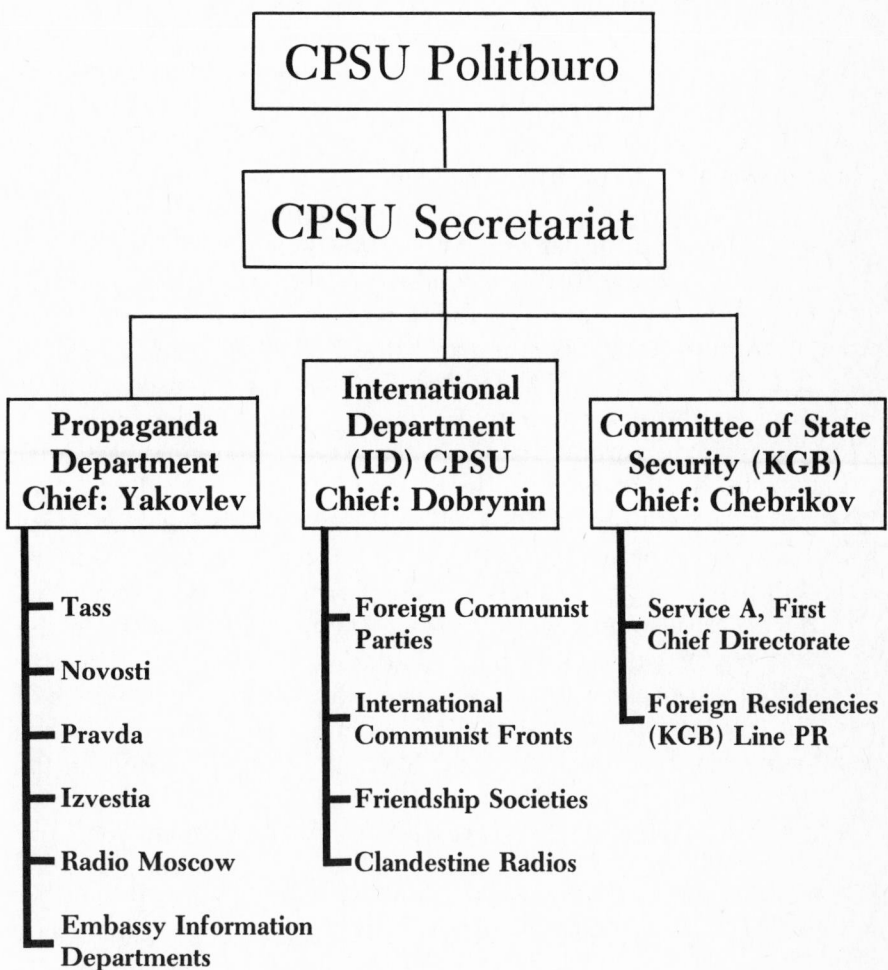

CPSU Politburo

CPSU Secretariat

| Propaganda Department Chief: Yakovlev | International Department (ID) CPSU Chief: Dobrynin | Committee of State Security (KGB) Chief: Chebrikov |

- Tass
- Novosti
- Pravda
- Izvestia
- Radio Moscow
- Embassy Information Departments

- Foreign Communist Parties
- International Communist Fronts
- Friendship Societies
- Clandestine Radios

- Service A, First Chief Directorate
- Foreign Residencies (KGB) Line PR

Note: It has been estimated that the Soviets spend $3–4 billion a year on active measures.

Figure 2

In the course of that broadcast Moscow said, "It is now possible to trace links between the CIA and the attempt in May 1981 on the life of Pope John Paul II. The assassin, Ali Agca, failed to carry out the assignment to the end. Yet the very fact of the assassination attempt is now used by the CIA in mounting a slanderous campaign against Bulgaria and the Soviet Union."[3]

The main practitioner of the overt element of this propaganda campaign is Iona Andronov, a senior journalist for the Soviet newspaper *Literary Gazette,* with a long history of KGB activity. According to Andronov, no one took an interest in Agca's motives "until a signal was given from the White House to launch the latest anti-Communist campaign." According to Andronov, "Dozens of Western newspapers, radio and TV stations immediately raised a hue and cry against Sofia and Moscow! . . . President Reagan ordered the CIA to go on using the 'Agca affair' to the maximum for propaganda in favor of a 'crusade against communism.'"[4]

Claire Sterling, in her criticism of the U.S. government, identified a U.S. diplomat in Rome who expressed his personal opinion that the evidence against the Bulgarians and Soviets was insufficient. Andronov took the story and stood it on its head. Claiming that this man is the "CIA resident," Andronov accused him of orchestrating the campaign to blame the Soviet Union and Bulgaria.[5] Andronov forgot that it is the KGB chief in a particular country who is called the "resident"; the CIA official is called "chief of station." A number of CIA officials have held that post since 1978, when Andronov claims that this particular diplomat was assigned to Rome. None of them was the person named by Andronov.

Andronov also makes good use of Theme 3. He quotes a leader of the bizarre political group headed by Lyndon LaRouche: "Nevertheless the assassination was prepared with the knowledge of the CIA. Do not be surprised! Remember a similar occasion when Kissinger was U.S. Secretary of State and was monitoring the activities of the CIA. It was he who sanctioned the murder of terrorists of the former Italian Prime Minister and Christian Democrat leader Aldo Moro." Andronov claims he responded, "Yet it seemed incredible that the CIA bosses had raised a hand against Pope John Paul II." Andronov quoted the LaRouche official as saying, "Apart from these bosses there are several traditionally rival cliques within the ranks of the CIA. There is a pro-fascist grouping among them, too. It is capable of acts which sometimes appear incredible."[6] The LaRouche group, which now calls itself right wing, actually began in the late 1960s as a faction of the Marxist-Leninist Students for a Democratic Society. Andronov attempted to identify the group as right wing to be able to attribute the false charge to a supposed non-Communist source.

The KGB contributed to the campaign by forging two secret U.S. government cables that purported to show that the U.S. government was orchestrating a press campaign to blame the Soviet Union and Bulgaria. First planted in the July 21, 1983, issue of the leftist Italian magazine *Pace E Guerra*, the forgeries were soon exposed. The KGB had made the mistake of not putting cable numbers on the forgeries. U.S. officials pointed out that cables are hard enough to find in the files when they are numbered; unnumbered cables would cause chaos. Although most of the Italian press exposed the Soviet forgeries, a book was published in France reproducing them in full and pretending that they were authentic. The book's author, Christian Roulette, has been a member of the French Communist Party for decades. An examination of the book, *Jean-Paul II, Antonov Agca, La Filiere* (Paris: Editions du Sorbier, 1984), reveals that large sections were reproduced from the writings of Andronov (sometimes attributed, sometimes not). Entire pages were taken word for word from Andronov's pamphlets and *Literary Gazette* articles. The book was made available to the French press by the Bulgarian Embassy in an attempt to defend Serge Antonov, the Bulgarian official arrested by the Italian police for complicity in the assassination attempt. Roulette's connections were revealed by the Milan newspaper *Corriere della Sera* on March 20, 1985; it reported that he had spoken at a Rome press conference organized by the Bulgarian press spokesman.

A similar book was published in West Germany, entitled *The Russians are Coming—in Time*, by Hubert Reichel. The legitimate "cover" on this book was no better than the one on Roulette's. A lengthy excerpt from the Reichel book, entitled "The KGB Attempt to Kill the Pope—How the 'Bulgarian Connection' Started from CIA Headquarters," appeared in *Unsere Zeit*, the newspaper of the West German Communist Party.[7]

Philip Agee is a defector from the CIA. He built a reputation for identifying alleged CIA officers and "exposing" supposed CIA activities. Philip Agee's magazine, *Covert Action Information Bulletin*, devoted an entire issue to "Disconnecting the 'Bulgarian Connection.'" This publication has replayed Soviet disinformation in the past. It even reprinted in full the most famous and widely used of the Soviet forgeries, the so-called Field Manual.[8] A large portion of the magazine's special issue was taken from the Roulette book, and footnote credit is given. The Roulette book is also credited with most of the pictures published by Agee's magazine.[9]

The International Association of Democratic Lawyers is an international Soviet front. According to the CIA, "Although restricted in membership by definition, the International Association of Democratic Lawyers (IADL) has been one of the most useful Communist front organizations at the service of the Soviet Communist Party."[10]

The IADL took up "the case" at its Twelfth Congress, held in Athens from October 15 to 19, 1984. After numerous delegates stood up to condemn the view that the Soviets and Bulgarians might be involved in the assassination attempt, the IADL, in the judicial mode, established "an international commission" to study the case.[11]

The "commission," while admitting that Agca had been to Bulgaria prior to the attempt on the Pope's life, suggested that this was meaningless, and of course that the Soviets and Bulgarians are innocent.[12]

Another international Soviet front involved in this "active measures" campaign is the International Organization of Journalists (IOJ). According to the CIA, "The IOJ is heavily infiltrated by Czechoslovak and Cuban agents. It operates a world-wide news service, offered practically free to Third World news media. A review of this IOJ service in any given country faithfully reflects current Soviet propaganda themes."[13]

The *IOJ Newsletter* and its magazine, *The Democratic Journalist,* have carried numerous articles aimed at their audience in the less developed countries promoting all the Soviet themes on this case. The *IOJ Newsletter* for October 1983 suggested, "This inflammatory campaign [i.e., news stories suggesting Soviet-Bulgarian involvement], threatening peaceful coexistence was seized upon quite willingly by some mass media of Western countries in the race for sensation and profit." *The Democratic Journalist* for December 1983 reproduced photocopies of West European newspapers implicating the Soviets and Bulgarians and suggested that such stories were violations of journalistic ethics.

Vitaliy Yurchenko was a high-ranking official of the Soviet KGB; he defected to the United States by walking into the U.S. Embassy in Rome in July 1985. He was brought to the United States and extensively debriefed. In November of the same year he shocked the American intelligence community by redefecting to the Soviet Embassy in Washington. In press conferences held in Washington and Moscow he accused the CIA of kidnapping him.

On August 9, 1986, the Soviet newspaper *Moskovskaya Pravda* reported an interview with Yurchenko. He supposedly claimed that the CIA had told him that they wanted him to say that the Bulgarians had plotted the attempt on the Pope's life together with the KGB. He further claimed, "They [the Bulgarians], according to the CIA prompting, were in charge of the practical organization of the participants in the plot, while the Russians gave them instructions and supplied the money." Yurchenko went on to say that the CIA wanted him to claim that he himself had gone to Sofia and had met Agca and had offered him three million West German marks to carry out the assassination.

The Soviets and Bulgarians have devoted a great deal of time, energy, and money to "prove" that they are innocent and that the United States is guilty in the attempt to assassinate the Pope. Journalists and academics like Claire Sterling, Paul Henze, and Michael Ledeen, who have presented arguments implicating the Soviets and Bulgarians, have been subjected to an extensive smear campaign by the Soviets and their surrogates. The surfacing of Yurchenko indicates that the campaign will continue. As a result of the Italian court's "Scotch verdict" (i.e., unproved), most of the world press still believes that the Soviets and Bulgarians were involved in Agca's crime. The U.S. government continues to refrain from commenting on the issue. But Soviet "active measures" continue: "the guilty flee where no man pursueth."

Notes

1. Konstantin Chernenko, Speech at meeting of Central Committee, Communist Party of the Soviet Union, June 14–15, 1983. *Information Bulletin.* (Prague, August 1983), p. 24.

2. Permanent Select Committee on Intelligence, U.S. House of Representatives, *Soviet Active Measures.* Hearings before the Permanent Select Committee on Intelligence, House of Representatives. (Washington, D.C.: U.S. Government Printing Office, 1982), p. 31.

3. *Foreign Broadcast Information Service, Daily Report,* III, January 12, 1983, p. A6.

4. Iona Andronov, *On the Wolf's Track.* (Sofia: Sofia Press, 1983), pp. 9–10.

5. Iona Andronov, *The Triple Plot*. (Sofia: Sofia Press, 1984), pp. 9–11.

6. *Wolf's Track*, op. cit., pp. 41–43.

7. *The Bulgarian Connection: The End of a Provocation*. (Sofia: Sofia Press, 1983), p. 9. Unattributed.

8. Permanent Select Committee on Intelligence, U.S. House of Representatives, *Soviet Covert Action (The Forgery Offensive)*. Hearings before the Subcommittee on Oversight of the Permanent Select Committee on Intelligence. House of Representatives. (Washington, D.C.: U.S. Government Printing Office, 1980.)

9. *Covert Action Information Bulletin* 22 (1985).

10. Permanent Select Committee on Intelligence, U.S. House of Representatives, *The CIA and the Media*. Hearings before the Permanent Select Committee on Intelligence, House of Representatives. (Washington, D.C.: U.S. Government Printing Office, 1978), p. 614.

11. *Democratic Lawyers Oppose the Inequities Against Antonov*. Documents of the Twelfth Congress of the International Association of Democratic Lawyers, Athens, October 15–19, 1984. (Sofia: Sofia Press, 1984.)

12. *Report of the International Commission of Study and Information on "The Antonov Affair"* (mimeographed, no date), circa 1985.

13. *The CIA and the Media*, op. cit., p. 603.

SOVIET
DECEPTION
AND RELIGION

Dr. William Fletcher

Ever since 1917 Western churchmen have been among the Soviet Union's strongest, most faithful supporters. In good times and bad, a small number of powerful Christian leaders have acted almost as partners of the Soviet State, praising its successes, ignoring its failures, and helping it whenever they can. Especially in foreign policy, these Western church leaders are quick to support all but the most brutal Soviet actions.

How they, as Christians, can support the atheistic Soviet regime is a mystery. Communism insists on atheism; it is bitterly hostile to any religion at all. No one has ever succeeded in marrying Marxism to religion; when it is tried, the Christian part always shrinks and disappears, and what is left is only the slogans of revolution, violence, and even terrorism. The Soviet Union, for its part, has tried for seventy years to crush religion, using a vast array of discrimination and force against the churches and religious believers. When Western Christians learn of the true situation of religion in the USSR, they are horrified, for no one could support the degradation and suffering that has resulted from Soviet religious policy.

And yet Soviet foreign policy is firmly and completely supported by some religious leaders. The Soviets are aware that such sympathizers in the West can be a huge asset, and they have laid down careful plans and policies to encourage, nurture, and even direct such sentiments among Western religious leaders. This chapter will survey this aspect of the Soviet confrontation with the West.

Spokesmen of Deception

What are the motives of these outspoken admirers of Soviet policies and actions? Even though they are united in their support of the

USSR, a great many dreams, desires, and opinions must have led them to this position. There are a number of possibilities.

Many of them may be motivated by politics and ideologies of their own. Some of the most liberal elements in the West have looked to the USSR with hope and longing as the land where their political beliefs and dreams come true. The most notorious of these extreme liberals was Dr. Hewlett Johnson, the "Red Dean of Canterbury." Praising the ideal of a classless society, he wrote:

> Such is the heart and intention of the Soviet Union. Such is the basis of its strength. It is scientific. It is moral. In both these respects at least it has outstanding points of contact with Christianity. . . .

> Jesus gave us the driving force, the vision, the appetite, the thirst to achieve. . . . Now the Soviet Union, aided by the abundance which science makes possible, turns vision into reality. It treats each child as a brother or sister, and assures to each sufficient food for adequate physical life, and education to high levels of cultural life. The opportunity, in short, to live a full, rich, human life. . . .

> Communism has, I would suggest, made a massive approach to a nobler Christian life and a nobler attitude to the Great Power which lies behind all life, to God. . . .

> Finally, a planned, Communist society seeks peace. It has peace at the heart of its productive life. A planned industrial economy has no need to struggle for markets. It knows how to consume all it produces. It has banished competitive war at home. It seeks to eliminate competitive war abroad. Hence Communist society is at its moral greatest in its quest for peace.[1]

It should be noted that Johnson wrote this in 1956, on the eve of Khrushchev's "Secret Speech," in which he made public the appalling cruelties of Stalin's rule. Nevertheless, Hewlett Johnson never changed; he never lost his enthusiasm.

Nor is he alone. A similar ideology may drive John C. Bennett's approach to Marxist revolutions. "Marxism has been the bearer of a true revolutionary imperative," he has said. He has gone further, however, to suggest, "Its anti-religious stance is a judgment upon the churches."[2]

Probably a large number of those religious leaders who praise the USSR are simply naive. Often protected by their profession, and seeking to practice Christian ideals in their own lives, many of these people credit others with that same Christian charity that they seek for themselves. They try not to excuse their own faults, and they try to be blind to the sins of others. From this attitude it is only a short step to a political view that sees evil only in their own country while ignoring much greater evils elsewhere. Thus, for example, the National Coalition for American Nuns joined enthusiastically in the campaign against the neutron bomb. "The USSR accuses the United States of defying our own human rights code by developing the neutron bomb," they stated. "We must agree in this one instance with the Russians."[3]

John M. Swomley, Jr., president of the Methodist Peace Fellowship, provided a good example of this naiveté when he advocated U.S. withdrawal from South Korea.

> If it is argued that the Soviet Union will replace the United States as the dominant power in the Far East, there are a number of possible responses. One is to let the Russians do it, earning the hatred that comes from trying to divert the current of nationalism; let their elite reap the consequences of expending resources and spreading manpower thin at the expense of the Russian people. Another possible response is to rejoice in the possibility that there may be forces within the Soviet Union and other Communist countries which would welcome the chance to demilitarize and disarm if they no longer had to compete militarily with the U.S.[4]

He did not say how he had been able to detect this yearning for pacifism in the present power structure of the USSR.

This trusting, naive acceptance very often fills the reports of visitors to the USSR. For example, Charles Smith, the outgoing president of the American Baptist Churches, returned from a visit with the strange report that Baptists in the USSR did not agree with President Carter's stand on human rights. Furthermore, he admitted that believers are harassed, but he felt that some of what Soviet Christians feel along those lines "is more psychological than real."[5]

Closely aligned to this approach, which wishes to see only good and not evil, is that group of apologists for the USSR who are pacifists. Pacifism has a long and honorable history in Christianity and other religions, and almost certainly pacifism would have surfaced with or without the encouragement of the USSR.

A great many denominations and church leaders gave prominent support to the recent nuclear freeze movement, an approach that pacifists in the West could join with some hope of success at home; there was no such possibility in the USSR. Naturally, Soviet foreign policy was vigorously in favor of this movement.

Many of the major organizations that began as pacifist bodies soon came to resemble certain other groups that are far from peaceful. The American Friends Service Committee, the Fellowship of Reconciliation, the War Resisters League, the Women's International League for Peace and Freedom, and many others began to join in a swelling chorus of anti-Americanism that soon became popular, indeed was a fad, among the American left. A great many churchmen and churches also yielded to the temptation to join in whatever was being promoted most loudly. Thus, for example, the antinuclear position of the National Conference of Catholic Bishops in their Pastoral Letter, while very welcome to the supporters of Soviet foreign policy, almost certainly was not the result of Soviet guidance.[6] Instead, it reflected what was temporarily sweeping the extreme fringes of the Western radicals and the media. Time and again, church leaders have been willing and eager to join in activities and statements friendly to the USSR when that has been the immediate goal of the political left.

Finally, a large and unknowable number of these religious apologists for the Soviet regime are driven by simple ambition. Eugene Carson Blake, for example, led the first U.S. church delegation to the USSR in 1956. Deeply ambitious to win the Russian church for the Ecumenical Movement, he was most generous and flattering in all his comments.[7] A decade later, having risen to become general secretary of the World Council of Churches (WCC), he was still careful not to offend his Russian members. In 1967, for example, his only reaction to an appeal to the WCC for aid to over two hundred Baptists in Soviet prisons was:

> The World Council of Churches is studying the document closely. Because of its concern for both religious liberty and unity within its member churches, it is seeking direct contact with the competent authorities in the USSR particularly with leaders of the Baptist church, who have been asked to comment on the document and evaluate it.[8]

Nothing more was heard from the WCC on this issue.

An even more open attempt to curry favor appeared during the American Broadcasting Company's two-hour special program on religion in the USSR in 1983. The Reverend Bruce Rigdon, the program's host, gave serious and encouraging attention to the Soviet peace theme in long segments. Soviet churchmen, some of them fairly obscure but very articulate, gave long and very impassioned expression to the views of peace that were currently being featured in Soviet propaganda, and ABC gave them large amounts of air time in its nationwide broadcast. It was clear that in this case, the show's producers were willing to pay this price for the State's permission to shoot the film in the USSR.

Nor is such deference confined to any one segment of Western religious leadership. Dr. William Bright, founder of Campus Crusade for Christ International, was approvingly quoted by *Moscow News* in 1978:

> As to "complaints of persecution because of religious beliefs," he emphasized, he has not heard any in the Soviet Union, although he was quite familiar with rumors of that sort at home. "Three weeks are evidently too short a time to make a final judgement but it is my belief that much of the criticism concerning the lack of religious freedom in this country is without basis or fact." He went on to say that the cases he personally was able to check out show this conclusion to be totally correct.[9]

A much more celebrated case occurred four years later. Statements by Dr. Billy Graham at a news conference following his visit to the USSR in 1982 caused a furor. In the course of the news conference he made a number of unusual observations. "Saturday night," he stated, "I went to three Orthodox churches. They were jammed to capacity. You'd never get that in Charlotte, North Carolina." Answering a question about the churches' relationship to the State, he made an unfortunate comparison that had huge implications: "Here the church is not a State church. It is a 'free' church in the sense that it is not directly headed, as the church in England is headed, by the Queen." Finally, he flatly stated, "I have seen no religious persecution during my stay in Russia."

Whatever their motives, a large number of Western church leaders not only go out of their way to avoid any possible offense to the USSR, they also charge ahead, trying to help many of its most ambitious plans in international affairs. This is an important corps of supporters for the USSR to use. Very little is needed to encourage them in their support. In fact, they are so ready to believe the best (and to deny anything that contradicts their fond hopes) that it takes very little to keep them from learning the true facts about their fellow Christians in the USSR. Content in their ignorance, they seem happy to stay misinformed about such dark matters as these.

Deception Organizations

In order to provide the structure for clergy to support Soviet plans, large organizations have not been used much. Even in the case of front movements, where the Soviets and their supporters are quick to create an organization for every occasion, such efforts are not needed in the field of religion. A very few organizations were more than enough to channel and direct the efforts of these Western churchmen and to encourage them to cling to their beloved misconceptions.

The World Peace Council (WPC) is the oldest of the organizations that the Soviets are using in the religious field.[10]

After its wartime and immediate postwar espansion had stopped, the Soviet government went on the defensive in international affairs until it could close the gap with the United States in atomic weapons. Noticing the deep currents of pacifism in a war-weary world, Stalin quickly made peace a major theme of Soviet foreign propaganda. From then on this was a constant part of the Soviet approach, the demand for peace. Soviet propagandists changed the meaning of the word, so that their concept of *peace* supported whatever the USSR was demanding at the time, and they tried to freeze out all other meanings of the word. They often succeeded.

The WPC was formed in 1949, and from the beginning it welcomed the Russian churchmen. Not only might they make the new organization more believable, they could also extend its influence into churches in the West. The chief spokesman for the Russian Orthodox Church in the WPC was Metropolitan Nikolai, and he entered into the spirit of things with enthusiasm. At the First USSR Conference for Peace in 1949, he proclaimed:

> Common people the world over are alarmed by the ring of a
> knife, rusty with human blood, as it is sharpened by the hand of
> a murderer. Death is again raising its ruthless scythe over the
> fields of the earth, preparing to reap a bountiful harvest. The

same dark forces that ten years ago hurled humanity into the abyss of indescribable suffering, again wish to hold a blood feast, for, being born to feed on human blood, they cannot live without it. . . . The transatlantic octopus is trying to fasten its greedy tentacles around the whole globe. Capitalist America, the rabid fornicatress of resurrected Babylon, having set up a world market, is trying to seduce the people of the world while pushing them toward war. But the common people of all countries are turning their eyes away from her shameless nakedness with a feeling of abomination. None of them are, or can be, enticed.[11]

It was with the beginning of the Korean War in 1950 that the WPC really came into its own. The USSR was fortunate to have a propaganda organization already in place and operational when that war began. The WPC played a prominent role in the Soviet efforts to mobilize public opinion against the UN forces in Korea, to block shipments of war materiel by demonstrations and dock strikes, and, in France especially, to stir up the turmoil and dissent that delayed and hindered the formation of NATO.

Nor were the Russian churchmen at all shy about joining the effort:

We see, then, that the spirit and the flesh of fascism have not disappeared, that there are some who are continuing the delirious dreams of the fanatic Hitler and are attempting to make them come true.

These representatives of the "superior" race have been and are committing mass rape of Korean women and girls, herding them from surrounding villages, making them drunk on gin and raping them.

Not stopping at such outrage, in some places they drove the unfortunates into tunnels which they blew up after machine-gunning the victims.[12]

As the Korean war died down, the Soviet peace movement began to fall apart. When public attention was no longer focused by an active war, it turned to other things. The WPC, by now thoroughly exposed by its own excesses as nothing more than an arm of Soviet propaganda, fell into total disrepute. As early as 1950, its headquarters had been expelled from Paris because of its political one-sidedness, and it had moved to Vienna. When Austria regained its independence, the WPC was expelled in 1955. It continued to use the shadowy International Institute for Peace, which sprang up at its former address in Vienna, for its mail, and finally it was able to find more permanent quarters in Helsinki, Finland. There it languished for twenty years, and its sad, futile meetings had no more influence or respect than the Trotskyite International.[13]

Only a new generation of Americans restored to the poor, tired, tainted WPC the gift of credibility. In 1975 officers of the WPC made a triumphal tour of ten cities in the United States. With startling naiveté, national and local church figures greeted them everywhere, welcoming them with open arms, arranging for them to meet people, especially in the high schools, and praising their one-sided opinions, which never differed in any way from the Soviet line.[14] Two years later the WPC was able to hold a highly publicized meeting in Washington, D.C., with representatives of some forty countries in attendance.[15] The Americans, with the help of their churchmen, had restored its fortunes as a front-line organization of Soviet propaganda.

Meanwhile, during the years when the WPC was in decline, Soviet attempts to sway Western churchmen concentrated on two other organizations: the Prague Christian Peace Council (CPC)[16] and the World Council of Churches (WCC).[17]

The CPC was started by the Czech theologian Joseph Hromadka in 1958. It was perhaps the clearest example of Khrushchev's revolution in Soviet foreign policy. Stalin divided the world into two camps: "He who is not for us is against us." Fellow travelers were required to toe the line, giving full support to every detail of Soviet propaganda, regardless of how outrageous it might be. Under Khrushchev the doctrine was changed. He invented a "zone of peace," a third group of nations that had broken away from their former colonial masters but that had not yet come to full, Soviet-style socialism. With this more flexible approach, Soviet foreign policy was able to seek a broader range of friends and allies. The rules were relaxed, and a new, more refined approach developed. At Soviet-sponsored meetings delegates were allowed a wide range of discussion, even including some disagreement with Soviet positions, in secondary matters. Soviet propagandists focused on a few key issues, and if they got full agreement on these, they let the delegates express almost any opinion on other matters.

The CPC was rather successful over its first ten years. Especially in Europe, some religious leaders seemed to feel that going along with the Soviets on one or two key issues was a small price to pay for the chance to meet together in dialogue. They were still careful not to offend their hosts, though. For example, at one CPC meeting where the issue was West German rearmament, one of the delegates proclaimed:

> It is certain, in this context, that the primitive anti-Communism of most of the western countries (the public mentality, the press, the government speeches), the revival in the German Federal Republic of a certain number of military or judicial personages who played a very definite role in the last war, the placing of American bases at the frontiers of the USSR, can only confirm that country in the conviction that it is encircled and this must necessarily flavor, in consequence, the action of those who are more strongly partisan to a hard policy, even envisaging the eventuality of a third world conflict. I am saying all this because I am speaking to the West. With my Soviet friends I have used quite a different language as you may imagine. I am not giving here any value judgement: what counts is not to say yes or no, whether the USSR is right, but to know what reactions are brought about by one attitude or another on our part.[18]

The CPC was perfect for the new, more subtle foreign policy of the USSR. Its broad acceptance in Western church circles gave Soviet churchmen an important avenue to spread their influence, and it was able to call attention to a large number of topics that would soon become important in Soviet international relations. In particular, by emphasizing the question of peace and Christian pacifism, it was able to work out theological and biblical positions supporting Soviet "peaceful coexistence" well before such questions were raised in the West. Thus it was the CPC that provided the positions that churches throughout the West, but especially in the United States, would soon adopt as the protests against the war in Vietnam began to grow.

These promising beginnings were brought to a halt by the Soviet invasion of Czechoslovakia in 1968. Hromadka, the CPC's founder, and an associate both condemned the invasion, and when Hromadka died shortly thereafter his associate was forced out of the leadership. Because East Europeans had proved unreliable, the Soviets put through a reorganization of the CPC in which all of its key offices were firmly controlled by Soviet churchmen. As a result, the movement's credibility was ruined, and it lapsed into the decline that had overtaken the WPC a decade earlier.

In the United States the invasion of Prague killed a three-year effort to establish a U.S. Committee for the CPC. But almost immediately a new organization sprang up in its place: Christians Associated for Relationships with Eastern Europe (CAREE).[19] Even though its tight relationship with the CPC was only thinly disguised, by the late 1970s CAREE had managed to gain some credibility among liberal church leaders in the United States. The National Council of Churches (NCC) gave it subcommittee status and some funds, and the NCC president, James Armstrong, joined the board of CAREE. More and more, the original plan to serve as a U.S. branch of the CPC could be fulfilled, with CAREE selecting delegates for expense-paid trips to CPC events in the USSR and elsewhere, nominating Americans to serve as CPC officers, and in general providing a conduit for CPC propaganda to reach a selected audience of U.S. religious leaders.

In its early years, the CPC had another use in the overall plans of the Soviet campaign to influence Western churchmen. A radical change in Soviet policy toward Western churches was about to begin, a change that involved what at first may have seemed a high-risk venture. Russian churches were being prepared to move into the Ecumenical Movement, which was a major international effort for Christian unity. The CPC, which was mobilized two years before these ventures began, was designed as a fallback position, so that if the move should backfire the USSR would still have its own, safe, "ecumenical" organization in the CPC. In fact, there was no problem, for Soviet churchmen in the Ecumenical Movement succeeded beyond the wildest hopes of the planners of Soviet foreign policy.

During the early years Soviet churchmen were very cautious in the Ecumenical Movement. Their main task was to secure and solidify their position in these international organizations. Soviet delegates to the World Council of Churches and the Baptist World Alliance (BWA) took a very low profile and, in fact, sometimes tried to restrain their more outspoken Western co-workers when support for the USSR was on the agenda.

In order to secure their position, the Soviets had to paint a false picture of the strength of their churches at home. Directly and by implication, Soviet delegates continually told of a kind, friendly government that guaranteed complete separation of church and state and gave the churches full religious liberty. In addition, the number of churches in the USSR was vastly exaggerated. On its entry into the WCC, the Russian Orthodox Church claimed that there were 22,000 churches in the Moscow Patriarchate. This was a wildly inflated figure, for since well before World War II the number of Orthodox churches the State allowed to function in the USSR never was more than 15,000, and by the time the Russians joined the WCC late in 1961, the regime's whirlwind campaign of closing churches had reduced their number to such an extent that in 1962 a Soviet source was able to boast that only 11,500 remained. Two years later 7,500 churches were left. Nevertheless the WCC never questioned the Russian claim and continued to treat the delegation from the USSR as if it represented a church three times its true size.

In the early 1960s Soviet churchmen had another important task in their dealings with the West. This was to shield Western churchmen from any hint of what was really happening in the USSR. In the late 1950s Khrushchev began an antireligious campaign that, if Western churchmen had learned of it, might have caused a scandal. A furious attack against religion took place; in many ways this campaign of the 1960s equaled and even surpassed the bitter extremes of the 1930s. Between 1960 and the fall of Khrushchev in 1964, this antireligious campaign shut down half the remaining churches in the country; harsh new laws against religious activity were enforced; children were separated from believing parents by force; thousands of believers, hundreds of priests, and at least three bishops were imprisoned; and some Christians were killed. But not a hint of this tragic situation was raised in Ecumenical circles. The West did not even find out about this antireligious campaign until the late 1960s, and this was due in no small measure to the fact that Soviet churchmen were deliberately promoting and encouraging the completely false view that all was peaceful and well with the Russian churches.

The dissenting movement is a fine illustration of this. Among the Baptists in 1961 and among the Orthodox four years later, the antireligious campaign triggered protest movements.[20] The Baptist movement was immensely effective; a year after it began, it could claim it had twice as many congregations as the legalized Baptists. A mountain of protests and appeals for help were sent, first to the BWA and then to the WCC; similar documents from the Orthodox protest piled up after 1965. Neither the BWA nor the WCC took any action at all, lest they offend their Soviet members. The Soviet churchmen went everywhere, putting out the fires and spreading the impression that the dissidents were merely unbalanced, fanatic, chronic complainers. They saved the Soviet government no end of embarrassment and perhaps salvaged the entire program of influencing Western churchmen.

By 1966 Soviet churchmen were firmly entrenched in the Ecumenical Movement, and they had changed their earlier low profile. Now they began to try to turn the WCC into an ally of the USSR. This reflected a change that was taking place in Soviet foreign policy. Khrushchev's subtlety was giving way to the more structured, controlled, bureaucratic approach of Brezhnev's elderly Politburo. Hereafter everyone working in Soviet foreign policy and their allies would be made to toe the line, to go by the book supporting the full range of Soviet international endeavors.

The WCC was always very liberal and supported programs of the Left. But it had been careful to avoid extremes that would anger the vast majority of its members. In the late 1960s this changed: to the delight of its Russian members, the WCC turned radically leftward. In particular, at its Uppsala General Assembly in 1968 it endorsed violence in revolutions against unjust (i.e., colonial, or in some cases capitalist) institutions. This change allowed it to align itself completely with Soviet foreign policy.

The transformation was absolute. The WCC was so committed to this new course that overt leadership by its Soviet members was not needed at all. The WCC General Assembly at Nairobi in 1975 provides an example of how the new approach worked.[21] A Swiss delegate introduced a surprise amendment from the floor criticizing the Soviet Union for its lack of religious freedom. The amendment drew overwhelming support from the delegates but not from the WCC leaders. The criticism of the USSR was only killed by a last-minute, desperate maneuver based on a technicality by a U.S. delegate, Robert Moss of the United Church of Christ. In the parliamentary maneuvering needed to delete the criticism of the USSR, the Soviet delegates were able to rely on their U.S. colleagues and kept quiet, except for the Russian Orthodox Bishop Leonid Makary, who complained, "The Assembly has no right to judge us. I don't like somebody outside imposing problems which don't exist."

As matters turned out, the Soviet success in virtually capturing the WCC turned out to be a mistake. To be sure, the USSR gained a faithful and sure ally. However, the WCC's excesses—such as its Program to Combat Racism, in which the WCC gave grants to violent and even terrorist organizations, many of them receiving direct arms aid from the USSR—resulted in the decline of the movement's credibility. Very soon many of the churches and large numbers of their members withdrew their interest and support completely. The influence of the WCC decreased, and its efforts became less effective.

In addition to these bodies, the USSR relies to some degree on special, highly publicized conferences and extravaganzas to gain the support of Western churchmen. The peace conference organized by the Moscow Patriarchate in 1982, which led to the surprising statements by Billy Graham, provides an example of how effective such meetings can be.

By and large, however, in seeking to influence Western churchmen the USSR relies less on organizations than on individuals. It is the highly skilled corps of Soviet clergymen active in foreign policy who form the front line of this effort.

Agents of Deception

The Soviet State has been able to profit from the services of a talented body of its own churchmen in its foreign affairs. These religious leaders in the USSR, many of them specializing in international (as opposed to domestic) religious affairs, share a large number of common traits. They are obedient to the dictates of Soviet foreign policy and almost never contradict or question it in public. They show great loyalty and patriotism as citizens of the USSR and, usually, as church members. Many of them are well equipped with languages and cultural preparation for work in the West, and some of them have great theological knowledge. Of course, there are differences among them. Perhaps the most interesting is the nature of their loyalty to Soviet foreign policy.

An unknown but probably small number of these Soviet religious leaders may be considered "wholly owned assets" of the Soviet State and its intelligence arm, the KGB. By the nature of things, such people are hard to detect, for they are paraded as clergymen and, of course, are careful to hide the fact that their only loyalty is to the State rather than to the church. Nevertheless, some few examples have come to light among the Soviet churchmen. In the 1960s, for example, the U.S. Department of State denied a reentry visa to the permanent secretary of the Exarch of the Moscow Patriarchate in New York on grounds of activities incompatible with his position as a churchman.[22] In the middle 1970s secret Soviet documents smuggled to the West gave much evidence—indeed, clearly stated—that Metropolitan Aleksii of Tallin was the KGB's chief informer on the other bishops of the Russian Orthodox Church.[23]

The most scandalous example came to light in 1974.[24] The case concerned a member of the foreign section of the Moscow Patriarchate of the Russian Orthodox Church, the Reverend Boris Kudinkin. He was a priest and, according to the Orthodox tradition, married. Claiming that his wife was dull and lacked the intellect he needed for true sexual fulfillment, Kudinkin seduced a middle-aged secretary from the Netherlands Embassy in Moscow. Not surprisingly, photographs of their sexual intimacies were used to get her to cooperate with the KGB. Filled with guilt and anxiety, she eventually suffered a nervous breakdown and was transferred out of Moscow. When the KGB tried to pass her on to a new case officer at her new duty station, his demands for secrets from the Embassy were so crude and greedy that she confessed to her own people, despite his threats to make the blackmail pictures public.

Such cases as this, fortunately, are the rare exception. But there have been many who have risen so rapidly in the Church that KGB pressure was widely suspected. It is possible that the KGB has inserted its own people into the theological seminaries, for all who apply are interrogated by the KGB, and certainly nobody is admitted without KGB permission. Especially during the furious campaign against religion in the 1960s, when several priests defected to atheism, there were rumors that at least some of them had been KGB from the beginning. However, there is not much evidence; and in any case, if a priest can be compromised and forced to serve the KGB, the end result is the same. Either way, the KGB gets what it wants.

A much larger group consists of priests who, though they may be sincere, serve the State out of weakness and fear. The Soviet regime has very tight control over the appointment of priests and pastors. Those who are strong enough to resist the State's desires are seldom promoted; those who refuse to cooperate are either removed from their posts or find themselves transferred to smaller and smaller remote villages. Certainly those who rise high enough to become active in foreign affairs do not do so without the permission of the regime. The KGB especially seeks those whose weakness and fear are combined with past mistakes that make them subject to blackmail.

Thus the system itself insures that a great many of the churchmen who meet with religious leaders in the West have few of the qualities of leadership themselves, but instead have been promoted because of their own weakness and fear. From all the evidence, it would seem that the present head of the Russian Orthodox Church, Patriarch Pimen, falls into this category.[25]

There is another group of Soviet church leaders, and no one knows how large it is: firm believers who consciously decide to serve the Soviet State in international affairs. Since World War II the Soviet regime has made it perfectly clear that unless churches are willing to collaborate, especially in foreign affairs, the local churches will come under the full fury of the hostile State. The antireligious campaign of the 1960s showed just what the State could do to religious believers. In order to keep the local churches open and to give the believers at least some chance to wor-ship—indeed, to keep some of them out of the Gulag—some Soviet priests and pastors make the bitter inward decision to bargain with the State for the life of their church. If this means deceiving some foreigners, that is a small price to pay to protect the thousands and millions of members of their own church. For some of these Soviet churchmen, at least, when the life of thousands of churches all across the vast country is at stake, even sinning against the truth by telling outright lies, when it cannot be avoided, may be considered worth it.

This was probably the case with Metropolitan Nikolai.[26] His speeches to the World Peace Council certainly showed that he was willing to go along with whatever Soviet propaganda required, no matter how false and even silly it might be. Even worse, in at least one known case he worked for the secret police against one of his own bishops to keep him from defecting to the West. And yet at the end of his life, when the time came to make a final choice, he chose the Church rather than the State.

In 1960, as the State was starting its furious attack against the churches, he wrote a defiant speech for a Soviet conference on disarmament. The speech insisted on the vital role that the Church has played all through Russian history and denounced the anti-religious campaign's attacks. It closed with a challenge: "Jesus

Christ Himself predicted indestructibility of the Church when he said: 'The gates of hell will not overcome the *Church.*'"

The State was swift to respond. He was removed from office at once and forced into retirement. The next year, within days after the Russian Orthodox Church had been accepted into the World Council of Churches, Nikolai died. Immediately there were rumors of murder, and to this day he is considered a saint by Orthodox people.

His successor, Metropolitan Nikodim, may have been of the same caliber, a churchman who decided to serve the State in order to safeguard the Church. A very talented man, Nikodim was young, well trained, a good theologian, and highly respected throughout the West and within the USSR as well. He was very, very shrewd: He was the one who came up with the subtle, plausible, but completely untrue argument that it was not the State that was closing churches but the Church itself, so that it could have a few large, strong churches rather than many small, weak ones. Although he served the State faithfully, in small, subtle ways he managed to get surprising benefits for the Church in return. After his premature death his memory, too, is revered among Orthodox people.[27]

Finally, it is possible that another group of these Soviet clergy sincerely believe what they say about Soviet foreign policy with a clear conscience. But in view of some of the horrors of Soviet activities abroad, where blackmail and terrorism abound, and especially in view of the atrocities of Afghanistan on top of the USSR's invasion of its own allies in Czechoslovakia and Hungary, this seems unlikely. And in view of the absolute demand that every Soviet cleric tell outright falsehoods and lies, some of them preposterous, in order to deceive Westerners about the true facts of the lives religious people are forced to lead within the USSR, it is hard to believe that complete sincerity is really possible.

The Results

It is important to note that the motivations of these Soviet churchmen make no difference in getting results for the State. Whether a Soviet church leader is acting out of a bitter compromise for the good of his church, or out of weakness, or because he is no churchman at all but a KGB officer makes no difference: he will have to do the same things anyhow.

Nor does it matter much what kind of meetings he has with Western churchmen. Whether he is in one of the organizations designed to deceive the West, or at special meetings, or even hosting Western visitors in the USSR, his first task, as far as the Soviet State is concerned, is to mislead the Western churchmen. He must at all costs keep from them any knowledge of the true situation of religion in the USSR, giving them whatever misinformation or even outright lies may be needed to keep them happy. At the same time he must lead them to support Soviet foreign policy. Whatever personal, religious, or theological benefits he may seek at the meeting, his task for the Soviet State, which he *must* fulfill, is to deceive the Westerners.

And his job is made so much easier by Western church leaders who want to be misled. Many of them seem ready to believe anything at all that praises the USSR, and they are deaf and blind to any criticism of the regime, its ideology, or its practices. When Western church leaders seek the real facts and examine the policy proposals in the light of their own faith and the results that such actions would bring, they are almost immune to deception. But when some Western churchmen are willing to be deceived and even want to be, they are the ideal victims for Soviet deception on religion.

By themselves, these deceived churchmen are not very important. However, when they can spread the deception and entice others to follow their leadership, they are a real problem.

The primary target of these churchmen in spreading their strange affection for the USSR and its policies is their own denominations and churches. This is their immediate audience, and most important, it is here that funds are supplied to support their activities. In some cases, such as the World Council of Churches, some of the people have already reacted against the excesses of their leaders by withdrawing their support. In recent years the WCC has had to absorb budget cuts because some Christians simply will not let their contributions be used for the radical causes the WCC supports. But at every level churchmembers should look carefully at how their leaders are using their donations. Where the leadership persists in wrongdoing, they should withdraw their support, or even their membership, entirely or, perhaps better, depose the leaders.

Among the public at large there is a less direct but still important concern; for this deception is designed by the Soviets ultimately against the lives and liberties of all people. Because of this common, shared concern, church leaders should be treated like anyone else when they speak outside their own area of religious subjects. When they support the USSR's politics, they should be held to the same standards of truth, knowledge, and facts that are expected of other leaders. Religious leadership does not imply any special expertise in world affairs. (Indeed, if a person has struggled to the top leadership in a religious bureaucracy there may be real questions as to whether he has any qualifications at all to speak out on matters outside his own church organization.)

Certainly such religious leaders should not be excused from telling the truth, and fairness should be a special obligation of those who claim the mantle of religion. When such people persist in spreading blatant deception and unbalanced and untrue claims designed to support Soviet policies, all credibility should be withdrawn from them, and the media and the public at large should look elsewhere for guidance. The key test, after all, is the test of truth.

And truth is ultimately the West's surest defense and its greatest hope. Time and again, Soviet deception has been shattered by the test of truth. The World Peace Council, the Christian Peace Conference, and even the more recent deceptions channeled through the World Council of Churches and other religious conferences—all will finally lose their credibility because the propaganda they proclaim is blatantly untrue. And today, as always, truth will win out over falsehood. A devotion to honesty and truth is the strongest, indeed the only, sure protection against Soviet deception in religious affairs.

Notes

1. Hewlett Johnson, *Christians and Communism*. (London: Putnam, 1956), pp. 58–59, 65, 116.

2. John C. Bennett, "Christian Responsibility in a Time that Calls for Revolutionary Change." In John C. Raines and Thomas Dean, eds., *Marxism and Radical Religion: Essays Toward a Revolutionary Humanism*. (Philadelphia: Temple University Press, 1970), p. 61.

3. *Commonweal*, August 19, 1977, p. 514.

4. *Christian Century*, September 29, 1976, pp. 813–15.

5. *Religious News Service*, June 27, 1977.

6. John Garvey, "The Ambiguous Pastoral." *Commonweal* (May 6, 1983), pp. 264–65.

7. William C. Fletcher, *Religion and Soviet Foreign Policy, 1945–1970.* (London: Royal Institute of International Affairs, Oxford University Press, 1973), pp. 125–26.

8. Ibid., p. 127.

9. *Moscow News* 4, February, 4–11, 1978.

10. Fletcher, op. cit., pp. 30–35.

11. *Zhurnal Moskovskoi Patriarkhii* 9 (September 1949). Reprinted in Nikolai, Metropolitan, *We Will Defend Peace!* (Moscow: The Patriarchate, 1955), pp. 16–24.

12. *Zhurnal Moskovskoi Patriarkhii* 3 (March 1951). Reprinted in Nikolai, op. cit., pp. 69–75.

13. Richard H. Shultz and Roy Godson, *Dezinformatsia: Active Measures in Soviet Strategy.* (Washington, D.C.: Pergamon-Brassey's, 1984), pp. 114–32.

14. "WPC Tours U.S.A." Booklet. (Helsinki: Information Center of the WPC, 1975).

15. *Daily World*, February 23, 1978.

16. Fletcher, op. cit., pp. 39–56.

17. Ibid., pp. 117–39.

18. *Christian Peace Conference*, March 1963, p. 59.

19. Rael Jean Isaac and Erich Isaac, *The Coercive Utopians.* (Chicago: Regency Gateway, 1983), p. 29.

20. Michael Bourdeaux, *Religious Ferment in Russia.* (London: Macmillan, 1968), and *Patriarch and Prophets.* (London: Macmillan, 1970).

21. *Religious News Service*, December 10, 1975; *Christian Century*, December 24, 1975, p. 1171; *Congressional Record*, December 9, 1975, p. E6550.

22. Fletcher, op. cit., p. 104.

23. Dimitry Pospielovsky, *The Russian Church under the Soviet Regime, 1917–1982.* (Crestwood, New York: St. Vladimir's Seminary Press, 1984), II, p. 392.

24. John Barron, *KGB* (New York: Reader's Digest, 1974), pp. 117–18.

25. Pospielovsky, op. cit., II, pp. 391–93.

26. William C. Fletcher, *Nikolai: Portrait of a Dilemma.* (New York: MacMillan, 1968.)

27. Pospielovsky, op. cit., II, pp. 360–458, et passim.

SOVIET
ECONOMIC
DECEPTION

Dr. Steven Rosefielde

Introduction

A quarter of a century ago the United States was the preeminent military power. Its forces were numerous and technologically advanced. Annual U.S. weapons expenditures were twice those of the Soviet Union, and the notion that the Soviets could catch up militarily with and surpass the United States seemed absurd. The gross national product of the Soviet Union was half that of the United States, and it was widely believed that the rigidities of the Soviet economic system placed it at a serious competitive disadvantage.

The Soviets, however, were undaunted. In the late 1950s they launched a massive arms buildup, continuing the pattern of the 1930s. It allowed them to draw even with the United States in the late 1970s and overtake it thereafter. Annual Soviet weapons outlays today exceed those of the United States by nearly 150 percent.

How has this come to pass? Part of the answer obviously lies in the morass of the Vietnam War and its aftermath; part in the competition for funds generated by Great Society programs; and part in the Soviet's single-minded pursuit of their national security goals. These explanations, however, are incomplete. They do not take account of the Soviet economic deceptions that have facilitated the deterioration of the U.S. military posture.

This essay explores this theme. It attempts to demonstrate that deceptive Soviet economic practices have greatly impaired U.S. deterrent capabilities.

In the postwar period Soviet economic deception has taken three predominant forms. The Soviets have deceived U.S. arms control negotiators into accepting treaty compliance costs that one-sidedly constrain U.S. ballistic missile modernization. They have encouraged Western observers to erroneously believe that the shortcomings of their economic system prevents them from posing a serious military threat. And they have deliberately falsified their official defense budgetary statistics to persuade the unwary that their military spending has not increased since 1970. These deceptive actions, individually and collectively, have significantly degraded U.S. military capabilities and turned the balance of power decisively in the Soviets' favor.

Compliance Costs and Degraded Force Capabilities

The first important form of postwar Soviet economic deception involves U.S. strategic ballistic missile modernization. The present U.S. land-based ICBM deterrent force is almost entirely comprised of aging Minuteman II and III missiles, many of which are two decades old. U.S. political authorities have been attempting to replace these weapons since the late 1960s without success, in considerable part because cost-effective, survivable basing modes have not been found. The Soviets, however, have not been similarly constrained. They have introduced two new generations of ICBMs since the late 1960s and are currently deploying a third, the SS-25. What explains this asymmetry?

The answer can be found in the way the Soviets fashioned the formal provisions of the SALT agreements and informally managed U.S. perceptions so that U.S. land-based ballistic missile modernization could only be attained by paying an exorbitant compliance penalty that the Soviets did not have to bear. This was accomplished by formally limiting launcher silos, and/or silo clusters, and by prohibiting mobile missiles, while informally persuading U.S. officials that the spirit of the accords prevented them from building undeployed ballistic missile reserves. As Soviet targeting capabilities improved, these restrictions left the United States with only one viable land-based modernization option consistent with the verification requirements of SALT: the MX system, deployed in multiple protective shelters (MX/MPS). The cost of these multiple protective shelters, however, was extraordinarily expensive, exceeding those of other land-based deployment modes by several billion dollars. In the cost-conscious political environment of the 1980s, these excessive compliance costs made the total cost of the program prohibitive, forcing the Administration to abandon the deployment of MX in the MPS basing mode. As a consequence, although the Soviets could not have gotten President Carter to explicitly forgo land-based ballistic missile modernization at the Vienna summit, they successfully used economic pressure to achieve this objective.

The economic pressure exerted on the MX program was unconcealed, and it could be argued, therefore, that it was not deceptive. This argument, however, ignores the fact that the U.S. side, in accepting the obligation to pay the SALT compliance cost, was encouraged to believe that the Soviets would be similarly constrained—an obligation it appears the Soviets felt no need to fulfill. Instead of building an MPS system of their own, paying the required compliance penalty, or forgoing ICBM modernization altogether, they chose to circumvent the spirit of SALT II by building concealed ballistic missile reserves. Defense Intelligence Agency (DIA) statistics indicate that the Soviets built an implied ICBM reserve of 815 missiles, capable of delivering 6,250 nuclear warheads during the brief period 1980-84.[1] The one-sided imposition of SALT compliance costs thus not only caused the United States to abandon the MX/MPS program, valued at 27 billion dollars in 1978 prices, without developing an operational substitute, but it has also allowed the Soviets to achieve an otherwise unobtainable strategic nuclear advantage with their concealed missiles.

Perceptions Management and Coercion

This success has been complemented by other initiatives aimed at making Western public opinion less resistant to Soviet geopolitical aspirations. These deceptive economic activities are subordinate elements of a larger deception process fostering what the Soviets call a favorable change in the "correlation of forces in the world arena." As noted earlier, they take two forms. The first seeks to assure the West that the Soviets do not pose a security threat because their domestic economic needs take precedence over other competing motivations. The second attempts to persuade the Allies that they should not squander their resources on defense because the Soviets terminated their arms buildup in 1970.

The purpose of both initiatives appears to be broadly the same: to increase Soviet military power by weakening Western defenses and reducing Allied resolve. More concretely, by managing Western perceptions the Soviets hope to reduce NATO's defense spending;

to obtain a pledge of "no-first-use" of Allied tactical nuclear weapons in response to a conventional Soviet attack; to undermine extended deterrence by having the Europeans renounce the U.S. strategic nuclear umbrella; and to evict U.S. troops from the continent. Once these objectives are achieved they can use either the threat or the reality of their superior conventional forces to obtain their hegemonic ends without fear of nuclear escalation.

The Soviets have been relatively successful in dispelling Western apprehensions about these ambitions by encouraging the widely held misconception that their economy cannot withstand a protracted arms competition. This misconception is predicated on the erroneous assumption that "command economies" based on State ownership of the means of production are unworkable. Western analysts routinely assert that the Soviet economy is a basket case; that market economies necessarily outperform command systems; and that if the Soviets should attempt to compete in the military sphere, this can only be achieved by impoverishing the civilian sector. Although the Soviets might pursue a course of this kind in the short run, it is argued that political realities will compel them to forgo guns for butter.

This seemingly plausible hypothesis, however, is not borne out by the facts. Soviet per capita consumption and weapons production have both grown uninterruptedly for more than a quarter of a century. According to CIA estimates, armaments and the standard of living rose rapidly at 3 and 2.2 percent per annum 1955–83, well above comparable U.S. rates.[2] Alternative estimates computed by the DIA and the author indicate a far higher rate of Soviet weapons growth, but the lesson taught by these statistics is the same. The Soviet leadership has not had to choose between guns and butter, and the population has not been impoverished by the arms buildup, however vigorously it may have been pursued.

This finding, which is compatible with modern theories of the Soviet system's economic potential, demonstrates that the Soviets were not driven to the Geneva summit because they recognized that their faltering economy would always prevent them from achieving their worldwide goals. The evidence suggests that, insofar as the past is a guide to the future, the Soviets can and will ceaselessly continue their arms buildup, tilting the balance of power increasingly in their favor without provoking domestic unrest, as long as the West is deceived into misperceiving the real dimensions of the threat.

It can be counterargued that the foregoing analysis glosses over the pronounced slowdown in economic growth that began in the mid-1970s. Aggregate Soviet economic growth 1975–83 was below the postwar norm. This decline, however, merely qualifies but does not reverse the conclusion that the Soviets will widen their military advantage in the years ahead. Both per capita consumption and weapons may increase more slowly than before, but recent rates of advance will be more than adequate for their purposes, especially if, as now seems certain, the surge in U.S. weapons production will be sharply curtailed.

It can also be counterargued that it is wrong to project long-term trends into the future because the Soviet economy has recently undergone profound changes. Consumer expectations have risen, while the quality of Soviet consumer goods has deteriorated compared with standards prevailing in the West. The rate of improvement of Soviet technology, especially in the consumer goods sector, has similarly declined, and weapons production, judged from the CIA's estimates, has been stagnant since 1976. Does it not follow therefore that the costs of guns in terms of forgone butter are high and that considerations of domestic political stability require the Soviets to satisfy consumer expectations by diverting resources from defense to consumption; by increasing access to Western consumer technology; by expanding East-West commerce; and otherwise accommodating the logic of peace?

Arguments of these sorts have enormous intuitive appeal, but they are mistaken. The Soviet Union is not a parliamentary democracy. The Communist Party of the Soviet Union is not responsible to the electorate and can easily disregard what it deems excessive consumer demands. It may of course honor elite preferences, but these can be satisfied at a comparatively low social cost evaluated in terms of forgone weapons outlays. Similarly, the Soviets long have had unfettered access to Western consumer technologies and can avail themselves of the opportunities they afford without curtailing their arms buildup. And finally, data obtained by the DIA establish that productivity in the Soviet military machine–building sector far exceeds that prevailing in the consumer goods sector. This means that any diversion of resources from weapons to consumer products would sharply reduce both the level of the Soviet gross national product and its growth potential. The evidence strongly suggests that the economy the Soviets fashioned to support their arms buildup in the postwar period cannot be painlessly converted to civilian purposes. Insofar as structural economic factors influence policy, they incline the Soviets toward coercion of Western nations, not toward enduring peaceful coexistence with them.

Deceptive Manipulation of the Soviet Defense Budget

The cogency of the preceding analysis, with regard both to the structural characteristics of the Soviet economy and to the leadership's international ambitions, depends significantly on the actual level and growth of Soviet weapons procurement. The Soviets recognize this, and it is possible to demonstrate that they have deliberately manipulated their published defense statistics to deceive Western observers on both scores. The evidence elaborated below is especially important because it clearly reveals that Soviet assertions of peaceful intent cannot be taken at face value.

The data in question are the annual official Soviet defense budgetary figures illustrated in Figure 3. These statistics indicate

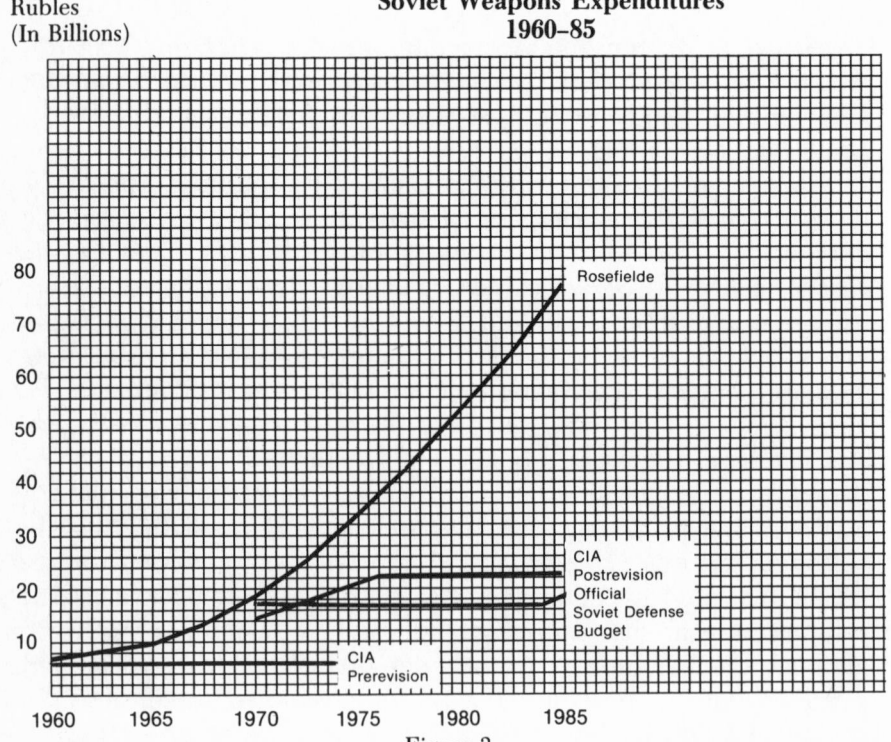

Rubles
(In Billions)

Soviet Weapons Expenditures
1960–85

Figure 3

that Soviet defense spending rose 6.8 percent per annum during the 1960s and then declined at 0.3 percent per annum until 1985, when it surged nearly 12 percent.[3] The pattern is implausible given the steady increase in the physical size of Soviet military programs, but the CIA accepted it as proof that its own direct cost estimates were accurate until 1975, when information obtained from the books of the Soviet Ministry of Defense established conclusively that Soviet defense outlays in 1970 were nearly triple the published budgetary value. Subsequent internal analysis by British scholar Raymond Hutchings confirmed the agency's revised assessment and led him to assert that "the official totals have entirely ceased to be believable, not only because of external evidence but because of their internal trends and the manner of their presentation."[4]

It follows directly that the Soviets have deliberately falsified their defense statistics in order to conceal the size, scope, and momentum of their arms buildup and to deceive world opinion about their real priorities.

Budgetary Deception and American National Security

The impact of the Soviet budgetary deception on the military balance can be best evaluated by dividing the problem into two parts, the first covering the period 1960–74, before the CIA obtained the "new information," and the second spanning the years thereafter. The ruble statistics displayed in Figure 3 demonstrate that until the "new information" was acquired, the CIA believed that the Soviets had not materially increased their weapons expenditures measured at constant 1970 ruble prices since 1960. Although this trend was sharply at variance with the physical evidence, the Agency took the position that the Soviets were satisfied with their subordinate superpower status and were not striving to overtake the United States.

The effect of the agency's statistics, supported by the official Soviet Defense Budgetary series on U.S. national security policy, defies precise measurement. It cannot be doubted, however, that they had a powerful impact on Western attitudes toward detente and defense spending. They created an environment in which disadvantageous treaty concessions of the sort previously described were facilitated and in which Western defense spending was excessively restrained.

The magnitude of the advantage the Soviets achieved in this way is partly suggested by comparing U.S. weapons expenditures from 1960 to 1974 with the author's estimates of Soviet outlays. These data, which are consistent with observed trends in the quantity and quality of Soviet weapons, indicate that starting from a position of substantial inferiority in 1960, annual Soviet expenditures overtook those of the United States in 1971, opening up a gap that portended a dramatic reversal in the military balance by decade's end. Had this trend been accurately reflected in the official Soviet defense budgetary statistics, or had the CIA's estimates been on target, it is reasonable to suppose that the United States' response to the Soviet arms buildup would have been swift and effective.

The influence of the Soviet defense budgetary deception on Western national security after 1974 is more difficult to describe. The CIA firmly repudiated the official Soviet defense budgetary series in 1976. Overnight it acknowledged that Soviet weapons outlays in 1970 measured in rubles were more than triple its prerevision estimate, but it also inconsistently asserted that its perception of the level and trend of Soviet military activities valued in dollars was unaffected by the "new information." As a consequence, while apprehensions were raised by the Agency's revised estimates of the Soviet defense burden (the military share of GNP expressed in rubles) and the increasing disparity between annual U.S. and Soviet dollar weapons expenditures caused by the continuing U.S. post-Vietnam War military builddown, the attitudes spawned by the budgetary deception persisted nearly to the end of the Carter years, as evidenced by the low levels of U.S. weapons expenditures and the SALT II accords.

Under the Reagan Administration, the United States has vigorously attempted to recover lost ground. U.S. weapons outlays during the 1980s have risen 12.0 percent per annum, double the Soviet rate.[5] But this positive development is likely to be reversed long before the gap in annual outlays is closed because the CIA's estimates continue to mimic the false trend displayed by the official Soviet defense budget. According to the latter, Soviet defense spending from 1975 to 1985 grew 0.9 percent per annum, while the CIA estimates that Soviet weapons outlays (Figure 3) over the same time frame increased 0.4 percent per annum. As a consequence, CIA dollar statistics erroneously indicate that annual U.S. weapons expenditures regained parity with the Soviets in 1984 and surpassed them in 1985, stimulating congressional calls for a complete reappraisal of Soviet international policy and U.S. national security outlays.[6] The pernicious influence of the Soviet budgetary deceptions thus persists a decade after it was exposed, warping informed perceptions of Soviet capabilities and aspirations.

Policy Implications

The preceding survey has demonstrated that the Soviets have effectively employed economic deception to degrade Western defense capabilities and obscure appraisals of their hidden motivations. It has been shown that while the United States is preparing to embark on the next round of detente in the wake of the Geneva summit, the Soviets will almost certainly persevere, rapidly increasing their relative military superiority at the West's expense. It is not difficult to perceive that one of their most important objectives is assured military dominance at all levels of conflict. This will allow them to press their expansionist goals in Europe and elsewhere. The appropriate response to this strategy is assured deterrence, maintaining sufficient conventional and nuclear forces to prevent the Soviets from imposing their will on the West. This goal can be pursued within or outside the framework of renewed detente, but the record suggests that if the latter course is chosen, it will require shrewder management than has been the standard hitherto.

Conclusion

The Soviets have adroitly utilized deceptive economic stratagems in the postwar period to enhance their relative military power. The measurable dollar value of these ploys may conservatively be fixed at several tens of billions of dollars, but these sums do not fully reflect their benefit.[7] Economic deception has significantly degraded U.S. strategic nuclear ballistic missile modernization, restrained Western defense spending, and dampened recognition that the military forces the Soviets have assembled are designed to provide the Soviets with assured military dominance. The Soviets may not ultimately realize their objective of overall military dominance, but if they do, a large share of the credit will be due to their skillful use of economic deception.

Notes

1. See Table 2 in the expanded version of this article, available from the author on request.
2. See Table 3 in the expanded version of this article.
3. See Table 4 in the expanded version of this article.
4. Raymond Hutchings, *The Soviet Defense Budget.* (Albany, N.Y.: State University of New York Press, 1983), p. 139.
5. See Table 6 in the expanded version of this article.
6. Senator William Proxmire, JEC Press Release, February 21, 1985: "It is time for Washington to take official notice that Soviet military procurement has been stagnant for the past seven years and to stop acting like nothing has changed."
7. See Table 1 in the expanded version of this article.

SOVIET
DECEPTION
AND DETENTE

Vladimir Bukovsky

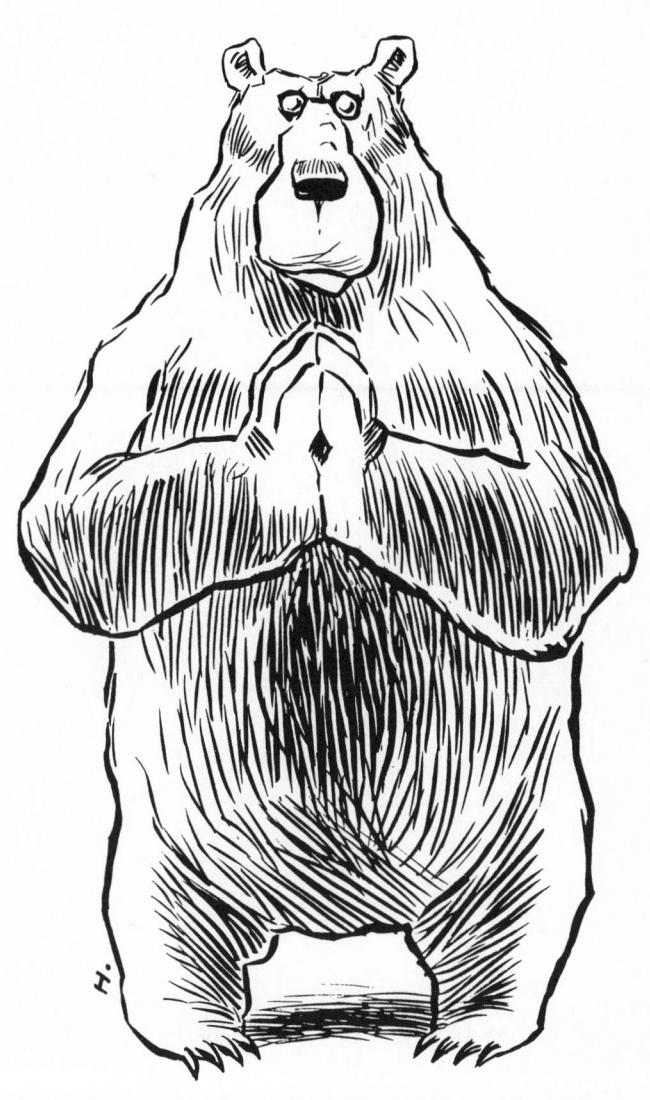

No matter how much evidence of Soviet deception has been amassed in the last forty years—violation of international treaties, manipulation of public opinion, subversion and terrorism, covert coups, and overt aggression—a large part of the Western public still finds it hard to believe. If nothing else, the sheer scope of Soviet activity and the utterly inhuman methods they employ make a "balanced" Western observer suspicious.

Even the most undeniable facts—like shooting down the Korean airliner a few years ago, or the invasion of Afghanistan—failed to change public opinion. Instead, the very absurdity of Soviet behavior in both cases has prompted many people to look for a more "rational" explanation or even for a justification of Soviet motives. And more often than not, these explanations tend to blame the Western governments rather than the Soviets.

This attitude is remarkably similar to the pattern of behavior displayed by a patient with terminal cancer: Whenever a person is confronted with something mind-boggling, something utterly horrible and beyond his control, he goes through a succession of mental states ranging from denial to guilt, and from fantastic rationalizations to acute depression.

Indeed, what can be more traumatic than facing a mortal enemy who stops at nothing and who can destroy the earth five times over? An enemy who subjugates country after country, slowly but steadily, for half a century, who penetrates every sphere of our life and ruthlessly exploits our every weakness—all for no apparent reason. Historically, the West has tried practically every possible remedy, from containment to detente, and nothing has worked. As Alexander Solzhenitsyn suggests, communism is like a cancer, and therefore, not surprisingly, our reaction to it is similar to that of a cancer patient.

So the most important reason for Soviet success is the reluctance of the Western public to face the danger, to recognize the source of the threat. Soviet behavior ceases to appear so frighteningly irrational as soon as we realize that they regard themselves as being at war with the rest of the world. Basically, people accept different moral standards during wartime, and many acts of violence and deception appear justified then by necessity. Thus, the sinking of the *Lusitania* by German U-boats in 1915 was probably a worse crime than shooting down a passenger airliner in 1983; the former incident killed at least four times as many innocent people. Yet we are inclined to see the sinking as more understandable, while the airline incident is viewed as a totally irrational act.

Similarly, when we read about Lawrence of Arabia, we are not particularly outraged by his skillful manipulation of feuding Arab tribes. Yet we refuse to believe that the Soviets routinely employ the same methods of warfare by supporting and manipulating all kinds of extremist groups around the world. The facts are undeniable, but it seems just too mean to be true.

And speaking of propaganda, have deception or disinformation not always been legitimate means of war, from the Trojan horse to the fake D-Day assaults? Every country's army has a special detachment for psychological warfare, dormant in peacetime and activated at the beginning of hostilities. The only difference in the case of the Soviet Union is that the entire country has become such a detachment, while the war itself has not been formally declared.

However, strictly speaking, we cannot blame the Soviets for waging an undeclared war against humanity. This war was actually proclaimed at the turn of the century by the founders of Marxist-Leninist ideology under the banner of "class struggle," and it has continued unabated ever since. Every five years at each Party Congress, the Soviet ruling clique solemnly reaffirms the declaration of war by pledging its full support to "liberation movements" and to the "forces of progress and socialism." The West simply does not want to pay attention.

The Western public has very little chance to survive unless it realizes that, willingly or not, it is at war with the Communist world. As Jean Francois Revel explains in his book *How Democracies Perish*, a democratic society has inherent weaknesses that make it an easy prey for a totalitarian enemy. But the more we come to grips with the reality of being at war, the less these weaknesses become.

After all, democracies did defeat a totalitarian enemy in World War II.

The second reason the West is so receptive to Soviet influence is closely related to the first. It is ignorance. Indeed, we know more about a remote galaxy or about a minuscule part of a living cell than about a political system existing just a few thousand miles away. Just one illustrative example: The death of each Soviet leader is automatically perceived in the West as a signal for change of the regime. The media, the public, and even so-called experts become terribly excited. They discuss in great detail the new leader's personality, his wife, his habits, his tastes, proclaiming him a "closet liberal" and a "peacemaker."

Apart from the usual wishful thinking, this example demonstrates remarkable ignorance. Even after sixty-nine years of Soviet existence the Western public as well as the decision makers still have not learned that the Soviet system is not an autocracy but a totalitarian regime in which the death of a leader changes nothing at all. And that is exactly why the Soviet system is so dangerous. Autocracies disappear with the death of autocrats; a Communist system continues. It is a machine that makes human characteristics irrelevant. Everyone in the Soviet Union is a "closet liberal," but they cannot come into the open.

And these Western decision makers, completely ignorant of the most basic principles of the Soviet system, are supposed to make vital decisions about defense and strategic negotiations, East-West relations, and the military budget!

Most depressing, however, is the level of knowledge among so-called experts, Sovietologists, Kremlinologists, and so on. A few notable exceptions aside, they are the least qualified to tackle the problems of East-West relations. On average, they are worse than the man in the street. At least common folks have common sense at their disposal. The expert is supposed to be sophisticated, that is, to have his own pet theory or prejudice. He is expected to be balanced—never mind the truth—and becomes prominent by saying what the media want him to say. It is hard to believe, but most of them don't even know the Russian language. Can you imagine a nuclear physicist who does not know mathematics and, therefore, cannot understand the simplest equation?

Who are these people? What are their credentials? Usually, somebody who worked a few years in the U.S. Embassy in Mongolia, or took a guided tour in the Soviet Union and then wrote a popular trash book, or, better still, someone who used to be a government official with "experience in dealing with Russians." More often than not, they proved to be a total disaster while in office. Nevertheless, the media will invite them on every occasion to hold forth with an appearance of a pundit. They never learned to distinguish Soviet people from the Soviet system, and they still honestly believe that Ivan the Terrible was the founder of the Soviet Union. Yet it is they who will be giving their "valuable advice" to the public, to the governments, and to students at the universities.

These modern astrologists have completely twisted public perception of the Soviet problem. Thanks to their efforts the Western public believes that there can be no precise knowledge of the Soviet Union, of its intentions and behavior, only guesses, which makes the public even more susceptible to Soviet disinformation.

They render any public debate on the subject of East-West relations quite meaningless. Once the truth is not an objective to be reached, your guess is as good as theirs. Disinformation is as good as information.

Another reason for the Soviet success is the ideological affinity of a certain part of Western society. By that I don't mean the extreme left or Communists but rather a certain tendency of those on the left of center to perceive danger only from the right. The very image of oppression imprinted in their minds is an image of a cruel man in the military uniform. It is a notion of personal power that terrifies them, while impersonal horror of the Soviet system does not penetrate their mental block.

Besides, to them the Soviet Union is a "revolution that went astray." That is to say, it is something that was made with good intentions but went wrong through somebody's mistake. Therefore, they feel obliged to justify the intentions if not the results.

People with such views actually constitute a large and very influential part of Western society. They are an excellent conductor for Soviet disinformation.

Their influence is indeed enormous, even if exercised indirectly through trends and standards they set for the society. Or should we say double standards, for they introduced a certain moral and intellectual dishonesty into our public debates, social attitudes, and reactions. Can anybody explain why it is all right to be a Communist and absolutely socially unacceptable to be a fascist? Nobody can. But if you try to treat a Communist with the same disgust as his less fortunate brownshirted colleague, Western society will brand you as "intolerant," "unpluralistic," and "undemocratic."

By the same token, it is quite all right to "remove" dictators like Ferdinand Marcos or Jean-Claude Duvalier (even though it requires interference into the internal affairs of a sovereign country), but it is absolutely unacceptable to support contras because they want to "overthrow the legally elected" government of Nicaragua. For some obscure reason, in these cases we must "negotiate" a "solution." In short, when we deal with a dictator, it is he who has a problem; when we deal with a Communist system, it is we who have a problem. The regime of apartheid is repugnant to our conscience; therefore all of us—left, right, and center—must be united against it. There are no talks, no summit meetings, no bridge-building or "citizen diplomats." Just embargo, disinvestment, boycott. However, in dealing with the Soviets, talking seems to be the best remedy: Embargos, we are told, are never effective because somebody else might take our place as trading partner. Boycotts will only increase "international tension." Again and again we are advised to be tolerant and pluralistic, ever ready to "understand" the other side. With such an understanding enemy, it is a wonder the Soviets bother to spend so much on their "active measures."

The Soviets, however, have a few problems of their own. Created according to a nineteenth-century doctrine—a doctrine that was obsolete even before it was implemented—the Soviet system is bound to export its ideology even if nobody believes in it any longer. It has to "liberate" mankind without alerting it and, above all, to make the world cover the expenses of its own "liberation."

What used to be a belief, a revolutionary passion of the founders, in due time became a structure, a social order, and a paid job for millions of people. Sixty-nine years after its creation, the Soviet system cannot survive without the ever-present threat of war, which gradually replaced the lure of the Communist ideology both at home and abroad.

At home, a threat of war is the only excuse for a totalitarian regime, lack of rights, misery, and privileges of the ruling elite. Abroad, it is the only means to keep the empire together, to spread further Soviet influence, and to blackmail the West into providing credits, goods, and technology. Therefore, peace has become the main subject of Soviet disinformation, while the "struggle for peace" has become a substitute for the "class struggle."

How does this work in practical terms? First, the Soviet Union generates constant conflict, either by shifting the balance of forces with the West or by its adventures in the Third World. Then the Western response is used to generate military hysteria at home and to profit from "peace hysteria" abroad. These two hysterias feed each other. When Soviet people see on their television screens millions of Westerners marching against "American missiles," clashing with the police, chanting slogans against their "war-mongering" governments, they begin to believe official propaganda: Nuclear war must be just around the corner indeed, if so many people brave the police and risk their freedom in antigovernment demonstrations.

On the other hand, when thousands of peace activists, "bridge-builders," and "citizen diplomats" visit the Soviet Union, they are confronted by genuinely concerned and scared people who ask them, "Why do Americans want to burn us in the nuclear holocaust?" These visitors see only people craving peace, traumatized by the losses of World War II, and Soviet officials with their inevitable toasts for *"mir i druzhba."* Dragged from one war memorial to another, these peace activists never understand the difference between the people and the system, and they will go home firmly convinced that "Russians" do not want war.

Of course, in the process of their trips these visitors are interviewed by Soviet media at every location. Surely, as respectful guests, they do not mention SS-20s or Afghanistan. They condemn Reagan's "militarism" and Star Wars program, thus strengthening even further the military hysteria of the Soviet population.

The opposite happens when Soviet people are allowed to visit the West. With their families being left at home as hostages, these carefully selected envoys simply repeat slogans of Soviet propaganda. Of course, Western people, as polite hosts this time, do not ask them about Afghanistan, either. Once again, we hear only about bad Reagan and the purely peaceful intentions of the Soviet Union.

One might ask: What do the Soviets stand to gain by driving millions of Westerners into peace hysteria? After all, missiles were placed in Europe, peace hysteria notwithstanding, and peace movements have never reached a sizable proportion of Western society. Shouldn't we consider their "struggle for peace," like their participation in the public debate, quite legitimate in a democratic society?

Even if we leave aside the unilateral nature of this "debate," which is never allowed to spread into Soviet territory, and even if we ignore the Soviet methods of conducting it, the advantages we are left with are still too enormous to be taken lightly. No real debate can give such an advantage and influence to one side over the other as to practically paralyze the will of the opponent.

To begin with, peace hysteria makes any decision to strengthen defenses (particularly nuclear forces) so unpopular that the Western governments become more and more reluctant to consider such measures while the Soviets are totally free to build their arsenal with impunity. Sooner or later, this will lead to Soviet strategic dominance, which will only increase Soviet pressure, making their blackmail more credible and scaring even more people into peace hysteria.

It constantly threatens to split the Western alliance.

It shifts the focus of public attention from the aggressive nature of the Soviet system as a threat to peace in our world, to the number of warheads, missiles, planes, and other quite innocent hardware. As a result Western governments are forced to engage in a senseless and self-defeating process of arms control negotiations, while the public perceives both sides as equally responsible for the ever-present danger of holocaust.

It gives priority to the question of security over the question of human rights in the Soviet Union, an issue too dangerous for the Soviet regime to be tolerated as a subject of public discussion. In 1980, while launching a new round of "struggle for peace," the Soviets came up with a slogan: "The peoples have the power to preserve peace—their basic right." (*Pravda*, September 24, 1980) The message was unmistakable and very effective: If you want to survive, forget about human rights in the Soviet Union. And the West did: "Better red than dead" became a rule of the time.

People of quite different professions—doctors, priests, lawyers, scientists—have suddenly become preoccupied with the craft of diplomacy, each of them claiming they were saving humanity by signing their own separate "peace treaties" with the Soviets.

Thus, justifying his decision to renew scientific exchange with the Soviet Union at the very moment when Dr. Sakharov was reportedly dying in exile, the president of the American Academy of Sciences, Frank Press, wrote, "Despite our continuous concern for Sakharov, there are some issues of such deep importance to the future of mankind that we have felt the necessity to continue talking about them with our Soviet counterparts. In this respect, arms control and international security are certainly of high priority." (*The Washington Post*, May 11, 1983)

Justifying their decision to bring to the "peace talks" in the

United States Dr. Marat Vartanyan—a person legally responsible for the abuse of psychiatry in the Soviet Union—Physicians for Social Responsibility wrote, "Although mistreatment of dissidents is repugnant to us, it won't result in the extinction of the species as the nuclear issue will. There is no issue that is worth the annihilation of life on earth." (*Times-Tribune*, September 24, 1985)

This sudden urge to save humanity by betraying one's moral values has overwhelmed the Western public. Everyone from American Catholic Bishops, who should be more concerned with a man's soul than with his survival, to the American Bar Association, which should know better than to seek cooperation with the modern version of the Gestapo, became vigorous champions of appeasement. Even Ted Turner believes that he saves mankind by paying for a huge Soviet propaganda show. Even a U.S. district judge, rejecting a final plea on behalf of the unfortunate Soviet sailor who tried to jump off his ship in New Orleans on the eve of the Geneva summit meeting, said, with a noble passion in his voice, "This District Judge is not going to do anything which jeopardizes the national interests of this country, including rendering a decision which runs the risk of creating a confrontation."

Once again this skillfully cultivated atmosphere of moral capitulation in the West, endorsed last year by the Nobel Peace Prize, has a double effect: At home it helps the Soviets destroy the human rights movement; abroad it prepares the ground for a new spell of detente.

Indeed, after years of artificially created tension and peace hysteria, no Western government can afford to reject the Soviet offer of detente, even though the most recent outbreak of this disease has left few illusions about its real nature. It became clear that the Soviet system cannot relax for any length of time without eroding. Detente is necessary to catch a breath, to lull Western vigilance, to gain access to Western technology and credits, to improve the military balance, and to grab as many countries in the Third World as time may permit, before the West becomes alerted once again. Then, a period of "Cold War" will follow, with all "progressive mankind" blaming "U.S. imperialism" for "overreacting" and for "not recognizing new political reality."

For the Soviets, detente is simply another version of the "struggle for peace," another weapon of psychological warfare. Aimed at softening Western resistance, as AIDS destroys the human immune system, it does not affect internal life in the Soviet Union, where the climate of Cold War never relaxes. Internally, detente is a period of increased repression; externally, it is a period of intense disinformation. Only in this way can the Soviets prevent rapid erosion of their regime, and it can be achieved only in a closed society, where all channels of communication with the outside world are strictly controlled and often disguised as "independent public institutions."

For the West it is a shameful period of self-censorship and self-deception, an attempt to buy peace by succumbing to the Soviet dictate. It is a time when appeasement triumphs.

Not surprisingly, detente always occurs when the Soviets need it most desperately. Due to a catastrophic decline of productivity caused by the general backwardness of the Soviet economy, they cannot successfully compete militarily with the West, nor can they support their ever-growing empire. These are the real reasons for periodic outbursts of detente or, to take the most recent example, the reasons behind Gorbachev's well-advertised economic reforms. If we give them a break, if we relax in military competition or reduce pressure on their empire, if we give arms control priority over human rights, if we accept that a threat to peace is created by the piles of weapons, not by the nature of the Soviet system, then what is the difference between us and pacifists? What is the difference between President Reagan and Physicians for Social Responsibility? The latter at least are more consistent when they openly proclaim priority of their "basic right" for peace over all the other rights and moral principles.

At the end of the Geneva summit a "new" agreement on cultural and scientific cooperation was solemnly signed. This agreement, however, is new only in name. In fact, it is a precise copy of a 1972 agreement that gives all advantages and exchanges to the Soviet Union. Once again, all the contacts between East and West will be channeled through official Soviet institutions, giving them the right to control information and people.

Apart from strengthening Party control over the Soviet population, this agreement also serves to confuse the Western public, equating phony Soviet institutions with their Western "counterparts." What is the difference, then, between the Reagan Administration and the American Bar Association, whose agreement with the Association of Soviet Lawyers was so widely criticized?

We are told once again, as in the 1970s, that "understanding" is the best way to achieve peace with the Soviet Union. But the choice is limited: One can have "understanding" either with the Soviet people or with the Soviet rulers.

Regrettably, President Reagan seems to choose the latter option. He finds it "counterproductive" to meet with Yelena Bonner or even to be photographed with Anatoly Shcharansky, but he welcomes Katya Lycheva, a Soviet "counterpart" of Samantha Smith. This is symbolic of the current trend in the East-West relations: exchanging Boy Scouts for Hitlerjugend in a quest of "understanding and peace." Once again the "quiet diplomacy" doctrine of the 1970s is revived and made an official policy of the United States. Open pressure is reserved only for Manila and Pretoria. What is the difference, then, between Carter and Reagan?

Meanwhile, several hundreds of American businessmen rushed to Moscow eager to improve "East-West economic relations." Credits and technology, goods, and loans are ready to be poured into the Soviet Union. The only remaining obstacle seems to be the Jackson-Vanik Amendment, and even that is under constant attack from left and right alike, including from Senator Dole.

Detente is upon us once again, although nobody seems to notice it. Conservatives don't want to criticize "their president," liberals are smart enough not to criticize their agenda, and both sides carefully avoid the very word lest its too-familiar sound disturb some bad memories. Oh no, we do not call it detente any longer. It is just a "more stable and constructive relationship."

Ironically, all of this happens at a time when the West does not need a break. The Western economy is strong and healthy, the West's military capability is improved, and the political atmosphere is much better than after the Vietnam War. Even Europeans have been cured from their "infant disease of leftism" (as Lenin once called it). It is the Soviets who need detente most desperately. Yet it is the West who is going to pay for it, saving in the process the bankrupt Communist system. We are going to witness a repetition of the same mistakes a second time within a single decade, something without precedent in human history, only because the West has no defense against Soviet psychological warfare.

COMBATING SOVIET DECEPTION: WHAT MUST BE DONE

Mr. Smith

As we have seen, Soviet strategic deception aims ultimately at the intellectual, moral, and physical disarmament of the United States. In the short term this may mean sowing sufficient confusion into our decision-making process so as to induce a disunity and paralysis that would render us incapable of acting decisively to prevent or overcome challenges to our strategic interests in various regional theaters. In the long term it means rendering us incapable of sustaining such deterrent forces that would be sufficient to resist a mortal Soviet threat to our security and way of life. To achieve such objectives, Soviet deception is aimed at each of the key targets in our society that have significant influence over our national policy decisions: opinion leaders, including the news media, the academic community, filmmakers and writers; the American public itself; the Executive Branch, including the President, his advisers, and the foreign affairs, defense, and intelligence agencies; and Congress. Because each of these four elements of our society has responsibility for affecting national defense decisions, each has a responsibility to combat Soviet deception in its own sphere.

Opinion Leaders

The various opinion leaders in our society—the media, the academic world, the purveyors of popular culture—have all been traditional targets of Soviet deception. Not only have the Soviets attempted to inject their disinformation themes into the writings of our reporters, columnists, scholars, novelists, and screenplay writers, but they have historically tried to penetrate the ranks of these groups with "agents of influence." Recognizing how these efforts have been done is the first step toward successfully combating them.

The penetration of our news media has been accomplished in several ways. The Soviets have been remarkably successful in controlling all the news regularly reported from Moscow. If a reporter files stories that put the Soviet regime in what the Soviets judge to be too bad a light, that reporter will be expelled, as many have been, from Moscow. If his newspaper replaces him with others who write the same kinds of stories—stories that do no more than describe the normal political realities of life in the USSR—then that newspaper will be denied a bureau in Moscow. Of course, no significant organ of the U.S. news media wants to be left without access to a post in Moscow. Given this situation, all Western reporters in the USSR must censor themselves to suit the Soviets if they want to remain there. Thus, the entire news product emanating from the Communist world is missing large chunks of the truth. As a result, most of what we get from our media has an element of deception built into it. We don't really hear the full truth until some of the better reporters return to the United States and write books of their recollections about the Soviet Union. But how many people read these books?

Soviet manipulation of the news goes much further, however. The Kremlin's experts at controlling information also use a variety of inducements to encourage reporters to write exactly what they want them to write. The more favorable a reporter's stories are to the USSR, the more access he will be granted to senior Soviet officials. He will be given exclusive interviews or exclusive "leaks" and scoops shared with him by a friendly Soviet "source" who, while adopting the guise of being a member of one or another Soviet government agency, will in fact be a KGB disinformation expert or an agent of the Communist Party Central Committee's International Propaganda Department. These various favors can make a reporter's life much easier in Moscow: more stories with less work, and more entry into the highest echelons of the Soviet leadership. But this is a system of corrupting the Western media.

If there is to be any real integrity to the news-gathering process by Americans in the USSR, this system of corruption should be exposed and resisted by the editors in the media themselves. The professional associations of newspapermen and broadcasters should incorporate into their professional codes of conduct special standards of behavior for reporters in totalitarian countries. The various organs of our media should also have reporters on Soviet and other Communist countries' affairs who do not reside in those countries.

One can learn immense amounts of information about the USSR from a variety of sources in Washington, D.C., alone, not to mention various European capitals. One major source of news and information on the Communist world is Radio Free Europe/Radio Liberty (RFE/RL), whose headquarters are in Munich. These radios receive voluminous amounts of news from Communist countries from various sources, including underground pipelines of information, radio and TV broadcasts from the Communist countries monitored by RFE/RL, and research reports prepared by RFE/RL's research staffs. One idea whose time has come is that RFE/RL establish its own wire service, to which newspapers and broadcasters around the world could subscribe.

All too often Western reporters detailed to Moscow have never studied Soviet or Communist affairs, nor do most of them speak Russian or any of the other Soviet languages. Thus many rely on their KGB-supplied interpreters to translate for them and to assist them in their reporting and interviewing. And, as *Wall Street Journal* correspondent David Satter has reported, some reporters even rely on interviewing their KGB-supplied maids to find out what the Soviet "man in the street" is thinking. Here again, the integrity of the news-gathering process demands that our major media insist that their reporters have expertise in the country, its ideology, its political system, and its language.

Another thing should also be kept in mind. Reporters in the USSR are uniformly restricted to certain parts of the country. Most of what reporters are permitted to see is Potemkin Village—a fake village of false fronts constructed to impress the visitor with certain features that the regime would like him to keep in mind. To give a complete and accurate portrayal of life in the USSR, reporters must do their utmost to see what it is that the regime wants to hide from them. They must also gather information that they can send through various confidential channels back to their respective newspapers to be published under the bylines of other reporters stationed outside the Communist world.

Another way the Soviets manipulate our news media is through recruitment of our journalists as "agents of influence." This may be done very directly, when a Western journalist is induced by financial rewards to write what the KGB would like him to publish. Within the past few years a French journalist, Pierre-Charles Pathe, and a Danish journalist, Arne Petersen, were exposed for acting as political "agents of influence" for the USSR. They often published stories already written for them by the KGB. There are other, more indirect means that the Soviets use to accomplish the same goals, however.

A KGB agent, for example, under cover as a Soviet "journalist," may befriend a U.S. journalist. In their conversations, the KGB agent may discover that the American is deeply opposed to the "arms race," its "irrationality," and its "hopelessness," while being fervently committed to working to help bring peace to this situation. The KGB agent may then declare that he believes in the same things. Why then, he will suggest, don't they both try to work together to publish articles in both their newspapers that decry the senselessness of the arms race? He will share with the American a few of his own articles that make these very points. Through relationships such as this, the KGB recruits Western journalists who never know that they have been recruited or are working in any way for the Soviets. Nevertheless, the KGB considers such indirectly influenced journalists as recruits in fact. As Stanislav Levchenko, former KGB agent in charge of "active measures" operations in Tokyo, has testified before Congress, he personally recruited many journalists, many of whom did not realize that they were being manipulated in this way. If journalists are to avoid being used as conduits of Soviet political influence and disinformation, they must educate themselves well about these techniques so as not to leave themselves vulnerable.

Another way the Soviets deceive us through our media is by having their propagandists appear as commentators on U.S. TV or as authors of U.S. newspaper columns. While it is useful for Americans to understand Soviet views on various international issues, editors should be much more sensitive to the differences between Soviet views that are expressed regularly in the pages of the Soviet press and those which are prepared specially as propaganda for U.S. audiences. To invite Vladimir Posner, a propagandist for Radio Moscow, to appear on U.S. TV, to introduce him as a fellow "journalist" (as if there were a free press in the Soviet Union), and to let him utter one propagandistic falsehood after another with no rebuttal by a qualified U.S. analyst is to serve as a direct agent of Soviet deception. Our major TV networks have a major professional, ethical, and civic responsibility to stop this form of complicity with and assistance to Soviet deception and propaganda.

The academic world is susceptible to similar manipulations.

The Soviets know that if they can inject certain key deception themes into the theories and writings of Western scholars, they can affect the entire direction of U.S. policy toward the USSR. It is very unlikely that our government would ever conduct a policy opposed to assessments reached by most of our country's experts on Soviet affairs. Indeed, those experts are consulted by our government as well as appointed to official posts, including key analytical jobs in the intelligence community. They educate scores of students, who end up working throughout the Executive Branch and Congress. And they often contribute columns to our national press and appear on television as commentators. If the Soviets can succeed in deceiving our Sovietologists, they may well succeed in deceiving the entire country.

The Soviets attempt to do this in several ways. One is by trying to corrupt scholars who wish to travel to the USSR and gain access to senior Party and government officials. Those who write certain truths about the USSR are often not even permitted visas to enter the country. Those who write what the Soviets like are conversely the ones who are most likely to gain the greatest access and suffer the fewest restrictions within the USSR. This latter point, of course, is not a hard-and-fast rule. Much depends on the subject matter being covered by the scholar in question. Nevertheless, as a general rule, this carrot-and-stick policy often induces many of our "experts" to censor themselves in the interest of being able to return to the USSR and gain more access. Some scholars are well aware of this game yet still have admitted censoring themselves in order to retain sufficient access to the Soviet Union. Such travel becomes a tool of their trade—i.e., fieldwork—and thus enables them to uphold their "scholarly reputation" within their profession.

Another method the Soviets use is to encourage scholars to adopt certain theories about the nature of Soviet foreign policy that are false. This is done by the repetition of various disinformation themes within the Soviet press, which is studied most closely by our scholars, both in academia and in the intelligence community. Soviet propaganda that endlessly harps on how many people the Soviets lost during World War II is repeated, among other reasons, to induce Western experts to adopt the theory that the Soviets operate from an extreme sense of insecurity due to external threats and thus pursue a foreign policy motivated principally by defensive concerns and desire for "peace." Thus some "experts" have put forward the theory that the Soviet invasion of Afghanistan, which has turned into a seven-year war of destruction against millions of innocent Afghans, was done for "defensive" reasons.

To avoid these and other methods of being manipulated into serving Soviet deception by repeating Soviet disinformation and engaging in self-censorship, America's experts on Soviet affairs have a solemn responsibility to uphold the highest standards of scholarship. Their professional scholarly associations should also adopt a professional code of behavior that takes into account the ways the truth may be compromised. Finally, experts in this field should do much more to acknowledge the risks of repeating disinformation in spite of all the best efforts a scholar may make to avoid doing so: it is not always possible for even the most brilliant analyst to distinguish truth from deception, given the vast number of ways deception can be injected by the Soviets into people's perception of reality.

Our popular artists are also targets of Soviet deception. If TV producers, novelists, playwrights, movie makers, and even artists, musicians, actors, and other celebrities can be deceived about Soviet reality, they can serve as powerful conduits of that deception into the consciousness of our society. While the Soviets may be less likely to focus their deception efforts directly on many of these people, their efforts to influence them indirectly command considerable resources within the Soviet disinformation and propaganda apparatus.

The Soviets will encourage joint film productions between U.S. and Soviet filmmakers. They utilize cultural exchanges as means of getting U.S. cultural figures to travel to the Soviet Union so that they can be presented a well-orchestrated image of Soviet reality, a Potemkin Village reality, which is in fact a false reality. The Soviets also use their own cultural programs from ballet to film and even sports as a special means of propaganda. The Soviets know that a pleasing cultural presentation can soften an audience's antipathy toward the Soviet Union, increase people's curiosity about Soviet life, induce people to perceive the Soviets as people who are "just like us" (and who therefore must love peace as well), and encourage people to be more susceptible to more overt political propaganda messages in the future.

To avoid being influenced by Soviet deception, popular U.S. artists have a special responsibility to be aware of the pitfalls of dealing with things Soviet. They should make an extra effort to consult a wide variety of experts in the field to sensitize themselves about the ways the script, screenplay, or novel they are preparing might be an unintended vehicle of Soviet strategic deception. To help educate the public about the dangers of deception, these same people could do a great service to the truth by applying their talents to new and creative ways of portraying the problem of deception to the public.

The American Public

Because the American people themselves are the ultimate source of political decision making, the Soviets always conduct their propaganda and deception efforts with the American public in mind. The Soviets are particularly interested in influencing those elements of the public that are organized and politically active. As we have seen, if they can succeed in deceiving U.S. Christians, for example, that there is freedom of religion in the USSR, or that the Nicaraguan Sandinistas are not Communists but agrarian reformers, or that the threat to peace comes from inanimate objects such as nuclear weapons rather than from the people whose fingers are on the nuclear button—the same people who are massacring hundreds of thousands of Afghans—then they will have gone a long way toward intellectually and morally disarming a significant portion of the U.S. electorate. If the leaders of the various Christian denominations can be brought to believe in such falsehoods, then they may easily be enlisted into the pro-Soviet "peace" movement or the pro-Communist effort to prevent U.S. aid to the democratic resistance in Nicaragua.

Thirty years ago, when the American public was much better educated about communism than it is today, a wide variety of private, fraternal, religious, and civic groups undertook significant efforts to educate their members and the public in general. Students in Sunday schools, for example, were taught that communism and religion are philosophically opposite and that anywhere communism rules, religion is the principal target of destruction, and if that is not possible, manipulation and control are practiced. This is no less true today than it was three decades ago. Yet because people have not worked to keep themselves informed, they can easily be deceived and even exploited by the Communists for propaganda purposes.

When evangelist Billy Graham went to Moscow to preach, he conducted a service in a church with a full congregation, many of whose members for this occasion were secret police. During the service some parishioners unfurled a large sign declaring that believers were indeed persecuted in the Soviet Union. Even after seeing this sign and witnessing the secret police remove the demonstrators, Graham publicly declared that there was freedom of religion in the USSR. Only later did he admit that his public pronouncements from Moscow were dictated by his desire not to offend his official Soviet hosts so that he could be permitted to return there in the future. Instead of permitting himself to be a tool of Soviet deception, the evangelist should have told the world some pertinent facts: that over 90 percent of the churches in the Soviet Union have been either closed down or destroyed since 1917; that the religious education of one's children is regularly treated as a punishable crime in the USSR; that the Russian Orthodox Patriarchate of Moscow is infiltrated and controlled by KGB agents, some of whom were his hosts; and that this Church is used by the Soviets as a major arm of the Soviet international propaganda apparatus. If America's religious groups were to work harder to keep their members informed of such facts, they would not be vulnerable to this kind of deception.

While religious groups are a special target of Soviet deception, others are also given special attention. U.S. business is one such target. The Soviets know that since business plays such a large role in American life, the political neutralization of significant portions of our business community can yield them strategic benefits. Thus the Soviets have long sought to develop trade relationships with U.S. companies. Once such relationships have been established, U.S. businessmen will get accustomed to the profits from those relationships. Once "hooked" in this way, these businessmen are less likely to say anything publicly that the Soviets don't like. They may even become an active lobby for a "detente" policy with the USSR so as not to jeopardize their profits. But as we have learned from history, "detente" can occur only when Americans censor themselves and stop telling the truth about the Soviet Union.

U.S. business is one of the great engines of our free society. It produces our great abundance of goods and services. It offers millions of Americans the chance to develop their talents to their fullest. But it can do these things only in a climate of political freedom. You would think, then, that U.S. business would be more active in supporting political forces working for a strong national defense—the defense of their life-giving freedom. Even those businesses that have a vested interest in a strong defense policy—the "military-industrial complex"—have been remarkably absent when it comes to active support for public education about the Soviet Union and communism. Such companies, as well as others not particularly involved in the defense business, could do much more: support prodefense research institutes and political action lobbies whose staffs work on telling the truth about the USSR; sponsor advertisements alerting people to the Soviet threat and Soviet deception techniques; distribute educational literature to stockholders; support universities whose faculties tell the truth about communism; and withhold support from universities whose faculties either confuse, misinform, or even deceive their students about Soviet affairs and communism. To conduct such a corporate public affairs policy requires some imagination, of course, and a break with some of the short-range strategies based merely on near-term profit calculations. It requires a long-range strategy that recognizes that a public alert to the Soviet threat and Soviet deception is much more likely to support a strong defense than an uninformed, complacent, or deceived public.

U.S. business as a whole should take its long-term political interests more seriously in general. To support a strong defense today means avoiding catastrophically costly wars tomorrow. In the field of public education about communism, the U.S. labor movement does more than the business community. It is labor, which has a history of fighting Communists within its own movement, that is ready to alert the public consciousness about the meaning of the Solidarity movement in Poland. It is U.S. labor that educates members of foreign labor unions about the methods of fighting communism and preserving freedom for their societies and their unions. To be sure, the U.S. Chamber of Commerce has taken a significant step in the formation of the Center for International Private Enterprise, which assists foreign countries in developing free enterprise systems.* But much more can be done to educate people about the principal threat to private enterprise: communism.

The large community of lawyers in the United States can also play a bigger role. Lawyers are among the most articulate and influential of our citizens. Once the American Bar Association

---

*Ed. Note: Inspite of labor's good record in this area, U.S. labor does have a tendency to support political candidates largely on domestic issues that are not supportive of national security.

(ABA) was more sensitive to the realities of communism than today. One of its standing committees was the Committee for the Study of Communist Strategy and Tactics (also called the Committee for Education on Communism), which published many excellent studies on communism. Unfortunately, this committee was disbanded, and the ABA no longer serves as an active player to keep the public informed. Instead, the ABA has served as an accomplice in another Soviet deception: it recently signed an agreement of cooperation and "mutual respect" with the Association of Soviet Lawyers, one of whose senior officers is the author of major recent Soviet anti-Semitic propaganda tracts. To proffer "respect" to the association of Soviet lawyers is to promote the idea of the moral equivalence of the United States and the USSR by encouraging the deception that Soviet lawyers are just like U.S. lawyers and that the USSR is run by the rule of law just as is the United States. In reality, Soviet lawyers serve as agents of the Communist Party and its whims. It is Soviet lawyers who have sent millions of political prisoners to their fate in the Gulag Archipelago. During World War II, would the ABA, for purposes of dialogue, mutual understanding, and peace, have signed an agreement of "mutual respect" with the Association of Nazi Lawyers?

The U.S. medical and scientific communities are yet another target of Soviet deception. Because physicians and scientists are also articulate and well-respected members of their communities, the manipulation of their voices to serve Soviet propaganda and deception is a major Soviet goal. To achieve this, the Soviets use quasi-front organizations like International Physicians for the Prevention of Nuclear War as a means of enlisting to their side the weight and prestige of naive and ill-informed Western physicians and scientists. Once such people join the chorus of those opposing U.S. nuclear weapons programs, they assist the Soviet effort to disarm the United States, to conceal through distraction the vast Soviet investment in nuclear arms, and to deceive the West about Soviet political and strategic intentions.

Just recently, in 1985, an American physician, Dr. Bernard Lown, joined a Soviet physician, Dr. Yevgeny Chazov, to represent International Physicians for the Prevention of Nuclear War in receiving the Nobel Peace Prize for its "efforts" to prevent nuclear war. Dr. Chazov, however, happens to be one of the very group of Soviet scientists who publicly denounced Dr. Andrei Sakharov, the father of the Soviet H-bomb and one of the USSR's foremost truly independent peace and human rights activists. This public denunciation was the Soviet Communist Party's way of justifying their persecution of Sakharov and their dispatching him to internal exile. Roping Dr. Lown and other Western scientists and physicians into what is in effect a Soviet front organization was the Soviets' way of giving international respectability to Chazov and his fellow physician-propagandists. That these propagandists and their dupes should have been given the Nobel Peace Prize for their propaganda only legitimizes the propaganda even further. If U.S. physicians want to do their part in combating Soviet deception and propaganda, they too have a responsibility to keep informed and to refuse to participate in Soviet propaganda efforts and front organizations.

U.S. scientists have an extra obligation when it comes to ensuring that the truth prevails. That is to see to it that not just those scientific theories that are exploited by Soviet propaganda, but others as well, get national publicity. Not long ago, popular politician-scientist Carl Sagan began to promote a theory that was still in its very speculative and infant stage as the conclusive findings of modern science: the theory of "nuclear winter." Because of the frightening implications of this theory and the importance intimidation plays in Soviet strategy, the vast Soviet propaganda machine was mobilized to frighten the world with this theory. "Nuclear winter" became Moscow's Party line overnight, and even the most prominent Soviet scientists were dispatched with multimillion-dollar travel budgets to promote the theory at conferences and on speaking engagements around the globe. Partly on the basis of this theory, New Zealand refused to permit U.S. naval vessels to make port calls, since some do carry nuclear weapons. As a result, since it did not want to carry its share of the mutual defense burden in the Pacific area, its action precipitated the breakup of the ANZUS alliance. Later, however, with further research, Western scientists began to cast grave doubts on the nuclear winter theory. The National Center for Atmospheric Research and the British Meteorological Office concluded on the basis of their studies that "nuclear winter" is in fact a myth and that the more accurate scientific term should be "nuclear autumn."

In spite of all these new conclusions, the Soviet propaganda machine continues to try to frighten people with nuclear winter, and Carl Sagan, far from correcting the record on the nationally prominent pages of *Parade* magazine, is nowhere to be seen. Meanwhile, no one has ever heard of nuclear autumn. And no one is alerted to the extent to which the Soviets selectively exploit certain scientific theories for purposes of strategic deception.

No matter which walk of life a citizen comes from, each must do his part to learn the truth and live by it for the sake of our consistent support of a citizenry that realizes that we have something here in the United States that is worth defending and that there is a major threat to our security that has not gone away. If our citizens take national defense for granted, if they think that it is somebody else's business and not theirs, they are seriously mistaken. As long as our citizens have the vote and can thus affect our national defense decisions, they must do all they can to make informed decisions. To do this requires a new national campaign to educate ourselves about the nature of communism, the Soviet system, its foreign policy, and its strategy of deception. If we can learn the truth about these things and act accordingly, we will always be able to keep our country free.

The Executive Branch

The Executive Branch of our government has the greatest responsibility to combat Soviet strategic deception for two reasons. First, it is in possession of more information about Soviet activities than any other element of society. Thus it has the responsibility to share this information with the Congress, opinion leaders, and the public so that they can make better-informed decisions. Secondly, the President is in the best position to lead. In this case this means leading the nation along the path of greater awareness and vigilance so that the correct defense decisions are made. It specifically means analyzing the Soviet strategy of deception and defeating it with a positive strategy of freedom through truth.

American Presidents over the last twenty years have a very sorry record on both counts. They have neither done much to inform the public nor exercised their powers of leadership. President Reagan has done more than others. During his 1980 campaign and the first two years of his presidency, he personally made a point of telling the people the truth about the nature of the Soviet system and its threat to the West. His Administration has done more than any of its recent predecessors in declassifying intelligence about the extent of Soviet military preparations. It has released the annual

Department of Defense report *Soviet Military Power,* reports on the Soviet use of chemical and bacteriological weapons, Soviet efforts to acquire sensitive Western technology, Soviet strategic defense, Soviet activities in Central America and other regions, and other related reports. His Administration has made major strides in monitoring and reporting Soviet propaganda, disinformation, and "active measures." Unfortunately, most of these reports have seen only limited distribution. The Public Affairs Bureau of the Department of State, which has principal responsibility for educating the U.S. public about foreign affairs, has failed to reach mass audiences with the simple, vital message about Soviet deception. Neither does it attempt to use modern means of mass communication, such as television and film; nor does it choose to designate Soviet deception as a high-priority item for one of its more effective operations—its speakers program.

The problem with the State Department's role in all this, of course, lies much deeper. It is a problem of U.S. government policy. It is next to impossible to combat Soviet deception, no matter how many limited-distribution reports the government may issue, when the U.S. government's policy itself involves reinforcing that very deception. *The question of how to combat Soviet deception is thus not just a question of what to do; it is also a question of what not to do.*

President Reagan came into office telling the plain truth about the USSR. Sometimes he was so direct ("lie, cheat, commit any crime," "Evil Empire") that he alarmed many people who felt that saying such things could only increase tensions with the USSR and possibly provoke it to be more dangerous than it already is. As long as the President told these truths, he succeeded in securing the necessary resources from Congress to redress many of the dangerous military imbalances in which we had found ourselves vis-à-vis the relentless Soviet military buildup. He demonstrated clearly that telling the truth is good for U.S. defense and is good ultimately for the peace with freedom that rests on that strong defense. Unfortunately, the truth's days were numbered.

The President found precious little support within his own cabinet for his policy of telling the truth. Not a single effort was made by either of his Secretaries of State to support publicly his charges about the Soviet Union's aggressive and mendacious nature. When some Americans were confused by the President's statements, questioning whether an entire country with its millions of people could so carelessly be branded as evil, nobody stepped forth to clarify that the President had been making a distinction between, on the one hand, the Soviet Communist Party leadership and its totalitarian and externally aggressive system, and on the other, the millions of people forced to live as victims of that system. To this day the Administration has failed to remind the American people of the distinction between the "Soviet Union," a creature of communism, and "Russia," a nation that is only a part of the Soviet Union, a nation whose spirit, customs, religious heritage, and cultural traditions have been smothered, twisted, and distorted by Soviet communism. Aside from the few instances when the President used brief, blunt characterizations of the USSR, not once has he or his Secretaries of State thoroughly explained clearly, calmly, and factually to a national audience what the nature of the Soviet system and its threat to our security are.

The President had to endure tremendous criticism for the few times he stepped forth to tell the truth. The criticism came from the vocal minority who never supported him in the first place, from such quarters as *The Washington Post*. It also came from the Soviets, who took the opportunity to utilize yet another deception to silence the President. Soviet propaganda against the President was achieving new heights for shrillness and bellicosity. Its purpose was to get the President to stop telling the truth. This was done by threatening the peace and threatening to increase the danger of nuclear war while distracting people's attention from Soviet behavior, such as its continued domination over Eastern Europe, its invasion of Afghanistan, its export of Communist revolutions all over the globe, and its persecution of its own people.

The Soviet gambit succeeded. The President apparently became convinced by his advisers that his truth telling, rather than being the vehicle to achieve peace through truth and strength, was an impediment to peace. He became convinced that it was politically dangerous to tell the truth and that the American people and the people of Europe did not want to hear it. Thus the President softened his talk about the bitter truths about the Soviet system.

For several years, Executive Branch agencies have been accumulating evidence of Soviet violations of arms control treaties. Yet the U.S. government has refused to warn the American people about the meaning and danger of these violations. Instead of taking a leadership role and telling the American people the truth, the President was convinced by his advisers that doing so would only be interpreted as an attempt to derail arms control. Rather than protesting that it is violations that undermine arms control and not reports of those violations, the President withheld any public comment on this until forced to do so by Congress.

Apparently convinced that the people did not want to hear the truth but rather thirsted for a more comforting atmosphere of U.S.-Soviet relations, the President began his own version of detente with the Soviet Union. Sanctions levied against the Soviets for their invasion of Afghanistan were lifted, while Soviet air attacks massacred Afghan villagers by the thousands. New trade with the Soviets was promoted; expiring agreements with the Soviets originally signed by former Presidents were renewed. A summit meeting ensued, with smiles and handshakes with the new leader of the "Evil Empire." During this entire period, with the exception of Secretary of Defense Caspar Weinberger, the Executive Branch was conducting a policy of silence about the Soviet threat. In the interests of achieving a friendly atmosphere at the 1985 summit and maintaining the "Spirit of Geneva" afterward, the President and his top foreign policy advisers followed a conscious policy of saying nothing that would offend Moscow. Since telling any truth about the Soviets and their foreign policy would offend them, self-censorship was the price the Administration had to pay to give the world the false impression that a more peaceful world had been achieved through diplomatic "success." But self-censorship was not the only price that had to be paid to win Gorbachev's cooperation in creating the new atmospherics: the Administration, perhaps without fully realizing it, also felt it necessary to behave in a way that ended up assisting the Soviets in some of their deceptions.

Principal among these deceptions is the false idea that all that is necessary to solve U.S.-Soviet differences are goodwill, negotiations, mutual understanding, and more goodwill. To promote this idea is to conceal the fact that as long as the Soviets remain Marxist-Leninists, they can never be a status quo power and reconcile themselves to the existence of U.S. democracy, whose very essence is an idea that represents a mortal threat to the Communist Party's hold on power—a mortal threat to the Soviet *system*.

In another example, the State Department and other Administration spokesmen have discussed the necessity of working with the Soviets to solve "common problems" such as terrorism. Indeed, in 1985 the Soviets became victims for the first time of Middle East terrorists when several Soviets were kidnapped in

Lebanon. Now that both countries had been victims, the Administration felt it could then say with a straight face that terrorism was a "common" problem that both sides had an interest in eliminating. Notwithstanding the fact that the Soviets have been the principal sponsor of international terrorism—providing terrorists with funds, training, weapons, explosives, transportation, forged documents, communications assistance, and safe haven (it should be understood that Marxist-Leninist morality does, in fact, justify robbery, terror, and, yes, even murder, in the name of "building world communism")—and notwithstanding the Soviets' abiding desire to conceal their role and deceive the world about it, the Administration was ready to pay the Soviet price for the atmospherics of "peace" by assisting them in their deception.

Another type of Soviet deception to which the U.S. government has been an accomplice has come in the form of Moscow's many "arms control" proposals. Every few months, the Kremlin consistently puts forth yet another "bold" and "original" proposal to limit or reduce nuclear weapons. Many of these are so patently one-sided that even the most devoted members of the arms control lobby have expressed their disappointment in the Soviet lack of seriousness. The purposes of almost all of these are threefold: One is to convince the Western public that the Soviets are offering serious arms reduction proposals; another is to stake out negotiating positions that are so audaciously one-sided that anytime they move away from those positions to the slightest degree in the direction of compromise they can claim to have made great concessions; and finally, they aim to evoke U.S. concessions in response, which they have succeeded in doing in the past. However, the extreme one-sidedness of the Soviet position puts the United States at an immediate disadvantage. If, on the one hand, the U.S. response is a much more reasonable one that comes close to a mutually acceptable position, the Soviets will be able to make a counterresponse that can be extremely one-sided, then claim to have made a major concession. If the United States does not respond to this, having gone as far toward compromise as the nation's security will permit, the Soviets will accuse the United States of not being willing to make further analogous concessions. If, on the other hand, the first U.S. response is just as one-sided as the original Soviet proposal (so as to avoid being put in a position of not being forced to make concessions), then Soviet propagandists and their echoes in the U.S. media will accuse the United States of not being "serious" about arms control and of not putting forth a sufficiently "negotiable" proposal.

By the very act of participating in this "arms control" process, which is wholly one-sided since public and media pressure can be placed only on the United States and not on the Kremlin, the U.S. government is at an immediate disadvantage. To make matters worse, however, the U.S. government has felt compelled to bend over backward to show that it is "serious" about arms control and that the President is really interested in peace. So to foster these impressions with the public, the Administration praises, or gives credit to, Soviet proposals that are outrageously one-sided, in hopes that by doing so it will encourage the public to believe that real progress is being made in the negotiations. Thus the Soviets make a preposterous proposal; then the U.S. government praises it and raises the public's hopes. This, unfortunately, is a deception of the U.S. public—the very deception that Moscow wants our public to believe. Finally, the Administration, after "studying" it, rejects the Soviet offer. Moscow then criticizes the U.S. government's intransigence.

Another way the U.S. government has facilitated Soviet deception has been by obscuring the criminality of certain Soviet actions. The follow-up to the Soviet shootdown of the Korean airliner is an example. The Soviets had declared the shootdown to be a legitimate act and even went so far so to declare that they would do it again given their "legitimate" security concerns. Then they launched a propaganda and disinformation campaign, claiming that the civilian airliner was a spy plane. Western apologists for the USSR later assisted Soviet propaganda by alleging that the Soviets mistook the airliner for a U.S. military reconnaissance aircraft. All this, of course, conveniently overlooked the fact that U.S. reconnaissance planes do not display exterior lights of the kind that civilian airliners do—lights that the Soviet fighter pilots identified, as revealed by U.S. intelligence radio intercepts. One of the most prominent U.S. government responses to this crime against scores of innocent people was to launch negotiations with the Soviets and Japan to reach an agreement to improve safety procedures in the Northern Pacific air corridor, an agreement that was later signed. The problem to be solved, however, was not "inadequate international safety procedures." Whether it was a Soviet military system programmed in such a way that no distinction is made between military and civilian aircraft intrusions, or a Soviet political system incapable of making amends for its deadly action, the problem to be solved was Soviet behavior. To identify the problem as anything else was to deceive the public about exclusive Soviet criminality in the matter.

Another form of U.S. government assistance to Soviet deception is to assist the Soviet efforts to distract attention from their aggressive actions around the world. At the 1985 Geneva summit the two sides signed an educational and cultural exchange agreement. While educational exchanges, if conducted with prudence and reciprocity, can be beneficial to U.S. understanding of the USSR, cultural and sports exchanges have consistently been used by the Soviets as a means of propaganda and distraction. Ballet dancers, musicians, and sportsmen all speak a universal language. Thus they can induce U.S. and other foreign audiences to ease their suspicion of the Soviets; after all, can a country that makes such beautiful music be so bad? Furthermore, such cultural and sports events with the Soviets, not to mention trade relationships, distract our attention from such things as the Soviet military buildup, the Gulag, and the war in Afghanistan.

To combat Soviet deception thus requires more than anything else a foreign policy that refuses to accept and assist Soviet deception in any way. U.S. Presidents must stop succumbing to the temptation of illusory, atmospheric improvements of relations with the Soviets. Each time they do, it is the truth that is destroyed; that is the price that the Soviets demand. Despite the repeated failure of every President since Franklin Roosevelt to parlay such improvement in atmosphere into benevolent changes in Soviet behavior, even a relative realist like Ronald Reagan has been convinced into repeating many of the mistakes of the past. What is needed is for our Presidents to tell the truth and to remind the electorate of the importance of telling the truth. They must also require the Department of State and other agencies like the FBI, the CIA, and the Defense Department to conduct major public education programs that inform the people about the realities of Soviet communism.

FBI Director J. Edgar Hoover published several books about communism, including a major study on Communist deception, *Masters of Deceit*. Although over twenty years old, Hoover's studies are completely valid today. More such studies should be produced and widely distributed. Since the FBI has such a large role to play in controlling the hostile intelligence presence in the United States—especially the Soviet presence—it can do much more to educate the public on the goals and methods of the Soviet intelligence services here, including their role in "active measures," disinformation, and deception. Greater public awareness can only benefit the FBI in doing its job.

Another example from the past offers a further suggestion. During World War II the great Hollywood director Frank Capra produced several excellent documentary films entitled *Why We Fight*. These were not hate-propaganda movies. They were factual portrayals of the politics, ideas, goals, and methods of the Nazis and a review of the ideas the United States stands for. Although we are not in a shooting war with Soviet communism, we are in a protracted low-intensity conflict with it—a battle of ideas, a competition of truth versus falsehood, a struggle for the survival of freedom. What we need today are constant reminders of "why we defend"—why we must have a defense budget, why we cannot be isolationist, why we must help others fight for their freedom, why we must stand up for what we believe.

The Department of Education has a role to play here. It can assess the level of ignorance in our nation's schools about Soviet communism and can encourage greater study of this subject. The Defense Department can expand its education programs on communism for U.S. military personnel. It can improve the Soviet areas studies programs at the service academies and war colleges. It can also play a much larger role in educating the public through publications, films, and speakers. The State Department can do the same for its own personnel, as well as improve its personnel placement policy. Currently, foreign service officers with no knowledge of Soviet communism whatsoever can be transferred from posts on other continents to policy-formulating positions on the Soviet desk at the State Department. Unfortunately, the general lessons in foreign affairs that an officer may learn in Africa or South America cannot serve as a replacement for education about Soviet communism.

The Central Intelligence Agency is not without responsibility. It is in charge of every significant defector who escapes from the Communist world. While these defectors are principally of intelligence value to the CIA, they may also be of tremendous value to the public at large as witnesses to the realities of communism. The public testimony of defectors can be some of the most powerful evidence available that attests to the nature of Soviet lies. Thus the

CIA can play an enormously constructive role in assisting defectors to write articles and books or in participating in other means of public education.

Finally, the President himself must play the most important role. He must not only steer policy in ways that do not contribute to Soviet deceptions, he must continue to tell the truth and insist that his cabinet and all his agency chiefs assist in this effort. He must make more nationwide TV addresses on freedom and truth. He must be photographed at events that remind the public of the realities we face. Once 'candidate' Reagan criticized President Ford for not seeing Alexander Solzhenitsyn at the White House. But President Reagan has not yet received him after six years in office. It is the vigorous use of the national spotlight that will get the message across. It is the courage to exercise leadership rather than merely being a follower that is required to utter that message.

The Congress

Members of Congress, as representatives of the people, are closer to the public than is the President. They have a variety of unique ways of reaching their supporters that should be harnessed as part of the overall effort to combat Soviet deception. Congressmen and senators have newsletters that are sent to millions of constituents. They enjoy the audio-visual facilities of the House and Senate recording studios. With these they reach local audiences on radio and TV. The proceedings of the House are broadcast on cable TV to an audience of millions. Such parliamentary devices as the "special order," where members can speak on various subjects, can be used as educational tools.

But for all the means Congress has at its disposal to educate the public, it must educate itself about Soviet deception and how it is a special target of deception efforts. Many Soviet deception activities are aimed especially at Congress for several reasons. First among these is Congress's role in controlling the government's purse strings. If Congress can be convinced that the Soviet threat either doesn't exist, or is less than originally thought, or is of a different character than once suspected, Congress can decide that the Defense budget need not be as large as the President thinks it should be to safeguard the nation.

Congress is also a special Soviet target because it can be played off against the Executive Branch in Soviet arms control negotiating strategy. The Soviets would much rather negotiate with Congress than with the President, whose agencies can construct a coherent negotiating strategy in full possession of the facts: the history of Soviet proposals, responses to U.S. proposals, compliance with existing agreements and trends in arms production. Congress may learn these facts; however, as an institution it is not designed with an eye to conducting external negotiations. There is no way Congress can construct a coherent negotiating strategy. Yet the Soviets continuously attempt to induce Congress to take seriously negotiating proposals that are solely for propaganda purposes, proposals that the Executive Branch would dismiss out of hand. Such propaganda pressure on Congress can have its effects. For example, after the Soviets walked out of the arms talks with the United States in 1983, the Administration sought funds from Congress to construct one hundred MX "Peacekeeper" missiles. Congress replied by permitting enough funds for only twenty-one such missiles—funds which would be withheld if the Soviets returned to the negotiating table. In effect, for the course of almost a year, Congress gave the Soviets a veto power over our MX missile program! Although many other factors went into Congress's decision, such as the absence of an "acceptable" basing mode for the missile, this action nevertheless told the Soviets of great disunity within our government—the kind of disunity the Soviets work hard to exploit.

The Soviets like Congress as a target for deception for another important reason. Congress can be more easily deceived than the Executive Branch. Most Congressmen are not well educated in foreign affairs, and these days even less so in questions of communism. Most do not have foreign policy advisers, and those who do have legislative assistants who are often just out of school and without any experience in foreign affairs. In contrast, Presidents who do not have foreign policy experience at least have the counsel of many advisers and entire agencies whose sole responsibility is foreign policy. Thus congressmen are even more likely to be vulnerable to deceptive propaganda than the President. When Speaker of the House Tip O'Neill relies for much of his information about Central America on a Maryknoll nun who is a relative of his and who used to work in the region rather than on voluminous intelligence systematically gathered by a wide variety of sources, he, for one, leaves himself vulnerable to the biases of one point of view—an extreme one in this case, given the role of the Maryknolls in their witting or unwitting support of the Communists in Nicaragua. In addition, it is much easier for the Soviets to conduct covert political influence operations on Capitol Hill than in the Executive Branch. Hiring procedures for congressional staff are much more informal than those in the foreign affairs agencies. There are no background investigations for most staff, and security in general, even among committee staffs, is notoriously lax. Thus the possibilities for Soviet agents of influence to join congressional staffs and conduct disinformation and deceptive propaganda are enormous.

Congress has a special responsibility to mind its own store in another key respect. A number of its current members are active participants in the activities of several Soviet front organizations. Some ten congressmen, for example, are members of the U.S. Peace Council, the U.S. branch of the World Peace Council, which is the Soviets' largest front organization. Soviet fronts by themselves are a major form of deception. They are designed to accomplish the work of the Communist Party of the Soviet Union under another guise. The Soviets often use fronts with pleasing-sounding names as a means of ensnaring non-Communists into assisting their political operations without being aware of whose cause they are serving. The World Peace Council, however, is too prominent and has been too well publicized for its collaborators to be unaware of its sponsors.

In testimony before the House Intelligence Committee in 1983, the FBI revealed the names of those members of Congress who were involved with this Soviet front organization. However, the chairman of the committee, Representative Edward Boland (D–Mass.) erased their names from the public transcript of the hearings. Far from exposing the complicity of members of Congress in a Soviet political deception, Congress has acceded to a cover-up and has assisted in deceiving the American people.

The fact that a single committee chairman could get away with this kind of a cover-up is, of course, mostly a reflection of his own misconduct and that of the House leadership who permitted such behavior; it is not an indication of active misconduct by the entire Congress. Nevertheless, the fact that this incident was permitted to pass on quietly without a political storm in Congress is evidence of a lack of sensitivity to the significance of Communist front organizations in particular and Soviet deception in general. This lack of sensitivity has thus rendered Congress much more vulnerable to the lobbying efforts of Communist fronts of all kinds. Thus fronts for such groups as the Nicaraguan Sandinista Communists have had much greater influence than they otherwise would if Congress were more willing to look into the origins and composition of such organizations.

Congress should thus do everything it can to educate itself about Soviet communism and its methods and themes of deception. This should include all members of Congress, not just members of the foreign affairs committees. This process will take a great deal of political courage; to open one's mind to greater knowledge of these subjects and then to impart that knowledge to others often involves colliding with some unpleasant truths that are often easier to ignore than to confront directly. It is much more comfortable for a member of Congress to avoid telling his constituents certain truths that many would rather not hear. Many Americans, although in my view not most, would rather look at the world the way they wish it to be rather than the way it really is. Many would prefer to avoid facing such ugly realities as the persecution and murder of the Jews by the Nazis. In spite of copious evidence of those crimes, we in the West avoided coming to grips with the implications of that evidence before it was too late. Many today would rather not face the possibility that the Soviets are indeed the active enemies of U.S. democracy and are actually working to destroy it through the various methods of low-intensity warfare. But to avoid facing the truth, however unpleasant, is to live in a fantasy world. And fantasy and wishful thinking can never be the sound basis for a national security policy in an unpredictable and imperfect world. Only truth can serve as that basis: "Ye shall know the truth, and the truth shall make you free."

Congress should therefore consider establishing a new caucus: a Coalition for Freedom Through Truth. The purpose of this coalition would be to combat the strategic deception efforts of the enemies of the United States. It would constantly remind the American people and even the President and his cabinet that there is a vast constituency in this country that is not afraid to hear the truth and that demands that the truth be told by those who are responsible for our nation's security. The coalition could press for hearings to be conducted on the subject of deception. Its regular agenda could consist of monitoring, supporting, and encouraging the truth-telling and antideception activities of the Departments of State and Defense and the U.S. Information Agency. It could regularly monitor the deception efforts of the Soviets and their proxies. It could keep the government sensitized to "semantic infiltration"—the use of deceptive words and labels—and simultaneously encourage "truth in labeling." It could work to establish several annual high school debate topics on the subject of Soviet strategic deception to educate the nation's students about this threat to our security. One such topic might be: "Resolved, that Soviet deception makes mutual and verifiable arms control impossible between the United States and the USSR."

Finally, such a coalition should spearhead an effort to raise some of the hardest and most unpleasant questions to greater levels of prominence in our public discourse. One of these questions, which the abovementioned debate topic gives rise to, is whether indeed the arms control process itself is nothing but a deadly form of strategic deception. The fact that we cannot verify so many of the most critical elements of the Soviet strategic arsenal due to Soviet camouflage, concealment, and deception is but one reason why this may be so. The fact that the Soviets have violated every arms limitation agreement they have ever signed may be another reason. Perhaps, indeed, the Soviets do not have a self-interest in limiting their own acquisition of arms. If there is no compliance, there can be no such thing as mutual arms control. There can be agreements, there can be unilateral disarmament by the United States, but there cannot be mutual arms control. If indeed it is true that for these reasons the achievement of mutual and verifiable arms control is impossible, shouldn't someone have the courage to say so and explain why? The very thought of the impossibility of achieving arms control is too much for some people to bear. That is why many pursue it and promote it as if with religious faith; for these people arms control is man's only hope on earth, man's only salvation. If such quasi-religious attitudes forbid us ever to let the truth intrude into our public discourse, we may indeed risk losing our freedom due to willful blindness born of superstition. Will Congress be the incubator of such blindness? Will it be the temple of superstition? Or will it strive to be a redoubt of courage and truth?

"One word of truth" is all that is needed, said Alexander Solzhenitsyn. That one word of truth can overcome the greatest tyrannies, resist the harshest repressions, and stave off the most violent aggressors. Truth is the most powerful weapon the United States has in its arsenal, and it can only be used for the good. What it takes is the courage to see the truth, the courage to utter it, and the courage to hear it. In the end, as Solzhenitsyn once again taught us, our freedom and national security are not built on a foundation of guns and missiles alone. They are the result of "stout hearts and steadfast men," people with the courage to live by the truth.

CONCLUSION

General Bernard A. Schriever

We started out in this study to show that verification is the Achilles' heel of arms control with the Soviet Union. As we tackled verification it became all too clear that the Soviets were and are now violating many of the arms control agreements they have made. It also became evident that one reason for their violations is that they are using the arms control process to deceive us into slowing down, while they keep building and while they strive for worldwide military supremacy. The Soviets intend to build and are building worldwide military supremacy in order to "significantly alter the strategic balance" in their favor because, as Dr. Joseph Douglass points out: "Superiority accelerates the process of the physical and moral defeat of the enemy and makes it possible to operate more daringly and decisively and to impose one's will on the enemy and to attack him more successfully."

While the Soviets are continuing to build military forces, they are deploying superior Soviet forces into every corner of the world, preaching "peace." But it is a "peace" of deception, a "peace of the Gulag," as Ambassador Nitze explains.

The Soviets gained immediate conventional military superiority over the United States when we rapidly demobilized after World War II and the Soviets did not demobilize. They maintained their huge ground forces after World War II and occupied all of Eastern Europe. It was generally agreed in those days that the Soviets with their huge army could overrun all of Western Europe in a few days, or at most in a few weeks. To prevent this we stationed U.S. atomic forces in Europe, and we built ICBMs that deterred a Soviet invasion of Western Europe. At the same time NATO forces (including U.S. ground forces) were stationed in Europe to form a "tripwire" force to deter the Soviets from launching a ground attack of Europe.

This strategy of deterring Soviet military expansion into Free Europe worked well in Europe. However, the Soviet strategy was and is a global strategy. They used the North Koreans to invade South Korea, and we did stop them. They used the North Vietnamese to invade South Vietnam—and we lost South Vietnam, along with Laos and Cambodia. They used terror to take over South Yemen. They are using terror and guerrilla forces to destabilize and seize Ethiopia, Angola, and El Salvador. Soviet Army forces are being used to massacre the people and to seize Afghanistan.

In Latin America, of course, they used infiltration, subversion, and guerrilla forces to seize Cuba, which they then armed heavily and are still arming. They seized Nicaragua and are building huge military forces there on the mainland of America. The Nicaraguans have announced that they intend to communize all of Central America. Obviously, this can only be attempted with Cuban and Soviet participation. As the Soviets achieve greater and greater military superiority they will use more and more military power in Central America as well as in other parts of the world. True, this is being executed under the cover of "national liberation"—under the cover of Marxist-Leninist deception, as Charles Dickens shows; nevertheless, it continues Soviet expansionism.

By 1968–69 the Soviets had achieved general military parity with the United States. Yet the Soviets continued to build more submarines, more ships, more ICBMs, more bombers, more fighters, more tanks, more guns, more military power of all kinds.

As of 1986 the Soviets achieved military superiority over the United States in practically every category of weapons. David Sullivan compares U.S. and Soviet military forces.

President Reagan has acknowledged that the Soviets have acquired strategic superiority over the United States, according to Dr. William Van Cleave. Arms control agreements have not slowed the Soviet buildup. If anything, the whole arms control process has been used by the Soviets to deceive the United States and to make it easier for the Soviets to achieve military superiority. How are the Soviets using this military superiority and how will they use it in the future?

End paper map shows the Soviet global power projection as portrayed in the 1987 Department of Defense publication *Soviet Military Power*. However, we have shaded the thirty-seven countries of the world that are Marxist-Leninist, and we have shown the countries with Communist parties, which is a major aspect of Soviet power projection not included in the DOD Study.

It is clear that the Soviets intend to project their power to control "world hegemony," as they call it, unless the free countries of the West unite to stop them. In my judgment the Soviets can be stopped. They can be deterred militarily by rebuilding our strategic deterrence, especially the Strategic Defense Initiative, while we greatly strengthen our political-psychological attack against the primary vulnerability of the Soviet system. But to rebuild our strategic forces and to build the Strategic Defense Initiative we must expose Soviet deception in space, as James Oberg describes, and we must ourselves be free to use space.

The whole foundation of Soviet society is deception, and the roots that feed this foundation are embodied in language—semantic deception, as Raymond Sleeper shows. This semantic deception forms the structure of the operating concepts of Marxism-Leninism. These false concepts provide the rationale and dynamism of the Soviet system and the relentless expansionism of Soviet world power. Communist systems are in fact based on power, force, repression, atheism, and relentless indoctrination in lies.

The Soviet system cannot withstand the light of truth. The very existence of a society and an ideology anywhere in the world that is based essentially on truth is a deadly threat to the structure of the Soviet system and to the world Marxist-Leninist movement.

We Americans experienced in the summer of 1986 a celebration of our American idea—the renovation and renewal of the symbol of the American idea, the Statute of Liberty.

The American idea was captured early in our history by Thomas Jefferson, when he wrote, "We hold these *truths* to be self-evident, that all men are created equal, that they are endowed by their Creator with certain unalienable rights, that among these are life, liberty, and the pursuit of happiness." A recent dictionary tells us unalienable means "that cannot be rightfully taken away." Thomas Jefferson's Declaration of Independence established the idea, and our Constitution, together with the Bill of Rights, created the structure of our government and the U.S. nation.

Most nations have a homogeneous population that has been living in that country for many years. This is not true with the United States. People have come from all over the world to create the United States. Many embraced the ideas of freedom and equality long before they arrived in the United States. Our outpouring on July 3–5, 1986, celebrated the renovation of our symbol of freedom, the Statue of Liberty. Central to the celebration was the realization that we are free, that it is truly the "sweet land of liberty." But this liberty, this freedom, is threatened by world Marxism-Leninism, an ideology that wholly suppresses freedom and liberty, an ideology that, as Dr. Michael Voslensky points out, is founded on lies and conspiratorial totalitarianism.

My family came to the United States when I was seven, in 1917. I embraced the American idea, as so many others have. I became an aviator and fought in World War II. I have served the United States ever since, and I am still working for the peace and security of our nation. Through those years I watched the evil ideology of Nazism grow and threaten the world. We freed the world of this dire threat; but in the process the Soviet Union has become a much more serious threat. Without its great military power the Soviets would not be the serious threat that they are. The growing military power of the Soviet Union, together with the Soviet ideology of Marxism-Leninism, constitute a mortal threat to the Free World.

There are some 157 countries in the United Nations. Some thirty-seven are now Marxist-Leninist, and as End paper map shows, the Soviets are projecting their power across the world. This is their goal, in their typically deceptive "Communist language":

> The victory of communism on a world scale will provide the necessary material and intellectual preconditions for the merging of nations. A communist economy developing according to a single plan and securing a degree of economic integration never known before will gradually be formed throughout the world. There will emerge a common moral code which will fully absorb all that is best in the character of each nation. There will be a common language, a common means of communication for all people. Mankind will become one united, fraternal community completely free of antagonism.[1]

The Fundamentals of Marxist-Leninist Philosophy, from which this quotation is drawn, is essentially the *Mein Kampf* of Marxism-Leninism. It lays down the philosophy of "class struggle," the destruction of capitalism, and the creation of a Marxist-Leninist world, just as Hitler's *Mein Kampf* specified the philosophy of a Nazi world.

The Soviet system is vulnerable. It is vulnerable to the truth: the truth of human rights, the truth of inalienable rights, the truth of religious freedom, the truth of freedom.

It is vulnerable to the truth about Marxism-Leninism. Marxism-Leninism has no spiritual grace, no transcending love; it is a system based on hatred—hatred of capitalists, hatred of one's government, hatred even for one's parents unless they are Communists. Marxism-Leninism preaches the hatred of individual freedom, because individual freedoms expose the falsenesses of communism. Marxism-Leninism teaches and endorses violence.

> The communists consider it unnecessary to disguise their views and purposes. They openly declare that their aims can be accomplished only through the overthrow by violence of the whole existing social order.[2]

This type of entreaty and justification for violence abounds in Marxism-Leninism.

As long as the Soviet Union is dedicated to world communism and the violent overthrow of capitalist society, we will have no peace. Soviet endorsement of violence involves the endorsement of nuclear war, conventional war, guerrilla war, terror, and psychological war.

I said earlier that the Soviet system is vulnerable. It is. The entire system is based on lies supported by military power and secrecy. The West can, if it has the courage and the conviction, keep its own military forces strong and can expose the falsenesses—the lies at the heart of the Soviet system—and cause it to change.

There are no freedoms in a Communist totalitarian system. There are only lies, secrets, power, and deceptions. If the deceptions and lies are exposed, the result must be that the system changes.

The Soviet system is vulnerable to truth: the truth about the state of human rights, the truth about the "freedoms" in the USSR, the truth about the false ideology of Marxism-Leninism, the truth about "socialist democracy" in the USSR, the truth about terrorism in the world rooted in Marxism-Leninism, and the USSR. We must proclaim and popularize a true concept of peace while exposing the false Soviet concept of "the peace of the Gulag." We must develop a strategy of "freedom through truth" to expose the deception of the Soviet Union. We must maintain military strength in order to enjoy the freedom to halt Russian expansionism and in order to be free to use the world's oceans and aerospace and through this freedom and the growing power of the world communications revolution "shatter the Soviet monopoly of information which is the foundation of the Soviet system." As Dr. William Kintner says, "free men must fight against hostile ideologies which are antithetical to peace. Governments ruled by the tenets of Marxism-Leninism must be transformed if the conditions for global peace are ever to be established."

I am convinced that if we commit ourselves or, more correctly, recommit ourselves to our basic rights and fundamental freedoms, not only for Americans but for all peoples, and if we remain committed to staying militarily strong, and if we embark on a vigorous program to transmit these values to the people of the Soviet system, we will see a transformation of the whole system.

I do not mean to imply that such a program is easy or that it will produce quick results. Through the years, Western society has developed institutions to enhance, to strengthen, and to expand the individual personality, namely the family, religion, the complex cultures of the West, and the system of private property with all its elements enabling home ownership, increased comfort, and easy travel. The Communist system is hostile to individuality and to the institutions that enhance individuality. Solzhenitsyn expresses the Communist hostility thus: "Communism is anti-people, anti-humanity."

Solzhenitsyn, in his letter to the Soviet leaders of September 5, 1973, recommended that they abandon Marxism-Leninism, abandon:

> the ideological lies that are daily foisted upon us, . . . restore some of the power of the Soviets, . . . once the Party has relinquished its Ideology, renounce . . . world domination, . . . save us from a war with China and technological "disaster" and pursue a goal of a stable, moral system. This is the only feasible and peaceful way you can save our country and our people. And yourselves in the bargain.

Such a strategy of peace through freedom and truth is a long-range goal. It will require wisdom, hard work, and dedication to develop and explain to the people of the United States as well as the Soviet Union.

I am convinced that once the American people (and other free people as well) understand the false Soviet peace—they will strongly support the *real peace* that all people desire. It is our opportunity for not only the rebirth of the American idea but our opportunity to share this powerful idea and the attendant benefits with the world.

Notes

1. *Fundamentals of Marxist-Leninist Philosophy.* (Moscow, 1974), p. 406.

2. *Izvestia,* December 5, 1928.

INDEX

A

ABM Treaty break-out violations,
44–45
Acheson-Lilenthal plan, 185
Active measures, 147
approval of, 282
goals of, 281–82
organizational structure for, 283
in South Africa, 159–60
used as term, 139
Afghanistan, Soviet invasion of, 80
African National Congress (ANC),
159–60
Agreed intelligence, 91
*Always in Readiness to Defend the
Homeland* (Ogarkov), 102
American public, as target of
Soviet deception, 343–48
Antisatellite weaponry
deception/lies about, 264–73
American satellites statistics,
265
Soviet killer satellites, 264, 266,
268, 271
Soviet possession of, 264–65
Anti-semitism, 128–29
Arms control
configuration of failure of, 61–62
deception/lies in, 32–39
SALT violations, 40–45
as source of Soviet superiority,
39–41

intermediate-range nuclear forces
(INF), 70–73
negotiation deceptions, 54–57
examples of, 54–55
type sought by Soviets, 81–82
See also. Strategic Arms
Limitations Treaty (SALT).
"Arms race," Soviet definition of,
223

B

Backfire intercontinental bomber,
Soviet break-out violations, 43
"Balance," Soviet definition of, 222
Baruch Proposal, 185
*Basis Principles of Operational Art
and Tactics* (Soviet manual),
102
Batista, Fulgencio, 233–34, 238
Biological/chemical weapons bans
Soviet violations of
Biological and Toxin Weapons
Convention, 46
Conventional Weapons
Convention, 47
Geneva Protocol, 47
Helsinki Final Act, 47
Montreux Convention, 47
SS-20 moratorium, 47
Biological and Toxin Weapons
Convention, Soviet violations
of, 46

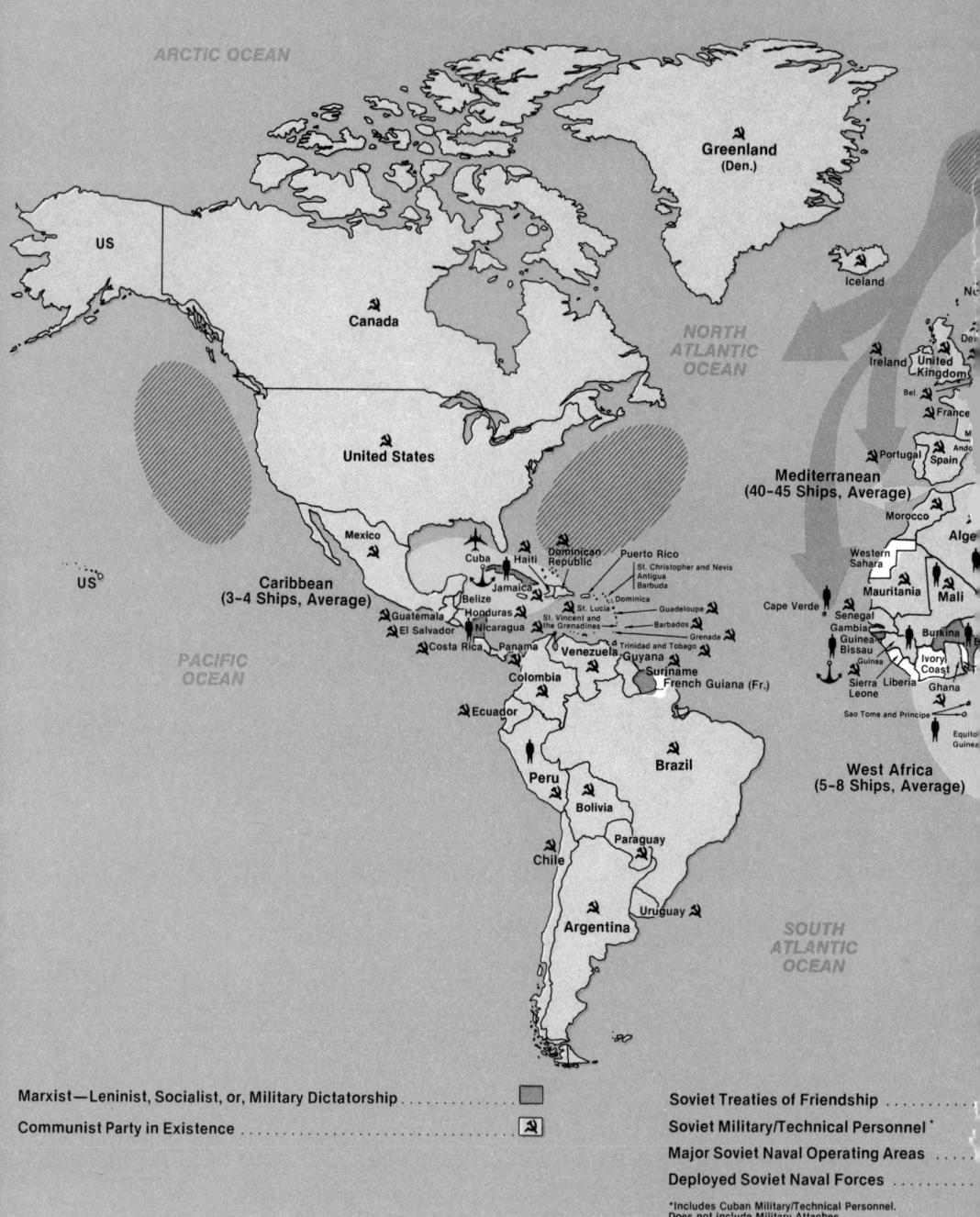

SOVIET GLOB

ARCTIC OCEAN

Greenland
(Den.)

US

Iceland

Canada

NORTH
ATLANTIC
OCEAN

Ireland   United
          Kingdom

Bel

France

United States

Portugal   Spain

Ando

Mediterranean
(40-45 Ships, Average)

Mexico

Morocco

Western
Sahara

Alge

US

Caribbean
(3-4 Ships, Average)

Dominican
Republic

Puerto Rico
St. Christopher and Nevis
Antigua
Barbuda

Cuba   Haiti

Jamaica

Cape Verde

Mauritania

Mali

PACIFIC
OCEAN

Belize

Dominica

St. Lucia

Guadeloupe

Senegal

Gambia

Guinea
Bissau

Burkina

Guatemala

Honduras

El Salvador   Nicaragua

Costa Rica   Panama

St. Vincent and
the Grenadines

Barbados

Grenada

Guinea

Ivory
Coast

Sierra   Liberia
Leone

Ghana

Venezuela   Guyana

Trinidad and Tobago

Suriname

French Guiana (Fr.)

Sao Tome and Principe

Colombia

Ecuador

West Africa
(5-8 Ships, Average)

Equito
Guinea

Brazil

Peru

Bolivia

Paraguay

Chile

SOUTH
ATLANTIC
OCEAN

Uruguay

Argentina

Marxist—Leninist, Socialist, or, Military Dictatorship . . . .

Communist Party in Existence . . . .

Soviet Treaties of Friendship . . . .

Soviet Military/Technical Personnel *

Major Soviet Naval Operating Areas . . . .

Deployed Soviet Naval Forces . . . .

*Includes Cuban Military/Technical Personnel.
Does not include Military Attaches.